THE SUNDAY WORD

The Sunday Word

A Commentary on the Sunday Readings

BY
HENRY WANSBROUGH

burns & oates

Published by Burns & Oates
A Continuum imprint

The Tower Building	80 Maiden Lane
11 York Road	Suite 704
London	New York
SE1 7NX	NY 10038

www.continuumbooks.com

British Library Cataloguing-in-Publication Data
A catalogue record for this book is available from the British Library.

ISBN: HB: 978-1-4411-4419-5

Library of Congress Cataloging-in-Publication Data
A catalog record for this book is available from the Library of Congress.

Typeset by Fakenham Prepress Solutions, Fakenham, Norfolk NR21 8NN
Printed and bound in India

Contents

Foreword by H.E. Cardinal Cormac Murphy O'Connor

It was St. Jerome who said, *Ignorance of the Scriptures is ignorance of Christ.* While every Christian is exhorted to a daily reading of the Bible, for many, the reading and listening to scripture occurs each Sunday at Mass. This is one reason why I warmly welcome *The Sunday Word* by Fr. Henry Wansbrough, OSB. Here is a distinguished biblical scholar opening up the richness of the Sunday readings to the adult Christian. There are many commentaries on the Sunday readings which serve only as a help to priests or deacons in preparing their Sunday sermons. This commentary, however, seems to me to have a much wider dimension, namely, it encourages both priests and people to reflect more deeply on the three readings of every Sunday. How do the stories of the Old and New Testaments, written many centuries ago, have a relevance to the present day? If the Word of God is 'alive and active' (Heb.4:12) it must be alive and active for all of us today. In these commentaries the background and shape of every passage is opened up and shared with us. This is a great achievement by Henry Wansbrough and we should all be grateful to him.

I hope this Commentary will be on the bookshelves of very many priests and people. It will certainly help all of us to appreciate and meditate on the Sunday readings and enable us to turn our thoughts and prayers to the God who has revealed himself to us in Jesus Christ and shown us his loving kindness.

+ *Cormac*

Cormac Card. Murphy-O'Connor
Archbishop Emeritus of Westminster

Foreword by the author

Soon after the publication of the Revised Lectionary, worked out as a result of the new and salutary emphasis in Vatican II on the place of scripture in the Church, I was asked by the editor of *The Catholic Herald* to write a weekly column on the Sunday readings. These were eventually gathered together and published as *The Sunday Word* in 1979; the book has long been out of print. Four years ago Dannie Firth started up *The Wednesday Word*, a child-friendly sheet aimed at taking the Gospel into the home of the high proportion of un-churched families of children in Catholic primary schools. Dannie asked me to help on the scriptural aspects. It soon became evident that a version for adult Christians would also be helpful. This book is the result; most of the commentaries have appeared as the parish version of *The Wednesday Word*.

Is it the same as the *Sunday Word* of 1979? I have not checked. I wrote the commentaries afresh without consulting the previous publication. I expect that some of my basic principles are the same as those of 35 years ago, but I hope that some of my ideas have developed. In any case, the copyright holders of the original publishers, Geoffrey Chapman, have tolerantly given their permission.

The idea of giving a question at the end of each reading was suggested to me by the receptionist to the Scottish Episcopal Conference, to whom I am most grateful. The questions may be useful for starting a train of thought. I hope the questions will not seem too flippant or irreverent.

Introduction

The Purpose of this Book

The treasure of the Church

The Bible has always been the greatest treasure of the Church. In the first generation of Christians, the apostle Paul was writing letters to the churches he founded around the shores of the eastern Mediterranean. Not surprisingly, the new converts were less than fully instructed in their new faith and had plenty of problems in their interrelationships with one another and with the surrounding Roman, Jewish and non-Christian cultures. Paul wrote to them in response to their problems, but establishing principles and teaching that still instruct and inspire us today. In the second generation of Christians, the oral traditions about Jesus came to be written down and so formed a record of what Paul called 'the Good News of Christ', the four gospels.

In the early second century an influx of gentiles, some of them highly educated, led to attempts to understand the Good News in terms of pagan and classical culture, neglecting its Jewish background. They produced their own versions of gospels, almost swamping the less educated and less wealthy Christians, with their Jewish-based account of God's revelation in Christ. By the end of the century there was a certain sobering up. Irenaeus of Lyons produced summaries of Christian doctrine that the Church found more appropriate to the traditional way of explaining Christianity, and orthodoxy began to have some meaning. At the same time Church leaders began to forbid the reading in church of certain of the writings that were circulating in Christian circles, and the idea of a regulatory canon of scripture began to be formed. Some of the writings circulating were felt not to give an authentic picture of Christianity. Writings excluded from this canon began to be confined to the sands of Egypt, to be redis-covered many centuries later. Also in the second century a Jewish canon of scripture began to be formed, distinguishing among revered religious writings between those that 'soiled the hands' (i.e. necessitated washing before and after handling) and those that did not. At the end of the second century a number of lists existed, detailing the books Christians held to be normative, that is, sure guides in matters of belief and behaviour. There is some variation on the fringes of this list, showing that some writings were accepted in some parts of the Church and not in others. Complete or almost complete uniformity was not achieved until about 400AD. Fostering and cherishing the Bible was, therefore, an early concern of the Church, both establishing which books expressed the sacred truth and presenting this truth to the Christian community. The principal means of proclaiming this truth was the public reading of the scriptures in the liturgy of the Church. In a non-literate age believers would also carry in their hearts an expansive treasury of the Bible on which they would meditate and pray.

Lectio divina

If we may believe the story of St Antony of Egypt, the monastic movement began with the prayerful listening to the scripture, when Antony heard the gospel passage: 'Sell all you have and follow me.' Monks of east and west were always encouraged to read the scriptures privately and prayerfully, as well as in the public offices of the Church. It was a prime way of coming to know God, God's dealings with the world and his chosen people, and the oscillating positive and negative reactions of that people, at one time passionately faithful, at another rebellious. St Benedict in his *Rule for Monks* (Chapter 48) prescribes that a considerable time each day should be set aside for such prayerful reading. In the Middle Ages the works of such writers as St Bernard of Clairvaux are so full of scriptural allusions that one can see that their minds were saturated with the scriptures from many hours of reading and meditation.

Perhaps the classic exposition of the method of prayerful reading of scripture, or *lectio divina*, is given by Guigo II, twelfth-century Prior of the Grande Chartreuse. He suggests four moments. It may or may not be useful to follow these steps. Whether this book is used for private prayer or for group discussion, there must be no compulsion to follow the steps through to the end. As soon as a prayer arises, or new thought or discovery suggests itself, it would certainly be wrong to suppress it and battle on to the end. Make use of the prayer or idea and enjoy that!

1. *Lectio* (reading) – a slow and careful reading of a limited portion, perhaps only a sentence, of scripture. This he compares to the initial taste of a grape in the mouth. First, the scriptural passage needs to be read slowly, carefully and with imagination. It is essential to remember that 'these things were written for our instruction' (1

Corinthians 10.8). The scriptures were written to enable believers
to learn about God and to communicate with God. A story may be
written in circumstances long past, a saying may be addressed to a
long vanished audience, but it has relevance now also to the present.
For instance, we do not know to whom the Songs of the Servant were
originally intended to apply. The human author ('Isaiah') may dimly
have envisaged that they had a meaning beyond the immediate application. However, the believer reads with a canonical reading, that is,
in view of the whole canon of scripture, including the final revelation
in Christ. If 'the Word of God is alive and active' (Hebrews 4.12), it
has something to say to us today.

2. *Meditatio* (meditation or reflection) – a careful study to enrich the
   reading by penetrating the meaning of the text, the full meaning of
   the words, the context and other connections. This Guigo compares
   to chewing the grape. It is for this stage that the present writing is
   intended. It is intended merely to begin opening up a passage. Far
   more may be done, especially if a particular commentary offered
   is unsatisfactory. The footnotes and marginal references of a good
   edition of the Bible may enable a reader to see more deeply into the
   significance and message of a text.

3. *Oratio* (prayer) – a turning to God in prayer, a lifting of the mind and
   heart to God. This is really the object of the whole activity. The prayer
   may be expressed in words – or even in song, dance or visual artistry
   – or may remain a silent reflection in awe, praise, thanksgiving,
   contrition or a thousand other emotions.

4. *Contemplatio* (contemplation) – the enjoyment of a sweetness
   and peace in God at some depth, 'a taste of the joys of everlasting
   sweetness'. This may or may not be granted. Guigo stresses that it is a
   special gift of God and it should not be expected.

Some books that may be helpful towards practising this way of reading
the Bible are:

E. Bianchi, *Praying the Word* (1998)
M. Magrassi, *Praying the Bible* (1998)
D. Foster, *Reading with God* (2005).

Vatican II and the scriptures
The stress of the sixteenth-century reformers on the principle of *sola
scriptura*, and especially Luther's stress on the 'plain meaning of the words',
with the implication that the meaning of the scriptures was always plain

without any guidance from the Church, resulted in a reaction from the Catholic Church. There grew a certain hesitancy towards the scriptures. In caricature, 'they' had the scriptures, while 'we' had the sacraments. It was as though 'they' were saved by the scriptures (if indeed they were saved), while 'we' were saved by the sacraments. Any Protestant household would possess at least a family Bible, whereas many zealous Catholic families had at best a Missal.

In the early years of the twentieth century this hesitancy towards the scriptures was only increased by the vigorous condemnation of the movement known as Roman Catholic modernism. This modernism was an over-zealous acceptance of the findings of nineteenth-century research in the fields of science, literature and archaeology, resulting in diffusion of opinions which the Church judged to be hasty and uncritical. The heavy-handed condemnations that followed scared both scholars and the wider believing public from looking too closely at the Bible. It was safer to leave the Bible in the deep freeze. The encyclical *Divino Afflante Spiritu* (1943) began the thaw, but it takes time for a thaw to penetrate right to the inside. It was still possible for an English bishop to say to me during the first session of the Council: 'Oh, you are a student of the Bible. I suppose that means you don't believe in it.' However, attitudes changed rapidly during the Council!

In its great document on the Revelation, *Dei Verbum*, the Second Vatican Council proclaimed that:

> In his love God chose to reveal himself in order to invite us into his friendship. The plan of salvation is expressed both in God's deeds throughout the history of salvation and in the words which make clear the mystery contained in them.

The Word of God is, then, God's loving gift of himself, to which the human response must be a response in loving faith. By reading and meditating upon the scriptures we get to know more about God and God's dealings with humanity, how human beings are created in the image of God to be his representatives in the world, preserving and continuing the divine creation. We learn also about the covenants, repeatedly made and repeatedly broken by human disobedience and rebellion, but still the basis of human relationship to God. We learn about the human personality of Jesus and his act of loving obedience, which annulled the state of human sinfulness. We learn about the position of the Risen Christ and how the scriptures express the humanity and yet the divinity of Christ. We learn more about the strivings of human nature and its contradictions, posings, yearnings, passions, unreliability – and much more. We learn about the Church, the Body of Christ, living with Christ's life and guided by his Holy Spirit, about the model of the early Church, its organization, successes and failures.

In accordance with this principle, the Council ordained that the lectionary used in the Eucharist should be revised to include a far wider selection of passages, enabling the faithful to hear all the principal passages of scripture. The resulting apportionment of readings is set out now.

The Shape of the Lectionary

The choice of readings for each Sunday can seem very random and irrational, if not higgledy-piggledy. It can seem as though there are three wheels (an Old Testament reading, a reading from the Epistles and a Gospel reading) all rotating independently. In fact, the sequence of readings is very carefully plotted. It is helpful for our understanding of the readings and the message they convey to know just why they are placed as they are.

The Gospels

The basic division is the allocation of Matthew, Mark and Luke to successive years. John is reserved for special occasions, mostly the seasons of Lent and Eastertide. For instance the great gospel readings about water, light and life are given on the third, fourth and fifth Sundays of Lent, in preparation for the prominence of those mysteries in baptisms which occur at the Easter Vigil. The Johannine readings of the Discourse after the Last Supper are given in the preparation for Jesus' departure from this world at the Ascension and his coming to the Church through the gift of the Spirit at Pentecost. Additionally, Mark is a little too short, so a series of readings from John's Bread of Life Discourse gives a little padding during the summer period of Year B.

Special seasons: Advent

Advent has two prominent features. The first readings are all taken from Isaiah, who is generally seen as the prophet *par excellence* of the coming of the Messiah. The gospel readings are carefully patterned:

- First Sunday of Advent: The last Sunday of the old liturgical year and the first Sunday of the new liturgical year are always about the end of the world, the final coming of Christ.
- The Second and Third Sundays concentrate on John the Baptist, the final prophet of preparation for the Messiah. On the Second Sunday he is preparing a community for the Messiah; on the Third Sunday he points out the Lamb of God.

- On the Fourth Sunday we turn to Mary as she prepares for the birth of her Son.

Special seasons: Lent

Lent also has two special features. It is the season in which the Old Testament comes into its own. The Gospel readings are preparing specially for Easter.

The first readings work methodically through the history of salvation in the Old Testament, each of the three years having the same pattern but with different readings. The basic idea is the series of covenants:

- Sunday One: the early myths about origins, before the covenant with Abraham.
- Sunday Two: the first covenant, with Abraham.
- Sunday Three: the great covenant with Moses on Sinai, the giving of the Law.
- Sunday Four: the covenant with David and the promise of the Messiah.
- Sunday Five: the new covenant promised by the prophets of the Exile.

The pattern of the Gospel readings is most fully seen in Year A (and the readings for Year A may be used also in Years B and C). All three years begin:

- Sunday One: the Testing of Jesus in the desert, for Lent is seen as a time of testing and trial. Jesus, Son of God, withstands the 40 days of testing in the desert which Israel, son of God, had (for 40 years) failed.
- Sunday Two: the Transfiguration, when the chosen apostles experience the divinity of Jesus on the holy mountain, to strengthen them against the coming torture and death of Jesus.
- Sundays Three to Five in Year A: three great Johannine passages to prepare for baptism or the renewal of baptismal vows at Easter. The gospel of Jesus and the Samaritan Woman teaches the mystery of living water in preparation for the washing and rebirth of baptism. The story of the Man Born Blind prepares for the enlightenment of baptism, and also builds up pressure from the blindness of the Jewish authorities. The Raising of Lazarus prepares for the gift of new life at baptism.
- Sunday Six is the Sunday of the Passion and the Sunday of Palms. The Gospel reading is the account of the Passion as given in the gospel of the year. John's Passion account is read on Good Friday.

Special seasons: Eastertide

Eastertide is the season of newness after the baptisms. The first reading is, unusually, taken from the New Testament, the Acts of the Apostles, describing the life and witness of the early Church. The second reading is taken from an appropriate New Testament document. Thus Year A has First Peter, which, at the time of the making of the Lectionary in the 1960s, was widely thought to be based on a baptismal instruction. Year B has First John, which concentrates on the love to be shown among disciples. Year C shows us the final glory of the Church as seen in the Book of Revelation.

The Gospel readings similarly have a clear pattern:

- Sundays Two and Three (Sunday One is the day of the Resurrection itself) recount the meetings with the Risen Lord.
- Sunday Four is Good Shepherd Sunday, with readings from John 10.
- Sundays Five and Six give readings from the final Discourse at the Last Supper, when Jesus is preparing the disciples for his departure and for the challenges of their mission in spreading the Good News. They are taken from John 14 and 15. Sunday Six is, of course, often ironed out by the Feast of the Ascension, which has its own readings.
- Sunday Seven has a reading from John 17, often known as the High Priestly Prayer, on the sanctification of Jesus by the Passion and of the disciples by the coming of the Spirit at Pentecost.

First readings

Outside Paschaltime these are all taken from the Old Testament. In Advent and Lent they have their own patterns (as above). At other times a heroic effort has been made to pair these with the Gospel readings of the day. This is the least satisfactory element in the lectionary, for the linking sometimes skews the Gospel reading away from its most central theme. Similarly, the Old Testament passage often loses much of its sense by lack of context. However, the presence of an Old Testament reading does at least keep before our eyes the importance of the gradual preparation of the People of God for the coming of Christ, for Christianity is the crowning of Judaism, and without Judaism makes little sense.

Second readings

Outside Eastertime these are all taken from the Letters of Paul (plus James and Hebrews). The little letters of 2–3 John and Jude simply do not fit in! During 'Ordinary Time' the pattern is as follows:

This pattern is best explained piecemeal. Each year begins with a group of readings from the First Letter to the Corinthians, that fractious and

Year A	Year B	Year C
1 Corinthians 1–4	1 Corinthians 6–10	1 Corinthians 11–16
Romans	2 Corinthians	Galatians
	Ephesians	Colossians
Philippians	Letter of James	
	Hebrews 1–10	Hebrews 11–12
		1–2 Timothy
1 Thessalonians		2 Thessalonians

Spirit-filled community that gave Paul so much trouble. Does this imply that the modern Church is the same?

Then Year A has the privilege of 16 readings from the great Letter to the Romans, which dwells on the process of the saving work of Christ. It is balanced in Year C by six readings from Galatians, which in a way is a preparation for Romans. In Years B and C we have respectively Ephesians and Colossians, those later letters, possibly by a disciple of Paul, almost a development and application of Paul's teaching to a later situation of the Church.

Year B receives the delightfully practical teaching of the Letter of James, and the noble Christology of Hebrews.

Finally, to prepare for the final coming of Christ, Years A and C conclude with the eschatologically orientated letters to the Thessalonians.

COMMENTARY ON THE READINGS

ADVENT AND CHRISTMASTIDE

Year A

First Sunday of Advent

First reading: The Vision of Peace (Isaiah 2.2-5)

With the beginning of Advent we turn to the idea of the coming of Christ, in history (that is, at Bethlehem), in mystery (that is, in the Church) and in majesty (that is, at the end of time). First of all, we turn to the vision of the peace that Christ brings, and for which we all yearn. The hill on which Jerusalem lies is not particularly high, but when Christ comes it will be a towering mountain, dominating the whole country. All nations will realize its importance and come to Jerusalem to draw salvation from it, the source of all salvation. The increasing concern of Israel for the salvation of the gentiles, which first comes to the fore in the post-exilic book, here reaches a highpoint. The permanent ending of war and strife is signalled by the remoulding of the weapons of war. You can't make war if you have converted your tanks into chicken houses and your aircraft carriers into skateboard parks – the modern equivalent of swords into ploughshares and swords into sickles. So Advent is a time of peace, peace between nations but also peace between families and within families, a time for reconciliation of quarrels as we prepare for the coming of Christ at Christmas.

Question: What can I do this Advent to increase peace?

Second reading: The Time is Near (Romans 13.11-14)

After his great exposition in the Letter to the Romans of the saving work of Christ, Paul goes on to encourage the Christians of Rome to be faithful. With the Resurrection, the final era of the world has begun. There is no room for delay: the night is nearly over and the children of light are coming into their own. Paul sees a pressing need for action, and much of his moral advice, especially in First Corinthians, is grounded on the assumption that the Second Coming of Christ at the end of the world is imminent. Did Paul get it wrong? He never says exactly how imminent it is, how soon the

Second Coming will occur, but we can safely say that he would have been surprised to discover that 2000 years would pass without any sign of its occurring. However, equally safe is it to say that timing is not his concern. The Second Coming remains imminent, in that there is no time to delay in mending our ways and preparing for this event. We are given an important reminder of this by our celebration of Christmas. Each year must really be a coming of Christ into our lives and our society.

Question: How can Christmas be to me a coming of Christ?

Gospel: Like a Thief in the Night (Matthew 24.37-44)
In each year of the three-year cycle the Advent Sunday gospel readings have the same pattern: the first is about the final Coming of Christ. In the second, John the Baptist is preparing a community of repentance to welcome Jesus' mission. In the third, John the Baptist points out Jesus as the Messiah. On the fourth Sunday we look to Mary, preparing for the birth of her Son. In this Sunday's reading about the Second Coming the accent is the same as in the Pauline letter: a pressing and urgent need to take action without delay. The Second Coming will be sudden and unexpected, and will seem as random as the threat of one taken, one left, or as a thief in the night when no protective preparations have been made. We do not even know whether the final confrontation, when each of us is brought face to face with the awesome presence of God, will be a unique event for each of us at death, or whether it will be a group event, as in Matthew's parable of the sheep and goats sent to right and left. There is no time in eternity, no waiting room! It will not be as any human mind can envisage it.

Question: Should we look forward to or dread the final meeting with the Lord?

Second Sunday of Advent

First reading: A Shoot from the Stock of Jesse (Isaiah 11.1-10)

From this reading the seven gifts of the Spirit are, rather artificially, taken. Seven is the perfect number, so this is intended to signify that the promised ruler will have all possible gifts of what we more generally call wisdom and understanding. He will be a ruler before whom one can stand in the secure knowledge that his judgment will be deeply fair and satisfying. The 'fear of the Lord' ensures that they will be in accordance with the divinely ordered bases of creation. Such is the Ruler whom we await at Christmas. It was surely these qualities that made Jesus such an attractive and charismatic figure, so that he could, as a wholly unknown stranger, pass those fishermen, and they would drop everything and respond to his call, 'Follow me'. Confrontation with his personality was shock enough and inspiring enough to cure sickness. His simple word gave assurance of forgiveness of sin. His command reduced the elements of nature to serenity. In the second half of the reading, we see the consequences, a return to the peace of the Garden of Eden. No more hostility, no more jealousy. Nature, even human nature, will not be red in tooth and claw.

Question: To you, what is the most attractive feature of the human Jesus?

Second reading: The Generosity of Christ (Romans 15.4-9)

Paul is here summing up his message to the Romans, a fragmented community of several house-churches, some drawn from Judaism, some from the gentiles. He has described and analysed Christ's work of salvation, the generosity of Christ in giving himself up for us, to win us back to the Father. Then he calls upon his hearers to imitate Christ's generosity. He speaks first to the Christians sprung, like himself, from Judaism, reminding them of the promises of scripture, the heritage of Judaism, which were to inspire them with hope, for God's promises are never failing and sure. Then he reminds them with a string of quotations (only the first of which is given, at the end of this reading) that God's promises were intended for the gentiles too, so that they too should praise God's name. Why are we given this reading in Advent? Because the perfect generosity of Jesus Christ in taking on this work of our salvation must be the model for our own generosity, both to those who are our natural friends and to those who are not, and because it must be the basis of our hope. However neglectful and ungrateful we are, Christ's work cannot have been in vain.

Question: In what way can I be more generous to prepare for Christmas, especially to those who are not my natural friends?

Gospel: John the Baptist's Call to Repentance (Matthew 3.1-12)

'Repentance' is an unattractive idea. It conjures up morose brooding over past sins and failures, a negative idea. This is not what John the Baptist proclaimed. His message was wholly positive. In both Hebrew and Greek, the concept is a change of behaviour, a change of direction. John is calling on them to change their ways, to change their scale of values, their whole direction of life. To reinforce his message he wears the clothes worn by Elijah, the prophet who was to return to announce the final coming of the Lord. He proclaims his message in the desert, that apocalyptic landscape of the arid and bare Jordan Valley, below sea level, where merchants would be crossing the Jordan on the road to the east. So he makes a deliberate claim to be this final prophet and to be preparing a way for the Lord. We see Jesus as the Messiah, the loving Saviour, but John was not yet proclaiming Jesus. He was proclaiming the threatening and imminent arrival of the sovereignty of God, when rotten trees would be cut down and evil swept away to be burnt in unquenchable fire. If we are to be open to the arrival of the Kingship of God, we may need to look to our scale of values. Am I the only person who matters to me?

Question: Is my scale of values compatible with the Kingship of God? How far do they coincide?

Third Sunday of Advent

First reading: 'The Eyes of the Blind shall be Opened' (Isaiah 35.1-6, 10)

Like all the first readings in Advent, this passage is from Isaiah, rejoicing in the coming deliverance. Most of the Book of Isaiah was written in a dark period of Israel's history, under the threat or the reality of defeat, devastation and deportation. The promises of a deliverer became all the more important and life sustaining. The prophet (or prophets, for the Book of Isaiah can hardly be the work of a single person) never wavered in his confidence that deliverance was sure. The prophecies prepare for the coming of the Lord, but it is the coming of the Lord God. On the one hand, there is not the clarity that would appear once Jesus had actually come: the prophecies do not make clear in what way or what form God would come to the rescue of his people. Would the promised Redeemer be God himself or a messenger or a herald of the end? At all events God would be at work. One the other hand, when Jesus came it was not immediately clear whether he was God, or whether God was at work in Jesus or whether Jesus was the final prophet. This became clear only on reflection in the light of the Spirit: 'The Word became flesh and dwelt among us.'

Question: Is the message of this reading encouraging or threatening?

Second reading: Waiting for the Lord (James 5.7-10)

The Letter of James is rarely read on a Sunday, indeed only once in this year. Yet it is full of comforting, homely images, like the farmer waiting patiently for the autumn and spring rains, or – less comforting – the judge waiting at the gates. Whether it was written by James who was the leader of the Christian community at Jerusalem is harder to determine. It may be an assemblage of the oral wisdom teaching of this important Christian leader, written up by a disciple. In any case, the Letter was written at a time when the eschatological fever of expectation had begun to wane, when Christians no longer felt that they were in the final generation of world history, and were prepared to settle down and wait for the coming of the Lord. Indeed, in contrast to the Paul's stress on the imminence of the Second Coming, for James the delay of the Second Coming is an incitement to patience. It will certainly happen, but there is plenty of opportunity beforehand for tolerance, both towards the annoying and tiresome people within the community and towards those persecuting the community from outside.

Question: Think of the most annoying person you know. Does God love him or her?

Gospel: Miracles of the Messiah (Matthew 11.2-11)

John the Baptist was expecting a Messiah of judgment, who would cut down the rotten tree and burn the useless chaff. When, in prison, he hears that Jesus is not doing this, he is puzzled and sends messengers to ask if Jesus is really the Messiah. Jesus sends back the message that he is fulfilling the prophecy of Isaiah – the passage we heard in the first reading. Jesus' concept of the task of the Messiah was healing, not punishment. He goes and seeks out those who need healing, both physical and moral. He does not wait for sinners to repent before gathering them in; he makes the first advance. Then he turns to praising the Baptist. It is a fascinating speculation whether Jesus was himself once a disciple of John the Baptist. After all, John says he did not recognize Jesus until he saw the Spirit coming down on him. He also says that Jesus, who came after him, has passed before him. This is a typical position of a rabbi, leading his disciples, and suggests that John had been Jesus' rabbi, then became his disciple. Jesus was fully man, and even he needed to learn as all human beings do.

Question: What healing can I do to spread the Kingship of God?

Fourth Sunday of Advent

First reading: The Virgin is with Child (Isaiah 7.10-14)

The readings of the last Sunday of Advent always turn to Mary, as she waits for her child to be born. The prophecy in this first reading was given in 736BC, when King Ahaz of Judah was about to be forced into an alliance, in a vain attempt to oppose the crushing military power of Babylon. Isaiah goes to him and warns him that the alliance would be fatal: he had better trust in the Lord. Isaiah promises a sign, which Ahaz refuses. He does not want to be convinced! What is this sign? The original Hebrew reads: 'A girl is with child and will bear a son', indicating that within a few months the threat will vanish and Jerusalem will be convinced that God is on their side – hence the boy will be called Emmanuel, in relieved gratitude. But the Greek translation of the Hebrew, made some 200 years before the birth of Jesus, translates 'The *virgin* is with child', which the evangelist Matthew sees as a prophecy of the birth of Jesus from the Virgin Mary. The symbolic name Emmanuel then becomes a promise of the presence of God in the world at our side.

Question: In what way can we experience the presence of God?

Second reading: Son of God in Power (Romans 1.1-7)

This reading gives us the beginning of the great Letter to the Romans, in which Paul lays out the saving work of Christ. After proclaiming his apostolic office, Paul lays out the two aspects of Jesus. In his introductions to the letters, Paul always briefly introduces or hints at the subject with which he is specially concerned in the letter. So here it is the dual aspect of Christ. If he were not both wholly human and the Son of God, his supreme act of obedience on the Cross would not have saved us. And yet, it is by his Resurrection that he lifts his followers to completion in the divine life, for we are baptized into his death and rise in his Resurrection. According to his human nature, he is a descendant of David, wholly human. At the same time he is Son of God in power through his Resurrection from the dead. Paul does not, of course, suggest that before the Resurrection he was not Son of God, but in some way the Resurrection put him in the position of his full power as Son of God. The Incarnation is the basis of all the theology of salvation.

Question: What can it mean that Jesus entered into his power at the Resurrection?

Gospel: Emmanuel (Matthew 1.18-25)

Matthew begins his gospel about the birth of Jesus with a long and elaborately formal genealogy of Joseph. But Jesus is the son of Mary, not of Joseph! The whole point of this story is that Joseph is not the genealogical father of Jesus, but adopts Jesus into his line of David. At first he is hesitant to do so, presumably thinking that he is unworthy to acknowledge the child as his own, and unworthy to bond with Mary who is with child by the Holy Spirit. But the angel insists ('Do not be afraid') that only Joseph can do this job. As soon as the child is born, he is given the name Jesus, and given it by Joseph. It is the father's prerogative to name a son, and by so doing Joseph takes the child as his own. We hear little more of Joseph, but what a joy it must have been to have Jesus as a son! What a relationship there must have been! What responsibility, too! When Jesus calls God his 'Father', he is using the concept that must have been formed in his mind by his adoptive father, Joseph, the perfect ideal of the loving father.

Question: What did Jesus and Joseph talk about as they walked to work together?

Christmas, the Nativity of the Lord, Mass During the Night

First reading: The Hope of Israel (Isaiah 9.2-4, 6-7)

This prophecy of Isaiah promises a joyful reversal after the threats of the Assyrian invasion of Jerusalem in 732BC. The devastating Assyrian armies had plundered the northern kingdom of Israel and seemed certain to repeat this exploit on Judah and Jerusalem in the south. Amazingly, they turned away. At the same time Isaiah promises a son of the royal line of David, who will bring peace with justice and righteousness. This son is described in exaggerated terms that we Christians see to be fulfilled only in Jesus, the Second David, the true Son of God. He will be Wonderful Counsellor, Mighty God, Everlasting Father, Prince of Peace, each pair of titles having a marvellous, transcendent air. Such promises sustained the hopes of the nation through the grim period of the Exile and the succession of foreign rulers which dominated the return from Exile. As the hated Roman occupation became more burdensome, the hopes of delivery through this promised heir of David became more and more vivid in Israel, as we see from the Jewish literature of the years immediately preceding the birth of Jesus. It is in terms of the heir to David and Son of God that Mary received the message of the angel at the Annunciation.

Question: In what way does Jesus fulfil these promises?

Second reading: The Appearing of Our Saviour (Titus 2.11-14)

The author of the letter sees God primarily as the Saviour, who wishes all people to be saved through Christ, also our Saviour. In the Old Testament, God is often called the Saviour of his people, but in the letters to Timothy and Titus this title is with equal frequency transferred to Jesus our Saviour, perhaps as a divine title. This reading is chosen to celebrate Christmas because it speaks twice of the appearing or manifestation (the same word in Greek) of our Saviour, and the Church Fathers often consider the moment of this Appearing at the Incarnation rather than the Resurrection to be the moment of salvation. It is celebrated as the moment when God became man so that man might be raised to the divine. Accordingly, the Eastern Church celebrates rather the Epiphany (or Appearing) of the Lord. However, the letter stresses that we must respond to this Appearing of the grace of God by preparing for the final Appearing. Thus the classic formulation speaks of the threefold coming of Christ: in history (at Bethlehem), in mystery (coming into our hearts) and in majesty (at the final coming in glory).

Question: Is it possible or useful to locate salvation at one particular historical moment?

Gospel: The Birth of Jesus (Luke 2.1-16)

Luke's account of the birth of Jesus stresses especially the poverty of the family: Christ comes to the poor and is greeted by the poor. Mary and Joseph are displaced persons, and can find no decent place for the baby to be born. There is no space in the living quarters and he has to be put in a feeding trough among the animals. He is greeted not by the rich presents of the magnificent Wise Men from the east, but by impoverished hired shepherds, guarding flocks in the winter night. He is born to be the patron of the homeless and of displaced persons.

But Jesus is also the fulfilment of the hopes of the Old Testament. The families of both John the Baptist and Jesus are eminently faithful to the prescriptions of the Law, waiting for the salvation promised to Israel. In the Temple, Jesus will be greeted by Simeon and Anna, the representatives of fidelity to the Old Law. The birth of Jesus at Bethlehem shows that he is born as the heir to the promises to David, that God would build David a house of everlasting sovereignty, whose king would be the son of God and would call God his Father.

Question: What can I do for someone poor or unhappy this Christmas?

Mass in the Day

First reading: All the Ends of the Earth shall see Salvation (Isaiah 52.7-10)

This reading, from the second part of Isaiah, written on the eve of the ending of Israel's exile in Babylon, is full of the joys of the impending return to Jerusalem. After the years of waiting and doubt, the author envisages a messenger coming into view on the mountains with the announcement of the good news of peace, salvation and the return to the ruins of Jerusalem. When the city was sacked and its people dragged (literally, on meat hooks) across the desert into exile, it had seemed that their God could not protect them. Now comes the confirmation that, after all, God is king and overcomes all opposition. Furthermore, a new dimension has opened out, for God brings salvation not merely to Israel but to the whole world, to 'the ends of the earth'. This is especially significant for Christians, since it was the expression used by the Risen Lord before the Ascension as his apostles are about to set out on their worldwide mission of bringing the good news to all nations. It is, therefore, a valuable reminder on the day of Christmas that the festival is not merely a family celebration but is the beginning of the Christian mission to bring God's hope and promise to the whole world.

Question: How can I be a messenger of good news announcing peace?

Second reading: The Heir of All Things (Hebrews 1.1-6)

The Letter to the Hebrews concentrates on the true humanity of Christ, who is also uniquely exalted, and also on Christ's priesthood. Here, at the opening of the letter, both these themes are sketched. Christ is higher than the angels, the very powers of God who accomplish the works of God and are the highest of all created beings. It is through these powers of God that God's will is accomplished, but Christ is incomparably higher than the angels. As 'the reflection of God's glory' and 'the imprint of God's being' Christ is spoken of in terms of God's Wisdom. In the Old Testament, God's Wisdom is seen as the image, the reflection, the emanation of God through which God creates, and by which God is mirrored in the world, the way in which God's power and goodness is perceived. At the same time, in history as man, Christ has made purification for sins and has been exalted to the right hand of God. The whole history of salvation is hinted in these phrases, which express both the approach of God to human beings by the incarnation, and the exaltation of humanity by the vindication of Christ at his Resurrection and Ascension.

Question: In this reading, which to you is the most powerful expression of the divinity of Christ?

Gospel: The Word made Flesh (John 1.1-18)

The Prologue of St John has a special place in Christian theology, and for centuries was recited at the end of the Mass as summing up the whole work of redemption. It begins with God's creation by the Word, and ends with the completion of the purpose of creation through the grace and truth of Jesus Christ. In the centre, comes the incarnation, which enables and invites those who accept Christ to become children of God. The gospel story of Mark begins at the baptism of Jesus, and the voice from heaven declaring that he is God's son. Matthew and Luke add the infancy stories to show that Jesus possessed and manifested these divine qualities right from his birth. John goes back beyond this, to meditate on the ultimate part in both creation and its fulfilment of the Word who became flesh. Perhaps the most exultant cry of all is 'we have seen his glory', for glory belongs rightly to God alone. This statement contains the paradox that Christ as a human being made visible this divine glory, and that it was his own glory, witnessed by the followers among whom he lived and moved. It is their tradition that will be expressed in the gospel story that follows and is celebrated through the year.

Question: What does 'we have seen his glory' mean?

Solemnity of Mary, Mother of God – Octave Day of Christmas

First reading: The Blessing of God (Numbers 6.22-27)

In its original setting in the Bible, this passage comes at the end of a series of laws. It invokes the blessing of God on his people. The triple repetition makes it a strong and insistent blessing, calling the presence and protection of God on his people. At a certain stage, in the 1960s, there was a great tendency to translate the Beatitudes in the Sermon on the Mount (Matthew 5) as '*happy* are the poor in spirit' etc. But God's blessing does not mean 'happiness' in the sense that the poor in spirit are singing and dancing, having fun. Rather, it means that God's protective hand is over them: nothing can go wrong, and God's guidance is looking after them, despite any appearances to the contrary. So, when the passage is read on this day, it does not mean that that Mary and her Son were always merry and having fun. Mary had the same troubles as any mother with a new baby, perhaps even postnatal depression. It does not mean that the baby Jesus never cried. Rather, God's protective hand was upon them in all their doings, their relationships and their troubles. For us, today, it means that this presence of the Lord was the beginning and guarantee of salvation.

Question: What is the difference between being happy and being blessed?

Second reading: Mother of God (Galatians 4.4-7)

In his Letter to the Galatians, Paul is not setting out to assert anything about the maternity of Mary. He is simply setting out to assert that we are no longer subject to the Law. Why not? Because Jesus, although a real man like ourselves, could call God his Father. As son and heir of God, Jesus is free of all restrictions and enslavements, and we too, plunged into Christ in baptism, as similarly heirs and free. All this depends on Jesus fully sharing our human nature. Paul just slips this in unquestioningly, 'born of a woman'. Where did he get his human existence from, if not from Mary? At the Council of Ephesus, Nestorius wanted Mary to be called *Christotokos* or 'Christ-bearer', but the Council insisted that the man Jesus, who was fully God, derived his whole being from Mary: she was *Theotokos*, 'God-bearer'. The whole person who was God was born of Mary, not just a human Christ. From Mary he derived his genes, his DNA, his flesh and blood, his temperament (which was also divine), his habits of mind, his warmth of personality. He was utterly, frankly and joyfully human, and yet those who opened their eyes and ears to him could not forebear reverencing him as only God may be reverenced.

Question: How much would Jesus have looked like his mother and had her characteristics?

Gospel: The Child in the Cattle Trough (Luke 2.16-21)
The cosy picture of the bright-eyed child in the clean wooden manger (with the ox and the ass peeping in from a respectful distance) is misleading. The picture is one of destitution. There was no room for the newborn in the normal living quarters, and the worried mother had to lodge him in the only space available, a feeding trough for cattle, perched on top of their fodder. That was where the ragged sheep minders found him. They, too, were the poorest of the poor, no sheep of their own, just hired for the night. Perhaps they got a drink of goats' milk or a crust of bread for their shivering pains. Matthew does at least have the baby worshipped by those rather splendid Wise Men from the east, with their noble and symbolic gifts. No gifts forthcoming from today's rough crew. As we worry about our post-Christmas waistlines, and set out on our prosperous New Year, it makes us reflect on where true blessedness lies, and who are the chosen ones of the Lord. Surely God could have rustled up more suitable worshippers for his Incarnate Son than these scruffy down-and-outs? No, I'm afraid not.

Question: Why is the material destitution of Mary and Jesus so strongly stressed?

Second Sunday after Christmas

First reading: The Wisdom of God takes Root (Sira 24.1-4, 8-12)

This wonderful poem, of which we read all too short an extract, celebrates the splendour of Jerusalem, where the Wisdom of God, the Law, took root. The author loves the Law, the Temple and Jerusalem with all his heart, as the gift and manifestation of God. God creates by his Wisdom, the master plan and agent of creation. Wisdom, expressed in the Law, is also the master plan guiding God's image and representative, which teaches us how to live as the image of God. So our author sees Jerusalem as the visible symbol of all the beauties of God's creation. We Christians, however, see Christ as this Wisdom of God, who took root in his Chosen People, and in Jerusalem – or at least in Bethlehem, seven kilometres away. For us, then, this hymn is a celebration of God's Wisdom in Christ, taking root in the human race. In Colossians, Paul hymns Christ as Wisdom, the firstborn in creation and the firstborn from the dead. In the great hymn at the beginning of Ephesians, Christ is described as the climax in whom all creation is summed up, in whom God 'brings everything together under Christ as head'. The completion of creation is, then, the fullness of the Incarnation that we celebrate at Christmas.

Question: Does it make any sense to speak of God or Christ as Wisdom?

Second reading: The Cosmic Plan of God (Ephesians 1.3-6, 15-19)

The sevenfold blessing, with which Ephesians begins, sums up God's plan of salvation for humanity. The climax is in the centre, 'to bring everything under Christ as head'. Christ is the Wisdom of God, the plan according to which and through which all things were created. Christ is also the completion of the creation, and the unity of all things in Christ is a special emphasis of the whole letter. All things are under Christ as head of creation, all nourishment for creation and all guidance of creation. In ancient medical science, the head was held to be the source of all these: all nourishment comes through the mouth, the brain thinks things out and makes the decisions on which the whole body acts. Christ performs for creation these functions which the head performs for the body. In earlier letters, Paul had written that the Body of Christ, which is the Church, is made up from many limbs and members, which all have different contributions to make to its wellbeing. Now he develops this image and differentiates Christ as the head of the whole Body as its guide, leader, nourishment and focus.

Question: Is the Body a helpful image for the Church?

Gospel: The Word made Flesh (John 1.1-18)

The gospel reading for this Second Sunday after Christmas is the same as that for Christmas Day itself. Perhaps, after all the celebrations of Christmas, there is room for a more sober thought. The climax is not at the end of the reading, but is in the centre: 'to those who believe he gave power to become sons of God'. On either side of this verse are rejection by his own people, and acceptance by those who see his Glory. This theme of acceptance and rejection runs right through the gospel of John, some accepting (the disciples, Nicodemus, the Man Born Blind), some rejecting (the Pharisees, the leaders of the Jews). The disciples accept at the Marriage Feast at Cana; the Jews immediately afterwards reject at the Cleansing of the Temple. You cannot remain neutral; you must either accept or reject. It is a great trial scene, and we judge ourselves by our reaction to Jesus. The Father has given all judgment to the Son, but the Son judges no one. The last dread scene is when the Jewish leaders pass sentence on themselves before Pilate and before Jesus crowned as king and seated as judge; they reject God's kingship by saying, 'We have no king but Caesar.' There is no need for sentence to be passed, for we pass our own sentence on ourselves.

Question: Does it make sense to say that we judge ourselves?

Feast of the Holy Family

First reading: Honour Your Father and Your Mother (Ecclesiasticus 3.2-6, 12-14)

The Book of Ecclesiasticus is a collection of wise instructions on how to behave in accordance with the Law. The author must have been an expert in the Law, living in Jerusalem. He sees the Law not as a tiresome set of rules to be obeyed, but as God's loving gift to his people, to show them how they should act to keep close to God. It is therefore to be treasured, a guide of inestimable value. The reading for today is a meditation and expansion on the commandment, 'Honour your father and your mother', explaining just how this should be put into practice. What was Jesus like as a baby? Did he cry? He must have done, to make his baby feelings known. Did he bawl and howl? Did he cry when he scraped the skin off his knees? Did he fall out of trees and break his arm? Did he make mistakes? Did he play pranks? He must have made jokes. He must have been a wonderful joy to his parents, loving, delightful company, full of the devastatingly simple wisdom of children. And they must have been loving, wonderful company for him, too, an anchor of affection and security.

Question: How to honour father and mother in later life – or to honour children?

Second reading: The Overcoat of Love (Colossians 3.12-21)

In an incredibly short space, the Letter to the Colossians gives a whole series of instructions on living in community: compassion, forgiveness, love and peace – not to mention gratitude. Love is a sort of overcoat, holding all the other qualities together. If we reflect on these and put them into practice, there can be no rivalry or hostility in the Christian community – even within a family, where the strains of Christmas often make love grow thin. However, a loving family is the model for the different relationships of a loving Christian community. God's fatherhood and motherhood is the model for human parentage, and Christ's devotion to his body the Church is the model for the devotion of spouses to one another. The reading begins with an inspiring reminder that we form the Chosen People of God; God's choice leaves us little alternative to the attempt to behave as God's people. The paragraph ends with the counsel to do everything in the name of the Lord Jesus; Christians are those over whom the name of the Lord Jesus has been called, making us members of his company and putting us under his power. This is the challenge really to act as God's people.

Question: Is it really possible to regard the Christian community as a family?

Gospel: The Flight into Egypt (Matthew 2.13-15, 19-23)
The flight into Egypt is a splendid gospel for the feast of the Holy Family. It tells of a time of the acutest danger, when Mary and Joseph must have been at their wits' ends to care for their precious child, and so most bound together as an endangered family, and at their most reliant on God in a situation humanly hopeless. The powerful, resourceful and pitiless Herod was a formidable threat; he would have no scruples about killing a few male children in the little hill town of Bethlehem.

There is also a further dimension: on many occasions, and especially here, Matthew depicts Jesus as a Second Moses: from the beginning Herod threatens Jesus' life just as Pharaoh had threatened Moses' survival as a baby.

Just as Moses went into exile after killing the Egyptian overseer, so Jesus also goes into exile, to return when the threat is past. Of both it is said, 'Those who wanted to kill you/the child are dead' (Exodus 4.19). Later Jesus will be seen as the Second Moses when he stays 40 days and nights fasting in the desert, and when he gives the Law at the Sermon on the Mount and at the Transfiguration.

Question: How can you bind your family more closely together in Christ?

Feast of the Epiphany

First reading: Camels, Gold and Incense (Isaiah 60.1-6)

This passage from the Book of Isaiah was written at a thrilling moment of Israel's development. They had returned from Exile in Babylon and were beginning to realize the universal task of Israel. The salvation promised to Israel was not just for the Jews but was for the whole world! Hence these cries of joy at all the curious camels and exotic nations thronging to Jerusalem. There is a similar opening out for us, too: Christ brings salvation not just to us, to those who come to our Church, but to the whole world – to all those grumpy, depressed, selfish, worried, suffering, disadvantaged people we meet in the street, most directly to Christians of every kind, but also to those who have not yet found Jesus. The Epiphany is the time at which Jesus 'went public', symbolized by the coming of the Wise Men from the east, the first people outside his own sphere to greet him. So we ought to go out into the street and shout for joy to alert people to what is on offer. Probably better to be a bit less crazy about it, and simply show the happiness it has brought to us by sharing our happiness in any generous way we can!

Question: What is the best way in which I can express my joy in Christ's salvation?

Second reading: God's Special Secret (Ephesians 3.2-3, 5-6)

The Letter talks about the 'mystery'. It really means God's great 'secret' to be revealed at the end of time. The climax of the long history of the world did indeed come at the Crucifixion and Resurrection, because all our hope is in Christ's Resurrection. That was the moment when history reached its highest point. This is the only Christian way of viewing the world, its slow evolution and then its history of human development, all directed to this point. We are much more aware these days that the immense universe, with stars millions of light years away, but still searching for the secret of the Big

Bang, is one great system of which we are a tiny part. When we think of angels hovering over Bethlehem, we really mean that all the power of God was focused on that one event. The Christian believes that one tiny baby, in his ancient equivalent of a nappy, presented to those Wise Men from the east, brought the secret of the universe to fulfilment. They represent all the races of the world, and far beyond, coming to greet the Saviour who was presented to the world on that day.

Reflection: Reflect on God's plan for the unimaginably huge universe, brought to perfection in one tiny baby.

Gospel: Wise Men from the East (Matthew 2.1-12)
The Wise Men, with their clever knowledge of astronomy and their lavish gifts, represent all that is best in worldly values. They also have a bit of magic about them, for frankincense and myrrh were used in spells, and the word for 'wise men' can also mean 'magicians'. They have real wisdom and its reward, and yet they lay it all at Jesus' feet. It might be worth asking at this beginning of the year whether we submit all our skills and comforts to Jesus. It is not humility – just a true scale of values.

The story also rests on the sharp contrast between King Herod and the Wise Men. Herod was a Jew, so he should have recognized and honoured the Jewish Messiah. Not at all! He tries to kill the Messiah. By contrast, the Wise Men, arriving from the equivalent of outer space, carry on their search until they find Jesus and humbly bow before him. This poses a nasty question: we Christians have all the guidance and encouragement of the Church, but how often we find those outside the Church, not even professed Christians, behaving in a more Christian way than we do ourselves!

Question: What skill can I submit to Jesus today?

Baptism of the Lord

First reading: The Servant of the Lord (Isaiah 42.1-4, 6-7)

Jesus knew the scripture; it was the only book he would have known. When he heard the Voice from heaven and he experienced the Spirit of God coming upon him, he must immediately have thought of this passage from Isaiah. He was, then, this mysterious Servant of the Lord about whom the scripture spoke. He was to bring Israel back to the Lord. He must have known that the Servant was to suffer and to reach his fulfilment only through bitter suffering and death for others. This realization must have been with him throughout his ministry, a dark shadow and a challenge to service. At the same time it was a confirmation of the love of the Father who was 'well pleased' in him. This was to be the model for all Christian suffering. We all know someone – we may even have experienced it ourselves – who has to suffer lovingly and generously in caring for others. The awesome privilege of suffering after the model of the Servant who is Jesus must draw respect and comfort for those who serve in this way. It is a confirmation of God's love for them.

Question: How can I tell what God wants from me?

Second reading: Peter Prepares Cornelius (Acts 10.34-38)

St Peter was making this speech at the house of the Roman centurion, Cornelius. Peter himself was still reeling from the shock of being told that foods (like pork) which he had, as a faithful Jew, all his life, considered unclean were perfectly acceptable. Now he is about to welcome into the Church a non-Jew, a gentile! Before he could even finish his speech, the Holy Spirit came down on Cornelius and his household, just as the Spirit had come down on the disciples at Pentecost. All this is the consequence of the coming of the Spirit on Jesus at his baptism. That was when Jesus began his mission, which is so strikingly described here as 'the Good News of peace'. Religion, and even Christianity, has so often been the cause of strife and quarrelling, rivalry between different Christian churches, rivalry between Christians, Jews and Muslims. We easily forget that the Spirit of Jesus is the Spirit of peace, openness, welcome. The Spirit of Jesus does not build barriers but dissolves them, does not inflict wounds but heals them, does not push people away but embraces them. Is this the community of Christ that I am trying to build in those around me?

Question: Do I put up any barriers, exclude anyone from Christ's love?

Gospel: The Baptism of Jesus (Matthew 3.13-17)

The account of the baptism of Jesus in Mark, the earliest gospel, is also the simplest. In Mark the Voice from heaven is addressed to Jesus himself, and there is no sign that others heard it; it is an experience of Jesus: '*You* are my Son.' In Matthew, the voice is addressed to the bystanders: '*This* is my Son.' This makes the private revelation into a public scene, a declaration that Jesus' work is about to begin. In the same way, our baptism is a public scene, a declaration that we are committed to Christ in his Church – even if we don't remember it! Matthew also records the little dialogue of John's unwillingness to baptize Jesus. Why should Jesus enter into the community of repentance that John was forming? He was no sinner! However, it was a gesture that Jesus was entering fully into the condition of all humanity. He shared fully in human nature, the nature of a fallen humanity. At the outset of his ministry, he must show this, for only so could he redeem the fallen human race. Jesus is not merely passive, for he himself joins with John in making the positive step: '*We* must do all that righteousness demands.'

Question: A quick review: what difference has baptism made to my life?

Year B

First Sunday of Advent

First reading: A Thrill of Hope (Isaiah 63.16-17; 64.1, 3-8)

Each Advent Sunday begins with a reading from Isaiah, for Isaiah is the great prophet of the Messiah. This reading is taken from the latest part of the Book of Isaiah. After the return to Jerusalem from exile in Babylon the Jews were passionately awaiting the coming of the Messiah. They were conscious that they had sinned and deserved their punishment, but still longed for the liberation from foreign interference that the Messiah would bring. After the coming of Christ we are in much the same position of waiting for the fulfilment of the sovereignty or kingship of God. Jesus brought the pledge of this kingship by his miracles of healing, his welcome to sinners, his teaching about the Kingdom and, above all, by his Resurrection from the dead. We no longer have any reason to fear death. We are conscious of our own failings, of our cooperation with evil, and long for the strength and fidelity that wholehearted membership of God's Kingdom would bring us.

Question: How do I need to change to become a fully committed member of God's Kingdom, to welcome the Messiah into my life?

Second reading: Waiting for the Lord Jesus (1 Corinthians 1.3-9)

This reading from the opening of Paul's first Letter to the Corinthians is full of the excitement of the Spirit. The young community of Christians at Corinth was full of the activity of the Holy Spirit, not just extraordinary things like speaking in tongues, but healing and teaching and guidance. Even being a good member of a family (husband, wife, parent, child) is an activity guided by the Spirit. All this was preparing for the final coming of Christ, for all Christian activity, no matter how humdrum, is given life and vitality by the Spirit of Christ. There was a freshness and enthusiasm that is sometimes lacking in our Church today. Paul does not hesitate to tell them that they were 'richly endowed with the Spirit'. So, of course, are we.

But he is going to go on and tell them that their squabbling is damaging their service of the Lord. Let us ask at Christmas for a new infusion of the Spirit that will help us to burst the bonds keeping us back from full service to the Lord.

Question: How is the Spirit visible in the Church today?

Gospel: The Watcher at the Door (Mark 13.33-37)
This brief parable of the master returning unexpectedly is typical of Jesus' vivid way of speaking. The message is typical, too, for Jesus was constantly stressing that there is no time to lose. In the gospel of Mark, especially, there is a feeling of hurry: in Chapter 1 alone there are 14 instances of 'immediately'! When Jesus came in his earthly ministry, he again and again challenged his hearers to make up their minds *now*, to change their ways *now*. He challenges us to do the same. We can hear the rattle of the returning Master's key in the lock. There is no time to hide the contrabands, to pull our uniforms straight before greeting the Master at his entry. Even if we do not think that the world's end is imminent, even if death is not threatening, every moment counts, every decision is for or against Jesus. Saints are rumoured to have said that, if they received the news that they were to die that night, they would carry on doing what they were doing anyway.

Is this really a Christian attitude? If we need to put things a bit more in order to prepare for the Lord's coming, is there any valid reason to delay? The four weeks of Advent are anyway a good time to clean things up for the Lord's coming.

Question: What do I need to change in my lifestyle?

Second Sunday of Advent

First reading: 'Console my People, Console them' (Isaiah 40.1-5, 9–11)

The reading from Isaiah for today is the joyful song that opens the second part of Isaiah. After the 70 years of the Exile, Israel is looking forward to the return to Jerusalem, aware that they are soon to be released from their captivity. They have 'served their sentence' in Babylon and their sin has been forgiven. The Lord will lead them in joy across the great desert as he led them across the desert at the Exodus, and will manifest his glory again. For Christians, the excitement is that John the Baptist picks up this message as he prepares the people for the coming of Christ. The coming of the Lord to Jerusalem was never wholly fulfilled, and we can see that the great fulfilment of this passage is in the coming of Christ to his own. He came to Jerusalem, yes, but has the divine glory been yet manifested? He brought the beginning of the Kingship of God, but it is for us Christians to show the glory and the love and the generosity of God to a world that has not yet seen the splendour of his coming. This is the daunting responsibility of those who bear the name of 'Christian', who see in Jesus the manifestation of God's reign.

Question: Has it any sense to say that the coming of Christ changed the world?

Second reading: The Lord Comes in the Night (2 Peter 3.8-14)

The Second Letter of Peter, probably the last of all the writings of the New Testament, here sets out to comfort Christians who were disappointed that the 'Big Bang' at the end of the world had not yet happened. The first generations of Christians had expected the world to come rapidly to an end – and yet it still goes on. In the first generation of Christians, much of Paul's moral teaching is shaped by the idea that the Second Coming will occur very soon. In the second generation, the author of this letter does not have such immediacy. He says that our task is to live holy lives in peace, and to wait in patience. The Second Coming is still imminent in the sense that we must live our lives in view of it, and we have no time to lose. But it will not occur tomorrow! From this point of view, the annual cycle of Church feasts and festivals, even of Christmas, is a reminder that God is in total control of his universe. For us the seasons roll round, but, for God, time is meaningless.

Question: Has the final coming of Christ any relevance for Christians today?

Gospel: A Baptism for Conversion (Mark 1.1-8)
Each Advent has two John the Baptist Sundays, the first when we see John preparing a community for the Messiah, the second when he points out Jesus as the Lamb of God. Today is the first of these. John chose a point where the busy road from Jerusalem to the east crossed the Jordan River. There he buttonholed all the busy financiers, merchants and other travellers and tourists, warning them to change their ways – and to change them now, before it was too late. 'I am too busy', no doubt they said, 'I have other things to worry about; I have a wife and family to feed.' John was forming a community of repentance, but not so much a community that wept 'Boohoo!' about its sins, as a community of people determined to set

the scale of values right. He meant them to stop going in one direction, to turn round and go in a different direction. Do we give ourselves a moment of pause to ask whether we have our priorities right? Where on our list of priorities does the entry of Christ into our lives come? John said rotten trees were going to be cut down, useless straw to be burnt. Do I need to feel the axe at my feet?

Question: What would happen if I turned my life round?

Third Sunday of Advent

First reading: Good News for the Poor (Isaiah 61.1-2, 10-11)

The Book of Isaiah reflects the thoughts and prayers of Israel over at least 200 years. The original prophet Isaiah was speaking in Jerusalem in 740BC. Further prophecies were added during the Babylonian Exile, and still more after the return from Exile. Through them all runs the promise that God will send his Spirit upon his Chosen One. In the first part, comes the wonderful promise of a sevenfold Spirit that we always associate with Confirmation. In the dark days of the Exile came the prophecy of 'my chosen one in whom my soul delights. I have sent my Spirit upon him', which is echoed at Jesus' baptism. Now, after the return from Exile, comes the prophecy of the anointed one to whom the Spirit has been given so that he may heal. All these are fulfilled in Jesus. Jesus also gives his Spirit to his followers, and it is our task, as we live by the Spirit, to heal, to bring good news to the poor and to bind up hearts that are broken.

Question: In what way is the Spirit at work in the Church today?

Second reading: Joy in the Lord (1 Thessalonians 5.16-24)

Writing to the Thessalonians, Paul gives his final blessing, asking that they may be kept safe for the coming of our Lord Jesus Christ. We are now waiting for the coming of Christ at Christmas. Paul means it in a very different sense. He was waiting for the coming of Christ at the end of the world, a triumphal procession in which we would join Christ 'in the clouds' as he presented the whole universe to his Father as God's completed kingdom. We don't see things in such dramatic, pictorial terms, but we do know that the whole universe is focused on God, and will reach its fulfilment only when his sovereignty is complete, when the world has been transformed by God's divine life in Christ. Paul himself, in 1 Corinthians 15, writes of the Resurrection in much more personal terms: it is a personal transformation after the model of Christ's own Resurrection. We will be drawn into the sphere of God and in some new way share in his divinity, strong instead of weak, incorruptible instead of perishable, glorious instead of contemptible, given life by the Spirit of God.

Question: What am I planning to do this Christmas to bring God's love and healing just one step further?

Gospel: A Voice Crying in the Desert (John 1.6-8, 19-28)

So, John the Baptist came as a witness to the light. In today's gospel reading, he seems rather to refuse witness. He is quite negative, answering with a stalwart and repeated 'No!' He witnesses only: 'There is one standing among you whom you do not know.' It is not always easy to find Jesus. All the way through the Gospel of John there are misunderstandings about Jesus, as people fail to recognize him for what he is: the Samaritan at the well, Nicodemus, Mary Magdalen beside the empty tomb, even Peter and the disciples as they fish on the Lake. We can easily become so wrapped up in our own troubles and worries that we fail to recognize the one figure who can bring their solution, although he is standing among us, the one who 'has the words of eternal life'. He may come to us in a way we do not like, as a corrective, blocking or diverting the way we had chosen. He may come as suffering, disappointment, failure or bereavement. All these may be acts of God's love, to show us the way, although we cannot see it at the time. It is just like John the Baptist, saying steadily 'No!', until eventually we turn around and see Christ as our true light.

Question: Does Christ confront us in a John the Baptist way? How?

Fourth Sunday of Advent

First reading: A King for Ever (2 Samuel 7.1-5, 8-11, 16)

At the height of his powers, King David wants to thank God for his lavish favours by building him a house. No human being patronizes God, and David was not allowed to build the Temple. But God replies with the promise that he will build David a House. The dynasty lasted for a couple of centuries. In one sense, David's House crashed into ruins when the last king of Judah was blinded and taken off into exile in Babylon. But the promise of an eternal kingship still inspired and encouraged the Jews in their Exile in Babylon. David's line still stands, not as a house built with human hands but as a House built by God. It is fulfilled in the eternal kingship of the Son of David who is also Mary's Son, and this fulfilment begins at the Annunciation. This is why so many phrases from the prophet Nathan's promise are echoed in the annunciation of the angel to Mary. 'Your sovereignty will always stand secure before me and your throne be established for ever', says Nathan. 'He will rule over the House of Jacob for ever and his reign will have no end', says the angel. Despite his faults, David remains the model of kingship in Israel.

Question: What docs Jesus' title as Son of David convey to you?

Second reading: The Last Secret (Romans 16.25-27)

This reading gives the final cry of excitement and triumph at the end of Paul's great letter to the Christians of Rome. His task is to reveal to the nations (not just to the Jews) God's secret plan, which has been brewing all through human history and now comes to its climax in Christ. This is the 'mystery' that God has finally revealed in Christ, for a 'mystery' is a sacred reality revealed only at the end of time. God has offered his friendship and his divine wisdom in Christ. Human beings respond with the 'obedience of faith', a keyword of the letter: we need only trust God's promises for all our weakness to be buried under God's glory. All we need do in this obedience of faith is to hang on to God's promises by our fingertips in our acceptance of God's promised help. Our celebration of Christmas is not just of a baby born at Bethlehem. It is of the climax of God's design for the world, the keystone of history. So we do not simply look back on it as a great event. Christians must see it as the anchor of God's design for the whole of history and for the course of each day.

Question: Is faith a matter of knowledge or of something else?

Gospel: The Annunciation (Luke 1.26-38)

As we prepare for the birth of Jesus, the final Sunday of Advent always focuses on Mary. What was the young girl Mary doing when the message came? Kneeling piously? Feeding the sheep? Fetching water? Sweeping the mud floor? What was she thinking? Engaged to be married, surely thinking about her approaching wedding to Joseph and about the children she would mother. Then came the message that she could accept or refuse, the message on which hung the future of the world: her child would be different from all others. How 'different'? Her thoughts were turned back to the promise to David. It had been read to her so often in the Bible, and now the words were drummed into her mind, 'his reign will have no end'. This would all be the work of the Spirit that she had so often heard read out in Isaiah; 'the Holy Spirit will come upon you', the Spirit that was to come upon the Servant of the Lord, the Spirit of Emmanuel, 'God with us'. Her young body was to grow, nourish and develop this child. Then she would have the child in her arms to cherish and shape as both Son of God and her own son (205).

Question: How is the Immaculate Conception related to Mary's motherhood?

Christmas Day

The readings given for Year A are used, p. 11

Feast of the Holy Family, Year B

In Year B for the first two readings either the readings of Year A (as on p. 17) or the following two readings may be used. For the Gospel Luke 2.22-40 is always used.

Alternative First Reading: The Promise to Abram (Genesis 15.1-6; 17.3b-5, 15-16; 21.1-7)

This reading from three different chapters of Genesis prepares for three features of the Lukan gospel of the Presentation and Circumcision in the Temple. Firstly, the Genesis story shows us the miraculous birth by which God's promise of descendants to Abraham was fulfilled, for Sarah was too old to have children in the natural way. Several such miraculous births occur in the Old Testament as signs of God's special care for his People, but never a virgin birth. Secondly, the divine promise fulfilled was a promise which would bring salvation not only to the Jews but to all nations, as many as the stars in the heavens, so 'a light of revelation to the gentiles' as Simeon puts it. Thirdly, the circumcision of Isaac is seen as a foretaste and type of the circumcision of Jesus in the gospel story. Especially with Simeon's prophecy to Mary of a sword which will pierce her heart, one is reminded that the shedding of Isaac's blood at circumcision is a preparation for the dreaded story of Abraham's offering of his son in sacrifice, just as the circumcision of Jesus is a preparation for the sacrificial offering of Jesus, the Son of God.

Question: Is it necessary to have an explicit belief in Christ in order to be saved?

Alternative Second Reading: Abraham's Trust in the Lord (Hebrews 11.8, 11-12, 17-19)

The horrific and dramatic story of the near sacrifice of Isaac in Genesis 18, on which this reading reflects, is appointed for reading both at the Easter Vigil and on the Second Sunday of Lent in Year B. It is the supreme example of Abraham's trust in the LORD. After his hopes of a line of heirs had been miraculously raised, they seemed about to be cruelly dashed again. And yet, even in this fierce test, he trusted in God until the very end, trusted that God would rescue him from this dreadful deed and that God would somehow assure his inheritance through Isaac. As Paul insists, it was not what Abraham did that justified him; it was his faith, his persevering trust against all appearances. As the list of Old Testament believers throughout this chapter of Hebrews makes clear, Abraham's unwavering trust in his sorrow is the model for the trust of Christians and all believers in the fulfilment of God's promises through thick and thin. By a slight extension, 'figuratively speaking', the saving of Isaac from death is also seen as a foretaste and type of the resurrection of Christ and of the Christian.

Question: What is the severest test to which your trust in God has been put?

Gospel: The Presentation in the Temple (Luke 2.22-40)

The story of the Presentation of the child Jesus in the Temple is dominated by Simeon's welcome, 'a light to enlighten the gentiles and the glory of your people Israel', and by his warning to Mary, 'a sword will pierce your heart'. Simeon reiterates the angel's promise that the child would fulfil the destiny of Israel and Israel's task to the nations. Much like any family life, the promised future included the delights of the growing, developing child, and the background fear that the great destiny of each child may include sorrow and even heartbreak. How much did Mary and Joseph know about the precious child they were nurturing? As he grew to independence, did he become more loving and supportive? How did his contemporaries find him? Was he a leader? Did he stand out from the pack? Each of us has a private picture of the child, the boy, the adolescent, the young man. All we know for sure is that 'the child grew to maturity' and that Mary 'pondered all these things in her heart', with Simeon's welcome and warning before her mind.

Question: What would Mary have felt and thought as she went home from the Temple?

Epiphany

The readings given for Year A are used, p. 19

Baptism of the Lord

The readings proper to Year A may also be used, as on p. 20

Readings proper to Year B

Alternative first reading: Preparing the Way (Isaiah 55.1-11)

The reading from Isaiah is positively bursting with ideas that prepare us for today's festival. To begin with, Isaiah proclaims the invitation to the rich messianic banquet. Perhaps we have had enough of rich food for the moment! But the picture of the Israelite relaxedly quaffing wine under his fig tree was an important part of the expectation of the Kingdom of God. Perhaps the social aspects of the banquet are more important in Jesus' frequent teaching about the banquet, and especially the warmth of the host and the company of the saints. But at Cana he does change the water into huge quantities of wine!

Second, there is the aspect of witness. The son of David is a witness calling to God the nations that do not know him, or the word of God that issues from the mouth of God and does not return without accomplishing his task. By our baptism we, too, are constituted witnesses for the world, accomplices of the word of God. But witnesses to what? The last part of the reading centres on the forgiveness of God, for God is nothing if not a forgiving God and the covenant nothing if not a covenant of forgiveness. The baptism of John, which Jesus himself underwent, is an invitation to change our ways and return to God.

Question: How can I prepare the way for the Lord?

Alternative second reading: The Love of the Children of God (1 John 5.1-9)

This is our first reading from the attractive First Letter of John, mostly about love, which is usually read during the Easter season. It slips in here to emphasize the mutual love of Father and Son, so fully expressed in the Baptism – 'with you I am well pleased'. By our own baptism, we share in this love. But, as with all love, there is a price to pay, not only in obedience to his commandments. It is a victory, a love that conquers the world. How it conquers the world is hinted by the mysterious reference that Jesus 'came by water and blood'. With John, there are always multiple layers of meaning. Does it mean the water and blood that flowed from his side as he was pierced by the soldier's spear on the Cross? Or is it – and this understanding lies deep in the tradition of the Church – that the water symbolizes baptism and the blood symbolizes the Eucharist? The sacraments flow from the side of Christ as he breathes forth, or gives over, his Spirit to the new community consisting of his Mother and the Beloved Disciple, the representatives of the Church. It is by the water and the blood that we meet Christ in these two basic sacraments.

Question: Is the crucifixion compatible with God's love for his Son?

Gospel: The Baptism of Jesus (Mark 1.7-11)
What can Jesus have experienced? It is described as 'the heavens torn apart', a voice, and the Spirit coming down like a dove. It must have given him the experience of being treasured, being embraced by the person whom he called 'Father'. But he is given a task, too, for the Spirit of God is an empowering Spirit. It must have felt like a new impetus, a thrill of challenge, a surge of energy and opportunity, an exciting new task. In this new Spirit, he went out to bring the good news of peace, gradually gathering his community and spreading God's healing love by his personality, his teaching and his healing. This is the power that baptism has given to us also, to bring God's healing and God's love, to build a community of love that reflects and extends God's own love. Jesus must have been daunted by the task. He knew it would test him to the limit of his endurance, but he knew he had received the power of God, and put his trust in his Father. He never promised us at baptism that it would be easy to live as Christians, but he did promise us that he would give us the surge of strength and power that is the Holy Spirit.

Question: Has my baptism empowered me?

Year C

First Sunday of Advent

First reading: The Branch for David (Jeremiah 33.14-16)

At the darkest moment of Israel's history, when the storm clouds of invasion were gathering, and the Babylonian conquest and exile seemed inevitable, comes this prophecy that the promise made long ago to David will not fail. Jerusalem will be sacked, but the promise remains that the city will be named 'the Lord is our Saving Justice'. The justice of God is not like human justice, conformity with the law. It is God's fulfilling his promises made to Abraham, Moses and David. So at this dire moment Jeremiah renews those promises that the stock of David will never fail, and gives a corresponding symbolic name to the city of David. Today's gospel speaks of another destruction of Jerusalem, that wrought by the Romans in 70AD, and looks beyond it to the final coming of Christ. So several layers are envisaged: the seeming loss of the promise at the Sack of Jerusalem by the Babylonians, which will be restored by the coming of Christ at the incarnation, and the destruction of Jerusalem by the Romans, which is the prelude to and promise of the final coming of Christ. In all these, the Lord is our Saving Justice.

Question: If Jesus is the 'righteous branch' promised to David, did he bring saving justice to the world?

Second reading: The Coming of the Lord Jesus (1 Thessalonians 3.12-4.2)

Paul gives instructions about living in holiness while waiting for the coming of our Lord Jesus Christ. Each year the Church reminds us of the final coming of the Lord, which is to be the end of the world as we know it. In the Old Testament, the 'Day of the Lord' is the day on which God will come to re-establish all things, to put wrongs right, to punish the wicked and reward the righteous. In the New Testament, from this earliest letter of Paul onwards, this Day of the Lord is the Day of the Lord Jesus. It is pictured as a day on which the Lord Jesus will come in a triumphal procession 'with all his holy ones', to be joined first by those who have died in the Lord, and then by those who are still living. For Paul, the triumph of the Lord is so dominant that he does not even mention or envisage punishments for the wicked. The Lord will triumph over all evil, sweeping all before him, and will carry all with him in his triumphal procession. Writing to the Corinthians he envisages that Christ will put all things under his feet, even the last enemy, death, and will then hand over the Kingdom to his Father.

Question: Is everything subject to Jesus, even the last enemy, death?

Gospel: Your Liberation is Near at Hand (Luke 21.25-28, 34-36)
With this reading, we begin the Year of Luke, for his gospel provides the readings for almost all the Sundays of the liturgical year that begins today. We begin at the end, for Luke sees the destruction of Jerusalem as the symbol and foretaste of final liberation at the coming of Christ. The horror of this day is represented by the cosmic disturbances, the collapse of all we regard as most stable and reliable, the eruption of the ocean and the collapse of the solar system. The Sack of Jerusalem by the Romans was certainly a decisive moment in the history of the Church, when the possibility vanished for ever of the Church remaining a branch of Judaism. In this sense, it was a liberation for the gentile Churches for which Luke was writing his gospel. It is also a symbol of the final liberation from the toils of evil in which humanity is embroiled, and so of the final triumph of Christ. It is a day for which we must prepare by our whole life, for revelation gives us no hint of when it will occur. The only hints are images of unexpected suddenness, like a trap being sprung (as here), a thief in the night or the pains of labour coming on a pregnant woman.

Question: If these prophecies are not to be taken literally, what do they mean?

Second Sunday of Advent

First reading: High Mountains Laid Flat (Baruch 5.1-9)

This part of the Book of Baruch is a meditation on Isaiah's promises for Jerusalem at the return of Israel from Exile in Babylon. It is, of course, taken up by John the Baptist in his proclamation that the high mountains will be flattened and the valleys filled in to make a smooth road for the

Messiah to cross the desert to Jerusalem. There were many aspects of the expected Messiah, the harbinger of God's Kingship. For Isaiah, it was a conquering hero, his garments stained with the blood of his victories. In this prophecy, the reign of God is more peaceful, a heartfelt dedication to God and the values of the divine sovereignty, for at this coming of God the names of Jerusalem shall be 'Peace through Justice' and 'Glory through Devotion'. True peace is possible only through the saving justice of God, when the people of God truly act as God's representatives, made in the image of God, and the envoys of his saving values. The ideal of God's Kingdom appears in the Garden of Eden before the Fall, when his representatives, Adam and Eve, lived in perfect harmony with one another and with God's whole creation.

Question: In what sense has the coming of Christ brought peace to the world?

Second reading: Filled with the Fruits of Uprightness (Philippians 1.3-6, 8-11)

Paul always begins his letters with a commendation and a blessing. The Philippians to whom he is writing were Paul's favourite community. The letter is full of friendship and affection. Here he commends the Philippians for their partnership with him in the gospel, and prays that God's work in them may be completed. So they may be ready for the Day of the Lord, which he envisaged to be imminent. The passage is chosen as a preparation for the coming of the Lord Jesus at Christmas – and Christmas shopping leaves no doubt about the imminence of that coming. It serves as a reminder that the traditional three comings of Christ cannot be separated. The coming in history was the birth of Jesus at Bethlehem. The coming in mystery is the coming of Christ into our hearts as we endeavour to mould ourselves as his faithful followers and to live out his values. The coming in majesty is the final coming of Christ in glory to gather his elect to himself, either at our homecoming in death or at the end of all things. The three comings lead on, one to another: the coming in history gives a new impetus to the Kingdom of God, the coming in majesty brings it to its climax, and the coming in mystery is our own repeated response.

Question: Which of these three comings of Christ is the most important for us?

Gospel: The Baptist's Message (Luke 3.1-6)
Each year the two middle Sundays of Advent centre on John the Baptist, preparing the way for Jesus. John came to prepare a community of

repentance who would be ready for the Messiah. This was to be a community not of those who went around moping about their sinfulness, but a community of those who had changed their ways and their whole system of values and priorities. The Hebrew concept that he proclaimed was a matter of turning round and going in the opposite direction. To be ready for the Messiah meant – and still means – such a radical change of attitude. John himself had prepared by going out into the desert, for the Messiah was to come striding across the desert, as did Israel at the exodus. John's clothing and his whole way of life showed his rejection of current materialism and his single-minded dedication. It is not primarily a negative point of view, for his quotation of Baruch (as in today's first reading) or of Isaiah shows that the flattening of the hills and the filling of the valleys is a preparation for the Kingdom of Peace and Justice. A good deal of positive planning and of spadework is needed if we are to be ready to welcome that Kingdom.

Question: What sort of change in my lifestyle is needed for me to welcome Jesus at Christmas?

Third Sunday of Advent

First reading: Rejoice, Daughter of Jerusalem! (Zephaniah 3.14-18)

Zephaniah prophesies that Jerusalem, the Holy City, sacked by the Babylonians, will be restored. It will be a day of overwhelming joy, when the Lord will truly be king in Jerusalem. After the Exile in Babylon, the Jews returned to Jerusalem, but they were continually dominated by one set of foreign rulers after another, tossed from one to another as the plaything of their powerful neighbours. They longed more and more to be free, to have God as their only ruler. When Jesus came, the kingship of God dominated his whole horizon, but they failed to recognize the kingship of God in his proclamation and his way of life. He was not the conquering hero they expected, and the citizens he gathered into his kingdom were the hungry, the poor, the persecuted, the disadvantaged, the alienated, the lost, the despised, the crippled and the sick. It was to these that he brought joy and rejoicing 'as on a day of festival'. If they failed to see God at work in his life, it was because they were looking for the wrong sort of God. If we want to share Christ's joy at Christmas, we must focus on the right kind of Kingship of God.

Question: Am I ready to rejoice at the coming of the Lord Jesus into our midst?

Second reading: Be joyful in the Lord! (Philippians 4.4-7)

The encouragement that begins this reading, 'Be joyful!', gave the third Sunday of Advent, halfway through the preparation for Christmas, its traditional name of Gaudete Sunday. However, it is all very well for Paul to tell us not to worry but to place all our desires before God. In the same vein, the Letter of James tells us that prayer must be made with faith, without a trace of doubt. Nevertheless, are our prayers always answered? How can they be, if you pray for rain while I pray for sunshine? The true prayer of petition is Jesus' own prayer, an embrace of the Father in loving confidence that God is just that, our loving Father. We can think we know what will make us happy, but the only true receipt for happiness is to leave it to God, in the knowledge that our human perception is short sighted and incomplete. Any further prayer must be provisional. It is almost a game: I think I know what will make me happy, but on another level I know that I don't know, that only God knows best. All I can do is to cast my worries onto the Lord and leave the rest to him.

Question: Should I pray for any specific thing, or leave it all to God?

Gospel: John the Baptist's Counsels (Luke 3.10-18)

In this second of the two Sunday gospels about John the Baptist, we first hear details about how to prepare for the coming of the Messiah. Luke is always aware of the dangers of wealth and money, so he concentrates on avoiding its misuse. First, he teaches equal sharing with the needy, no hoarding but generosity. Then he turns to financial exploitation; tax collectors had to pay for the right to collect taxes, and would be tempted to extort a nice margin to cover their own needs. In the same way, soldiers could be tempted to abuse their power of intimidation by bullying those they were meant to protect. The second half of John's task is to point away from himself towards Jesus, who will baptize with the Holy Spirit and with fire. Luke's gospel and the Acts of the Apostles are full of the Holy Spirit. Luke must have been vividly aware of the working of the Spirit in the Church, in its ministers of all kinds and in the life of the Christian communities. He warns also of the fierce fire that will purge away impurities; for John the Messiah is a stern figure who will burn away the rubbish in human hearts to make room for the Spirit.

Question: How would John the Baptist tell me to clean up my life?

Fourth Sunday of Advent

First reading: The Ruler from Bethlehem (Micah 5.1-4)

On this final Sunday of Advent all the concentration is on Mary as she prepares to give birth to her Son. The prophecy of Micah reminds us that God's standards are utterly different from human standards. Bethlehem was an insignificant little hilltop town, the home of the smallest clan of Judah, in an insignificant and oppressed country. Yet it had two moments of greatness, one when David was anointed king there, the other when Jesus was born. David was the youngest of his father's sons, left to look after the sheep when all the others were summoned. He stands in the long tradition in the Bible that God chooses the younger or less distinguished, Abel instead of Cain, Jacob instead of Esau, Joseph the youngest of all Jacob's sons. Jesus seemed to have no visible father at all, and Mary no roof over her head for the birth of her first child. We cannot dare to estimate any person's value in God's eyes, but amid all our striving, all the pushing and shoving for priority, we do have a lurking suspicion that those nearest to God, most marked by the image of God, are the humblest and least distinguished of people. Mary was among them.

Question: Does the Church give special honour to the poor?

Second reading: 'I am coming to do your will' (Hebrews 10.5-10)

As we prepare for Christmas we are reminded that Jesus came to overtrump the disobedience of Adam by his own perfect obedience. It was not the suffering of Jesus itself that redeemed the world, as though suffering had some value in itself, or paid some penalty. The medieval theology that suggested this tied itself in knots about the recipient of this payment: God or the devil? Neither recipient works out! In Romans, Paul is quite clear that the redemptive factor was Jesus' obedience even to the point of suffering on the Cross: 'Just as by one man's disobedience many were made sinners, so by one man's obedience are many to be made upright.' Adam is the image of human disobedience, the disobedience of us all. Today's reading from Hebrews tells us that Jesus was given a body to express his obedience. By his bodily obedience, the guarantee and expression of his full humanity, he brought all bodily men and women back to God. By our bodies, we express our obedience, in sickness and in health. Jesus, too, in his baby's body, his child's body, his youthful body, his fully mature body, expressed his obedience to his Father. In so doing, he prepared for the ultimate expression of loving obedience on the Cross.

Question: What is lacking in my obedience to God?

Gospel: The Visitation (Luke 1.39-44)
Luke's account of the birth and infancy of Jesus is built on the comparison and contrast of the two stories of John the Baptist and Jesus: the Annunciation to the parents, the birth of each, the joy on earth and in heaven, the circumcision, the growth of the child. In each incident, John is shown to be great, but Jesus greater still. Only in this incident do the two families meet, the two stories cross. The two mothers meet each other to marvel at the destiny of their children. The journey from Nazareth to even the nearest of the towns in the hill country of Judah (traditionally Elizabeth's home is located at Ain Karim, now on the outskirts of Jerusalem) would have been arduous, a week's walk for a fit young woman. This special exertion and generosity shows her love and care for her elderly relative, as well as the natural excitement of the two in sharing their motherhood. Luke has already told us that Mary was filled with the Holy Spirit. Now Elizabeth, too, is filled with the Holy Spirit as they share and exchange the praise of God for the gift of their child.

Question: Is there anyone to whom a visit from me would bring special joy at Christmas?

Christmas Day

As in Year A as on p. 11.

Feast of the Holy Family, Year C

In Year C for the first two readings either the readings of Year A as on p. 17 or the following two readings may be used. For the Gospel Luke 2.41-52 is always used.

Alternative First Reading: The Promsie of a Son (1 Samuel 1.20-22, 24-28)

The stress of these readings is not so much on the domesticity of the Holy Family as on leaving the family in the service of God. This is something which many Christians are called upon to do, though it is often the warmth and love of the early years in the family which enables them to do it. The birth of Samuel was regarded as a special act of God. The concept of miracle did not yet exist, since there was no concept of 'the laws of nature' which could be observed or broken – science was not yet sufficiently steady and predictable. Samuel's birth was, however, a special act of God's mercy, since Hannah had long been barren. The child was an answer to prayer. There is therefore a certain similarity to Mary's virginal conception of Jesus. However the chief emphasis of today's readings is on the presence of the child (Samuel and Jesus) in the Temple as a sign of their entire dedication to God. In Samuel's case he leaves his family because he is presented to the LORD in the Temple by his mother. In the case of Jesus he 'escapes' from his family, and his unique position in the Temple and his unique relationship with his divine Father is acknowledged by his parents.

Question: How does a family provide the basis for a holy life?

Alternative Second Reading: God's Children (1 John 3.1-2, 21-24)

On Holy Family Sunday this lovely reading from the First Letter of John takes its clue from the saying of the child Jesus in the gospel. He is wholly absorbed in his Father, with the total absorption of a 12-year-old, star struck and unaware of anything else in the world. On this relationship of Jesus to his Father depends also our relationship with God our Father. By our faith expressed in baptism, we too are God's children, bathed in his love, pampered by his lavish gifts, and committed to doing whatever pleases him, like young children to any loving father. Furthermore, it is repeatedly stressed in this letter that the vertical relationship of love to the Father has its equivalent in a horizontal relationship to our brothers and sisters around us: we cannot claim to love our heavenly Father, whom we cannot see, unless we love the members of our family whom we can see. On a human level it is important for our understanding of Jesus that we should realise that Jesus' concept of love, of family, of fatherhood was founded on the pure, generous and unstinting love of his human parents. It was the love of Mary and Joseph which taught the child Jesus what a fully loving relationship was.

Question: How can human love enrich our concept of God's love?

Gospel: The Child Jesus in the Temple (Luke 2.41-52)
This little incident, the only one told of Jesus' youth, has two attractive lessons for us. First, it is a joy to see Jesus behaving just like any other 12-year-old. He was a real child, and a child of that age goes off exploring, adventuring, frog hunting, sure that the all-powerful, all-knowing parents will know where he or she has gone. Parents meanwhile worry themselves sick at the unexplained disappearance. Mary, the young mother, knows her son and the ways of the 12-year-old. She does not scold or expostulate, but just accepts him with love and relief. Second, Jesus' reply gives us a glimpse of his relationship to the Father. Whether the correct translation is

'in my Father's house' or 'on my Father's business' matters little. Just as his questions to the teachers showed his wisdom, no doubt as yet unsharpened, so his reply to Mary shows his total absorption with his Father, inarticulate also. Jesus' human mind needed to develop and become fully articulate. Even he needed to go on learning and clarifying to himself who and what he was. We learn only gradually who and what we are. A child's development – even a divine child's development – is not to be rushed.

Question: Am I content to await God's good time?

Epiphany of the Lord

First reading: The Glory of the Lord has risen upon You (Isaiah 60.1-6)

Many of the most glorious passages in the liturgy are taken from this third part of Isaiah, written after the return of Israel from captivity in Babylon. They are full of optimism and a new self-confidence. What is more, they show an awareness of Israel's mission to the world. This had already been included in the promise to Abraham that 'all nations will bless themselves in' him – picked up by Mary in her *Magnificat*. But now there is a new consciousness that the choice of Israel was not just for themselves, but so that they could bring light to all the nations. This is expressed in terms of the sunrise that suddenly brings light to a grey world. All they need to do is simply to lift up their eyes and see the throngs of peoples eagerly coming from the remote deserts to draw salvation from Israel. How aware are we that our mission too is to bring light and salvation to a darkened world, that the message of God's love entrusted to us is given to us not only for ourselves but for all?

Question: Does the church bring light to all those around? If not, whose fault is it?

Second reading: The Climax of Creation (Ephesians 3.2-3a, 5-6)

The message of the Letter to the Ephesians is that the mystery hidden from the beginning of the ages has in Christ at last been revealed. In the first century there was great expectation of a defining and transforming event. In Christ, this event had taken place. In the earlier letters, Paul had already referred to it. Now two other dimensions have become clear. The division between Jews and gentiles is no longer valid, for in Christ all nations are summoned to the salvation promised to Abraham. This was only the completion of the promise that in Abraham all nations would bless themselves. Second, in Christ creation was brought to its completion. Just as all creation was created in Christ, the Word and Wisdom of the Father, just so all creation was summed up and brought to a head in Christ. As Christians we believe this, but to what extent do we live by it? Do we see all creatures, and especially all human creatures, as united with us and making sense only in Christ, even if they do not realize it. What confidence and joy this should give us!

Question: Do I see all human beings as chosen by God?

Gospel: The Coming of the Magi (Matthew 2.1-12)
The contrast is overwhelming: Herod, the King of the Jews, the nation prepared since all ages to welcome the coming of God to set all things right, fails to recognize the coming of the Lord. He is so blind as even to make every attempt to liquidate this herald of the completion of history and of Jewish hopes. By contrast, the trio of Wise Men from the east, the traditional home of natural wisdom, show their conviction of the turning point of history by journeying over desert and mountain to welcome and pay homage to the Lord. The evangelist is clear that this is the fulfilment of Isaiah's prophecy of the coming of peoples from the East to pay homage to the Lord. Especially in eastern Christianity is the festival of the Epiphany (rather than the birthday of Jesus) seen as the manifestation of Christ to the world. This is the meaning of the Greek word 'epiphany': it was first used of the manifest coming of the Roman emperor on a state visit, for he was regarded as a deity to whom worship and adoration were due.

Question: Which is the more important day, Christmas or Epiphany?

Baptism of the Lord

First reading: My Chosen One in whom my Soul Delights (Isaiah 42.1-4, 6-7)

In the Book of Isaiah occur four songs about a Servant of the Lord. The fourth is familiar from Good Friday's liturgy, for it is about the servant's triumph through rejection and suffering. Today we are given the first of the four songs. The servant is the Lord's Chosen One, on whom the Lord confers his Spirit, with the mission of bringing true justice to the nations. Jesus refers to himself frequently as servant. He must have had these poems in mind. In his human mind, the opening of the first song must have echoed in his head as he set off after his baptism on his mission to bring the sovereignty of God to a new degree of realism. The coming of the Spirit and the voice from heaven constitute a sign that determines his way. In so many ways, this prophecy is echoed in his behaviour, his gentleness, his light to the blind, his freeing so many captivities of human distortion, his zeal for God's will, and finally in his supreme act of service and love. Is this our programme too?

Alternative first reading: 'Console my People, Console them' (Isaiah 40.1-5, 9-11)

The reading from Isaiah for today is the joyful song that opens the second part of Isaiah. After the 70 years of the Exile, the Israelites are looking forward to the return to Jerusalem, aware that they are soon to be released from their captivity. They have 'served their sentence' in Babylon and their sin has been forgiven. The Lord will lead them in joy across the great desert as he led them across the desert at the Exodus, and will manifest his glory again. For Christians, the excitement is that John the Baptist picks up this message as he prepares the people for the coming of Christ. The coming of the Lord to Jerusalem was never wholly fulfilled, and we can see that the great fulfilment of this passage is in the coming of Christ to his own. He came to Jerusalem, yes, but has the divine glory been yet manifested? He brought the beginning of the Kingship of God, but it is for us Christians to show the glory and the love and the generosity of God to a world that has not yet seen the splendour of his coming. This is the daunting responsibility of those who bear the name of 'Christian', who see in Jesus the manifestation of God's reign.

Question: What are the chief obstacles today to the mission of the Church?

Second reading: Jesus Begins in Galilee (Acts 10.34-38)

In this reading, we are given Peter's address to Cornelius the centurion, the first gentile to be received into the community of the followers of Jesus, a decisive step in the opening of God's blessing on the world. Each of Peter's addresses, however, begins the history of Jesus' mission at the Baptism. In the selection of a successor to Judas, the chief conditions were discipleship, company with Jesus from this first moment of baptism, and witness to the Resurrection. The example of Jesus' life and activity must be familiar to enable us to see what the implications of living out the sovereignty of God must be, how we too can be the servants of the Lord. That is why familiarity with the four gospels is so important. These four different faces of the prism that make up the gospel of Jesus Christ all have their contribution to make to our intimate knowledge and love of Jesus.

Question: Which is your favourite gospel and why?

Alternative second reading: Saved by Baptism (Titus 2.11-14; 3.4-7)

The sentence in this reading that seizes the attention is: 'He saved us through the waters of rebirth and renewal by the Holy Spirit. Is it referring to Jesus' baptism or to yours and mine? My guess is that in the original letter it referred to our baptism, but that, by putting it forward on the feast of the Baptism of the Lord, the Church is referring it to Jesus' baptism as the model of your and my baptism. We received in our baptism the same rebirth as children of God and the same renewal in the Holy Spirit as he did in the Jordan. The image of birth from the waters is a fascinating one, and can be taken on many levels, the ocean as the great, turbulent earth mother from which all life derives, the source of life and fertility for plants, animals and humans, the 'waters' of each mammal's birth. By the waters of baptism, we are given a wholly new life as adopted sons of God. In Luke's account of the Baptism of Jesus, the coming of the Spirit has the main focus. On us, too, the Spirit comes at baptism and empowers us to do all kinds of good work beyond any human ability.

Question: How is the Spirit active in this particular local community?

Gospel: The Coming of the Spirit (Luke 3.15-16, 21-22)

Luke does not tell us who baptized Jesus. In Luke, the story of John the Baptist ends with his promise of one who will baptize with the Holy Spirit – then John is arrested. At the baptism itself all Luke's concentration is on the coming of the Spirit. Indeed, it is hardly an account of the baptism at all, for the baptism is only a time marker for the coming of the Spirit 'when Jesus, after his own baptism, was at prayer'. Jesus' mission begins with the coming of the Spirit. In the same way, in Luke's second volume, the Acts of the Apostles, the mission of the apostles begins with the coming of the Spirit at Pentecost. It is as if Luke wants to show the importance of the Spirit from beginning to end of the Christian life. And this is the case: in both writings, the part played by the Spirit directs all the action. The same is still true in the Church today, although often human stubbornness and blindness do their best to retard or impede this leadership and guidance by the Spirit. Most of us are artistes at blocking the Spirit when the Spirit's promptings are inconvenient.

Question: Is the dove a good symbol of the Spirit?

LENT AND EASTERTIDE

Year A

First Sunday of Lent

First reading: The Garden of Eden (Genesis 2.7-9, 16-18, 25; 3.1-7)

In Lent, the readings are especially carefully chosen. The first readings work through the history of salvation, starting with the story of un-salvation, which makes it all necessary, the Fall of Adam and Eve. Presented in the form of a historical story, this is not really history of what happened long ago to the first man (Adam means generically 'man') and woman. Rather, it is an analysis of what happens to us every day, an image of how sin happens: we are subtly tempted to go against what we know are the divine commandments for life. Look at the way the serpent flatters Eve to make her pleased with herself and so fall all the easier! We fall, come to our senses and find ourselves naked and defenceless. Even so, God does not desert the creatures he loves. He comes to their aid, to help them over the worst: he himself sews garments for them to ease their shame, and finally – a few verses later – promises that evil will not eventually prevail. Other cultures have other stories of how evil comes into being, but only the Hebraeo-Christian story ends with the assurance that evil will be conquered, that the seed of the woman will crush the head of the serpent.

Question: Does the story ring true? Fit it to your own experience!

Second reading: The Second Adam (Romans 5.12-19)

Paul's letter to the Romans sets out in glowing confidence and clarity the process by which evil was overcome. Just as the representative of all humanity, Adam, turned away from God, and by his disobedience set humanity on a course leading to disaster, so Christ, by his supreme act of loving obedience, turned back the course of human destiny. Only Christ, who was not only the supreme Man, but more than man, could so reverse the course of history and bring to God the homage of the human race that would wipe away and extirpate the rebellion from God wrought by

47

human disobedience. We know full well that we were born into a world in which evil begets evil, fraud begets fraud, violence begets violence, jealousy begets jealousy. Salvation consists in the conscious act of putting our faith in Christ, in the reversal he achieved. This is normally – but not always – expressed in baptism, by which we enter into Christ and clothe ourselves in his redemption. So the one man, Adam, prefigures the one Man, Christ. Only the direction is reversed. Adam is paradigm of rebellion from God; Christ the paradigm of loving obedience to God.

Question: Can those who have never heard of Christ enter into his salvation?

Gospel: The Testing of Jesus (Matthew 4.1-11)

By putting this scene of the testing of Jesus at the beginning of Lent, the Church shows that it sees Lent as a period of testing. Matthew sees this moment as the testing of God's Son, as the People of God Israel – God's son, whom he brought out of Egypt into the desert – was tested for 40 years. We may also see it as the time when Jesus reflected on the mode of his mission. His mission was to bring the Kingship of God to a new realization: how should he do this? The Tempter suggests false ways, which Jesus rejects, one after another, each time with a word from scripture, the Word of God. He rejects the idea of the Messiah merely producing the luxury of the plenteous messianic banquet (stones into food). He rejects the idea of a startling personal miracle that none could gainsay (the leap from the Temple). He rejects the suggestion of entering into league with the Tempter's own values of pride and dominion (rule over the world). At the same time Jesus shows himself to be the Second Moses, the founder of a new People of God: like Moses, he spends 40 days and 40 nights fasting; like Moses he is taken up onto a high mountain, from where he can see not merely all the territory of the Holy Land, but all the kingdoms of the earth.

Question: What is the chief fault that tempts the Church away from the way of Christ today?

Second Sunday of Lent

First reading: The Call of Abraham (Genesis 12.1-4a)

Each year on this Sunday we have a reading about Abraham, for with him the history of salvation begins: God prepares a people, the family of Abraham, which will eventually issue in his Messiah, Jesus. Here we have the first beginning. God calls Abram to leave his country, his family, his comfort zone, to go out into an unknown land and an unknown future. Abram has no security beyond the simple promise of God that God will bless him and his family, with a blessing so great that all nations will recognize it and use the very name of 'Abram' as a blessing. In a fierce and arid land, which offers no protection to strangers, he has no family, no children to support him. He is to become a wanderer over the earth, not knowing the goal of his wanderings. He does not ask for the credentials of this voice that calls him. He does not seem even to have any concept of God, and yet he follows this call. Just so, the first disciples at the Lakeside will, without a word or a question, follow God's Son when he calls them. Abram's trust in this voice is the model for all personal trust.

Question: What for me are the real implications of unconditional trust in God?

Second reading: The Response to God's Love (2 Timothy 1.8-10)

This reading is put before us by the Church as an encouragement to persevere in our Lenten resolutions. In his earlier writings, Paul had often seen his own sufferings and those of other Christians as completing those of Christ. Not that there was anything faulty about the sufferings of Christ, but the members of Christ's Body, the Church, must share in the destiny of the suffering Christ. Now the recipients of the letter are called upon to share the sufferings of Paul in prison, not to earn salvation but as a response to the grace of salvation. The word 'grace' has been much misunderstood, as if 'grace' were an independent gift, a thing in itself. In fact, the word is used in the New Testament to express the love of God or of Christ, particularly the burning human love of Christ. Primarily it is a loving divine or human relationship. When Mary is addressed as 'engraced' or 'full of grace', it means that she is the special recipient of God's love, which, in turn, makes her more lovable. So here the 'grace granted to us in Christ Jesus' is the loving way in which God has regarded us from the beginning of time, although its fullness has become visible only at the Appearing of Christ Jesus.

Question: How can I best respond to the grace of salvation?

Gospel: The Transfiguration (Matthew 17.1-9)

Each year on this second Sunday of Lent we read the account of the Transfiguration. It was the moment at which the disciples were shown the divinity of Jesus on the Holy Mountain. The scene is reminiscent of Moses' encounter with God on Sinai, when his face, too, shone like the sun. Moses and Elijah are present because they are the two Old Testament figures who experienced the presence of God on the Holy Mountain. With his usual impetuous generosity, Peter attempts to 'freeze' the moment. The public declaration of Jesus as God's Son at the Baptism is repeated, but with the addition that Jesus is the authorized divine teacher; Matthew is alert to the implications for the Church of the presence of Christ as Teacher. The cloud is also a symbol of God's presence, to which the human response can only be to fall to the ground in fear and reverence. The awesome moment of revelation cannot, however, last, and Jesus brings his disciples back to the dire realities before them with the reminder that his death must precede the revelation of his glory at the Resurrection. Until they have experienced the limitless generosity of his death, and the vindication by God of this love, they are not ready to spread the message of Jesus.

Question: Why are the disciples forbidden to spread the message till after the Resurrection?

Third Sunday of Lent

First reading: Water from the Rock (Exodus 17.3-7)

In each Lent, the first readings dwell on the Old Testament progress of the history of salvation; the third Sunday is always about Moses. In this year, Year A, the incident is chosen to pair with the gospel reading about living water. Christ is the living water of salvation, an image of which is the water provided for God's people when they were tortured by thirst in the desert. It was not just that they could do with a bit of a drink, as we in a well-watered country experience. When you run out of water in the desert you lose all strength, all will to advance, and eventually wilt to death. On two separate occasions, the story is told of Moses striking the rock, and the rabbis held that the rock followed them through the desert. Paul interprets the rock as Christ, who always provides for his people, but with most of them God was not well pleased. They continued to rebel and complain about their hardships and to long for 'the leeks and onions' of their slave life in Egypt. With the same ingratitude, we continue to neglect the salvation offered us, absorbed in any passing pleasures we can find.

Question: How do you use water? Is water of life a good image for the gifts of God?

Second reading: Peace with God through Jesus (Romans 5.1-2, 5-8)

Gradually explaining the mystery of salvation in his great Letter to the Romans, Paul has outlined a world sunk in evil. Then he meditates on Abraham's trust in God's promises, the same unwavering trust that is our only way to salvation, an unshaken conviction that God will come to our rescue in our shame and our failures. But what is the means by which God fulfils his promise of obliterating the evil that grips the human race? It can only be the obedience of Jesus, shown in his loving and obedient death on the Cross, which outdoes the disobedience of the whole human race, represented in Adam's sin. It is not the gore and suffering that are in themselves salvific – like a price paid for human delinquency – but the total extent of the love shown in unflinching obedience to the Father's will. It was love for the Father, but also love for us, for whom he was to establish the Kingship of God on earth. Paul seems to argue that, although in normal terms we were not worth dying for, Christ *did* die for us, just as in his ministry he did not wait for sinners to repent, but actively and unconditionally called them back to himself.

Question: What evils grip the human race today, and what can Jesus' work do to solve them?

Gospel: The Samaritan at the Well (John 4.5-42)

In this lively dialogue, Jesus almost seems to be teasing the Samaritan woman, deliberately leading her into misunderstanding about what he means by living water or about the conditions of worship. Nothing daunted, she gives as good as she gets, replying with a cheeky series of sarcastic questions, gradually edging nearer to the truth: an open-minded Jew – greater than our father Jacob – a prophet – and finally acknowledging him as the Messiah. With its serious message it is a lovely example of Jesus' willingness to engage with people as they are, and of his openness with women. On these last three Sundays of Lent before Palm Sunday in Year A, the Church lays before us the three great symbols of the baptisms that will be celebrated at Easter. This concerns not only those who will be baptized at the Easter Vigil, but all those who are invited to renew our baptismal promise and commitment at Easter. Then we enter afresh into the living and nourishing water of God's love that surpasses any food or drink, into the light that enlightens the blind (the Cure of the Man Born Blind) and true life (the Raising of Lazarus).

Question: In prayer, should we treat Jesus as the Samaritan Woman does?

Fourth Sunday of Lent

First reading: David Anointed King (1 Samuel 16.1, 6-7, 10-13)

In the sketch of the preparation for the coming of Christ which the Church lays before us during Lent, the fourth Sunday brings us to the story of David, with whom the promises of a messianic king originate. As founder of the messianic kingly dynasty, David is the figure of the reality that will be fulfilled by Jesus. Here we have one of the three biblical versions of the discovery of the future king (the others being the story of the young musician at Saul's court and the story of the young warrior slaying the giant Goliath). Here the lesson is that God does not choose as human beings do, although David is obviously an attractive young lad. He would turn out to be a leader of charisma, who could twist anyone round his little finger. God also chose Cain's younger brother Abel, and the youngest of Jacob's 12 sons, Joseph. We constantly have difficulty in accepting that our achievements contribute nothing to God and do not earn his favour. David, the adulterer and murderer, learnt the hard way that we can rely only on God's merciful forgiveness.

Question: Why is David the model of the messianic king?

Second reading: Rise from the Dead and Christ will shine on you (Ephesians 5.8-14)

This reading is obviously chosen to prepare for the gospel reading, in which Jesus brings sight to the blind man. Light is one of the archetypal symbols of hope and encouragement. Without light we are crippled until, as the psalmist says, with the dawn man goes forth to his work and activities. In the Old Testament, God is light who lives 'in inaccessible light'. In the New Testament, this attribute of God is transferred to Jesus, for Jesus proclaims that he is the light of the world. In the final book of the Bible, the Book of Revelation, victorious from the conquest over evil, God and the 'Lamb once slain' together constitute the light of the new city of God, so that neither sun nor moon is required. The reading ends with a positive little couplet, possibly an early Christian hymn adopted into the reading, about Christ as the light who by his Resurrection bursts through the deepest darkness of all, the darkness of death. Even in the darkness of Lent, preoccupied with the coming Passion of the Lord, we look forward to his liberation and ours in the glory of the Resurrection at Easter.

Question: Is Jesus truly the light of the world for me?

Gospel: The Cure of the Man born Blind (John 9.1-41)

The second of the three great Johannine readings about water, light and life featured in the baptisms of Easter gives us the splendid account of Jesus bringing light to the blind man in the Temple. It is full of Johannine contrasts and irony. The 'Jews' or the Pharisees think they have the light and knowledge, but the more they abuse the man born blind, the clearer their own darkness and ignorance become. The more they try to thrust him away from Jesus, the more they push him into seeking refuge in him. Much of the colouring of the scene comes from the controversies towards the end of the first century, when the Pharisees were the only branch of Judaism to survive after the destruction of Jerusalem by the Romans. The New Testament shows that there was bitter opposition between those Jews who accepted the divine claims for Jesus, and those who rejected them. This is especially clear in the fear of the blind man's parents that they would be excluded from the synagogue if they accepted that Jesus' grant of sight was a sign of his divine mission. The doughty and pugnacious man born blind has no such hesitation!

Question: Where did these opponents of Jesus go wrong?

Fifth Sunday of Lent

First reading: The New Spirit (Ezekiel 37.12-14)

At the darkest moment of Israel's history, when they are hopeless exiles in Babylon, the prophet Ezekiel foretells a rebirth. In a great vision, of which we read only three paltry verses, he sees a valley full of dead bones. The Lord commands him to breathe on them and, in Hebrew, the same word is used for breath and Spirit. Ezekiel breathes on them the enlivening Spirit of the Lord. The bones come together, are covered with flesh and sinews, and become 'a great, an immense army'. Directly, the prophet is foretelling the rebirth of Israel as a nation, that they will return to life once again in the Promised Land, given life as a nation once more. We can, however, read this prophecy in the light of the biblical revelation as a whole, and see that it is hinting at and mysteriously suggesting a further meaning. In this fullness of meaning, the Church has always understood the prophecy as a promise of personal Resurrection through the Spirit of God. We are on the threshold of the celebration of the Resurrection of Christ at Easter, and so of our own Resurrection. This reading partners today's gospel reading about the new life given to Lazarus.

Question: What is this Resurrection to which we look forward?

Second reading: The Gift of the Spirit (Romans 8.8-11)

In the preceding chapters of the Letter, Paul has described and analysed the process of salvation through Jesus' offering of himself in loving obedience to his Father, and our own integration into Christ by being plunged into him in baptism, and so joining him in his death and Resurrection. This eighth chapter is the chapter of the Spirit, considering how we are transformed by the Spirit of Christ, now become our own spirit, through which we live. The Spirit of the Risen Christ is already in us and is empowering us, but our bodies are not yet transformed, as they will be in the final Resurrection. In the later Pauline epistles (Colossians and Ephesians), this is expressed differently: God has already brought you to life with Christ. You have already been raised up: it remains only for this risen life to be revealed with him in glory (Colossians 2.12; 3.4). The Spirit of God and of Christ, described in the Johannine writings as the Paraclete or Helper, leads us into all truth, giving us an ever deeper appreciation of God's gifts to us. The Spirit also gives us strength and zeal to do God's work in all our ways of life.

Question: How can the Spirit change our lives?

Gospel: The Raising of Lazarus (John 11.1-45)
The third of these great Johannine gospel readings on the Sundays of Lent, leading up to and preparing us for the baptisms of the new members of Christ at the Easter Vigil, grips us with the story of Jesus' gift of life to his friend Lazarus. This is not the same as the gift of life to us by Jesus in the Resurrection, for Lazarus returns to ordinary human life, and will die again, whereas the Christian Resurrection transforms us into a new way of life, giving us a life that is a participation in the divine life. But the Resurrection of Lazarus is the last and greatest of Jesus' signs, his marvellous works that point towards and hint at this final gift of divine life. The first of the signs was the transformation of the water of the Law into the wine of the messianic wedding banquet at Cana. These signs show us who Jesus really is. As well as showing the divine power of Jesus – for only God can give life – they also show the real, human love of Jesus for his friends. He is upset by Lazarus' death and weeps for him, sharing the human sorrow of his family as he shares our sorrows, too.

Question: Is death something to fear?

Palm Sunday

Today's liturgy concentrates on two very different events: the triumphal entry of Jesus into Jerusalem as Messianic King and the events of a few days later, culminating in this agonizing and shameful death. This seeming end point was to be reversed by the explosion of new life in the Resurrection after three days, an explosion which constituted God's vindication of Jesus' loving obedience and the affirmation that it has overcome and wiped out the sin of Adam, human sin.

The Gospel of Palms (Matthew 21.1-11)

How much time did Jesus spend in Jerusalem? The Gospel of John recounts four separate visits to Jerusalem, whereas Mark (and Matthew and Luke, who follow Mark's outline) compresses all Jesus' Jerusalem ministry into one visit, inaugurated by this solemn entry. As all the gospel incidents, this event is recounted by the evangelists in the light of their fuller understanding of the meaning of Jesus after the Resurrection. We see the colourful festal atmosphere of crowds going up to Jerusalem for a festival, waving palm branches as banners in their enthusiasm, and, of course, singing as they march. Jesus and his disciples join in. But it may be only later that the significance of this event was grasped: this was the fulfilment of the prophecy of Zechariah about the messiah coming into his inheritance, to complete his God-given mission and to proclaim peace to the nations. Matthew especially, writing for a community steeped in Judaism, actually quotes the prophecy and also the psalm verse about 'him who comes in the name of the Lord'. He stresses that Jesus is this Son of David, whose eschatological kingship is about to be established.

The Mass

The Mass begins with the usual two preliminary readings. These help us to understand the shocking story of the gospel. First Isaiah 50.4-7 presents this first Song of the Servant of the Lord. Jesus saw himself as this Servant who would give his life to save his people, fulfilling the destiny foretold long ago by the prophets. Then Paul's exultant hymn in Philippians 2.6-11 explains how Jesus' disregard for his own due honour won him the homage of all creation to the glory of God the Father.

The Passion of Christ according to Matthew

The accounts of the Passion given by the four evangelists are not identical. The basic outline of these dreadful events was clear enough. It is confirmed by the contemporary Jewish historian Josephus, who tells us that Jesus was crucified by Pontius Pilate at the instigation of the Jewish leaders. The task of the gospel writers is not to relay to us the raw facts, but to help us understand their significance. Each stresses a particular aspect. For instance, John underlines that this was the triumph of Jesus: he shows his divinity already at the arrest scene. He himself yielded up his Spirit only when he had completed his task Matthew's preoccupation with Judaism dictates that he show in detail how the events accord with God's plan revealed in the scriptures. Almost every incident is told in such a way that hearers familiar with the scriptures would catch allusions to the biblical writings: nowhere is this more obvious than in the account of the death of Judas. Although Pilate the governor must bear the final responsibility, Matthew also stresses the pressure put on him by the crowd manipulated by the politically adept Jewish authorities, culminating in the horrific cry, 'His blood be on us and on our children' – an allusion to the sufferings undergone by the next generation during the siege of Jerusalem by the Romans. The significance of the events is further underlined by the apocalyptic earthquake at Jesus' death, and by the immediate release of the blessed dead, who come at last into the Holy City.

Easter Sunday

First reading: Peter Instructs Cornelius (Acts 10.34, 37-43)

Peter was speaking to Cornelius. Cornelius was the Roman centurion who already reverenced God and had had a vision that he should invite Peter to come and instruct him. Peter shows that Jesus was a real human being. He went about, bringing God's peace to everyone he could meet. Nevertheless, he was executed as a criminal. So God reacted by raising him from death to a life that was totally new. This was the fulfilment of all the promises made to Israel, bringing to completion God's plan in creation. Life moved into a new gear. Peter expresses this that God has appointed the Risen Jesus to judge the living and the dead. The Jews expected that at the end of time, at the completion of all things, God would come to set everything to rights, to judge things according to their true worth. Now Peter says that Jesus is the one who will be this judge. Jesus is the Lord who will bring all things to completion and to judgment. By his rising from the dead, Jesus comes to this position of supreme authority over the whole world. Paul put it that he was 'constituted Son of God in power' by the Resurrection.

Question: What do you find the most encouraging aspect of Easter?

Second reading: New Life in Christ (Colossians 3.1-4)

This reading is the visible tip of an iceberg, of which much more lies below the surface! Paul here tells us that all our interest must be in heavenly things, the things of Christ, because we share Christ's life. What is more, that life is no ordinary life. What does all this mean? We share Christ's life because faith in Christ means that we put all our trust and hope in Christ. We have been baptized into Christ, that is, by baptism we have been dipped into Christ as into a river, and come up soaked with Christ, or dripping with Christ. I am growing into Christ, share his inheritance, his status as son of God. The wellspring of my life is no longer the ordinary, natural life which enables me to live, breathe, digest, feel, see, sing and play, love and hate. It is the Spirit of Christ that spurs me to generosity, service, kindness, self-control, peace and openness. This life, says Paul, is still hidden, and will be fully manifested only at the coming of Christ. But if I am to be true to my profession of faith in baptism, the principles on which I operate must be those of this risen life of Christ.

Question: How can I help non-Christians to appreciate the wonder of Easter?

Alternative second reading: The Paschal Lamb (1 Corinthians 5.6b-8)

Paul is obviously referring to the Jewish festival of the Passover, at which a lamb was sacrificed. This festival was originally the meal commemorating the move of pastoral nomads at the beginning of spring from their winter to their summer pastures. A lamb was sacrificed as an offering to the gods. After the exodus from Egypt the festival came to celebrate the great trek of 40 years through the desert, and the Covenant of Moses on Sinai, when Israel became God's people. When Israel settled down and became agriculturalists, this festival coincided with the Week of Unleavened Bread, marking the beginning of the wheat harvest, when all last year's wheat products and leaven were cast aside as corrupt and outdated, 'past their sell-by-date'. Leaven is, after all, fermented, and so, in some sense at least, corrupt. Thus, the Passover Festival became associated with total newness. At the Last Supper Jesus sealed the New Covenant and gave himself to his disciples as the new paschal lamb, the sacrifice of this New Covenant. Paul uses this symbolism to indicate that Christians are people of total newness. Their conduct must be purged of all the old corruption and marked by a new freshness, the innocence and purity of new life.

Question: How can I help non-Christians appreciate the wonder of Easter?

Gospel: The Empty Tomb (John 20.1-9)

There are several accounts in the various gospels of the discovery of the empty tomb. The slight variations between them show all the marks of oral tradition, for in genuine oral tradition each 'performance' is different. Different people tell the story slightly differently, stressing different aspects. This story stresses the proof that the tomb really was empty, for the apostles examine the evidence carefully. Other accounts concentrate less on the evidence and more on the message, that they will meet the Risen Lord in Galilee. It was important to establish that the tomb was empty, to prevent the charge that the meetings with the Risen Christ were simply ghost appearances. Apart from the proof that this was a real, living and bodily person, these meetings stress two factors, the power of the Risen Christ and the commission given to the disciples. They are to go out into the whole world and spread the message, always accompanied by and strengthened by Christ himself. In this account, Simon Peter is clearly the senior, authority figure, to whom the Beloved Disciple defers. But it is the love of the Beloved Disciple that immediately brings him to faith.

Question: Is the empty tomb the chief evidence for the Resurrection?

Second Sunday of Easter

First reading: A Community of Peace (Acts 2.42-47)

The first readings throughout Eastertime this year are about the earliest community of the followers of Jesus (they had not yet acquired the name 'Christians') at Jerusalem. From time to time Luke, the author of that history of the earliest spread of the Christian message called 'The Acts of the Apostles', gives a summary of their lifestyle. This passage is the first of these summaries, placed just after the birth of the Church at Pentecost. It is a picture of peace, generosity and devotion, summed up in grateful praise of God. Luke is showing us the quality of a community where the Spirit of God is given free play; he is giving us an ideal to strive for. It is a community to which anyone would wish to belong, a community in which love prevails, where each member is attentive to the needs of others. It is not surprising that their number was constantly on the increase. Are the pillars on which it stands the two types of prayer, in the Temple and in the Eucharist, or the resultant human goodness of generosity and joy? Perhaps, as in any community we experience, there were tensions beneath the surface, but the warmth of trust in the Lord breathes through the account and promises a solution to every problem.

Question: What is the most attractive feature of this Christian community?

Second reading: A Sure Hope (1 Peter 1.3-9)

Throughout the Easter season this year we read this First Letter of Peter. Whether it was actually written by the fisherman, the enthusiastic and impetuous leader of the Twelve, or simply attributed to him, is still discussed by scholars. The answer makes little difference to the positive message of the Letter, which is full of the optimism of the new Christian movement, the love, confidence and joy of looking forward to the promised inheritance. Traditionally, the Easter Vigil is the time for new baptisms, and so new births into the Church. Even if we were baptized long ago, we can still benefit from the occasion to refresh our newness in Christ. New birth into Christ brings with it a promise of an inheritance. Just as an earthly inheritance can change a whole situation and way of life, even a change of personality, so does our entry into Christ. Of course, it brings with it responsibilities and duties, and the reading mentions the trials which test us like gold. I know that I, for one, still have a lot of dross which needs to be purged before I can confidently stand before the Lord and claim my inheritance as a son of God.

Question: Is my baptismal freshness tarnished or enriched or both?

Gospel: The Peace of the Risen Christ (John 20.19-31)

This passage from John's Gospel has all the more significance because it brings the Gospel to a close. The story of the breakfast party with the Risen Christ on the shore of the Lake of Galilee is a sort of appendix. The storyline of the main Gospel ends with Thomas blurting out 'My Lord and my God'. The Gospel therefore ends, as it began, with the only two unmistakable declarations in the New Testament of the divinity of Jesus. 'The Word was God' and 'My Lord and my God' bracket the Gospel, showing the purpose and angle of the whole, to show that Jesus is God. It complements the other gospels: they show a man who is also God, whereas this Gospel shows a God who is also man. It is with the divine authority that Jesus confers on his Church the divine power to forgive. Real forgiveness is indeed Godlike. It is not simply 'forgive-and-forget', but forgiveness in the knowledge that a hurt has occurred. Just as a bone, broken and merged together again, can be stronger than it was before it was broken, so forgiveness can create a real link of love on both sides, a treasured secret of divine graciousness between forgiver and forgiven.

Question: Am I part of the Church's divine power to forgive?

Third Sunday of Easter

First reading: The Meaning of Resurrection (Acts 2.14, 22-28)

Pentecost was the birthday of the Church, the moment when the Christian Church was born. This reading from Peter's speech at Pentecost explains not so much the actual even of the gift of the Spirit, but the event which lies behind it, the Resurrection. Peter sees it as predicted in the psalm; the Holy One of the Lord can never remain lying in the corruption of the grave. His Resurrection is the revelation of true and permanent life. It brings to a conclusion the whole plan of God for the world. The scriptures of the Old Testament teach us the ways of God with the struggling and recalcitrant human race, its highs and lows, its joy in the Lord and its betrayals. We can see ourselves in it at every stage of this history, mirroring our own hopes, promises, failures. But running through it all is the certainty that God will fulfil his promise to Eve to bring good out of evil. So the Resurrection of Christ is God's acceptance of the loving obedience of his son, expressing and renewing the loving obedience of the human race, which we, unaided, could not provide. By raising Christ to life God shows his final acceptance of Christ's rededication of human loyalty.

Question: What does it mean to say that you share Christ's risen life?

Second reading: The Blood of the Lamb (1 Peter 1.17-21)

In the Middle Ages, when ransoming was a current practice for setting captives free, theologians debated to whom the ransom of Christ's blood was paid: was it to God or to the devil? However, the real context of this passage is Old Testament sacrifice, and particularly sacrifice for sin. In these rites, the blood is valuable not for the pain it represents but for life. There can be no reconciliation without blood, according to Leviticus 17.11, for blood represents life. The blood of a living creature belongs to God because it represents the God-given life. Once the blood is shed there is no more life. So in Hebrew thought the blood is a cleansing and enlivening agent, renewing life. It takes away and overrides the deadness of sin. The blood of Christ cleanses us, since it represents the divine life which is given to us. So in the Book of Revelation the garments of the martyrs are washed white (the colour of victory) in the blood of the Lamb, that is, they receive new life. This also explains the importance of the Eucharistic blood of Christ, which gives us Christ's own divine life and enables us to live with his life.

Question: Is there any advantage in receiving Communion from the chalice?

Gospel: The Journey to Emmaus (Luke 24.13-35)

This attractive and delicate story is the story of the journey to faith in the Risen Christ: it occurs in any Christian instruction, and especially in the Eucharist, formed from instruction based on the scriptures, and then brought to its fulfilment in the sacrament. The two disciples (are they man and woman, as so often in Luke, perhaps Cleopas and his wife?) start off deep in depression and disappointment. But they are open minded and willing to learn as the Stranger explains to them from scripture the meaning of events. Their hearts burn within them at the Stranger's words, but their eyes remain closed. It is only in the sacramental meal that they recognize the Risen Christ. This is the story of any Christian instruction, culminating in the Eucharist, for the Eucharist is a sacrament of initiation, bringing us to the intimate, personal encounter with Christ. Once they have been enlightened and have learnt the profound meaning of the events, the truth of the scriptures and the Resurrection, then the disciples return to the Holy City and carry on their own Christian apostolate by spreading the news of the Resurrection. This is the shape of the Christian vocation which we all receive, to assimilate and pass on the meaning of Christ's Resurrection.

Question: Is the Old Testament a book for Christians?

Fourth Sunday of Easter

First reading: The First Conversions (Acts 2.14, 36-41)

Last Sunday we heard Peter's explanation of the Resurrection as the fulfilment of God's plan as outlined in the scriptures. Now we hear the practical consequences: baptism to wash away sin and to receive the Spirit as Christ did at his own baptism. From the very beginning Luke shows that baptism and the promises are for all, not just for the Jews. All are welcome into Christ's company. But we must first understand what Peter (and before him Jesus and even John the Baptist) meant by 'repentance'. It is not a doleful moping over sin. It is a change of life, a complete change of scales of values. The Greek word means a changed mindset. The corresponding Hebrew word means turning round and going in the opposite direction. It is a serious business, not to be undertaken lightly. We think we did it at baptism, or when we took on Christianity for ourselves. In fact, a more careful scrutiny tells us of all kinds of unswept corners where the old standards and scales of value remain lurking, breeding and reproducing. The Christian is baptized into Christ and into Christ's death in order to rise to new life with Christ, but even St Paul acknowledges that he remains caught up in doing the evil he wants to avoid.

Question: Is it possible to take on Christ's life and yet to sin?

Second reading: The Example of Christ (1 Peter 2.20-25)

The most striking element in this passage is that it is addressed primarily to slaves, exhorting them to bear with the harsh treatment of their masters after the model of Jesus' own acceptance of harsh treatment. What is striking is that the author does not in the least question the institution of slavery or see injustice in the harsh treatment that slaves tended to receive. It was not for a millennium and a half that the treatment and the institution itself of slavery was seen to be incompatible with Christ's teaching on the equal dignity and limitless value of every individual human being. As the Pope pointed out on his recent visit to Britain, credit for the extension to slaves of this important principle of social justice must be given to Christian political movements in Britain. However, the wider principle remains, that we all suffer to a greater or lesser degree, and that this is a priceless opportunity to draw close to the suffering Christ, and consciously to share in his redemptive suffering. Neither must the suffering of others in union with Christ be neglected. It is easy to despise the poorer and more neglected members of society, and to forget that, by their very disadvantages, they can be the chosen favourites of the Lord.

Question: In practice, does slavery still exist in the modern world?

Gospel: The Good Shepherd (John 10.1-10)

In each year of the three-year cycle of readings this Sunday is designated Good Shepherd Sunday, with readings from the parable given in John 10. In the first two Sundays after Easter the meetings with the Risen Lord are described, but after that the most important truth about the Risen Lord which the Church puts before us is that Christ is the Good Shepherd. In the Old Testament, God is the Shepherd of Israel, and indeed in the neighbouring pastoral nations, too, the protective deity of the nation is commonly called their shepherd. As the pastoral ancient world well knew, the duty of the shepherd is to care devotedly for the sheep, with no regard to the personal cost to himself. Ezekiel repeatedly castigates the recent shepherds of Israel for their failure to care for the sheep and for managing the flock for their own personal advantage. It is especially striking that in all four gospels the divine title of Shepherd is transferred from God to Jesus himself, at least implying not only that Jesus is the perfect shepherd, but also that he is the incarnation of that divine Shepherd, fulfilling the duties which had hitherto been credited to God alone. By his selfless generosity he is the model for all rulers and leaders of nations.

Question: Are you a sheep?

Fifth Sunday of Easter

First reading: The Appointment of Deacons (Acts 6.1-7)

There are two really striking features about this story. The first is that the first officials appointed in the Church are called 'servers' or 'servants', which is what 'deacons' means. St Paul will stress, writing to the Corinthian community, that any job in the Church is a service to the community. It is not a dignity to be proud of, except in so far as it is a sharing in the service given by Christ himself, the Servant of the Lord. The most important part of it is to attend to the needs of the community, not to preen oneself on getting a grand position. The second feature is that even so early in the life of the ideal early community a squabble occurs. One group feels that it is being neglected. The split may even be worse that Luke allows us to see, for all the new officials appointed belong to one of the two parties, the Hellenists. This is not going to ensure an even distribution of food between the two parties! Is a completely different organization being set up, so that the deacons are, in fact, a leadership parallel to that of the apostles? Even in a good community reconciliation of differences needs to occur constantly.

Question: Is there any split in your community that needs to be reconciled?

Second reading: A Royal Priesthood (1 Peter 2.4-9)

The background of this reading is the covenant between God and his people of Israel on Mount Sinai. There the mountain was so sacred that the people were not allowed to approach it. Now the author tells us that the new people of God, chosen by God, is so sacred that we can huddle close to the rock that is Christ. In the old dispensation, Moses alone was holy enough to approach the mountain and offer sacrifice; now it is the whole people. The whole people now constitute a royal priesthood and a consecrated people that can offer sacrifice. One of the principal emphases of Vatican II was that the Eucharistic sacrifice is offered by the whole people, not by the priest alone. Yes, the priest does have a special function, that of presiding at the Eucharist, and without this presidency the Eucharist cannot take place. Nevertheless, it is the sacrifice of the people as a whole, which the laity offer just as much as the priest. The reading also uses another Gospel image: the people of God is a house built of living stones, a living holy Temple, joined to the foundation stone who is Christ.

Question: What difference does it make that the Mass is the offering of the people as a whole?

Gospel: Jesus warns of his Departure (John 14.1-12)

As the festival of the Ascension approaches Jesus begins to prepare his followers for his own departure from the world. There are two aspects of this. First, Jesus speaks of the final purpose, union with the Father, and his preparation of a place for us there. 'There is plenty of room', he says, suggesting not that there are plenty of separate cubicles for different sets of people (bishops, babies, monks and maniacs), but that there is no lack of space. No problem of 'only one wins the prize' in this case. The second aspect is preparation for the future Church on earth, and the almost shocking promise that in the absence of Jesus – but in the strength of his Spirit – his people will do 'even greater works'. Paul teaches that believers 'make up what is lacking in the sufferings of Christ', for in every age the Church fills up the measure of Christ's sufferings; it is a Church that shares its Master's trials. In the same way, in every age, the Church must carry on the works of Christ. In John, the 'works' of Jesus are the marvellous deeds, beyond human powers, which show who Jesus is. We too are called on to perform marvellous deeds, beyond human powers, works of grace and generosity.

Question: In heaven what will our relationship with other people be?

Sixth Sunday of Easter

First reading: The Gospel spreads to Samaria (Acts 8.5-8, 14-17)

The story of Acts is the spread of the gospel to 'the ends of the earth'. The first few chapters described the ideal Church at Jerusalem. All this was shattered by the persecution that erupted into Stephen's martyrdom. We missed out that story, reserving it for St Stephen's feast on Boxing Day. The effect of things getting too hot in Jerusalem is that the Word of the Lord begins to spread beyond the city, and first to Samaria, the country region just north of Jerusalem. The peace of God's Kingdom comes to the Samaritans in the form of liberation from sickness and the torment of various diseases. Luke notes for us the joy which this brings, a joy that is the sign of the Kingship of God. It is notable that the distinction between the gift of faith and the fuller gift of the Spirit is already marked in the same way as the distinction in the modern Church between baptism and confirmation. The apostles come to administer the sacrament, just as nowadays the bishop comes, marking the unity of the Church and the special position of the successors of the apostles.

Question: Is the presence of the Spirit in the Church a matter of joy to me?

Second reading: Defence of the Faith (1 Peter 3.15-18)

This final reading from the first Letter of Peter gives a heartening model for defence in persecution. In modern society, any persecution faced is more likely to be verbal mockery or contempt than blood shedding. A Christian stance on moral issues can so easily incur charges of narrow mindedness or blindness. It is not always easy to keep one's temper and give a fair and helpful reply 'with courtesy and respect', expressing the consequences of the Christian hope. Such a reply just might strike a chord deep down, rather than an explosive or sarcastic riposte, which merely deepens the divide. This can be a real and important Christian witness. The final sentences of the reading are helpful here, for the accounts of Jesus' trial stress that Jesus himself was silent 'like a lamb before its shearers' as the Suffering Servant of the Lord, in fulfilment of the scriptures. The Passion account is full of irony and mockery, from the High Priest, from Pilate, from the soldiers; but if Jesus himself did not explode at the false accusations and mockery, but retained his dignified silence, we, too, should keep our cool and reply with courtesy.

Question: How do you reply to mockery of the Catholic or Christian stance?

Gospel: The Advocate whom the Father will send (John 14.15-21)
Only in John is the Spirit whom the Father will send called 'the Advocate' or 'the Paraclete'. Both names have the same derivation and the same meaning, but the former is from the Latin, the latter from the Greek. It means someone 'called to one's side' as a helper, principally as a defender in a lawsuit. The word 'Paraclete' also suggests comfort and strength, as implied in the quality *paraclesis* or perseverance. In the discourse after the Last Supper, when Jesus is preparing his disciples for their future task, there are four separate sayings about the Paraclete. The Paraclete is sent both by Jesus and by the Father, but always from the Father's side. The Paraclete, the Spirit of truth, will teach the disciples everything and lead them into all truth, witnessing to the Father. The Paraclete is 'another Paraclete', that

is, other than Jesus, who will make Jesus present when Jesus is no longer physically with them. The close link and interplay between these three figures gives us not only the beginnings of the theology of the Trinity, but also a lasting confidence that Jesus is never absent from his Church. With the guidance and patronage of the Paraclete the Church enters more and more deeply into the understanding of the divine mystery.

Question: Have you ever felt especially helped by the Spirit of Jesus?

Sunday of the Ascension

The first two readings come each year. The gospel and its commentary is for Year A only.

First reading: The Ascension (Acts 1.1-11)

How are we to envisage what happened at the Ascension? Two feet disappearing into a cloud? It is mentioned only in the Acts, and the other gospels seem to imply that the Risen Christ was glorified on the day of the Resurrection itself. Luke, the author, is putting across several messages. First, the 40 days since Easter should not be carefully counted. In biblical language, '40' makes just 'a fairly long period', often a period of preparation, like Jesus' 40 days being tested in the desert, or Israel's 40 years of the Exodus. For all that time Jesus has been preparing his apostles. Second, it is the definitive parting of the physical Jesus, after which the Risen Christ is no longer with his disciples. It is now the Spirit of Christ which is at the heart of the Church, inspiring all its activity. Third, Luke represents Jesus as a prophet (and more than a prophet), so he leaves his disciples in the same way as the prophet Elijah, who was taken to heaven in a fiery chariot, leaving his disciple Elisha to carry on his work, filled with a double share of his spirit.

Questions: In what way is the Ascension an encouragement? How would you explain the Ascension to a non-Christian friend?

Second reading: Christ is Supreme (Ephesians 1.17-21)

The blessing that forms the core of this reading gives the sense of the Ascension for the Church. It is not the manner of Christ's departure that is important, but the exalted position of Christ, and the power of God which raised Christ from the dead. This same power has called us to be believers, made us rich in the glory of his heritage, and has given us the strength to follow Christ. As Christians, we believe that Jesus was divine not only from birth but from the moment of his conception. It was then that the Word of God became flesh. And yet something further happened at the glorification of Christ in his Resurrection. Paul says he was 'constituted Son of God in power' at the Resurrection. Is this the same as the claim which the high priest declared blasphemous, 'You will see the son of man seated at the right hand of the Power and coming on the clouds of heaven'? In the final scene of the gospel of Matthew, Jesus declares, 'All power in heaven and on earth has been given to me', and the Book of Revelation shows the Risen Christ sharing the throne of God.

Question: Are there evil spirits abroad in the world? How does the existence of evil fit with God's power?

Gospel: A Final Commission to the Disciples (Matthew 28.16-20)
For Matthew, this is a momentous climax. Jesus is on the Holy Mountain. But, where is this mountain? We do not know; but that does not matter. The importance is that Jesus is commissioning his followers as the Second Moses. Just so he taught the Sermon on the Mount on the Holy Mountain, as Moses had given the Old Law on Mount Sinai. He is the glorious Son of Man of the prophecy of Daniel, to whom all authority on earth was given; but to him is given all authority in heaven and on earth. As Jesus sends them out, he promises that his divine presence will be always with them. It is in the strength of that presence that they will pursue their task. This promise provides the final bracket of the Gospel, as the name given to Jesus by the angel provided the opening bracket: 'They will call him "Emmanuel", a name which means "God is with us".' The divine presence of God in Jesus and in his community is the clue to the whole Gospel of Matthew. In the centre of the Gospel, it is again stressed, 'Where two or three are gathered together in my name, there am I in the midst of them.'

Question: Why does Matthew present Jesus as the Second Moses? Does it mean anything to me?

Pentecost Sunday

All three readings come each year, although other readings may be used in Years B and C

First reading: The Birth of the Church (Acts 2.1-11)

The ministry of Jesus starts with the coming of the Spirit at his Baptism, and so the ministry of the Church begins with the coming of the Spirit at

Pentecost. There can be no witness to Jesus or to his message, no spreading of the Kingship of God, without the Spirit of Jesus. Another lesson from this parallel is that the task of the Church and the life of the Church are the same as those of Jesus himself: to bring God's Kingship to its fulfilment by bringing healing, love and joy through the message of the Risen Christ. The rushing wind and the tongues of fire are an allusion to the coming of God's Spirit upon Moses and the elders in the Old Testament. So the new message is the fulfilment of the Old Testament, breaking out beyond the boarders of Judaism to include all peoples of the world. The union of all these peoples, all understanding one language in their own way, is a deliberate contrast to the scene at the Tower of Babel, when the Lord split up all the peoples of the world by their inability to understand one another's languages. The list of unpronounceable peoples is itself a witness to the universality of the Church!

Questions: How can the Church claim to be the Spirit at work in the world? Mention three outstanding ways in which the Church shows Christ at work today.

Second reading: The Body of Christ (1 Corinthians 12.3-7, 12-13)

The slightest glance around a church full of people is enough to show the variety within the Christian community. But it needs the hints given us by Paul to remind us that every member of that community has his or her own special gift to contribute. Mercifully, these gifts are all different. It is valuable to reflect on the natural gifts that we find all around us. It is also valuable to reflect how dull, or even intolerable, life would be if I lived with a lot of clones of myself, all with the same gifts and the same faults as me! Every one of us contributes something different and valuable in its own way, whether it is the baby squeaking as a sign of new, developing life or the older person contributing wisdom, experience and even the suffering of Christ. The other inspiring thought is that all these varied and diverse people go to make up the Body which is Christ. We all have experience of various corporate bodies, organizations and companies, but none of these other bodies makes up a person. That Person is Christ, since as Christians we all live and operate through Christ's Spirit.

Question: Who is the most Christ-like figure for you in the present or recent past?

Gospel: The Gift of Peace (John 20.19-23)

At first sight, this is a surprising gospel reading for Pentecost, but, of course, the event of Pentecost came too late to be a subject for the gospels, and we read the account of another incident where the Risen Christ gave the Spirit to his disciples. There are two emphases in the account. The first is peace. Christ brings peace to his disciples with the double greeting of peace, and peace is a Christian watchword. Peace was the song of the angels at Jesus' birth. Each of Paul's letters opens with a greeting of peace. The Letter to the Ephesians proclaims that Christ is our peace, the reversal of all worry, strife, envy, jealousy, self-seeking ambition. 'Go in peace' is Jesus' dismissal of those he cures, and also the dismissal at the end of Mass. Peace was Jesus' bequest to his disciples after the Last Supper. The second watchword is forgiveness, for God was always known as a God of mercy and forgiveness, as Jesus came to show by his constant approach to sinners. But the Lord's Prayer shows that if we do not ourselves forgive, we block God's forgiveness of ourselves too.

Question: 'Forgiveness is the only sure path to peace.' Does this cause any difficulties?

Trinity Sunday

First reading: The Definition of God's Name (Exodus 34.4-6, 8-9)

This is one of the really very central passages of the Bible. In Judaism, the special name of God (sometimes written 'Yahweh') is never spoken. For two reasons. It is too sacred and awesome to be pronounced, for the name somehow makes the personality present. It is also too intimate: we do not bandy around in public the special family name by which we are affectionately known by our nearest and dearest. So where the name occurs in the Bible, a conventional 'the LORD' is used. The name itself was revealed to Moses at the Burning Bush, but not its meaning. Here for the first time the meaning is given, 'The LORD, the LORD, a God of tenderness and compassion.' Only when God has to forgive Israel for its first, heinous but rapid, rebellion, is the meaning of the name revealed. And this meaning is echoed again and again down the scriptures, in Deuteronomy, in Psalms, in Jeremiah. Even Jonah has to admit it when, to his fury, Nineveh is forgiven! This is the way Israel loves to picture its God, as a God of forgiveness. The Prologue of St John and the Parable of the Prodigal Son are no new inventions.

Question: Is 'God of forgiveness' the most important concept of God?

Second reading: A Trinitarian Blessing (2 Corinthians 13.11-13)

This reading, concluding with the Trinitarian blessing, is the finale of this Letter to the Corinthians. The interrelationship of the three Persons of the Trinity is a theological elaboration, reached only gradually in Christian meditation. Paul, however, already often mentions the three Persons in parallel, making some distinction between them or at any rate between their functions in the story of salvation. When he mentions one he seems at the same time to be conscious of the influence also of the other Persons of the Trinity. The constant triple mention of each of the Persons in itself suggests equality, each playing a special part, as 'It is God who gives you a sure place in Christ, giving us as pledge the Spirit in our hearts' (2 Corinthians 1.21), or 'You have been justified in the name of the Lord Jesus Christ and through the Spirit of our God' (1 Corinthians 6.11). Rather than prying, so to speak, into the personal interrelationships of the three, the scripture limits itself to mentioning the part played by each in our creation, salvation and sanctification. God, whom we also address as *Abba*, Father, is the initiator. It is through the work of Christ that we are justified, saved, redeemed, reconciled. The Spirit is at work in transforming us in holiness.

Question: What would you like to add to St Patrick's cloverleaf image of the Trinity?

Gospel: God so loved the World (John 3.16-18)

At first sight, this part of the dialogue with Nicodemus seems to mention only the Father and the Son. A chief concern of the Gospel of John is to show the relationship of loving obedience between Father and Son. The love and equality in a perfect relationship between a human father and a son is the nearest reflection of such love that we can envisage. In complete trust and confidence, father gives to son everything that is his. His only interest is the advancement of the son. Son's only care is to please his father and to be as close to father as he can be, in word, action and relationships. Each has a vibrant and continuous bond of love for the other. Such a relationship may be rare in human family life, but it can model for us a pale reflection of the loving relationship between the Father and the Son. And the Spirit is, in fact, mentioned because the love itself is the living bond uniting the two. We must, however, appreciate that any such language limps and belittles the divine relationship, which is of a different order of perfection and intensity. Human language can never begin to render the divine reality, which is utterly beyond our comprehension.

Question: What is the best human image for the Trinity?

Sunday of the Body and Blood of Christ

First reading: The Gift of Manna (Deuteronomy 8.2-3, 14-16)

Here the Church sets before us the model for the Eucharist, that is, God's care in feeding his people during the 40-year desert trek of the Exodus from Egypt. During this time the Israelites were fed with manna; they called this 'bread from heaven', so that it has become the model for the Eucharistic bread. As in all folktales, the story has gradually grown in the telling, but originally manna seems to have been the wholly unexpected and seemingly miraculous provision of a sweet substance exuded from a tamarisk bush. The Hebrews did not know what it was, and, with a wordplay typical of the Bible, etymologized it as *manhu*, the Hebrew for 'What is it?' The reading also stresses that this heavenly gift was a symbol of divine Wisdom, God's revelation of himself given from heaven. Hence the saying, quoted by Jesus to Satan during his Testing in the Desert: 'Man does not live on bread alone, but on every word that comes from the mouth of God.' The manna became the symbol and reminder of God's unfailing care for his people throughout their journey, just as the Eucharist is the expression of God's care for his people today.

Question: How does the Eucharist reveal God's love?

Second reading: The One Body of Christ (1 Corinthians 10.16-17)

Paul, in writing to that difficult and divided community at Corinth, chides the people for their disunity and selfishness. There were some rich members of the community, who got to the Eucharist early, took all the best places, and proceeded to unpack their hampers and feast, while the latecomers – presumably the workers and slaves – justifiably felt excluded and remained hungry. In the strongest terms, Paul insists that the Eucharist must be the symbol and expression of unity, and that those who prevent it being so are making themselves 'answerable for the body and blood of the Lord'. Paul seems to use 'the body of Christ' interchangeably of both the Eucharistic bread and the Eucharistic body, which is the community, united in the celebration of the Lord's Supper. It is difficult to see when he means one, and when the other. He obviously regards them both as equally important and equally sacred. Later in the Letter he will explain that the community is an organism, in which everyone has their own, individually special part to play, all living with the Spirit of Christ as the life-giving principle. Unless this life is truly shared it is distorted and fails of its purpose.

Question: How is it possible to make the Eucharist an expression of unity?

Gospel: The True Bread of Life (John 6.51-59)

This is the final section of Jesus' great discourse in the gospel of John on the Eucharist, delivered in the synagogue at Capernaum. It is in the form of a synagogue sermon, commenting in turn on the phrases of Psalm 78: 'He gave them bread – from heaven – to eat.' Jesus explains that these words are truly fulfilled not by Moses' historic gift of manna in the desert, but by the Father's continuous and repeated gift of Eucharistic bread. The discourse has the same pattern as the Mass, instruction followed by eating. The first two sections of the discourse were about God's gift of revelation in Christ, which is accepted and assimilated by belief in the teaching of Jesus. Now we come to the final section on God's gift of Christ as food. Particularly striking are two points. First, the stress on eating: the word used for '*eat* my flesh' is full of the reality of eating; it really means 'chew', and designates the sacramental eating as a real assimilation of the nourishing food. The second point is that 'my flesh for the life of the world' links firmly to the Last Supper: the Christ that we receive is the Christ at the very moment of his redemptive act of self-offering.

Question: How does Christ nourish us in the Eucharist?

Year B

First Sunday of Lent

First reading: The Covenant with Noah (Genesis 9.8-15)

Lent is a time when the first reading really comes into its own. On the Sundays of Lent the Church leads us step by step through the preparation of the People of God for the supreme event of Easter, the Resurrection of Christ. In each year of the three-year cycle of readings the first Sunday starts with the Bible story before Abraham. This year it is the promise to Noah that God will never again let a destructive flood devastate the earth. The first thing Noah does on emerging from the ark is to sacrifice to God in thanksgiving for his deliverance. To this God replies with his promise, guaranteed by the reassuring sign of the rainbow, which binds together earth and heaven, a sort of glorious pathway to heaven.

Each of the covenants God makes with his people emerges from evil. There is no pretence that we are not fallible, sinful human beings. Time after time the human partners fail and break the covenant. Time after time God forgives and offers a covenant again, until the new covenant in the blood of Christ. A good way to start Lent, acknowledging our sin and welcoming God's invitation to start again.

Question: How can Noah's covenant help my Lent?

Second reading: The Pledge of a Good Conscience (1 Peter 3.18-22)

Lent reaches its climax with the renewal of our baptismal promises at the Easter Vigil on Holy Saturday night. This reading begins to prepare for it. Noah's emergence to new life from the waters of the Flood (amid devastation and destruction) is compared to, or made a symbol of, emergence to new life from the waters of baptism. Water is the source of all life. Just look at the way people so often carry a little water bottle around with them! Although you don't really appreciate water as the source of life until you have been lost in the desert without any water, getting more and more desperately thirsty and weaker. See a drooping flower revive when it is given a few drops of water! The waters of baptism are a symbol not only of washing away sin, but more importantly of new life in Christ. To 'baptize' means to 'dip' in water. By baptism we are 'dipped' into Christ's death. We emerge from the water soaked through with the risen life of Christ, so that henceforth Christ is our life. The reading encourages us to prepare for the renewal of this life at Easter by getting our conscience in order. This needs thought, commitment and prayer, so that we are ready with 'the pledge of a good conscience'.

Question: What are the great symbols of Lent? Is there any modern symbolism like water?

Gospel: Jesus is Tested in the Desert (Mark 1.12-15)

Each year the gospel reading for this Sunday is about Jesus' testing in the desert. Mark's emphasis is distinctly different from that of Matthew and Luke. No details of the testing, but rather Jesus' sojourn in the desert is rather almost a return to the peace of the Garden of Eden. The desert of Judea, between Jerusalem and the Jordan Valley, is a noble and dignified solitude of smooth, sandstone hills. Nothing grows, of course, but wild camels and the occasional leopard prowl around. There Jesus was 'with the wild animals' as, led by the Spirit, he made his preparation for his mission. In what way was he tested? We may presume that in solitude and prayer he was working out the implications of the Voice from Heaven at his Baptism. How was he to run his course as the beloved Servant of the Lord? Precisely how was he to bring the presence Kingship of God into people's lives? The '40' is often used in biblical accounts for a period of preparation, as Israel's 40 years in the desert, or the apostles' 40 days of preparation between Easter and Ascension. We may use our 40 days to reflect on how we may bring God's presence to bear in and through our lives.

Question: Is testing the most important aspect of Lent?

Second Sunday of Lent

First reading: The Sacrifice of Isaac (Genesis 22.1-2, 9-13, 15-18)

Every parent must be moved by this terrible and touching story. How could a parent do such a thing? And the boy was Abraham's last hope for the survival of his family, granted to him to fulfil God's promise. The narrative becomes slower as they approach the point. Note how Isaac is allowed to carry the wood, but Abraham carefully carries anything on which the child might hurt himself, the fire and the knife. One can imagine the jaunty boy trotting along beside dad, bouncing questions at him, and dad's monosyllabic answers as he nears the moment he dreads. Yet he trusted in God right up to the brink of disaster, somehow confident that God would rescue him from this terrible deed. As Paul stresses, it was not anything Abraham did that justified him, not his obedient action, but his total trust in God. Can I claim such total trust in God's love?

The tradition of the Church sees in this tragic story a 'prequel' of God's offering his only, beloved Son for the salvation of the human race, a mysterious preparation for that supreme offering which we celebrate at Easter. The goal of this season of Lent is kept before our eyes as we advance along the way.

Question: How could a loving father do this?

Second reading: Paul rejoices in God's love (Romans 8.31-35, 37)

Paul reflects on God's love: if God loved us sufficiently to deliver up his son for us, there is no limit to his love. Paul begins the letter by exposing the human race as mired in sin. Of this the sin, the disobedience of Adam – and 'Adam' means 'man' in Hebrew – is the symbol. Then Paul shows that the perfect, loving obedience of the Second Adam, Christ, to his Father unravels our disobedience, and set us steady again in God's love. The Cross is the supreme act of love: Jesus loves his Father even to death. God accepts this death out of love for the human race. Nothing, continues Paul, can separate us from this love, not life or death, not human or superhuman powers. As an example of this love, he then shows how even the Jews who rejected Jesus remain God's beloved people. In the end, they, too, will be saved by that love.

Question: Do you see Christ's obedience as the heart of his sacrifice?

Gospel: The Transfiguration (Mark 9.2-10)

As the time of the Passion approaches the foreboding of the disciples grows. Jesus sustains them by this vivid experience of his more than natural nature. On the Holy Mountain of revelation, they see him transformed. It was a real visual experience, albeit described in symbols familiar from the Bible, brilliant white clothes and so on. Moses and Elijah are seen there because they also had experienced the vision of God on the Holy Mountain. For Moses, this was at the giving of the Law on Mount Sinai; for Elijah, in the cave of Mount Horeb. The disciples were frightened, confused and overcome at the awesome experience, and yet comforted in a way which made Peter want to prolong it. This will later be the rare reaction of Christian mystics, a reassuring terror and a frightening homelessness, the awareness of a presence that is at the same time awesome and comforting, an experience that cannot fully be put into words. The Voice from Heaven is an echo of the Voice at Jesus' Baptism. There, however, it was addressed to Jesus, whereas here it is spoken to the disciples, proclaiming Jesus as authorized teacher, the extension of that same divine voice.

Question: Is fear the right attitude we should have to God?

Third Sunday of Lent

First reading: The Ten Commandments (Exodus 20.1-17)

The ten commandments are not harsh rules, but an invitation to Israel, showing them how to be God's people: if you wish to keep close to God, you must behave in a way compatible with God's own nature. They come in an order opposite to the priorities of the modern materialistic world, for God comes first, then values of persons, and values of things and possessions only at the end.

We need to think of them not as prohibitions but as expressing positive values. So 'keep holy the Sabbath day' implies freedom of worship and freedom for leisure. 'Honour your parents' includes not only obedience of children, but real parental care for children and of adult children for aged parents, as well as other family values. 'No adultery' means fostering the marriage bond and continually deepening it. 'No false evidence' includes the right to free speech, and a good reputation, free of slander, no brainwashing or distortion by school systems or by the media.

Many of these laws come in other ancient law codes, but in Israel they have a different meaning, for here they are the guidelines for living under divine protection and in the company of the Lord.

Question: Is any of the ten commandments more important than the others?

Second reading: The Scandal of the Cross (1 Corinthians 1.22-25)

This reading is all about power and wisdom: 'The Jews demand miracles (works of power) and the Greeks look for wisdom.' These are two measures of success in the normal terms of our modern materialistic society. Power comes in the form of wealth, authority, command, being the boss. Wisdom results in the respect and reputation accorded to a person: he or she makes the right decisions. But where are these in the crucified Christ? He was a prisoner, powerless, horribly tortured, mocked and derided. He commanded nobody. There is no respecting a tortured prisoner. God's standards are different, and we heard them in the form of the commandments in the first reading. It was these standards that brought Jesus to the situation of the Passion, for these were the standards he had sought to live out and show to people by his way of living and acting. This was the Kingship of God which he came to proclaim and to spread. In the first reading, we heard the demanding, positive standards for membership of God's people. Now, in this second reading, we receive strength and comfort from the reassurance of the model of Christ, the only ideal of the Christian.

Question: What are the qualities of true wisdom?

Gospel: The Cleansing of the Temple (John 2.13-25)

According to John, this scene took place at the beginning of Jesus' ministry, on the first of Jesus' four visits to Jerusalem. At each subsequent visit the Temple authorities lay in wait for Jesus, increasingly keen to eliminate him, but unable to do so until his hour had come. The other gospels place as the final climax both this incident and all other scenes of Jesus in Jerusalem. Whichever is correct, the incident is the basic cause of Jesus' arrest and tortured death. By his action, Jesus had demonstrated that the worship carried out in the Temple was vain in God's eyes and must be superseded. To the Temple authorities, this was intolerable, and he must be removed. Again, Jesus demanded a complete reversal of standards. His puzzling saying about building the Temple anew in his body was at last understood by his disciples to mean the Temple that was his Body, the Church. The material building that had been the centre of worship was no longer important. Henceforth all worship would take place in any place, but within the Christian community. The community – or the Church – was now the place of sanctification and of prayer to God.

Question: What was Jesus trying to show by his demonstration in the Temple?

Fourth Sunday of Lent

First reading: The Broken Covenant (2 Chronicles 36.14-16, 19-23)

In the first readings for Sundays in Lent, we have worked through the promising but tragic history of Israel, a history of promises by God, of broken promises and fresh starts by Israel. We have seen this in the stories of the covenant with Noah, Abraham's obedient trust, the commands given to Moses to keep Israel faithful to the Lord. Now we come to the final disaster, inevitably brought on by Israel's repeated failure and infidelity. This whole history of Israel was composed with the background theme that fidelity brought prosperity and that a healing punishment was the inevitable consequence of desertion of the Lord. In this final chapter, the historian looks back at the ultimate disaster of Exile in Babylon, and the return of a renewed Israel to the Holy City. Even then the promised blessing of God seemed long delayed. They were an oppressed little community, huddled round Jerusalem, harassed by their neighbours and dominated by one foreign power after another. After some years they did summon up energy and resources to rebuild the Temple, but they continued to yearn for the decisive intervention of God that would enable them to serve their Lord in freedom and total dedication.

Question: Is material prosperity really a blessing?

Second reading: The Grace of God (Ephesians 2.4-10)

The Letter to the Ephesians is usually considered to be the first commentary and reflection on Paul rather than from the Apostle's own hand, reflecting on the salvation won by Christ. After the record in the first reading of the repeated failures of Israel, the message, twice repeated, that salvation is by grace alone, is particularly apt. Grace here means not a substance poured into our souls to provide some sort of salvific energy, but is the unmerited favour and choice by God. It is a personal relationship rather than a material, rather even than a spiritual gift. God has smiled on each of us and invited us into his friendship. In the light of this gift of friendship, we are strengthened and encouraged to serve him, so that this gift of his friendship becomes an ever stronger and more important element in our lives. God shows us his love and we respond. So he shows us even grater love. But the greatest gift of all is his Son and the salvation, the new life won for us by Christ.

Question: What are the difficulties in having a personal relationship with God?

Gospel: Nicodemus (John 3.14-21)
After Jesus' conversation with Nicodemus comes this reflection on his visit. Is it Jesus' reflection or the evangelist's? The text does not make it clear. Throughout the gospel of John, people are coming to Jesus and judging themselves by their reactions to Jesus. The Father judges no one, but has

given all judgment to the Son. In his turn, the Son does not judge, but we judge ourselves by our reaction to him. So at the wedding at Cana the disciples believe in him and see his glory. In the Temple, the Jews refuse belief and are condemned. Then comes Nicodemus in secret and in fear. He is sitting on the fence, afraid of the Pharisees, but by the time of the burial he has decided for Jesus. After Nicodemus comes the Samaritan woman, cheeky and unbelieving at first, but won over by Jesus' playful persistence. And so on: the Jews on one side, the man healed at the Pool of Bethzatha on the other; the Jews on one side, the man blind from birth on the other. The decision is ours too: when confronted by Jesus do we come to the light that our deeds may be known, or do we shun the light?

Question: How can we be afraid of the light?

Fifth Sunday of Lent

First reading: The New Covenant (Jeremiah 31.31-34)

For Christians, this reading from Jeremiah can be called the climax of the Old Testament. It is certainly the climax of the history of Israel that we have been following in the first readings of the Sundays of Lent. The exile to Babylon seemed to be the end of the road. Israel had lost king, country, Temple and cult. They had been unfaithful to their Lord once too often, and at last the covenant was left in tatters. Paradoxically, however, this was the moment of advance, the moment that brought Israel to be a world religion, by which all humanity could benefit from the salvation promised to Abraham. The covenant was to be renewed, not, as previously, dependent on the institutions, Law and cult of Israel, but open to every individual, an individual commitment to the Lord, written on human hearts. 'No need for everyone to teach brother'? Yes, we must still learn from one another and accept the guidance of the Church, but the bond is between God and the individual, no longer the race as such. This is 'the covenant in my blood for the forgiveness of sin' to which Jesus refers at the Last Supper. He sees it ratified in his blood, as the first covenant was ratified in the blood of animal sacrifice. The forgiveness it brings is the final forgiveness, pre-echoed in God's forgiveness of the sin of Israel down the ages.

Reflection: What important lesson have I recently learned from someone else?

Second reading: Jesus' Prayer (Hebrews 5.7-9)

The wonderful second reading is the heart of the Letter to the Hebrews that dwells on the priesthood of Christ. Here the author prepares us for the coming celebration of the Passion by reflecting on the double aspect of the human fear and pain of Jesus, and his complete, loving obedience. It says his prayer was heard. What prayer? Not the prayer to be spared death, for that prayer was not heard. Rather the deeper prayer, the prayer at the heart of his burning desire to establish the kingship of God in human hearts, bringing peace between heaven and earth by his perfect obedience. How then did he 'learn obedience through suffering'? The secret of the Cross of Jesus is that here he reached the perfect obedience to his Father, giving everything to his Father's will. His whole life and ministry had been devoted to the Father's will, to establishing the Father's Kingship on earth. Now it reaches its highest point. His perfect obedience overrode and expunged the disobedience of Adam, that is, the archetypal disobedience of the whole human race. So by accepting defeat, pain and humiliation he obtained for himself and for all victory, bliss and exaltation to glory.

Question: What have I learnt from suffering, my own or someone else's?

Gospel: Exaltation through Suffering (John 12.20-33)
This moving gospel reading is the immediate prelude to the account of the Last Supper and the Passion. It is full of Jesus' dread and confidence at what he knows is approaching. In the gospel of John, there is no agony in the garden before Jesus' arrest, for in John the story of the Passion is so shaped that it is clearly the triumph of the Son of man. There is no mention of humiliation or mockery. Jesus remains in control from the beginning, when he permits the guards to take him into custody, until the end, when he calls out that he is ready to die: 'It is complete.' This is all the hour of the exaltation of the Son of man, when Jesus is raised up in every sense. All the more important, then, for John to show before the Passion that the cost for Jesus was real, with this little dialogue in prayer between Jesus and his Father. This is John's equivalent of the prayer in the garden. The second reading from Hebrews shows that there were in early Christianity strong but slightly variant traditions of Jesus' prayer before his Passion. All express his very human fear, his unshakable commitment to his task and his loving confidence in his Father's care.

Question: What are my real fears? Can I entrust them to God?

Passion Sunday

Gospel of Palms: Jesus Enters Jerusalem (Mark 11.1-10 or John 12.12-16)

The procession of palms is joyful and sad at the same time. It is the triumphant entry of the Messiah as King into his holy city. The crowds were celebrating and singing the psalm for the festival as they entered the city, not knowing that they were, in fact, welcoming the Messiah at the coming of the Kingship of God. Often in Mark the actors in the story do not realize the full significance of their actions, as when the Roman soldiers later mock Jesus as King, which we know he is. As Christians, we believe that the Kingship of God was fulfilled or established by the death and Resurrection of Jesus, the drama that begins with this entry and ends at the story of the empty tomb. John tells us that it was only afterwards, when Jesus had risen from the dead, that the disciples realized the significance of the event. The Resurrection was the keystone of the arch, which at last made sense of everything, showed everything in a new light. John also tells us that this was the humble king of the prophesy, riding, not on a triumphant warhorse but on a humble donkey.

First reading: The Song of the Servant (Isaiah 50.4-7)

In the Book of Isaiah occur four songs, of which this is the third, sung by a mysterious Servant of the Lord. It is not clear who this Servant is, but he is totally dedicated to the service of the Lord, a disciple who listens devotedly. Through suffering, this Servant brings to fulfilment the salvation that the Lord intends for Israel and for the world. Jesus saw himself in the terms of this Servant, and the four songs feature throughout the liturgy of Holy Week.

Second reading: Raised high through suffering (Philippians 2.6-11)

This hymn was probably not written by Paul himself, but taken up by him into the letter, a very early Christian hymn. It celebrates the triumph of Jesus through his selflessness. The assertions at the end are staggering. The hymn claims for Jesus the titles and the worship that are due only to God. What is more, this acknowledgement of Jesus does not detract from the glory of God, but is precisely 'to the glory of God the Father'. This is perhaps the fullest statement in Paul of the divine glory of Jesus, and it is won by his humiliation in death.

The Passion according to Mark

Jesus deserted

The gospel of Mark is concerned to show Jesus as a real, human person. So the story of the Passion begins with the very real fear and horror of Jesus in the garden. Mark represents Jesus as almost beside himself with apprehension at the torture that he knew he would suffer. Again and again he returns to seek companionship from his disciples, to find them callously asleep. The Passion story ends, too, with a loud cry of agony as Jesus breathes his last.

The divine Jesus

The core of the Passion story is the trial scene. Before the high priest, Jesus acknowledges that he is the Messiah of Judaism, and the Son of the Blessed One. To these titles he joins 'Son of man'. In the Book of Daniel, the Son of man is a glorious figure who triumphs over persecution to receive from God all power on earth. So now Jesus claims to share God's throne as that Son of man. It is for these divine claims that is rejected as a blasphemer and handed over to the Romans.

The triumph of God

When Jesus cries out on the Cross, 'My God, my God, why have you forsaken me', he is not in despair, but is beginning Psalm 22. The Psalm begins in persecution, but ends in the triumph of God and the vindication of the sufferer. This gives the meaning of his Passion: by it, Jesus brings the triumph of God and his own vindication by God. The Cross is the moment, not of abandonment by God, but of the most complete union of Jesus to the Father. Jesus here establishes the Sovereignty of his Father by his total, loving obedience. This is why the centurion proclaims, 'Truly, the man was Son of God.' It is also significant that here for the first time in the gospel a human being recognizes Jesus as Son of God. And he is not a Jew but, rather, a gentile – the beginning of the spread of the gospel to all nations of the world.

Easter Sunday

First reading: Peter Instructs Cornelius (Acts 10.34, 37-43)

Peter was speaking to Cornelius. Cornelius was the Roman centurion who already reverenced God and had had a vision that he should invite Peter to come and instruct him. Peter shows that Jesus was a real human being. He went about, bringing God's peace to everyone he could meet. Nevertheless, he was executed as a criminal. So God reacted by raising him from death to a life that was totally new. This was the fulfilment of all the promises made to Israel, bringing to completion God's plan in creation. Life moved into a new gear. Peter expresses this that God has appointed the Risen Jesus to judge the living and the dead. The Jews expected that at the end of time, at the completion of all things, God would come to set everything to rights, to judge things according to their true worth. Now Peter says that Jesus is the one who will be this judge. Jesus is the Lord who will bring all things to completion and to judgment. By his rising from the dead, Jesus comes to this position of supreme authority over the whole world. Paul put it that he was 'constituted Son of God in power' by the Resurrection.

Question: What do you find the most encouraging aspect of Easter?

Second reading: New Life in Christ (Colossians 3.1-4)

This reading is the visible tip of an iceberg, of which much more lies below the surface! Paul here tells us that all our interest must be in heavenly things, the things of Christ, because we share Christ's life. What is more, that life is no ordinary life. What does all this mean? We share Christ's life because faith in Christ means that we put all our trust and hope in Christ. We have been baptized into Christ, that is, by baptism we have been dipped into Christ as into a river, and come up soaked with Christ, or dripping with Christ. I am growing into Christ, share his inheritance, his status as son of God. The wellspring of my life is no longer the ordinary, natural life that enables me to live, breathe, digest, feel, see, sing and play, love and hate. It is the Spirit of Christ that spurs me to generosity, service, kindness, self-control, peace and openness. This life, says Paul, is still hidden, and will be fully manifested only at the coming of Christ. But if I am to be true to my profession of faith in baptism, the principles on which I operate must be those of this risen life of Christ.

Question: How can I help non-Christians to appreciate the wonder of Easter?

Alternative second reading: The Paschal Lamb (1 Corinthians 5.6b-8)

Paul is obviously referring to the Jewish festival of the Passover, at which a lamb was sacrificed. This festival was originally the meal commemorating the move of pastoral nomads at the beginning of spring from their winter to their summer pastures. A lamb was sacrificed as an offering to the gods. After the exodus from Egypt the festival came to celebrate the great trek of 40 years through the desert, and the Covenant of Moses on Sinai, when Israel became God's people. When Israel settled down and became agriculturalists, this festival coincided with the Week of Unleavened Bread, marking the beginning of the wheat harvest, when all last year's wheat products and leaven were cast aside as corrupt and outdated, 'past their sell-by-date'. Leaven is, after all, fermented, and so, in some sense at least, corrupt. Thus the Passover Festival became associated with total newness. At the Last Supper Jesus sealed the New Covenant and gave himself to his disciples as the new paschal lamb, the sacrifice of this New Covenant. Paul uses this symbolism to indicate that Christians are people of total newness. Their conduct must be purged of all the old corruption and marked by a new freshness, the innocence and purity of new life.

Question: How can I help non-Christians appreciate the wonder of Easter?

Gospel: The Empty Tomb (John 20.1-9)

There are several accounts in the various gospels of the discovery of the empty tomb. The slight variations between them show all the marks of oral tradition, for in genuine oral tradition each 'performance' is different. Different people tell the story slightly differently, stressing different aspects. This story stresses the proof that the tomb really was empty, for the apostles examine the evidence carefully. Other accounts concentrate less on the evidence and more on the message, that they will meet the Risen Lord in Galilee. It was important to establish that the tomb was empty, to prevent the charge that the meetings with the Risen Christ were simply ghost appearances. Apart from the proof that this was a real, living and bodily person, these meetings stress two factors, the power of the Risen Christ and the commission given to the disciples. They are to go out into the whole world and spread the message, always accompanied by and strengthened by Christ himself. In this account, Simon Peter is clearly the senior, authority figure, to whom the Beloved Disciple defers. But it is the love of the Beloved Disciple that immediately brings him to faith.

Question: Is the empty tomb the chief evidence for the Resurrection?

Second Sunday of Easter

First reading: Christian Sharing (Acts 4.32-35)

On the next six Sundays of Eastertide we hear the story of the earliest Christian community. Each Eastertide the Church puts it forward as a model for us, giving important aspects of their life. This first reading stresses the unity of the community, and the mutual caring to ensure that no one is in want. This care of those in need, and particularly in financial matters, remains a strong challenge to us today. The care for the needy remains a strong emphasis throughout the Bible, from the earliest part of the law codes of Israel until the Letter of James and beyond. As man and woman are made in the image of God, we are to care for one another and for those in need as God cares for us; this is part of the human obligation to foster life and to care for creation.

The gospel of Luke especially stresses the dangers of wealth and the need to use wealth responsibly and generously. This is followed through in the Acts of the Apostles as part of being 'one in heart and mind'. The other feature of their life together is the bold proclamation of the Resurrection of the Lord.

Question: How far is the model practicable for a modern Christian community?

Second reading: Begotten by God (1 John 5.1-6)

The second readings for the Sundays of Eastertide this year are all from the first Letter of John. The main topic is Christian love. It is quite significant that this Sunday's passage is out of order. It centres on two overarching aspects of Christian love, which are vital for any genuine manifestation of that love. The first aspect is that this love, which conquers the world, is built on faith in Jesus as Son of God. 'The world' here stands for all the evil and godless attitudes standing in opposition to Christian values. By raising Jesus from the dead God has shown the vanity of these attitudes, and has made the victory of Christian love over them sure. These are the true values that in the end will prevail. The second aspect in that by Christian love we are raised to be sons of God, co-heirs with Christ and able to cry 'Abba, Father' truly to God. To the Hebrew mind to be a 'son of' is wider than mere physical generation. It involves respect, devotion, obedience, keeping an eye on, careful conformity in desire, ability and behaviour. It is much like being 'in the image of', but closer, stronger, more heartfelt and more intimate.

Question: Which imagery do you prefer, to be a son of God or in the image of God?

Gospel: Jesus in the Upper Room (John 20.19-31)
Two aspects of this meeting are especially striking. This is the last scene of the gospel of John, for Chapter 21 is an appendix. At the end, before

the concluding reflection, Thomas gives the only direct acclamation in the New Testament of Jesus as God. Nowhere else is Jesus directly hailed as 'God', although there are ways in which he is equivalently so presented. So in a way this acclamation of the Risen Christ is the climax of the New Testament. Second, it is striking that Jesus' final blessing is of peace and forgiveness. The mission of all Christians is to bring these to a troubled world. Throughout the Bible God is a God of forgiveness. The Old Testament consists of a series of covenants of forgiveness, each in turn broken by God's Chosen People. The covenant with Noah after the Flood, the covenant with Abraham, with Moses after the worship of the Golden Calf, finally the new covenant promised by Jeremiah when unfaithful Israel is being exiled to Babylon. Christianity is not for the perfect but for the sinner, surrounded by sinners. Forgiven sinners must bring forgiveness to all those around them.

Question: How far is the authority of the Church compatible with individual judgment?

Third Sunday of Easter

First reading: Peter's Speech to the Jews (Acts 3.13-15, 17-19)

This reading is the final section of Peter's speech to the people of Jerusalem after Pentecost, when he is explaining to the crowds the significance of the first miracle worked by the apostles in the power of the Spirit. Like all the speeches in Acts, it is not a word-for-word, tape-recorded report, but is a sample of Peter's preaching to the Jews. He lays the blame for Jesus' rejection squarely on them, but shows that it was just as scripture had foretold. All the speeches end with an invitation to repent. This does not mean simply to get all weepy about past sins, 'how dreadful and wicked I have been'. It means that the listeners, and we, must change our ways, adopt God's and the Risen Christ's system of values. To convert means I was going in one direction; now I turn round and go in another. Then the way I look at the world becomes different. I see things from a different angle, God's and Christ's angle.

This sort of conversion does not so much look at the past with regret as look at the future with confidence. It is the new determination that allows God to wipe out our sins.

Question: What difference does Christ's Resurrection make to my life?

Second reading: Our Advocate with the Father (1 John 2.1-5)

This second reading advances one step further than the first. The first is about conversion, the second about blotting out former failures. Jesus Christ is our Advocate with the Father, 'standing at the right hand of the Father', because he takes our sins away. How does he do this? By his act of obedience on the Cross Jesus wipes out the disobedience of Adam, that is, of all humanity. Adam (which means 'man') is the figure of all humanity, and Adam's sin is the symbol of all human sin, a sort of 'prequel' of all sin, an act of turning away from God, of independence and disobedience. On the Cross Jesus was perfectly united to the Father, in an act of utter obedience in love, to which the Father in love responds, with a renewal of love for all humanity.

For us, too, it is true that if we know God, if we have any appreciation of God and any personal bond to God, we cannot but obey him. God's commands are not arbitrary, but are the way of keeping close to God. By the command of love God reveals himself and invites us to be like him.

Question: In what sense is the world renewed by the Resurrection?

Gospel: Fish for Supper (Luke 24.35-48)

The two disciples had met Jesus on their way to Emmaus. There Jesus had used the Eucharistic meal to reveal himself to them, for the Eucharist is always an occasion for us to get to know the Risen Christ better. Now he meets the whole group of disciples in their refuge, the Upper Room. It is perhaps the same incident as the one we heard last Sunday, but this time there are different emphases. Now the stress is on the meeting with a real person, not just a ghost. That is why he eats a piece of fish. The important lesson of this is that, in our Resurrection to true life, it is the whole person that is raised, not just the soul. Christian teaching is that a person is an animated body. We work out our salvation with fingers and toes and other bodily members, and all will be raised to life. It is not just a matter of thoughts and intentions! The whole body is baptized into Christ and is the instrument of our salvation. The body will be changed, and St Paul tells us that it is stupid to ask what sort of body we will have in the Resurrection, but I will be raised as a whole person.

Question: Will we have bodies in heaven?

Fourth Sunday of Easter

First reading: The Healing Power of Jesus (Acts 4.8-12)

The Acts of the Apostles shows that the Church carries on the life of Jesus. Under the leadership and power of the Spirit it represents the Risen Christ in the world of the first century and of today. So Peter and Paul work the same sorts of miracles as Jesus as signs and works of power. They heal people, raise the dead, forgive sins and spread the Good News of the sovereignty of God, just as Jesus did. In less spectacular ways also the life of the community still continues the work of Jesus. Peter explains that all this is done 'in the name of Jesus'. The name signifies the power of a person. So we are baptized in, or even into, the name of Jesus, and in this way take on his personality and his power in the Spirit. We become the company of Jesus. It is in his name or power that we hope. In the early years of the Church Christians were known as those over whom the name of Jesus had been pronounced, that is, those who have entered under Jesus' patronage and who trust in his name.

Question: In what ways could your local Church carry on the life of Christ more faithfully?

Second reading: The Love of God for his Children (1 John 3.1-2)

From beginning to end this first letter of John is a meditation on Christian love and its implications. The innermost motivation of all Christian activity is the awareness that we have been raised to sonship of God and to being co-heirs of God with Jesus. Both women and men have been raised to this sonship, for only sons (not daughters) could inherit. This sonship enables us to call God 'Father'. When Paul speaks of this, he uses the Aramaic word 'Abba' as a sort of talisman and guarantee that we can pray 'Father', using the same address as Jesus himself used. 'Abba' is not a children's word like 'Daddy', as has sometimes been supposed, but is the expression of a warm and responsible adult relationship. Just as Jesus' sonship of the Father consisted in doing perfectly the Father's will, and being about the Father's business in his whole life, so the Christian, spurred on by this relationship, is drawn to a heartfelt obedience. This must be a challenge to us: is the mainspring of our activity to act as sons of the Father, being truly his representatives in the world and striving to bring his will to completion in all that we do?

Question: Does the scripture help to show us what is meant by being 'sons of God'?

Gospel: The Good Shepherd (John 10.11-18)

Each year on this Sunday there is a reading from John about the Good Shepherd. To think of ourselves as woolly and cuddly sheep, obedient to the shepherd, would be a mistake. Sheep are renowned as being silly, contradictory creatures, always starting off in the wrong direction, getting themselves into tangles and difficulties. In the Holy Land, they are scraggy beasts, pastured on rocky, often dangerous ground, amid boulders and rocky cliffs, threatened by wild animals and marauders. It was not simply a matter of the shepherd sitting on a rock and idly playing his pipe. He needed to be on the alert to save the sheep from hurting themselves. So Jesus as the good shepherd is kept well occupied by our foibles, our stubbornness, our mistakes and our fears. Again, as in the other two readings, there is the reassurance of a close relationship with the Father. Jesus knows us intimately, just as he knows the Father. It is questionable whether in real life a shepherd should lay down his life for his sheep: what would happen to the remainder of the flock? But it is an expression of his whole-hearted devotion to the sheep, and an assimilation to the case of Jesus.

Question: Are you a sheep?

Fifth Sunday of Easter

First reading: Paul's Fearless Proclamation (Acts 9.26-31)

This reading is the first news that we have had that the Church has spread beyond Jerusalem. Paul has received his vision of the Risen Christ and has joined the disciples, being baptized at Damascus. Then, according to his letters, he went off to Arabia for three years before going up to Jerusalem. Paul's arguing with the Hellenists (or Greeks) is a foretaste of his bringing the gospel to those beyond the borders of Judaism. His fearless proclamation of the gospel message, both in Damascus and in Jerusalem, is a character-istic of work of the early missioners. We have already come across it in the fearless proclamation of the message by Peter before the Jewish authorities. It will continue throughout the Acts of the Apostles, even till the end, when we see Paul proclaiming the message during his captivity in Rome. How are we to spread the gospel fearlessly? Perhaps mostly by sticking up for Christian principles in moral behaviour, such as the protection of life, the rights of the poor and disadvantaged, fearlessly facing the issues of justice, war and peace, and sexual morality. But it must also be a proclamation in love and peace.

Question: Have we any causes for fear in making our proclamation of Christ?

Second reading: The Two Commandments (1 John 3.18-24)

These two commandments will dominate the rest of the letter. They are not exactly the classic two commandments of the Law, reiterated by Jesus, to love God above all and our neighbour as ourselves. The two commandments of God here are, first, to believe in the power or name of the Risen Christ, and, second, to love one another. One might say that belief in the power of the Risen Christ is an application of love for God, an aspect that is especially relevant during Eastertide. The saving power of Christ flows out from God's care for ourselves, and belief in it must both be a response in love and provoke love and gratitude. It must also make us fearless before God, full of the love that casts out fear, since the power of Christ's Resurrection is a guarantee of God's acceptance of Christ's sacrifice for us. It saves us from our own sin and disobedience. It brings also fearlessness before a hostile world, with the fearlessness of which we heard in Paul's preaching in the first reading. It must also inspire fulfilment of the second commandment, love of neighbour. Such belief, issuing in love, forms the criterion for knowing that the Spirit is dwelling within us.

Question: What does real love of neighbour involve?

Gospel: The True Vine (John 15.1-8)

A vine is an extraordinary plant. It can grow to a huge size, spreading over a huge area, a whole garden wall or trellis work, from one single root, and produces a rich sap that yields grapes at the end of countless little branches. And then there is the business of pruning: cut it back thoroughly on all its many shoots and tendrils, and it seems only more determined to grow thick and strong. So the vine was the symbol of Israel, drawing from the Lord a sap that penetrated to all its shoots, and lovingly pruned by the gardener in a way that best encouraged its growth. The image was taken over by Jesus for his own community, the new Israel. Pairing with last week's picture of the good shepherd, it is one of the greatest of John's images. It perfectly sums up the two emphases of today's other two readings. The only source of fruitful energy for the Christian is union with and dependence on the life flowing from Christ. Without that, the branches wither and die; a trimming cut off from a vine no longer has any chance of life. The vine itself at pruning season looks stark, rough and suffering. It is, in fact, bursting with new life.

Question: Have I benefited from the vinedresser's pruning knife?

Sixth Sunday of Easter

First reading: The Conversion of Cornelius (Acts 10.25-26, 34-35, 44-48)

Jesus was the Messiah of Judaism, bringing to completion the promises made to Abraham. It came as a surprise to the first Christians that the salvation brought by Jesus was meant not just for Jew alone but for all the peoples of the earth. This is the scene where it happens. Peter has been prepared for it by a vision which annulled the Jewish food laws. Then he was summoned to bring the gentile Cornelius to the faith. Now, even while he is speaking to Cornelius and his household, the Spirit takes matters (so to speak) into his own hands and comes down upon Cornelius. A gentile Pentecost. Today also we are happy to think of our own group as the chosen ones, neglecting the breadth of God's love and desire that all people should turn to him and be saved. We can read again and again that Jesus actually went out of his way to welcome lepers, prostitutes, tax collectors, and we still find it hard to believe that to God they are not 'undesirables'. God has no favourites, but it is much more comfortable for us to stay snugly wrapped up in our own neat cocoons.

Question: How far does the message of Christ extend beyond Christianity?

Second reading: Christian Love (1 John 4.7-10)

At this time the Jews regarded gentiles as 'dogs'. This did not mean beloved pets, for dogs were either frightening guard dogs or filthy scavengers. The first reading showed us God actually taking gentiles to himself by sending the Spirit upon them. The second reading now meditates on the nature of that love. The old niggardly saying, 'I love him but I can't stand the sight of him', will not do if God is love itself and love itself is the nature of God. If God is not only the source of love and of life, but simply is love itself, even the distant 'wishing somebody well' from my heart is not enough. Would any of us be satisfied and comfortable with the idea that God doesn't actually like me but wishes me well in a distant sort of way? Love generates affection, respect, trust, a desire to come closer to the other. It is comforting to know that I am a son of God and can call God 'Abba', but the consequence is more daunting, that you too – whoever you are – are also the closest member of my family, despite all your faults.

Question: Do the faults of your own family impede or enhance your love?

Gospel: The continuing Love of Jesus (John 15.9-17)

Like so many of the great discourses of Jesus in the gospel of John, these are not a shorthand record of Jesus' words, but will have been written up afterwards. Most probably there were several slightly different versions of what Jesus said at the Last Supper. In any case, one can see that the author has in mind two different levels, both Jesus' own historical situation at the Last Supper and the situation of the early Church, where the disciples are being hard put to the test in their mission. They need encouraging by Jesus' own example of his sacrifice and by his promise of real friendship: they are friends, not servants, specially chosen by Jesus to bear fruit that will last. So we, too, are welcomed as friends, chosen and commissioned by Jesus to go out and bear fruit, but reminded that we must be prepared to pay the price. There is no fruit without pruning. Jesus had just given the example of service by washing the feet of his disciples. If we are to share the joy of Jesus, we must be ready to join him also in laying down his life for his friends.

Question: Do we ever have to make hard choices for Christ?

Seventh Sunday of Easter, Ascension

First reading: The Ascension (Acts 1.1-11)

How are we to envisage what happened at the Ascension? Two feet disappearing into a cloud? It is mentioned only in the Acts, and the other gospels seem to imply that the Risen Christ was glorified on the day of the Resurrection itself. Luke, the author, is putting across several messages. First, the 40 days since Easter should not be carefully counted. In biblical language, '40' makes just 'a fairly long period', often a period of preparation, like Jesus' 40 days being tested in the desert, or Israel's 40 years of the Exodus. For all that time Jesus has been preparing his apostles. Second, it is the definitive parting of the physical Jesus, after which the Risen Christ is no longer with his disciples. It is now the Spirit of Christ that is at the heart of the Church, inspiring all its activity. Third, Luke represents Jesus as a prophet (and more than a prophet), so he leaves his disciples in the same way as the prophet Elijah, who was taken to heaven in a fiery chariot, leaving his disciple Elisha to carry on his work, filled with a double share of his spirit.

Question: What is the essence of the Ascension: feet disappearing into a cloud, or the completion of Christ's vindication?

Second reading: Christ is Supreme (Ephesians 1.17-21)

The blessing that forms the core of this reading gives the sense of the Ascension for the Church. It is not the manner of Christ's departure that is important, but the exalted position of Christ, and the power of God that raised Christ from the dead. This same power has called us to be believers, made us rich in the glory of his heritage, and has given us the strength to follow Christ. As Christians, we believe that Jesus was divine not only from birth but from the moment of his conception. It was then that the Word of God became flesh. And yet something further happened at the glorification of Christ in his Resurrection. Paul says he was 'constituted Son of God in power' at the Resurrection. Is this the same as the claim that the high priest declared blasphemous, 'You will see the son of man seated at the right hand of the Power and coming on the clouds of heaven'? In the final scene of the gospel of Matthew Jesus declares, 'All power in heaven and on earth has been given to me', and the Book of Revelation shows the Risen Christ sharing the throne of God.

Question: Christ is 'the first fruits from the dead'; did the Ascension change him in any way?

Alternative second reading: The Gifts of Christ (Ephesians 4.1-13)

This alternative reading has two crucial passages, divided by a puzzling section. The Letter to the Ephesians was probably written by a close follower of Paul rather than the apostle himself. In many ways, it sums up and develops Paul's teaching. The puzzling bit in the middle is a specialized piece of Jewish exegesis, brought in by the quotation of Psalm 68 (67).18. The point of the passage is not the rather contrived explanation of 'ascended', but the fact that Christ's return to the Father ensured the gifts of the Spirit. These gifts are detailed both before and after the quotation. The earlier part is almost a reflection on Paul's plea to the Corinthians in First Corinthians 1–3, urging them to abandon their squabbles and work together: 'one Lord, one faith, on baptism', a unity of Christ's followers for which we are still hoping and praying ever more urgently. After the quotation comes what could also be a reflection on the later teaching of First Corinthians 12–14 about the gifts of the Spirit. Through the Spirit every member of the Church has their own special gift, their own special contribution and ministry to building up the body of Christ

Question: How should we balance the disagreements between Christians and the need for unity?

Gospel: The Conclusion of the Gospel of Mark (Mark 16.15-20)

This final blessing on the mission of the disciples summarizes events narrated in the Acts of the Apostles, events that show the power of the Spirit at work in their mission. Finally, the account of the Ascension itself is given, modelled on the account given in the Acts, the assurance of the power of Christ that stands behind all the works of his followers and believers. Most of these activities would not be expected in today's Church, but the first and the last are still the task of the Church. Casting out evil spirits and healing may not be done so dramatically as in the gospel miracles, but it is still the Christian's task to bring goodness where there is evil and healing where there are wounds. We have many opportunities in the course of the day either to foment anger and enmity or to soothe it, opportunities to roughen a wound or to smooth it down. As we know from our failures to do this, such works are the works of the Spirit of Christ, supporting our own weakness and triumphing over our own leanings towards evil.

Question: What would you say are the marks of Christ's presence and power at work in the Church?

Pentecost Sunday

The readings for Year A, as on p. 67, may be used in any year. The alternative second and third readings for Year B only are given after the readings for any year.

First reading: The Birth of the Church (Acts 2.1-11)

The ministry of Jesus starts with the coming of the Spirit at his Baptism, and so the ministry of the Church begins with the coming of the Spirit at Pentecost. There can be no witness to Jesus or to his message, no spreading of the Kingship of God, without the Spirit of Jesus. Another lesson from this parallelism is that the task of the Church and the life of the Church are the same as those of Jesus himself: to bring God's kingship to its fulfilment by bringing healing, love and joy through the message of the Risen Christ. The rushing wind and the tongues of fire are an allusion to the coming of God's Spirit in the Old Testament upon Moses and the elders. So the new message is the fulfilment of the Old Testament, breaking out beyond the boarders of Judaism to include all peoples of the world. The union of all these peoples, all understanding one language in their own way, is a deliberate contrast to the scene at the Tower of Babel, when all the peoples of the world were split up by their inability to understand one another's languages. The list of unpronounceable peoples is itself a witness to the universality of the Church!

Questions: How can the Church claim to be the Spirit at work in the world? Mention three outstanding ways in which the Church shows Christ at work today.

Second reading: The Body of Christ (1 Corinthians 12.3-7, 12-13)

The slightest glance around a church full of people is enough to show the variety within the Christian community. But it needs the hints given us by Paul to remind us that every member of that community has his or her own special gift to contribute. Mercifully, these gifts are all different. It is valuable to reflect on the natural gifts that we find all around us. It is also valuable to reflect how dull, or even intolerable, life would be if I lived with a lot of clones of myself, all with the same gifts and the same faults as me! Every one of us contributes something different and valuable in its own way, whether it is the baby squeaking as a sign of new, developing life or the older person contributing wisdom, experience and even the suffering of Christ. The other inspiring thought is that all these varied and diverse people go to make up the Body which is Christ. We all have experience of various corporate bodies, organizations and companies, but none of these other bodies makes up a person. That Person is Christ, since as Christians we all live and operate through Christ's Spirit.

Question: Who is the most Christ-like figure for you in the present or recent past?

Gospel: The Gift of Peace (John 20.19-23)

At first sight this is a surprising gospel reading for Pentecost, but, of course, the event of Pentecost came too late to be a subject for the gospels, and we read the account of another incident where the Risen Christ gave the Spirit to his disciples. There are two emphases in the account. The first is peace. Christ brings peace to his disciples with the double greeting of peace, and peace is a Christian watchword. Peace was the song of the angels at Jesus' birth. Each of Paul's letters opens with a greeting of peace. The letter to the Ephesians proclaims that Christ is our peace, the reversal of all worry, strife, envy, jealousy, self-seeking ambition. 'Go in peace' is Jesus' dismissal of those he cures, and also the dismissal at the end of Mass. Peace was Jesus' bequest to his disciples after the Last Supper. The second watchword is forgiveness, for God was always known as a God of mercy and forgiveness, as Jesus came to show by his constant approach to sinners. But the Lord's Prayer shows that if we do not ourselves forgive, we block God's forgiveness of ourselves too.

Question: 'Forgiveness is the only sure path to peace.' Does this cause any difficulties?

Alternative second reading: The Works of the Spirit (Galatians 5.16-25)

In writing to the Galatians, Paul insists that it is not necessary for Christians to obey the prescriptions of the Jewish law. To prove this, he appeals to the works of the Spirit that they can see among themselves: these must come from Christ, not from the law. Since Paul adduces them as proof, the works of the Spirit must have been clearly visible. The behaviour of Christians must have been distinctly and noticeably different from that of others. In the modern world, does the behaviour of Christians mark them out unmistakeably? Now Paul gives a full list of works of the Spirit and their opposites, the works of the flesh, that is, the works of natural, unreformed and selfish behaviour. Christ has sent his Spirit so that our behaviour may be completely changed, and so that we may live with his life. The works of the flesh are not merely the gross, 'fleshly' distortions of greed, avarice and sexual licence, but include also such failings as envy and quarrels. Paul's list is a useful little checklist to apply to our own way of life. Has the coming of the Spirit made a difference to us? Are we notably more Christ-like than many of the good pagans around us?

Question: What does Paul mean by 'the flesh'?

Gospel: The Advocate (John 15.26-27; 16.12-15)
In Jesus' final instructions to his disciples, gathered together at the Last Supper, he gives them four little promises about the Advocate whom he will send, send from the Father. 'Advocate' is really a legal term, in both English and the original Greek, and the Spirit will 'testify' on behalf of Jesus. The certainty and definitiveness of this terminology is important. In other sayings, Jesus promises that the Advocate will lead his disciples into all truth, enabling them to understand what they cannot yet grasp. With these promises, therefore, we are celebrating the continuing presence of the Spirit, leading the Church into all truth, into a continuously fuller and more profound understanding of the mystery of Christ. It is through the Spirit that, under the guidance of the Church, each generation and culture is enabled to assimilate and express – sometimes with a wobble or two – the great truths in its own terms, each generation building on the truths perceived by previous guidance. There must be a constant renewal in our personal understanding, under the guidance and testimony of this Advocate speaking through the Church. The Advocate guides our minds, but, above all, the mind of the teaching Church.

Question: What aspect of Christian teaching is the Spirit stressing to us in these days?

Holy Trinity Sunday

First reading: The God of Love (Deuteronomy 4.32-34, 39-40)

Why a reading from Deuteronomy on the feast of the Trinity? Because the Book of Deuteronomy is primarily about the love of God, the revelation of God's awesome, forgiving love to his people. Love is the nature of God. We can never understand God, or what we mean by three Persons in one nature. Rather than the Church giving us a reading that might get us a tiny step nearer understanding what we might mean by that, the Church gives us the heart of the revelation to Jews and Christians that God is love. Other religions feel their way towards this staggering and daunting truth, but to us it has been revealed. The revelation of God as love is a personal revelation, inviting us to a response in love, inviting us into a personal relationship with God as love. All the instructions that God gives us are simply meant to show us what that love means and how we can respond to it and stay close to God as own God's people. In the beginning man and woman were made in the image of God, and if I am to remain close to God I must shape my desires, my activities, my relationships to be like those of God.

Question: Why do we pray to God *through* Jesus?

Second reading: Son, Father and Spirit (Romans 8.14-17)

The Trinity is often treated like a mathematical and philosophical problem. No attempt to understand the intra-Trinitarian relationships of the three Persons can get very far. The reading which the Church gives us, instead, gives an inkling of our triple relationship with God. The basis is Jesus' own prayer, in which he called God 'Abba', the dignified and affectionate word in Jesus' own language by which a son addressed his father. The staggering next move is that Jesus told us that we might use the same form of address; so we use it, even in Aramaic. It is, however, only because Christ has given us his Spirit as our spirit that we can do so. This Spirit is also the Spirit of the Father. Sometimes in the gospel it is Jesus, sometimes it is the Father who sends the Spirit. We can say that the Spirit gives us access to the Father and to the Son, or that the Father gives the Spirit of the Son, or that the Son gives us his Spirit. In this way, the Trinity, each Person in a different way, imparts to us the love of God and draws us into God's own love.

Question: Why do we pray to God *in* the Spirit?

Gospel: Baptism into the Trinity (Matthew 28.16-20)

On a superficial level, this gospel reading seems chosen because of the Trinitarian baptismal formula. It is the only time this formula comes in the scripture, and it is remarkable that the Trinitarian liturgical formula was already developed while the New Testament was being written. At a deeper level, this reading of the final five verses of Matthew gives a wonderful Trinitarian view of the work of salvation. The words of the Risen Christ, 'all authority in heaven and on earth has been given to me' are reminiscent of the vision of the exalted Son of Man in Daniel, who comes to the One of Great Age, seated on his throne, and receives from him all power on earth. Only Christ receives all power in heaven too, as 'the Son of God in power'. In this power, he sends out his disciples, promising his divine presence always. The promise of Christ's divine presence in his Church now, at the end of the gospel, balances the promise at the beginning in the name Emmanuel, given by the angel for the child. Emmanuel means 'God with us'. So the permanent presence of Christ is the message of the whole gospel.

Question: If Christ is present in his Church, why is it so sinful?

Sunday of the Body and Blood of Christ

First reading: God's Covenant with his People (Exodus 24.3-8)

The first reading gives the story of the clinching of the Covenant on Mount Sinai, the moment when Israel became God's people, took on themselves the joyful obligations of the Law. The Law was God's gift to Israel, explaining what they must do to be his people. It was not a set of constricting obligations but a liberating set of instructions. Obedience to the Law was a response in love to a gift in love, to behave towards God with the generosity which God showed to his people. They must now behave towards others as God had behaved towards them, respecting the widow, caring for the orphan, welcoming the stranger. 'Be holy as I am holy', said the Lord. This reading is particularly apt at the Mass for Corpus Christi because, just like the Mass, it includes both instructions and sacrifice. In the first part of the Mass, we listen to God's revealing Word, which tells us in various ways how to behave if we are to be God's people. Only after committing ourselves to God's Word can we go on to join in the new alliance. That alliance, too, was celebrated by sharing a meal, for the communion sacrifices were a shared meal, and by sharing the blood, which is the life of Christ.

Question: How does Christ nourish us in the Eucharist?

Second reading: The Blood of Christ (Hebrews 9.11-15)

Blood plays an important part in all three readings of this Mass, and it is essential to understand its function in both Israel's and our own sacramental system. Blood is an obvious symbol of life. Total loss of blood means total loss of life. As blood flows out, so life ebbs away. Therefore, just as life belongs to God, so blood belongs to God. In Israel, it is therefore sacred. In recognition that life is the gift of God, blood may not be consumed. Sacrifice in Israel was not appeasing an angry God, by offering the death of an animal instead of my own death. Rather, it was a joyful a sharing with God, the sharing of a meal, and the granting of new life. Death releases the blood, which can then be sprinkled over the offerers to symbolize fresh life from God. The Letter to the Hebrews contrasts the old sacrifices and old sharing of blood, 'the blood of goats and bull calves', with the gift of Christ's blood. How much more is the new life, given by the blood of the divine Son of God! This is the rich purpose of receiving the blood of Christ from the chalice.

Question: What is the difference between the Christian and the pagan idea of sacrifice?

Gospel: A New Partnership (Mark 14.12-16, 22-26)
The original, Old Testament covenant was sealed by a death and by the sharing of the blood between God (signified by the altar) and his people as a sign of new life. Israel broke that covenant by persistently refusing to keep true to the way of life which the covenant enshrined. Now Jesus' new covenant engages us in a new alliance and gives us new life. The story told in this reading is the warranty and guarantee that, each time we receive the Body and Blood of Christ, we are bound anew into his covenant. The story is told in almost exactly similar terms in each of the first three gospels and in Paul's first letter to the Corinthians. It must have been learnt and repeated by heart. There is just enough difference to show that Mark and Matthew reflect the tradition of the Hebrew communities, while Paul and Luke reflect the tradition of the Greek-speaking communities. It must have been repeated again and again from the very first years of Christianity. Each time we repeat these words, we are re-entering Jesus' covenant. There should be a health warning. The Mass is dangerous: are you ready to commit yourself to the Kingdom, to engage in a new and personal alliance with Christ and to live with his life?

Question: What obligations do we take on by receiving the Eucharist?

Year C

First Sunday of Lent

First reading: A Wandering Aramaean (Deuteronomy 26.4-10)

The first readings during Lent each year are wonderfully arranged to lead us from the very beginnings to the immediate preparation for Christ, each Sunday working further forward in the history of God's promises to his People. This year begins with the profession of faith about God's care of his People, which Israelite priests had to make when presenting their offering. Surprisingly, it begins not with the promises to Abraham but with the wanderings of the nomadic tribes down to Egypt. It was first in Egypt that God made them his people, rescuing them from slavery. In this version of the history of Israel, the decisive moment was not the call of Abraham but the exodus from Egypt. But in following Sundays we will work forward through the call of Abraham, the call of Moses, the first Passover in Canaan and the promise of a New Covenant at the return from the Babylonian Exile. It is a record of God's constant care as he prepares the People for the coming of his Son at the incarnation, and the full revelation at the Cross and the Resurrection of Easter.

Question: In what sense are Christians still a Pilgrim People?

Second reading: Profession of Faith (Romans 10.8-13)

In these chapters of the Letter to the Romans, Paul is struggling with the problem of the salvation of the Jews: how is it that the People so carefully nurtured for so long should refuse to acknowledge that Jesus is the fulfilment of God's plan of salvation? To Paul, himself a fervent Jew, it was agonizing that so many of his own people should refuse to acknowledge Jesus. But he saw that their refusal opened the door to the gentiles. The Christian community at Rome was composed of both Jews and gentiles. It was important for Paul to show that even scripture proclaims that the door is open to all who profess their faith in Christ, not one party to the exclusion of the other: so, no distinction between Jew and Greek. This is, however, a very different profession of faith from the profession in the first reading: that was a belief in a Lord God who rescued from Egypt. This is a belief that the Lord God raised Jesus from the dead, and raised him to the status of Lord. Paul never uses the word 'God' of Jesus, but does call him by the special personal name so sacred that it is never pronounced in Hebrew. The word used then and now is 'LORD'.

Question: Is there any special reason why Christians should be concerned about the salvation of the Jews?

Gospel: Jesus is Tested in the Desert (Luke 4.1-13)
To remind us that Lent is a time when we are tested out, the gospel reading of the First Sunday of Lent is always about the testing of Jesus. But our fasting or whatever the extra little offering we make to the Lord during Lent may be, we enter into solidarity with the hardship undergone by Jesus in his Passion. Of course, Lent is not a matter of testing out how far we can push ourselves (some sort of self-torture). Rather it is a period of preparation for the Passion and Resurrection, like the 40 years of Israel in the desert, preparing for the Promised Land, or the prophet Elijah's 40-day preparation, or the 40 days during which Christ prepared the apostles between Easter and the Ascension. The point of Jesus' 40-day fast is to give some force to the devil's first taunt. To each of the devil's taunts Jesus replies with a word of scripture: if you rely on God's word you are unshakably safe, for God has created and arranged everything. Matthew and Luke have a different order for second and third temptations: Matthew climaxes with Jesus as the Second Moses, like Moses seeing all the territories from a high mountain. Luke ends the scene as he begins and ends his gospel, at Jerusalem, the turning point of the gospel.

Questions: If the Devil came to distract you from your Christian vocation, what would he/she dangle before you? In the solitude of the desert, Jesus prayed to his Father. Do you find solitude helpful in prayer?

Second Sunday of Lent

First reading: The Covenant with Abram (Genesis 15.5-12, 17-18)

There are different stories of exactly how God's pact with Abraham (or Abram) was made. There is no doubt that it was a promise of lasting protection for Abraham and his descendants. This version takes the form of an ancient sacral covenant, of a kind known from other ancient Near

Eastern sources. The offerings are cut in half, and the parties making the pact pass between the halves, as a symbol that they will observe the pact faithfully until the two halves come together again. Such covenants were frequent between equals, or between overlord and vassal, but no such covenant is known between a deity and a human being. It perhaps marks the inequality that only the awesome symbols of God here pass between the halves of the offering: Abraham cannot impose conditions on God! Neither can Abraham do anything to earn or justify this promise: he can only trust in God, for he himself remains a nomad without a settled territory to call his own. Only his descendants will inherit the land and become as the stars of heaven. The awesome mystery of the scene is increased by the deep sleep (the same sleep as fell on Adam for the creation of Eve) and by Abram's terror.

Question: What do you need to do to fulfil your part of the bargain with God?

Second reading: Citizenship of Heaven (Philippians 3.17–4.1)

Last Sunday's second reading moved one step higher from the first reading, from the Israelite profession of faith in God to the Christian's profession of faith in Christ as Risen Lord. So this Sunday Abram's promised ownership of the land is gazumped to the Christian's citizenship of heaven. In this world, we are aliens rather than citizens, in that our final values are not those of this world. We cannot rest in contentment except in the expectation of the Risen Lord coming in triumph to assume lordship of all things. This, rather than food or any material goods, must be the basis of our whole system of values. To modern conventions, Paul's occasional encouragement to follow his rule of life or to imitate him seems boastful and complacent. He sees himself as the servant of Christ, suffering for Christ, just as Jesus suffered as the Servant of the Lord. Paul's sufferings are the badge of apostleship. In other passages, however, he shows that he is as aware as any of us of his own failings and of his inability to live up to his ideals.

Question: If you are to live in the world, is it unavoidable to compromise your Christian standards?

Gospel: The Transfiguration of Jesus (Luke 9.28-36)

Each Lent the gospel reading of the Second Sunday is the Transfiguration, preparing the chosen three disciples and ourselves for the coming Passion. It is a scene of Christ's heavenly glory, his clothes bright as lightning, and his glory extending even to Moses and Elijah. These two personalities are here privileged to speak to Jesus because each had a vision of God on the Holy Mountain, Sinai or Horeb respectively (in the Old Testament, these are two names for the same mountain). The Voice from heaven at the baptism had been addressed to Jesus himself (in Mark and Luke); now the Voice is a public declaration of Jesus' Sonship, and authorizes him to all as the Chosen Teacher. Luke centres the scene especially clearly on the Passion by stressing that they were speaking of the 'exodus' he was to accomplish at Jerusalem – again the Lukan stress on Jerusalem. The fact that the disciples are praying, and are the same three disciples as are present at the Agony in the Garden, is a strong link to the Passion of Jesus. It is also part of Luke's stress on prayer, for Luke mentions Jesus' prayer and the importance of prayer on several occasions and in several parables (the Unjust Judge, the Friend at Midnight, the Pharisee and the Tax Collector).

Questions: What do you find the best form of prayer? Can you improve it during Lent? Jesus was transfigured on the Holy Mountain. What makes a mountain holy?

Third Sunday of Lent

First reading: Moses at the Burning Bush (Exodus 3.1-8, 13-15)

In our Lenten progress through the story of God's people, we come to the crucial moment of the revelation of God's name to Moses. This is a decisive moment, because to give your name is a sign of trust and friendship. Someone who has your name has power over you in all kinds of ways, so you give it only to those you trust. The Hebrews, descendants of Abraham, are at a low point, a mere rabble of oppressed immigrants, lacking land or security, marked out for extermination by a powerful bureaucratic state. It is as if God had waited for this moment to raise them up, to create them as a coherent group with a leader who could stand up for them in God's name. God does not yet give the meaning of the name; perhaps 'I am who I am' even means 'You mind your own business'. It is something to do with Being, and the Greek translation of the Bible understands it as 'Pure Being', 'the One who Is'. In the Hebrew Bible the meaning of the name is given later on Sinai, after Israel's worship of the Golden Bull, when God passes before Moses crying out the name, 'The LORD, the LORD, a God of mercy and forgiveness.' This is the meaning that will echo down the Bible in passage after passage.

Question: What qualities in God are most important to you in your approach to God?

Second reading: The Rock which is Christ (1 Corinthians 10.1-6, 10–12)

As in the previous two Sundays, the second reading moves the first reading into a higher gear. God revealed his name to Moses in the desert, led the Israelites across the sea and cared for them in the desert with manna for food and water from the rock to drink. Now Paul explains to us that the real meaning of the rock is Christ who nourishes us. How 'the rock that followed them'? Paul uses the current rabbinic explanation of the two accounts of Moses striking the rock for water: it is not two accounts of the same incident, for they are separate incidents. The same rock accompanied the Israelites on their journey through the desert. However, Paul is writing to chide the Corinthians on their undisciplined behaviour, especially at the Eucharist. Despite the wonders that accompanied the Israelites, the desert wanderings were a time of infidelity and rebellion that even the God of mercy and forgiveness was compelled to correct. Let the Corinthians learn their lesson! Even though their Christian life was marked by plentiful gifts of the Spirit, they must repent of their wild behaviour.

Question: Is Christ a rock that follows you around in life? Does he give you water?

Gospel: Time for Repentance (Luke 13.1-9)

We have seen Luke's stress on Jesus' message of repentance and forgiveness. At the beginning of Jesus' ministry, Peter must admit his sinfulness before he is called to be an apostle. At the end, the good thief acknowledges his guilt and is welcomed into Jesus' kingdom. This gospel reading, with its historical examples and its parable, reinforces the Old Testament lesson of repentance, the constant theme with Luke. In the Parable of the Pharisee and the Tax Collector, the latter wins through: his prayer is only 'God, be merciful to me, a sinner.' Every proclamation of the gospel in Luke's Acts of the Apostles ends with an appeal for repentance. Repentance means not simply bewailing our sins but doing something about it, changing our way of life, our scale of values. However, we are made in the image of God, and cannot expect God's forgiveness unless we too follow God's example and show the same forgiveness to others. The sinful woman who loved much was forgiven much (Luke 7.36-50). Neither is Luke the only evangelist to stress this point. Matthew adds at the end of the Lord's Prayer the saying of Jesus that underlines the importance of the single petition, 'Forgive us our sins as we forgive others.'

Questions: What is the most rotten part of your fig tree that you really need to change? Would the sacrament of reconciliation help? What sort of injury do you find it hardest to forgive? An affront to your pride, your pocket or your person? Is there anyone you have not forgiven?

Fourth Sunday of Lent

First reading: Passover in the Plains of Jericho (Joshua 5.9-12)

We are working through the history of Israel towards the promise of the New Covenant which is the central point of Easter. In this year's readings, the whole period between the Exodus from Egypt and the promise of the New Covenant at the time of the Babylonian exile, some 600 years later, is represented by this moment of arrival in the Promised Land of Canaan. This is the moment when the provisional arrangements of the desert wanderings come to an end. The idea of manna is based on an edible honey-like excretion of a desert plant. The stories of the desert wanderings are folk history, not modern research history. It is best to think of manna as the symbol of God's wonderful protection and feeding of Israel in the harsh and almost uninhabitable conditions of the Sinai desert. The reading describes a double celebration, bringing together two festivals. The Passover in origin is a feast of wandering nomads, as they move at the first full moon of spring from their sheltered winter pastures to cooler summer pastures. The Festival of Unleavened Bread, by way of contrast, marks the beginning of the wheat harvest, a feast of a settled agricultural people. For Paul, it represents the newness of Easter, the freshness of the New Covenant.

Question: Would it help you and your family to make more of religious festivals? How could you do so?

Second reading: Reconciled in Christ (2 Corinthians 5.17-21)

As we approach the commemoration of Christ's Passion and Resurrection we begin to focus more carefully on these events. The New Testament uses a variety of images for the event: Christ was glorified (using the idea of the awesome divine glory), raised to the right hand of God (using the imagery of Psalm 110), exalted to heaven. We were redeemed like freed slaves, ransomed like hostages, reconciled like estranged friends. When Paul uses this images there is no question of appeasing an angry God, who is to be reconciled by exacting from his innocent Son the punishment due to us sinners. No, man does not reconcile God, but God always does the reconciling. It is a divine action that takes place in Christ. How could God make the sinless one into sin? In Hebrew, the same word is used both for 'sin' and for 'sin offering'. Either Paul is using language of the Hebrew cult to express Christ as a sin offering or he means that Christ was put in the position of sinners. Paul likes playing with words. In either case, the heart of the action on Calvary is the full expression of the unitive, divine love of Jesus and his Father.

Question: Do you see God as angry and vengeful? Is there any truth in this idea?

Gospel: The Prodigal Son (Luke 15.1-3, 11-32)

Who is the hero of the story? What should its title be? Some call it the parable of the Powerless Father, for the father is powerless to do anything but welcome his son. Clearly, the principal message of the parable is that we can count on God's forgiveness, whatever we do. The contrast is also between the two sons. The younger insults his father: all he thinks about is his inheritance, as if he wished his father already dead. All the same, the father is eagerly on the watch, and forgets all his dignity to run and welcome his returning son. And to persuade the elder son to join in the party, he even leaves his dinner guests at table, going out into the field to urge the jealous elder brother to join in. Forgiveness and love is his whole motivation. The elder son responds to his father with insults, 'that son of yours', inventing guesses about sexual loose living, of which there is no suggestion in the story of the younger son. It is a splendid example of Luke's delicate, witty and subtle characterization. The anti-hero's little speech to himself as he wonders how to solve his problem is also typical of Luke, and occurs in several of his parables.

Questions: Which brother comes out of the story best? Have you ever felt like the elder brother? Would the story lose or gain anything if the parent were a mother?

Fifth Sunday of Lent

First reading: The New Exodus (Isaiah 43.16-21)

During Lent we have been working through the story of Israel preparing – or being prepared – for the coming of Christ: Adam, Abraham, Moses, the monarchy, and now the promise of a new beginning. For that is what Easter is. This part of Isaiah was written during the Exile of the Jews in Babylon, a traumatic event that seemed to them the end of all their hopes. Permanent exile and slavery, far from their beloved Jerusalem. 'There we sat and wept', says the Psalmist. But the prophet whose work is attributed to Isaiah set out to re-invigorate them with the promise that they would return to Jerusalem, and that the wonders of the Exodus from Egypt would be renewed. No need to recall the past, for there would be a road across the desert and miraculous supplies of water for the travellers. The desert would bloom afresh (for the slightest supply of water brings the withered plants to life in the spring) and the curious beasts of the desert, jackals and ostriches, would praise the Lord. There is a lesson for us, too. Our trust in God teaches us – and our own experience eventually grudgingly reinforces this – that seemingly total disaster can become a source of strength and instruction.

Question: In what way would you wish to be transformed by the new beginning of Easter?

Second reading: Pushing ahead for Olympic Gold (Philippians 3.8-14)

As we prepare for the celebration of the Passion next week, we read of Paul's own struggle, in the letter to his special friends at Philippi. He is tired, probably already quite senior, and longs to finish his race and be with Christ in tranquillity. The games and athletic contests were the football tournaments of the ancient world. Corinth, where Paul spent so long, was the centre for the Isthmian Games, more important than the Olympics, and Paul often uses imagery of running and even boxing. He knows the thrill of the contest, but at the same time he recognizes that all our power comes from the Resurrection of Christ. Christ endured and was raised by the Father. Often for us Christianity consists of enduring slights, insults or neglect and replying with a cheerful word or gesture that dissolves the hurt and seeks to renew friendship and genuine relationship. There is no need aggressively to turn the other cheek; it needs more of the courage of Christ to reply with a positive advance. If I can bring myself to ask, 'What would Jesus have done?' I am already sharing in his strength. The aggression of the athlete is redirected!

Question: Apart from his suffering and death, what do you find most inspiring about Jesus' life story and his character as seen in the gospels?

Gospel: The Woman taken in Adultery (John 8.1-11)

Why this reading from John in the middle of the Year of Luke? All the other gospels during this Lent have been from Luke. The answer is that it is an independent, floating story that does not fit the Gospel of John. In early manuscripts of the gospels, it floats around in various positions before it becomes anchored as an example of Jesus' saying just before, 'Our Law does not allow us to pass judgement on anyone without first giving him a hearing' (John 7.51). It fits in this year because the tone of the story and the theme of welcome for the repentant sinner are both thoroughly Lukan, constantly stressed in Luke, for example, by the Parable of the Prodigal Son. What did Jesus write on the ground, or was he just doodling to allow the accusers time to reflect on their self-righteousness? It is made clear throughout the Gospel of Luke that you cannot be a follower of Christ without first admitting your sinfulness. Peter in the boat tells Jesus to leave, for he is a sinner. Zacchaeus promises to make multiple restitution for his embezzlements. The woman at the supper weeps for her sins at Jesus' feet.

Questions: What do you think Jesus wrote on the ground? Would it sometimes be better to be less judgmental?

Passion Sunday

Gospel of Palms: Jesus Enters Jerusalem (Luke 19.28-40)

This reading gives us the triumphal entry of Jesus into Jerusalem at the end of the long journey. In Luke, the cheers are concentrated not merely on the Kingdom, but on the King himself, who comes in the name of the Lord. Their cries echo but excel those of the angels at the nativity, 'Peace in heaven and glory in the highest heaven!' For Luke, Jerusalem is the hinge, the turning point where the gospel ends and the Acts of the Apostles begins, the spread of the Good News to the ends of the earth. For the last 10 chapters all the concentration has been on this journey up to Jerusalem, where Jesus is to suffer and so rise again, but there has been an air of tragedy about the journey. Jesus' death has been constantly in mind, for it has been stressed that no prophet can perish away from Jerusalem. As Jesus enters the city he weeps over its refusal to accept him, just as he did in13.34-35, and as he will do as he leaves Jerusalem for execution.

First reading: The Song of the Servant (Isaiah 50.4-7)

In the Book of Isaiah occur four songs, of which this is the third, sung by a mysterious Servant of the Lord. It is not clear who this Servant is, but he is totally dedicated to the service of the Lord, a disciple who listens devotedly. Through suffering, this Servant brings to fulfilment the salvation that the Lord intends for Israel and for the world. Jesus saw himself in the terms of this Servant, and the four songs feature throughout the liturgy of Holy Week.

Question: How can I be more positive about bearing suffering for the sake of Christ?

Second reading: Raised High through Suffering (Philippians 2.6-11)

This hymn was probably not written by Paul himself, but taken up by him into the letter, a very early Christian hymn. It celebrates the triumph of Jesus through his selflessness. The assertions at the end are staggering. The hymn claims for Jesus the titles and the worship that are due only to God. What is more, this acknowledgement of Jesus does not detract from the glory of God, but is precisely 'to the glory of God the Father'. This is perhaps the fullest statement in Paul of the divine glory of Jesus, and it is won by his humiliation in death.

Question: What would it be like to meet Jesus, a human being, yet divine? How would one react?

The Passion According to Luke (Luke 22.14–23.56)

In Luke's version of the story of the Passion of Jesus, many of the details are different from those of the other evangelists. This merely means that Luke stresses different aspects, for the narratives are as much commentaries on the significance of events as straight narratives:

1. At the Last Supper Luke gathers together sayings of Jesus on the future of the Church and how the leaders of the community should behave: they should serve their brothers and sisters, not like the arrogant leaders of secular regimes. Luke places here the promise to Peter, that he will strengthen his brothers.
2. Luke stresses that Jesus is in control of the whole sequence. At the Agony in the Garden, instead of the three distraught prayers of Jesus, there is only one, and Jesus is in perfect control, kneeling down and standing up again, rather than throwing himself on the ground. At the end, instead of 'My God, my God, why have you forsaken me?', Jesus tranquilly yields his own life into the Father's hands, obediently completing his Father's will.
3. At the trial scene there is no sign of the High Priest or of any verdict. It is more a disorderly rabble who hustle Jesus to Pilate and produce trumped-up charges. Pilate does not sentence Jesus, but merely hands him over to them 'to deal with as they pleased'. Jesus, in contrast, continues his mission of bringing peace by the reconciliation of Pilate with Herod.

4. The crucifixion scene itself is a scene of conversions: Jesus continues right to the end his mission of bringing reconciliation. The women of Jerusalem mourn for Jesus. Jesus forgives his executioners. He welcomes the good thief into paradise. The centurion gives praise to God, and the crowds go home expressing their repentance. By contrast, it is the holy women who fulfil the Law of repose on the Sabbath.

Questions: Do I obey Jesus' instructions, 'Pray that you enter not into temptation'? Why does Luke stress so heavily this scene of forgiveness at the Cross?

Easter Sunday

The same readings are used in each year of the cycle.

First reading: Peter Instructs Cornelius (Acts 10.34, 37-43)

Peter was speaking to Cornelius. Cornelius was the Roman centurion who already reverenced God and had a vision that he should invite Peter to come and instruct him. Peter shows that Jesus was a real human being. He went about, bringing God's peace to everyone he could meet. Nevertheless, he was executed as a criminal. So God reacted by raising him from death to a life that was totally new. This was the fulfilment of all the promises made to Israel, bringing to completion God's plan in creation. Life moved into a new gear. Peter expresses this that God has appointed the Risen Jesus to judge the living and the dead. The Jews expected that at the end of time, at the completion of all things, God would come to set everything to rights, to judge things according to their true worth. Now Peter says that Jesus is the one who will be this judge. Jesus is the Lord who will bring all things to completion and to judgment. By his rising from the dead, Jesus comes to this position of supreme authority over the whole world. Paul put it that he was 'constituted Son of God in power' by the Resurrection.

Question: Do I really believe that Jesus is 'son of God in power' by his Resurrection? Do I act as if I believed it?

Second reading: New Life in Christ (Colossians 3.1-4)

This reading is the visible tip of an iceberg, of which much more lies below the surface! Paul here tells us that all our interest must be in heavenly things, the things of Christ, because we share Christ's life. What is more, that life is no ordinary life. What does all this mean? We share Christ's life because faith in Christ means that we put all our trust and hope in Christ. We have been baptized into Christ, that is, by baptism we have been dipped into Christ as into a river, and come up soaked with Christ, or dripping with Christ. I am growing into Christ, share his inheritance, his status as son of God. The wellspring of my life is no longer the ordinary, natural life that enables me to live, breathe, digest, feel, see, sing and play, love and hate. It is the Spirit of Christ that spurs me to generosity, service, kindness, self-control, peace and openness. This life, says Paul, is still hidden, and will be fully manifested only at the coming of Christ. But if I am to be true to my profession of faith in baptism, the principles on which I operate must be those of this risen life of Christ.

Question: What should I do this Easter to prove to myself that I live with the new life of Christ?

Gospel: The Empty Tomb (John 20.1-9)
There are several accounts in the various gospels of the discovery of the empty tomb. The slight variations between them show all the marks of oral tradition, for in genuine oral tradition each 'performance' is different. Different people tell the story slightly differently, stressing different aspects. This story stresses the proof that the tomb really was empty, for the apostles examine the evidence carefully. Other accounts concentrate less on the evidence and more on the message, that they will meet the Risen Lord in Galilee. It was important to establish that the tomb was empty, to prevent the charge that the meetings with the Risen Christ were simply ghost appearances. Apart from the proof that this was a real, living and bodily person, these meetings stress two factors, the power of the Risen Christ and the commission given to the disciples. They are to go out into the whole world and spread the message, always accompanied by and strengthened by Christ himself. In this account, Simon Peter is clearly the senior, authority figure, to whom the Beloved Disciple defers. But it is the love of the Beloved Disciple that immediately brings him to faith.

Questions: If Jesus were not risen, how would my life be different? What is the best way in which I can 'proclaim the Good News' of Christ's Resurrection?

Second Sunday of Easter

First reading: The Early Community (Acts 5.12-16)

Before he tells us of the spread of the gospel to the ends of the earth, Luke, the author of the Acts of the Apostles, tells us about the ideal community in Jerusalem. He stresses their unity, their prayer together, their common ownership of all their possessions, their generosity to those in need, and their steadfastness under the persecution by the authorities who refused to accept their message. It is the model for any Christian community, which all our Christian communities need to strive to imitate, a real centre of the love and confidence of Christ. In today's reading, he tells how in the early community the same signs and wonders of healing that Jesus himself had worked are worked also by the apostles, and especially by Peter. It is a theme throughout the Acts that the followers of Jesus, filled with his Spirit, continue his work and live with his life, expressing the power of the Risen Christ, who remains with them always. Luke also wants to underline that Jerusalem is being given a second chance: they had rejected Jesus, but now are given a second chance at the hands of his apostles, the witnesses to his Resurrection. Hence the comment that the numbers of believers increased steadily. The martyrdom of Stephen will mark the end and the failure of this second chance.

Question: What work of Christian healing can I do now?

Second reading: A Vision of the Lord Christ (Revelation 1.9-13, 17-19)

The first reading during Eastertide is about the beginnings of the Church. During this season of Eastertide in Year C the second reading is about the end and completion of the Church, taken from the Book of Revelation. This, the last Book of the Bible, was written to assure Christians, struggling under persecution from the Roman Empire, that the Risen Christ would eventually bring his Church to triumph and release them from all sorrow and sadness. It uses extravagant cosmic imagery to emphasize God's total control of the universe, heaven and earth, and all that is in them. It is very imaginative, drawing heavily on the imagery of the Old Testament and on the symbolism of numbers. The narrator is the Apostle John, exiled to the Greek island of Patmos, and it begins with a vision of the Risen Christ in all his glory. 'Son of man' was Jesus' favourite way of referring to himself. Here the 'Son of man' is also reminiscent of the Son of man in the prophet Daniel's vision, to whom God gives all power over the universe. The seven lampstands (seven is the perfect number) represent the seven local Churches of Asia to whom the Book was primarily addressed.

Question: This vision of Christ was written down to inspire and energize a real Christian community; does it inspire and energize mine?

Gospel: Jesus in the Upper Room (John 20.19-31)

Two aspects of this meeting are especially striking. This is the last scene of the gospel of John, for Chapter 21 is an appendix. At the end, before the concluding reflection, Thomas gives the only direct acclamation in the New Testament of Jesus as God. Nowhere else is Jesus directly hailed as 'God', although there are ways in which he is equivalently so presented. So, in a way, this acclamation of the Risen Christ is the climax of the New Testament. Second, it is striking that Jesus' final blessing is of peace and forgiveness. The mission of all Christians is to bring these to a troubled world. Throughout the Bible God is a God of forgiveness. The Old Testament consists of a series of covenants of forgiveness, each in turn broken by God's Chosen People. The covenant with Noah after the Flood, the covenant with Abraham, with Moses after the worship of the Golden Calf, finally the new covenant promised by Jeremiah when unfaithful Israel is being exiled to Babylon. Christianity is not for the perfect but for the sinner, surrounded by sinners. Forgiven sinners must bring forgiveness to all those around them.

Questions: Should there be any limit to Christian forgiveness? What constitutes the 'peace of the Risen Christ'?

Third Sunday of Easter

First reading: The Apostles in the Dock (Acts 5.28-32, 40-41)

By the time this hearing before the Sanhedrin occurs, the apostles have already been arrested twice for proclaiming the Good News of Jesus. The first time only Peter and John were arrested, interrogated and given a warning. Now it seems to be a whole group of the apostles. They were arrested, delivered from prison by an angel – another sign that God looks after his own people – and voluntarily went to face the Sanhedrin. The task of the apostle is first and foremost to proclaim the Resurrection of Jesus and his new life, a positive message of encouragement. Is our message of Christianity to those whom we meet always a message of encouragement? Does it always set out to inspire new life? All the way through the Acts of the Apostles, we see the interplay of harassment of Christ's messengers and protection by God. Peter is arrested and is about to be executed when he is delivered from prison by an angel. Later on, Paul is imprisoned and delivered from prison by an earthquake. It is no surprise that the same harassment, mockery and persecution continue throughout the history of the Church.

Question: What sort of hardships do I endure for the sake of Christ?

Second reading: The Lamb in Glory (Revelation 5.11-14)

The second reading from Revelation shows us a scene in the heavenly throne room, the Lamb sacrificed enthroned. In fact, this is the second half of the scene, the first half of which shows God enthroned in glory. Now we see the triumphant Lamb on the same throne, being accorded the same honours by the 24 elders and by all living creatures as were accorded to the Lord God. Note the sevenfold acclamation! Then there is a fourfold acclamation from the four animals, which already in Ezekiel's vision of the divine throne represent the solidity of the universe. The surest indication that, already in the early Church, the Risen Christ was seen as fully equal to the Father is the equality of worship accorded to them both by the whole of creation. It is precisely as the sacrificed Lamb of God that Jesus enters into the sanctuary, seated on the throne of God and presenting the very sacrifice that we present in the Eucharist. There is no time in God, and this sacrifice is 'once and for all'. The sacrifice on our altars is no new sacrifice but is the sacrifice of obedience which Christ presents in permanence to his Father.

Question: Has this scene of the enthronement of the Lamb any implications for real life?

Gospel: Jesus meets his Disciples at the Lake (John 21.1-19).
This epilogue to the Gospel of John shows an extraordinary link at the oral tradition stage to Luke's version of the Call of the Disciples: the same unsuccessful fishing all night, the success at Jesus' command, and the commission to proclaim the gospel. As in so many encounters with the Risen Christ, he is an awesome figure, the same person but mysteriously changed, so that they have difficulty recognizing him. In addition, it has the touching scene of Peter's restoration: a triple declaration of love and loyalty is extorted from Peter to compensate for his triple denial, and a triple commission is given to him, concluding with the repeat of his call, 'Follow me' – as the promise of his martyrdom still echoes in his ears. While Matthew's gospel concludes with a promise that the Risen Christ will be always with his Church, this gospel paints it occurring in practice: Jesus feeds his followers at the picnic breakfast. Why the 153 fish? For the Venerable Bede it is too obvious: put together the numbers from 1 to 16, to this add 10 for the Commandments and 7 for the days of creation, and you get 153. There may be more to it than that!

Questions: Is Peter's protestation of love an example for our own recovery from sin? How can I become more aware of Christ's presence in the Eucharist?

Fourth Sunday of Easter

First reading: Paul turns to the Gentiles (Acts 13.14, 43-52)

As we watch the Christian message spreading to the ends of the earth, three times Paul is rejected by his own people, the Jews, and forced to turn to the gentiles: once here in Asia Minor, once in Greece and, finally, in Rome. Each time he does so with a biblical gesture, shaking the dust off his feet, shaking out his cloak, finally in Rome quoting the fulfilment of Isaiah. Was Luke anti-Semitic, then, to paint the picture with such crackling emphasis? Perhaps in God's providence this Jewish rejection was the means by which the gospel reached beyond Judaism. If the Jews had accepted Jesus, would Christianity have remained merely a Jewish sect? In his letters, Paul is bruised to the bone by the failure of his people to accept their promised Messiah, and their failure remains a mystery. The witness of the Jews as the suffering servant of the Lord continues in another direction, helped no little by Christian anti-Semitism. Paul attests that they will be converted in the end, but how they will finally be grafted into the vine stock he cannot say: 'How deep are the wisdom and knowledge of God' (Romans 11.33).

Question: What can I do to help the Christian mission to all nations?

Second reading: The Innumerable Gathering of the Redeemed (Revelation 7.9, 14-17)

In his vision, John sees the countless numbers of the redeemed as they will be gathered at the throne of the Lamb. Their palms are the palms of victory and their robes, curiously washed white in blood, are the sign of integrity and innocence. The Book of Revelation was written at a time, whether of bloody persecution or not, when the temptation was overwhelming to submit to the dominance of Rome. This was not only political but also religious, for the Lord Emperor was worshipped as a god. In every city, there was an altar to Rome and Augustus. The greater the city, the greater the Temple. Worship of the Emperor and Rome set the whole tone for society. To join this worship was the only way to success and prosperity. Yet if Augustus is Lord, Christ cannot be Lord. Christians had to opt out, and many will have paid with their blood. The victory was not by arms but by endurance. Today also Christians must opt out of many aspects of society – and yet also vigorously opt in, to bring the Christian values as a leavening of society. We cannot stay comfortably huddled round the throne!

Question: Do I give too much ground to the idols and standards of contemporary society?

Gospel: The Good Shepherd (John 10.27-30)

The figure of the Good Shepherd is the nearest approach to a parable in John's gospel. It is so important that the Church puts it before us on the fourth Sunday of Easter in each of the three cycles of readings. Apart from its obvious sense of Jesus looking after his sheep – and silly, confused sheep at that – this image receives special sense from the figure of the shepherd in the Old Testament. God is the primary shepherd of Israel, who pastures his sheep in pastures green so that they fear no evil (Psalm 23). In Ezekiel 34, God promises to free Israel from the self-centred shepherds who keep the sheep for their own advantage, and to send them a true shepherd after his own heart, a second David, who will tend them as God himself would care for them. Thus, in putting before us each year in Eastertide, this proclamation that Jesus is the Good Shepherd, the Church is affirming the Risen Christ as the divine Shepherd who tends his flocks. Particularly in these verses, we see the unity of the Risen Christ and the Father in shepherding the sheep, just as in the Book of Revelation we saw the unity of the Lord God and the Lamb, both revered on the one throne.

Questions: What is involved in imitating Christ as shepherd? Do you ever feel like a sheep in search of a shepherd? Could the parish help?

Fifth Sunday of Easter

First reading: The End of Paul's First Missionary Journey (Acts 14.21-27)

Antioch was a big city, one of the largest in the ancient world. On the Mediterranean coast of Syria, it was at the end of the trade route from the east. So it had a busy commercial life, and there was a large colony of Jews among the traders. A considerable group of them accepted Jesus as Messiah and Lord, and it was at Antioch that the followers of Jesus were first called 'Christians' or 'Messianists'. Other Jews thought the Messiah had not yet come. The community there had appointed the well-trained and eloquent Paul to accompany Barnabas (Barnabas was still the leader) in spreading the Good News about Jesus as the Messiah. At the end of their journey, they reported back to the community at Antioch. It is significant that Barnabas and Paul appointed elders in each community. This was the normal constitution of a Jewish community. A synagogue is still ruled by a body of elders, of whom one is chosen to preside. Obviously, in spite of the upset of which we read last Sunday, these Christian communities felt themselves to be like the other Jewish communities, although accepting Jesus as Messiah, and living by his Spirit.

Questions: To what extent should my behaviour as a Christian be different from that of others? Is it my business to attempt to change them?

Second reading: The New Jerusalem (Revelation 21.1-5)

Like so much of the Book of Revelation, this prophecy of the New Jerusalem is heavily dependent on the prophets of the Old Testament. In the dark days of the Babylonian Exile the prophet Ezekiel had foretold that God would rebuild Jerusalem as a new city where God would dwell, a city named *Hephzibah*, 'My pleasure is in her'. The prophets had long spoken of the relationship of Israel to God as that of a bride to her husband, a bride who was often unfaithful. Then Isaiah had foretold a joyful marriage feast in which God would be the bridegroom and Jerusalem the bride, the final wedding of God to his people. God's bride, Israel, who had so often been unfaithful, would at last be wedded to him for ever in fidelity and happiness. This was the intended meaning of the marriage feast at Cana and of the parables of Jesus about a wedding feast of the great king, to which the poor and the outcasts would be invited. Here the Book of Revelation promises just such a festival to those who have sustained the grimness of Roman persecution. Now, as we celebrate Christ's triumph over death, we look forward to this same unalloyed happiness of God's presence and his love.

Question: If God lives among us now, where and how can I most find him?

Gospel: The Commandment of Love (John 13.31-35)

From now on till Pentecost we read in John the great final teaching of Jesus at the Last Supper about the future of his Church and his disciples. From the sayings of Jesus, the evangelist has composed a great discourse of Jesus about the obligations, duties and dangers that will come on his disciples after his own death and Resurrection. There were probably slightly different versions of this discourse, which were handed down by word of mouth; the slight impression of repetition results from the evangelist putting three versions one after another. As we approach the Birth of the Church at Pentecost we need to listen to how Jesus envisaged his community. This reading gives the essentials. At the head of the Christian community stands the glorified Son of Man, in whom God himself is glorified. But this is no distant figurehead, for he will come to be present among his disciples. And how? In the love his disciples show for one another. One is reminded of the legend about the aged St John, wheeled into the church at Ephesus. When asked for the message of Jesus, all he would say was, 'My little children, love one another.'

Questions: What in practice does this love mean for you? Does it really make sense to say, 'I love him with a Christian love, but I just don't like him'?

Sixth Sunday of Easter

First reading: The Council at Jerusalem (Acts 15.1-2, 22-29)

This was the crucial meeting of the whole Church at Jerusalem where the decision was made that Christianity was not only for Jews but was open to the gentiles too. Paul's activity in receiving gentiles into the Church had created a crisis: was not God's promise to Abraham limited only to Jews? Was it not limited only to those who observed the prescriptions of the Law? Could the Spirit of the Risen Christ really dwell in and activate the uncircumcised? The staggering breakthrough achieved here totally altered the course of history. The discussion at the meeting is omitted from this reading, which jumps to the concluding instructions, but it is a model for a community discussion: in the awareness of the presence of the Spirit, they heard the facts of the case, listened to the opinions on both sides of the question put forward by experienced leaders, and then made their decision in the Spirit. The letter of instructions that follows is also a model of its kind, firm in its decisions, but firm also in its appreciation of individual consciences. The restrictions imposed on gentile Christians were designed to make fellowship with Jewish Christians possible without outraging their sensibilities.

Questions: How do I get to know God's will for me? Would it be helpful if I took more part in parish life?

Second reading: The Holy City of Jerusalem (Revelation 21.10-14, 22-23)

The description of the New Jerusalem, the bride of Christ, begun in last week's reading, continues to be highly symbolic. The 12 gates (drawn from Ezekiel's prophecy) face the four quarters of the compass, to show that it embraces the whole universe and is four-square solid. They symbolize the 12 tribes of Israel and so also the 12 apostles. The richness and contentment is hinted by the sparkle of precious stones, not only diamonds but many others too. The dimensions of the city are vast: a cube, of 1500 miles in each direction. No need for the light and warmth of the sun, for the Lord God and the Lamb provide a single source of its nourishment and illumination. No need for a sacred area, for the presence of the Lord God and the Lamb make the whole city a sacred area. This is the ultimate goal of creation, when all is absorbed into God, the ultimate fulfilment of 'Thy Kingdom come'. The Letter to the Ephesians expresses it as the whole universe 'headed up' into Christ, making sense of creation and bringing creation to its completion.

Question: If I really lived in the presence of God, what would be the most daunting thing, what the most encouraging thing?

Gospel: The Promise of the Spirit (John 14.23-29)
In these final discourses of Jesus at the Last Supper, as he sketches the outlines of his future Church, come four passages promising the coming of a Paraclete or Advocate, the Holy Spirit. 'Paraclete' and 'Advocate' mean the same: someone called to your side as a supporter, often in a legal situation. The Father will send this Paraclete, in the name and power of Jesus, so that the Paraclete will make Christ present in the Church, not physically but in a new way. The Paraclete will strengthen Jesus' disciples with Christ's own strength. The Paraclete will lead the disciples into all truth, so that they gradually come to a fuller understanding of all the implications of the teaching of Jesus. Like any legal advocate, the Paraclete will provide the followers of Jesus with power in teaching and argument to withstand opposition. This is the power that will guide the Church in ages to come, not only the official teachers of the Church, the successors of the apostles, but all the faithful who preserve and enrich the tradition of the Church by their prophetic office. The decree of Vatican II on the Church leaves no doubt that not only the call to sanctity but the prophetic office also extends to all the members of the Church, an inspiring and awesome responsibility.

Questions: For what special task do I most need the Paraclete's guidance? For what do I most need the Paraclete's strength?

Seventh Sunday of Easter, Ascension Sunday

On the Feast of the Ascension the first reading is the same in years AB and C. The gospel reading is different for Years A, B and C. For the second reading the passage set for Year A may always be read, but an alternative is provided.

First reading: The Ascension (Acts 1.1-11)

How are we to envisage what happened at the Ascension? Two feet disappearing into a cloud? It is mentioned only in the Acts, and the other gospels seem to imply that the Risen Christ was glorified on the day of the Resurrection itself. Luke, the author, is putting across several messages. First, the 40 days since Easter should not be carefully counted. In biblical language, '40' makes just 'a fairly long period', often a period of preparation, like Jesus' 40 days being tested in the desert, or Israel's 40 years of the Exodus. For all that time Jesus has been preparing his apostles. Second, it is the definitive parting of the physical Jesus, after which the Risen Christ is no longer with his disciples. It is now the Spirit of Christ that is at the heart of the Church, inspiring all its activity. Third, Luke represents Jesus as a prophet (and more than a prophet), so he leaves his disciples in the same way as the prophet Elijah, who was taken to heaven in a fiery chariot, leaving his disciple Elisha to carry on his work, filled with a double share of his spirit.

Questions: In what way is the Ascension an encouragement? How would you explain the Ascension to a non-Christian friend?

Second reading: Christ is Supreme (Ephesians 1.17-21)

The blessing that forms the core of this reading gives the sense of the Ascension for the Church. It is not the manner of Christ's departure that is important, but the exalted position of Christ, and the power of God that raised Christ from the dead. This same power has called us to be believers, made us rich in the glory of his heritage, and has given us the strength to follow Christ. As Christians, we believe that Jesus was divine not only from birth but from the moment of his conception. It was then that the Word of God became flesh. And yet something further happened at the glorification of Christ in his Resurrection. Paul says he was 'constituted Son of God in power' at the Resurrection. Is this the same as the claim that the high priest declared blasphemous, 'You will see the son of man seated at the right hand of the Power and coming on the clouds of heaven'? In the final scene of the gospel of Matthew, Jesus declares, 'All power in heaven and on earth has been given to me', and the Book of Revelation shows the Risen Christ sharing the throne of God.

Question: Are there evil spirits abroad in the world? How does evil accord with God's power?

Gospel: The Ascension (Luke 24.46-53)

In his two-volume history, Luke has two versions of the Ascension, one at the end of the gospel (today's gospel reading), one at the beginning of the second volume (our first reading today). The emphasis of the first reading was on the open endedness of the mission of the apostles: they were to wait till the Spirit came, after which they would continue their mission until the return of Christ – whenever that was going to be. It is a bracket opening a clause, which will be closed only at the end of the world. The emphasis in the gospel reading is on the final blessing of Christ as he departs, and on the joy and thanksgiving that this imparts. There is a sense of completion, for the gospel began in the Temple with the annunciation to Zechariah, and it ends in the Temple with the disciples praising God. There is also a sense of beginning, as the Good News is to spread from Jerusalem to all nations. In either case, the challenge is there: Christ must now play his part through us, his followers. If we act in the Spirit, Christ is acting. If we do not, the Spirit is stifled.

Question: Can you see any signs of Christ's presence in the world today?

Alternative second reading: Christ Enters Heaven to Present his Sacrifice (Hebrews 9.24-28; 10.19-23)

The reading from Acts presents the aspect of Christ's departure from his disciples, leaving them to carry on his work. This reading from Hebrews presents the aspect of Christ's arrival into the presence of God, although that arrival is in no way tied to the event narrated in Acts. The stress is on the fact that Christ permanently presents to the Father the sacrifice by which he redeemed the world, and on the confidence this should inspire in us. Christ can be represented as continually presenting his sacrifice because in the Resurrection there is, of course, no time. He has removed sin once and for all. The letter is addressed to Hebrew priests, presumably new adherents to Christ, who still yearned for the rites of the Temple – and here specifically for the rites of the annual Day of Reconciliation – and needed to be reminded that Christ's sacrifice far surpasses the ineffectual sacrifices of the Old Law.

The 'sprinkling' and 'washing with water' must be allusions to baptism, by which we are plunged into Christ's death, become one with him, and share in his risen life; it is this that gives the full assurance of faith.

Question: Why was Jesus' self-offering so valuable to God?

Pentecost

The readings for Year A as on p. 67 may be used in any year. The alternative second and third readings for Year C only are given after the readings for any year.

First reading: The Birth of the Church (Acts 2.1-11)

The ministry of Jesus starts with the coming of the Spirit at his Baptism, and so the ministry of the Church begins with the coming of the Spirit at Pentecost. There can be no witness to Jesus or to his message, no spreading of the Kingship of God, without the Spirit of Jesus. Another lesson from this parallel is that the task of the Church and the life of the Church are the same as those of Jesus himself: to bring God's Kingship to its fulfilment by bringing healing, love and joy through the message of the Risen Christ. The rushing wind and the tongues of fire are an allusion to the coming of God's Spirit upon Moses and the elders in the Old Testament. So the new message is the fulfilment of the Old Testament, breaking out beyond the borders of Judaism to include all peoples of the world. The union of all these peoples, all understanding one language in their own way, is a deliberate contrast to the scene at the Tower of Babel, when the Lord split up all the peoples of the world by their inability to understand one another's languages. The list of unpronounceable peoples is itself a witness to the universality of the Church!

Questions: How can the Church claim to be the Spirit at work in the world? Mention three outstanding ways in which the Church shows Christ at work today.

Second reading: The Body of Christ (1 Corinthians 12.3-7, 12-13)

The slightest glance around a church full of people is enough to show the variety within the Christian community. But it needs the hints given us by Paul to remind us that every member of that community has his or her own special gift to contribute. Mercifully, these gifts are all different. It is valuable to reflect on the natural gifts that we find all around us. It is also valuable to reflect how dull, or even intolerable, life would be if I lived with a lot of clones of myself, all with the same gifts and the same faults as me! Every one of us contributes something different and valuable in its own way, whether it is the baby squeaking as a sign of new, developing life or the older person contributing wisdom, experience and even the suffering of Christ. The other inspiring thought is that all these varied and diverse people go to make up the Body that is Christ. We all have experience of various corporate bodies, organizations and companies, but none of these other bodies makes up a person. That Person is Christ, since as Christians we all live and operate through Christ's Spirit.

Question: Who is the most Christ-like figure for you in the present or recent past?

Gospel: The Gift of Peace (John 20.19-23)
At first sight, this is a surprising gospel reading for Pentecost, but, of course, the event of Pentecost came too late to be a subject for the gospels, and we read the account of another incident where the Risen Christ gave the Spirit to his disciples. There are two emphases in the account. The first is peace. Christ brings peace to his disciples with the double greeting of peace, and peace is a Christian watchword. Peace was the song of the angels at Jesus' birth. Each of Paul's letters opens with a greeting of peace. The letter to the Ephesians proclaims that Christ is our peace, the reversal of all worry, strife, envy, jealousy, self-seeking ambition. 'Go in peace' is Jesus' dismissal of those he cures, and also the dismissal at the end of Mass. Peace was Jesus' bequest to his disciples after the Last Supper. The second watchword is forgiveness, for God was always known as a God of mercy and forgiveness, as Jesus came to show by his constant approach to sinners. But the Lord's Prayer shows that if we do not ourselves forgive, we block God's forgiveness of ourselves, too.

Question: 'Forgiveness is the only sure path to peace.' Does this cause any difficulties?

Alternative second reading: The Spirit of Christ in me (Romans 8.8-17)

Paul's letter to the Romans is all about the process of salvation. What difference did the death and Resurrection of Jesus actually make to me and my condition in the world? This passage is the climax; it plants the flag on the summit and leaves us to live a full Christian life in peace, tranquillity and hope. There have been three stages. First comes the work of Christ: Jesus' loving, obedient death on the Cross undid, washed away or healed, the disobedience of Adam, that is, the disobedience of the whole human race (Romans 5.12-21). What is that to me? So, stage two: by baptism, I express my faith in Christ. By myself I am helpless and hopeless, so I put all my trust in Christ. In baptism, I am plunged into Christ, plunged into Christ's death, and come up soaked and dripping with Christ's risen life (Romans 6.1-11). Stage three: permeated with, or vivified with this risen life of Christ I am adopted to sonship of God and can cry out '*Abba,* Father' with the voice of Jesus himself. The inheritance of Jesus as Son of

God is now my inheritance. So Pentecost is the celebration of the Spirit of Jesus alive and active in every Christian.

Question: What difference does the presence of Christ's Spirit make to me?

Gospel: The Paraclete (John 14.15-16, 23-26)
In Jesus' final speech to his disciples after the Last Supper, preparing them for life after the Resurrection, he several times mentions a mysterious figure, the Paraclete. 'Paraclete' is Greek for 'advocate', someone called to your side to help, to guide you through a tricky patch. In Hebrew mythology about the Last Judgment, there would be an Accuser and an Advocate on either side. Jesus will send – or in other passages the Father will send – this Advocate to his followers as his own presence when he is no longer there, to guide the Church into all truth. That is the inspiring situation: the Church and each of its individuals will continue to deepen our understanding of the mysteries of God, over the centuries and over the years of our life. Before the Spirit was given, even the disciples who had been with Jesus throughout his ministry failed to understand his real significance, and certainly lacked courage to proclaim it. The coming of the Paraclete was the booster rocket that set off the Church on its course and keeps it on course. Now it is the duty and privilege of each of the members of the Church to fulfil the prophetic office of the Church, understanding more deeply and declaring more clearly the truth about Christ in the world.

Question: How can I fulfil the prophetic office of the Church?

Trinity Sunday
First reading: The Wisdom of God (Proverbs 8.22-31)

How did we Christians come to see God as a Trinity of Persons? With a noble sense of reverence, the Israelites saw God as so infinitely other than the world that it became difficult to understand how God could mix with the world, even how God could 'dirty his fingers' by creating the world. The solution was that God must have created the universe by his Wisdom, the 'master craftsman by his side' in the work of creation. God's Wisdom is in a way the same as God, but yet not exactly the same. But is God's Wisdom itself created? It is not clear whether God 'created' or 'possessed' Wisdom, for the Hebrew word, different from the word used for 'creating' the universe, is given both senses by different ancient translators. So there is in God something that both *is* God and *is not* the same as the Creator. The Wisdom of God is also similar to the Word of God by which God created, 'He spoke and it came into being' (in the Creation Story in Genesis 1). In the New Testament, Jesus is known both as the Wisdom of God and as the Word of God. The first thing we know about God is that we cannot know about God. Nevertheless, the Bible is groping towards the idea that there is diversity within God. This is the beginning of the understanding of the Trinity.

Question: 'God is love.' But if God is totally other, what can this mean?

Second reading: The Three Persons at Work (Romans 5.1-5)

When Paul wrote his letter to the Romans, the theology of the Trinity was still waiting to be worked out. The interrelationship between the three Persons did not begin to be elaborated by theologians for a couple of centuries yet, or what is meant by calling them three 'Persons'. Paul calls the Risen Christ 'Lord', using the sacred name that may be used only of God. However, already Paul shows an awareness that three different modes are involved in human salvation, the divine action that brings human beings back to God. He often has a triple formula like the one in this reading, using different language of God, Christ and the Spirit. *Through our Lord Jesus Christ* we are brought into *peace with God*, and the love of God is poured into our hearts *by the Holy Spirit*. Human language is so totally inadequate to express truths about God that it will be long before any satisfying formula is found.

Question: Can we distinguish the function of the three Persons of the Trinity in the work of our salvation?

Gospel: Father, Son and Spirit (John 16.12-15)

We can learn a little about the Trinity from this passage. Think of a perfect relationship between a father and a son: complete understanding between them, loving care from the father, loving obedience from the son, complete support from both sides. As soon as one has an idea, the other expresses it, to the perfect satisfaction of the first. As soon as one starts an action, the other has completed it, to the delight of the first. Then the son sends his own spirit, which *is* not himself, but *represents* himself fully, makes him present when he is not there and does his work exactly as he would do it. Two other images, perhaps rather cheeky: three men on a bench outside a pub or three women with supermarket trolleys, all three chatting in perfect harmony and understanding and complete exchange of ideas, plenty of humour, laughter and warmth. They are so attractive that you would love to join them but don't dare. They are so welcoming that they invite you to join them. They are so loving that you feel you have found happiness as never before. These are wretched images to express unity in diversity, but one must at least try to understand. Read the gospel again!

Question: Can you think of an image for three Persons in one Nature?

Sunday of the Body and Blood of Christ

First reading: The Blessing of Melchizedek (Genesis 14.18-20)

Melchizedek is a historically mysterious figure, king of Salem, who suddenly appears from nowhere to greet Abraham and bless him. In gratitude, Abraham gives Melchizedek one-tenth of the spoil he has just won in battle. The only other mention of Melchizedek in the Old Testament is in Psalm 110, where he is the priest-king of Jerusalem. The early verses of this Psalm are frequently used in the New Testament to show the exaltation of Christ to the right hand of the Father at the Resurrection: 'Sit at my right hand until I make your enemies your footstool.' In the New Testament, the whole psalm is therefore understood of Christ, and so in the Letter to the Hebrews the verse, 'you are a priest according to the line of Melchizedek' (originally addressed to the priest-king of Jerusalem) is understood to refer to Christ's priesthood. Christ is a priest not in the line of Aaron, but in the line of Melchizedek. The Letter further argues from the fact that Melchizedek blesses Abraham that Melchizedek's priesthood is superior to that of Abraham and Aaron. So, by this slightly involved explanation, in this first reading we are celebrating the priesthood of Christ, superior to the priesthood of the Old Law.

Question: What does it mean that all Christians share in the priesthood of Christ?

Second reading: The Lord's Supper (1 Corinthians 11.23-26)

From several points of view, this is one of the most precious passages of the New Testament. To begin with, the terms 'received' and 'passed on' are technical terms of the rabbinic process of oral tradition; they show that what Paul is about to say is part of the tradition conserved in the Christian community. Second, it shows us that the repetition of this rite was seen to bring to the participants participation in the death and Resurrection of the Lord Jesus – worthily or unworthily. And Paul's purpose is to rebuke the Corinthians for taking part in the Eucharistic supper without due seriousness. Third, it shows some of the most precious aspects of the Eucharistic meal: it is the sealing of the new covenant in the cup of

Christ's blood, that covenant that brings to each individual the union with the Father wrought by Christ's death. Fourth, as Paul's chief rebuke to the Corinthians is that they are disunited and selfish at their Eucharist, treating it just like an ordinary dinner, neglecting one another's needs, it is a reminder to us that the Eucharist is a celebration of the Body of Christ, in which we are all united in love, and in which we all depend on one another. Is this really our impression of the Sunday Mass?

Question: Which of the aspects of the Eucharist is most important to you?

Gospel: Jesus gives Food to the Crowds (Luke 9.11-17)

On the feast of the Body and Blood of Christ should we not have the gospel reading about the institution of the Eucharist at the Last Supper? No, the Church puts before us this reading of the wonderful gift of food by Jesus. It is a sort of open-air picnic Eucharist that begins with Jesus talking to them about the Kingdom of God; this is what happens in the earlier part of our Eucharist, as we listen to the readings and the homily on them. Then he heals those who are in need of healing, and that means all of us, for we are always in need of healing in various ways. If you don't think you need to be healed, don't come to the Eucharist. Only then does he raise his eyes to heaven, bless the bread and distribute it, just as Jesus gives himself to us in the Eucharist. A sign of the generosity and plenty of Jesus' gifts in the Eucharist is given by the 12 baskets of leftovers, ready for consumption by the 12 tribes of the new Israel. In the same way, on the feast of the Body and Blood of Christ we share joyfully in the sustenance which Jesus gives to us and to the huge numbers of his followers across the world.

Questions: How can I participate more fully in Jesus' gift of the Eucharist? Better preparation beforehand? Reflexion afterwards? Fuller attention during the Mass?

ORDINARY SUNDAYS OF THE YEAR

Year A

Second Sunday of the year

First reading: Israel, Servant of the Lord (Isaiah 49.3, 5-6)

We are about to set out, in the Ordinary Sundays of Year A, on a journey through Matthew's account of Jesus' ministry. In the gospels themselves of Mark, Matthew and Luke, the reader accompanies the disciples in learning only gradually who and what Jesus is. In the arrangement of the lectionary, however, put before us by the Church, the gospel reading of this first Sunday is from John, showing clearly who Jesus is, this year 'the Chosen One of God'. The first reading from Isaiah, written in the dark days of the Babylonian Exile, introduces a Servant of the Lord, formed in the womb to be the Lord's Servant and to bring light both to Israel and to the nations. Is this an individual whose mission is to bring Israel back to the Lord, or is it the nation of Israel, destined to bring the gentile nations to the Lord? Despite the failure to recognize the Messiah, the faithful of Israel still bear witness 'to the ends of the earth' to God's promises. It is remarkable that already at this stage of revelation the universalist task given by God is seen to be to bring the whole world within the orbit of the salvation promised to Israel.

Question: To what extent am I called to follow Christ as the Servant of the Lord?

Second reading: The Beginning of First Corinthians (1 Corinthians 1.1-3)

One-third of this great letter is read at the beginning of each of the three years of the cycle. Paul greets them as the 'holy people of God', but – like the pilgrim Church today – they were far from uniformly holy. But they were chosen to be holy, so by that same divine choice given a designation to be holy. Corinth was a turbulent city. It had been sacked by the Romans for rebellion. But it lay on the narrow neck of land between the Aegean

131

and Adriatic Seas, and so was a vital resource for shipping between eastern and western Mediterranean. After 100 years it was rebuilt, and 100 years after that, when Paul was writing, it was again a boom town, with two harbours, an international games more famous than the Olympics and a large segment of Jewish population. Paul spent 18 months evangelizing the city before being driven out by the Jews. However, he kept in close contact and wrote them several letters. It was not an easy relationship: the Corinthians were arrogant and quarrelsome. Paul does not hesitate to correct them. He calls them babies whom he can feed only on milk, which must have upset the city elders among them!

Question: What would your reaction be if Paul called you a baby to be fed on milk?

Gospel: The Lamb of God (John 1.29-34)

In contrast to the other gospels, where the reader observes the disciples discovering gradually who Jesus is, John gives us a week between the baptism and the marriage feast of Cana, during which Jesus is given increasingly significant titles by those who meet him: Rabbi, the Messiah, Son of God, King of Israel. Perhaps the most significant of all are those given by the Baptist himself, Lamb of God and Chosen One of God. Lamb of God overarches the gospel, for it comes again at the Crucifixion. According to John Jesus dies at the moment the paschal lambs were being slaughtered in the Temple, and John alone refers to Jesus the scriptural saying 'Not one bone of his will be broken' (John 19.36), originally part of the instructions for the sacrificing of the lamb at the Festival of Passover (Exodus 12.46). In the Book of Revelation, Jesus is represented standing 'as a Lamb that seemed to have been sacrificed'. It is, therefore, an image both of his suffering and of his triumph. It links up with the picture of Jesus as the Suffering Servant of the Lord who moves through suffering and humiliation to vindication and to the triumph of God.

Reflection: Reflect on Jesus as the Lamb standing as if sacrificed.

Third Sunday

First reading: Light in the Land of Darkness (Isaiah 9.1-4)

This prophecy of Isaiah is chosen as the first reading because in the gospel reading, Matthew sees its fulfilment in the healing activity of Jesus in Galilee, the region once allotted to the two northern tribes of Zebulun and Naphthali. Not long before the total collapse of the Northern Kingdom of

Israel they were invaded and devastated by the mighty power of Assyria. They are therefore given as the archetype of the ruined territory that will be restored to light, joy and rich harvest when God comes to save his people. In fact, Galilee has rich soil and wide plains. The Jewish historian at the time of Jesus is lyrical about the abundance and variety of fruit grown there. The prophecy of restoration is expressed in the past tense (*'have seen a great light'*) to emphasize its certainty: it is so sure that it can be described as if it had already happened, a tense known as 'the prophetic past'. The passage of Isaiah goes on, after our reading, to speak of the child to be born, who will achieve this transformation. He will be 'Wonder Counsellor, Prince of Peace'. Such was the background of hope which gave their full meaning to Jesus' deeds as he brought divine healing and restoration in Galilee.

Question: What is the most important element that would restore our country to God's service?

Second reading: A Divided Community (1 Corinthians 1.10-13, 17-18)

It is hardly surprising that the Christians at Corinth were a divided community; there were so many different levels of employment and wealth, financiers, dockers, tent makers, administrators and many others in that town with its double port, its booming trade, its biennial games and supporting trades. Paul shows us that there were also cliques claiming different personal loyalties. Some claimed to be Paul's own followers. Apollos was a Jew from Alexandria and a notable orator; perhaps he had the intellectual following. Cephas is the Aramaic name for Peter; his following may have been Christians sprung from Judaism who wanted to keep their Jewish practices in food, circumcision and Sabbath observance. Paul will have none of this party politics, one group hurling slogans at another. They would not even come together as a genuine community at the Eucharist. Paul had baptized people to be not his own followers but followers of Christ. Later in the letter, he will explain that Christians must form a single organic body, all working together in harmony, each with a special task and special gifts, but all contributing to the wellbeing of the whole. This is his basic vision of the Christian body, all living with the one life of Christ.

Question: Are there any echoes of such disunity in your community?

Gospel: The Call of the First Disciples (Matthew 4.12-23)
This is the beginning of Jesus' ministry. Matthew first introduces us to Galilee, characteristically quoting the scriptures to show that they are

being fulfilled, and in what way. Galilee is called 'Galilee of the gentiles' only in this passage, and it was not a particularly notable feature of Galilee. Archaeology shows that Jewish observance was strong in the region. Contemporary literature shows that there was a lively tradition of prayerful charismatic rabbis with a warm devotion to the Lord. Jesus begins his ministry by proclaiming the imminence of the Kingdom of God, which will be the subject of all his activity. Then he begins to form the new Israel by calling his team together. The Christian imagination tends to combine this scene with the scene with the Baptist in the Jordan Valley in the gospel of John, which gives at least Peter and Andrew some knowledge of Jesus. But today's narrative must be heard on its own, and the staggering factor is that this is the first time at any rate the sons of Zebedee have set eyes on Jesus. As he passes by he calls them, and such is the electrifying power of his charismatic personality that they simply drop everything and follow this total stranger – immediately, as the evangelist stresses each time.

Question: Do I ever follow Jesus' call immediately and unconditionally?

Fourth Sunday

First reading: Blessed by the Lord (Zephaniah 2.3; 3.12-13)

Before the Babylonian Exile, Israel tended to equate material prosperity with divine blessing: those who prospered did so because of the Lord's blessing; those who did not must in some way be blameworthy. The Exile put an end to all that, and the consequent puzzlement is visible in the Book of Job. These verses from the prophecy of Zephaniah show the new and more satisfying analysis: it is the humble of the Lord who will receive divine blessing, those who seek refuge in the Name or Power of the Lord and recognize their entire dependence on him. The nation of Israel was the plaything of the great powers on either side, dominated first by one, then by the other. This is the spirituality of the powerless Remnant, not giving themselves airs or trusting in their own strength. It is perfectly and consciously exemplified in the personnel of the Lukan Infancy Narratives, where Zechariah and Elizabeth, Mary and Joseph, Simeon and Anna humbly obey the law and await the salvation that is to come to them from the Lord. This spirit was not the strong suit of the Corinthians to whom Paul writes! It is partly exemplified also in the Beatitudes that will form the gospel reading.

Question: What, then, is true Christian humility? Is it to say that I am no good at anything, or to recognize my talents and be grateful for them?

Second reading: Reversal of Values (1 Corinthians 1.26-31)

The Corinthians seem to have been particularly pleased with themselves, so that Paul mercilessly lavishes his sarcasm on them. In their bravado and their complacency, they were happy to rely on their own resources, and expected to be saved by them. Paul repeats to them the lesson of Zephaniah. The public reading of the letter must have embarrassed those at whom it was aimed, and the vigour of Paul's criticism was perhaps the reason why his relationships with this community continued stormy for some time. For us, however, the positive teaching is a treasure, that Christ is for us our wisdom, our strength, our holiness and our freedom. Only through Christ can we achieve our ambitions and grow to full human maturity, by participating in these qualities of Christ. Once incorporated into Christ by baptism, we already share in his wisdom, holiness and strength, and even in his freedom, if only we rely on that and not on ourselves. Paul goes on to say that Christ is the Wisdom of God, a teaching elaborated in the later epistles (possibly written not by Paul himself) to the Colossians and Ephesians.

Question: Isn't it a blessing that none of us is conceited or cliquish?

Gospel reading: The Beatitudes (Matthew 5.1-12)
These eight blessings stand at the head of the Sermon on the Mount, pointing out eight ways in which we can welcome God into our lives. They are ways of living out God's blessing. The first and the last knit them all together with 'theirs is the kingdom of heaven'. Luke also begins his Sermon on the Plain with four such blessings – only his blessings are more on those who are materially poor and in need, whereas Matthew's concentrate on the spiritual attitudes required of the Christian, 'poor *in spirit*, hunger and thirst *for justice*'. Jesus came to proclaim the Kingship of his Father, and these are ways of living it. For each of them, do you know someone who exemplifies the attitude? Which is your own favourite? For most of them there are gospel incidents in which Jesus sums them up, like the entry into Jerusalem on a donkey as the gentle king, or the love he shows in his welcome to sinners, or his bringing peace to those tortured by disease or contempt, or his purity of heart in his single-minded preoccupation with his Father's will, and, finally, his acceptance of persecution for what he knew to be right.

Question: Are any of these qualities more basic than others?

Fifth Sunday

First reading: Authentic Conversion (Isaiah 58.6-10)

Look out! Lent is not far away! We need to start thinking again about genuine conversion, turning back to the Lord. This passage comes far on in the Book of Isaiah, written when the Jews had returned from exile in Babylon, but still things were not going right for them, still the favour of the Lord did not seem to be upon them. It makes a good examination of conscience: do I invite the homeless poor, share my advantages with others? Am I at peace with my family? Do I seek to dominate by the 'clenched fist', the wounding word, the put-down that can shrivel someone up? Isaiah is contrasting genuine service of the Lord with the merely exterior practices of religion, the conventional ways in which we may seem to be 'holy' people. In fact, however, holiness is all a matter of the heart, and – at any rate in this text – mostly a matter of seeing and serving God in other people. That is the only way our light can really shine in the darkness, and our own wounds be healed over. As in the Beatitudes, God's demands always have a promise attached.

Question: How would you define holiness?

Second reading: The Secret of Paul's Success (1 Corinthians 2.1-5)

What was the secret of Paul's success? At times he seems to us boastful, 'Take me as your pattern' (4.17) or 'Be united in imitating me' (Phil 3.17). He boasts of his faultless Jewish ancestry: 'Are they Hebrews? So am I' (2 Cor 11.22), etc. He claims to have undergone for Christ more sufferings and persecutions than others (2 Cor 12), to have been perfect in the law (Phil 3.6), to have outstripped his contemporaries in his zeal for the law (Ga 1.14). He claims that he speaks in tongues more than any of them, and yet he does not make much of it (1 Cor 14.18). Yet here he insists that he came among the Corinthians in weakness, in fear and great trembling in order to make known the power of the Spirit. In the same way, he will later admit that he holds the treasure of the light of Christ in fragile pots made of earthenware (2 Cor 4.7). There are some wonderful rhetorical passages in Paul, where he exploits to the full the literary and oratorical training he had received, but, in the last analysis, one must admit that his power consists simply in the power of his message and the promises of Christ.

Question: Is Paul conceited or boastful?

Gospel: Salt and Light (Matthew 5.13-16)

Matthew here takes two piquant images from the words of Jesus that he found in Mark's Gospel and builds them up. Immediately after the Beatitudes, with which he began the Sermon on the Mount, he shows that these Christian attitudes are not just for our own benefit but are to change the world. The first is a warning, the second a promise. Christians are to be salt for the whole world. Imagine a perpetual diet of food without any tang or taste, bland and insipid! This would be the world if Christians did not spread the message of Christ, did not impart to the world the flavour brought by Christ's message. What would the world be without that message and challenge of the generosity and salvation of Christ which we profess? Yes, of course, much of the same message may come to the world through other great world faiths, but the full challenge and the full promise is in Christ. The same is true for the second image, that of light. Imagine a world of darkness, in which we had to feel our way and are never quite sure of shapes and purposes! And then what a difference occurs when the sun rises over the horizon or the light is switched on. Such is the difference that Christianity – and our Christianity – must make to the world.

Question: How should the Christian set out to be salt and light to today's world?

Sixth Sunday

First reading: Contrasts (Ecclesiasticus 15.15-20)

A reading from Ecclesiasticus is rare enough for us to remind ourselves of the origin of the book. It is one of the Wisdom Books of the Bible, written towards the end of the Old Testament period, when prophecy had come to an end. The fierce corrections of the prophets and their inspiring promises of coming salvation were no more, and the word of the Lord came in collections of wise sayings to guide conduct, inspired by acute awareness that the Lord was the source of all wisdom. This collection of wisdom was brought together by a sage and experienced scribe of the law at Jerusalem named Ben Sira. It was taken by the author's grandson to Alexandria in Egypt and translated into Greek for the Greek-speaking Jews there. Only recently have manuscripts been discovered containing most of the Hebrew original. In today's passage, Ben Sira sets out the contrasting choices that face us, to which we can freely reach out our hands. It is one of the chief passages in the Bible stressing our own free will. Of our own volition we may turn to good or to ill. God calls for our love and response, but does not force us, for love must be a free act.

Question: How can I express my love for God and for his loving plan?

Second reading: The Wisdom of God (1 Corinthians 2.6-10)

Among the recipients of this letter of Paul's were philosophers who prided themselves on their wisdom, the Greek understanding of the nature of things and the structure of the universe. The wisdom which Paul teaches is beyond human understanding. What, then, is the point of it? First, it concerns the mystery hidden throughout the earlier history of the world and of humankind. The plan of God has been working itself out throughout history, throughout affectionate and tender, forgiving dealings of God with human beings. But it has been made clear only by the coming of Christ into human history as the keystone that makes sense of the whole structure. Second, we can still not fully understand it. We still have not fathomed the meaning of life and all its strange and unpredictable twistings and turnings. And yet we are assured by the Spirit of God that there is a meaning, and that this meaning is for our glory. Whatever goes wrong, as well as whatever goes right, is so arranged for our glory. Third, this same Spirit which penetrates the meaning of everything, even the depths of God, is the divine Spirit that lives in us and informs us as Christians.

Question: What seeming disasters in your life have, in fact, turned out to be part of the saving plan of God for you?

Gospel: Jesus corrects the Law (Matthew 5.17-37)

Jesus is the completion of the Law of God, given to Israel through Moses. He has come not to sweep it away but to perfect it. In this part of the Sermon on the Mount, Matthew has gathered together six instances (four this week, two next Sunday) of the ways in which Jesus brings the law to perfection. The first factor to notice, however, is that Jesus does not hesitate to adjust the divine law on his own authority, for he too has divine authority. Each correction begins with a statement of the Old Law and boldly goes on, 'But I say this to you …'

Each of the corrections has its own character. The first is about enmity, the sixth about love. About enmity, it is not enough merely to forego violent injury; we must even expel enmity from our hearts, positively seeking reconciliation, whether the offence is our fault or not. About lust, it is similarly not enough to forego acts of lust; we must not even harbour such thoughts in our hearts. About divorce, the easy toleration of divorce in the Jewish law is swept away, and Jesus uncompromisingly calls it fornication. About truth, it is not enough to keep a legal oath; we must be people on whose every word there is reliance. These are Jesus' demanding standards.

Question: Which is the most difficult of these demands?

Seventh Sunday

First reading: Love of Neighbour (Leviticus 19.1-2, 17-18)

This passage from Leviticus is taken from a series of regulations in the law called the 'Holiness Code'. Israel, God's own People, must set about treasuring and imitating God's own holiness. So there are regulations that express the awesomeness of God by demanding reverence and care towards God's sanctuary and towards those special processes of life, conception, birth and death, where the presence of God breaks in on human consciousness. God is felt to be specially present in these sacred moments of sex, when human beings combine to create life, and in the moments of passage to life and from life. There are also regulations that ensure that God's People treat the poor and unfortunate as God himself treated them when they were poor and downtrodden in Egypt. This is to be holy as God is holy. In particular, there must never be vengeance, but between the individual members of God's People the same love and forgiveness which God himself shows to his People. Jesus himself will take up this demand not only in today's gospel but also in the story of the Great Commandment, where he puts love of neighbour on the same level as love of God (Mark 12.28-34 and parallels in Matthew and Luke).

Question: Do we honour God and recognize the divine presence at these sacred moments of life?

Second reading: The Temple of God (1 Corinthians 3.16-23)

Paul is coming to the conclusion of the first section of his letter to the Corinthians. He has been chiding them for their conceit in grouping into separate cliques, making themselves followers of the various Christian leaders who have taught them at Corinth. 'Cephas' ('rock') is the Aramaic name for Peter, which also means 'rock'. Apollos was a Jewish teacher from Alexandria. 'No!' says Paul, 'the human leaders [including himself] are nothing, but you all belong to Christ.' He aptly uses the analogy of building, for Corinth had recently been rebuilt and was continually expanding. The foundation of the building is Christ. Different materials may be used, but on the one foundation there is only one building. Furthermore, this is no ordinary building, but is the Temple of God. In it each stone is holy, because the Spirit of God lives in the Temple of the Christian community no less surely than the Spirit of God dwelt in the Temple of Jerusalem. Later in the letter, Paul will develop this image to show that every element, every member of this holy Temple that belongs to Christ, has its special part to play. Each stone in the building is equally important.

Question: Can a divided parish form a single Temple for God?

Gospel: Jesus completes the Law (Matthew 5.38-48)

Following on from the four adjustments of the law in last Sunday's gospel come two more, perhaps the most demanding. The Law of Moses had limited revenge: only a tooth might be taken for a tooth, only an eye for an eye, not life itself. Jesus, however, will not tolerate even this limited vengeance; he allows none at all. Again and again in the course of the gospel, Jesus returns to this need for unconditional forgiveness. We daringly engage ourselves to it whenever we say the Lord's Prayer, 'Forgive us just as we forgive...'

The final demand, however, is the most challenging of all. There is, in fact, no passage of the canonical scripture that encourages 'hate your enemy'. In any case, just as God lavishes his benefits of life, sun and rain on good and evil alike, so we must put no limits to our love. Only in this way – think of the first reading! – can we attempt to honour and imitate the holiness of God. This is what it means to be a son of God, 'sons of your Father in heaven': only by following in his way and by fulfilling his designs can we be integrated into his family. There can be no enmity in Christianity.

Question: Can I really forgive with no trace of animosity?

Eighth Sunday

First reading: A Mother's Love (Isaiah 49.14-15)

In the Bible, God is normally regarded as a father. By analogy with the genetic theory that the father is the one who sparks into action the process of procreation, God is the Father of all things. God is also often seen as the disciplinarian, who corrects, forms and, as necessary, punishes his People. In general, a mother is seen as a softer, more affectionate and tender figure than a father, someone to whom the child can go running in tearful distress and be sure of finding comfort rather than the deserved sternness of a father. In reality, of course, there is no sex or gender in God, so that God's love does not have gender characteristics. Sometimes, God is represented as a loving and utterly caring parent, whose gender remains indeterminate, as in Hosea 11.1-4. Even a father can be tender and indulgent at times! But it is also important that there are passages, as this passage of Isaiah, in which God is compared to a mother, whose limitless affection can never be broken, will never turn away or be exhausted. This is a tenderness that, in the gospel stories, Jesus shows to those who approach him, the tax collectors, the woman who was a sinner, the adulteress.

Question: Is God more fairly imaged as father or mother, both or neither?

Second reading: The Servant of Christ (1 Corinthians 4.1-5)

'People must think of us as Christ's servants', begins the reading. Paul thinks of himself as the servant of Christ, just as Jesus thinks of himself as the Servant of the Lord. There is a handful of sayings of Jesus that obtain their full sense only if they are seen as alluding to Isaiah's prophecies of a Servant of the Lord who would draw Israel back to fidelity to the Lord, and would reach his fulfilment only through suffering and humiliation: 'the Son of Man came not to be served but to serve, and to give his life as a ransom for many' (Mark 10.45). Paul speaks of himself and his suffering for Christ in the same way, except that, whereas Jesus is the Servant of the Lord God, Paul is the servant of the Lord Jesus. Especially when he writes comparing himself to those who claim to be 'super-apostles', he refutes their claims by protesting that he has suffered more and been more bitterly persecuted on behalf of Christ than they have (2 Corinthians 11.22–12.13). So Paul sees himself as carrying on and completing the saving work of Christ. In the same way, it is through suffering and humiliation that he will be raised up at the last day.

Question: Why must God's servants always suffer?

Gospel: Trust in God's Care (Matthew 6.24-34)

At the beginning of this passage, we are told that you cannot serve two masters, a lesson that, in the gospel of Luke, is illustrated by the parable of the Crafty Steward. Unscrupulously, when he receives notice to quit, he defrauds his master by cutting down the sums owed by his master's debtors, and so wins their friendship, which will continue to support him (Luke 16.1-13). In Matthew's Sermon on the Mount, this whole passage, promising God's care for his faithful, comes after the requirement that we should serve God 'in secret', not blazoning our good works before onlookers. That passage is omitted from the semi-continuous reading of the Sermon because it is used at the beginning of Lent, on Ash Wednesday, so here we go straight on to the promise of a reward for faithful service. It is a commonplace of philosophers that no amount of worrying will increase our safety or comfort, but we need Christian faith to find our satisfaction and security in the divine protection. God's loving, maternal care does not preclude prolonged suffering, leading St Teresa of Avila to exclaim to Jesus, 'If you treat your friends like this, it is no wonder that you have so few of them.'

Question: Is it really possible to serve two masters, fairly satisfactorily?

Ninth Sunday

First reading: The Choice – a blessing or a curse (Deuteronomy 11.18, 26-28)

This passage is set in careful parallel to the gospel reading. It represents the end of the discourse of Moses in which he proposes the terms of the Covenant on Sinai. The choice set before Israel is whether they obey and flourish or disobey and perish. The whole of the subsequent biblical history of the People of Israel until the Babylonian Exile illustrates this choice: when they are faithful to the Covenant they flourish, when they are unfaithful they perish at the hands of their enemies until this correction by the Lord drives them back to repentance and fidelity.

The instructions to fasten the words on the hand and on the forehead were taken very literally and are still the basis of the *tefillin*, worn by orthodox Jews on forehead and hands at prayer, a little black box containing a minute copy of these verses. In accordance with verse 20, they are fastened also on the doorposts of the house; these are called *mezuzoth*. The injunctions may, of course, also be understood less literally, as instructions to keep the terms of the Covenant always vividly in mind and faithfully in practice.

Question: Do we have any such reminder in Christianity? Would it be useful?

Second reading: The Theme of the Letter to the Romans (Romans 3.21-25, 28)

We have finished our annual section from First Corinthians, and now, for the next 16 weeks of Ordinary Time, we read Paul's great letter to the Romans, the longest stint of any one letter. It deserves this, as Paul's fullest explanation of the salvation won by Christ's death and Resurrection. Paul's problem in writing to the Roman Christians, a mixed community, sprung from Jews and gentiles, was to show both that Christians are dependent on Judaism, as heirs of the promises made to Abraham, and that there is no longer any need to obey the Jewish law. Thus he stresses that Abraham was saved by his faith as a free gift, not by any meritorious action or act of obedience. So we too may be saved by our simple trust in God's will to save. By his supreme act of love on the Cross, Jesus reconciled humanity to God, by his obedience undoing and 'overtrumping' the disobedience of Adam, that is, of humanity.

Our reading of the letter begins in the middle of Chapter 3. The earlier part of the letter has shown that all people, both Jews and gentiles, are sunk in evil, and are in dire need of redemption.

Question: If I am saved by my faith in God's will to save, what is the point of good works?

Gospel: Conclusion of the Sermon on the Mount (Matthew 7.21-27)
The Sermon on the Mount, like the presentation of the Covenant, ends with both a threat and a promise. The threat is daunting: it is not enough merely to call on the Lord, to proclaim our devotion in words. If this assertion is to be real, we must proclaim it also in our actions. Matthew stresses the need actually to do the will of God: 'thy will be done', we pray in the Lord's Prayer, just as Jesus himself prayed this prayer in his Agony in the Garden. The dire threat of exclusion is repeated in the Parable of the Ten Virgins: the five thoughtless ones hear these very words when they arrive late and knock on the closed door.

The Sermon ends with a brilliant pair of parables, for Matthew likes to reinforce his lessons by a couple of parables: the Mustard Seed and the Leaven, the Hidden Treasure and the Pearl, the Darnel and the Dragnet, the Ten Virgins and the Talents. He also likes to put together in his parables contrasting personalities such as the two builders mentioned here: the Ten Virgins, the Two Sons, the Playing Children, the Sheep and the Goats. We are left in no doubt of the importance of this first great outline of Christian conduct.

Question: What is the central message of the Sermon on the Mount?

Tenth Sunday

First reading: God's Love (Hosea 6.3-6)

Hosea is the prophet of God's love. He had the searing experience of being married to someone who made herself easily available to all comers. Yet he continued to love her to distraction and call her back to himself again and again. 'Mad', you may say, 'unrealistic'. Yet his task as prophet was to show that God acts the same towards his people. At this time Israel was riddled with financial malpractice, sexual libertinism and deviation and materialistic values. All they were interested in was a soft bed, sex and drink. Precisely then Hosea proclaimed once again that God's forgiveness has no limits. After Israel's first rebellion, worshipping the idolatrous Golden Calf, God proclaimed to Moses that his sacred Name actually *means* 'a God of tenderness and forgiveness'. In today's passage, Hosea chides Israel for knowing all about God's love ('that he will come to us is as certain as the dawn') but refusing to turn back and seek that forgiveness. It is chosen because it obviously illustrates the frame of mind of Jesus, the God Incarnate, who goes out to link arms with despised sinners and tax collectors, actually choosing one for his inner circle of disciples to constitute the New Israel.

Question: Am I prepared to admit, even to God, how damaged and faulty I am, and to ask his forgiveness?

Second reading: The Faith of Abraham (Romans 4.18-25)

In the second readings, we are now working steadily through the Letter to the Romans, perhaps the greatest, or at least the most comprehensive, of all Paul's letters. Before he goes on to explain how Christ's act of salvation saves us all, Paul spends a chapter meditating on the faith of Abraham. Abraham was obviously the father of the Jews among the Christian community at Rome, but Paul teaches that he was the father and model in faith of the gentiles, too. The gentiles would also be saved by a faith in God's promises like that of Abraham. There could be no question that Abraham earned his salvation by anything he did. It was simply that, as time went on, and the situation seemed more and more hopeless, he continued to put his trust in God's promise. God would do the seemingly impossible and give him a son. The son would carry on his name and make him the father of many nations. The same trust in God's promises, fulfilled in Christ, is the only hope to which we can cling today. On this occasion it might be worth remembering that Muslims, too, are our brothers and sisters in this: they, too, see Abraham as their father in faith.

Question: What, in fact, do I rely on in life? What is my order of priorities?

Gospel: The Call of Matthew (Matthew 9.9-13)

Nobody likes tax collectors (or parking attendants). What made it worse in this case was that they were working for the hated enemy, the Romans. But Jesus positively chose them as his company. He called Matthew to follow him, and then went and had dinner with a group of them. He must have known that they were lonely and worried by their isolation, and wanted to heal them, just as he wants to heal us. So he went out of his way to call the sinners, not even asking them to repent first, but just because they needed him. He wasn't worried that they were despised or even hated, or that they were cut off from all the normal practices of religion. What scandalized the 'people who went to church' was that Jesus seemed positively to enjoy the company of these dirty sinners. He did the same with Zacchaeus, the chief tax collector of Jericho, who must have been a rogue. Three times in this gospel Jesus says, 'What I want is love, not sacrifice.' He didn't care whether they 'went to church' or kept the rules. He must have known that there was good in everyone, if only it is allowed to come to the surface.

Question: If Jesus preferred the company of sinners, why try to be good?

Eleventh Sunday

First reading: God Chooses Israel to be his own Possession (Exodus 19.1-6a)

This reading records the special moment when God chose Israel to be his own possession, a kingdom of priests, a holy nation, formed of 12 tribes, just as in the gospel reading Jesus will chose Twelve to be the nucleus of his holy Kingdom. God had led them out of slavery in Egypt with a purpose: they were to be gradually formed and enlightened to bring God's Good News to the whole of creation. First, they were given the Law (the Ten Commandments come just after this passage), which would teach them how the people of God must live out their vocation. 'Be holy as I am holy', acting in the image of God, completing God's work of creation. It was not going to be a smooth path. They rebelled already in the desert, hankering after the 'leeks and onions' of Egypt, and the history of Israel was to be a constant series of rebellion, recall and forgiveness – just like our relationship with God, full of failure and return. Formation always involves a fair amount of buffeting and correction, spiritual growing pains as well as physical. Like ours, their learning process was slow and full of mistakes, but, in the end, they brought salvation into the world in the person of Jesus.

Question: What can it mean that we are a kingdom of priests?

Second reading: The Proof of God's Love (Romans 5.6-11)

Paul uses several different images to convey the unique work of Christ. Here he uses 'reconciled', 'justified', 'saved'. Is there any difference between them? We *have been* reconciled and justified by Christ's death, and we *shall be* saved by his life, presumably by his risen and glorious life after the Resurrection, which will lead us to share with him in glory; this is still in the future, the end product. But we have already been reconciled with God. The enmity that we, the human race, put between ourselves and God by our constant rebellion has been dissolved by the overwhelming act of Jesus' love for his Father. The love of Christ surpasses the disobedience and hostility of Adam, the human race, in which we all shared. Paul also says that we have been justified or made righteous by Christ's death. Human righteousness, being right with God, is always dependent on God's own righteousness. God's righteousness is his fidelity to his promises to save. In fulfilling those promises, God is being true to himself and his word, and so is righteous. We are brought under that same righteousness by the fulfilment of the promises in Christ. So we are already reconciled and justified, and will be saved by Christ's life.

Question: If I have already been put right with God, can I just float along and leave it all to God?

Gospel: The New Israel (Matthew 9.36–10.3)

Jesus was concerned about his people. He wanted to bring to them the Kingdom of his Father, so he set out to heal them, and sent others out to do the same. His aim was to bring them the peace of God, to help them by ridding them of their worries, their sickness, their embarrassment at being lost sheep without a shepherd (God was always the shepherd in Israel). When he set up the 12 apostles he was making a New Israel, a new set of 12 tribes, as a permanent healing body, to make sure that the Kingdom of the Father and its peace and generosity would always be available. He was not setting up a clergy, a set of leaders, but appointing his own helpers in spreading God's Kingdom. That is what every Christian must do. Do I make it my business to spread the Kingdom or the Kingship of God? Am I a labourer in the harvest, trying to bring God's peace and healing to all the sick sheep? After all, I was made in the image of God, and God gave me the task of following on his creative work. And then Jesus called me, too, to work with him.

Question: Am I supposed to cure the sick and cast out devils?

Twelfth Sunday

First reading: The Persecuted Prophet (Jeremiah 20.10-13)

Jeremiah was the last prophet in Jerusalem before the Babylonians sacked the city and took most of the inhabitants into exile as slaves in 586BC. He was sent as a final warning, to tell them all, from the king downwards, that disaster was impending if they did not amend their ways and turn back to the Lord. The authorities didn't like it, and accused him of sabotaging the morale of the citizens. He was arrested and dumped in an empty water storage pit to keep him quiet. He himself was a gentle soul and hated delivering this fierce message, complaining to the Lord about his tough and unpalatable task, and the persecution he suffered. But he stuck to his guns, and when the king tore up the threatening message he sent, Jeremiah merely repeated it – with more besides. He also had a message of hope, that eventually the Lord would give them a new covenant, with a new heart and a new spirit, so that they would again be the People of God. This reading is chosen to show in the Old Testament the courage and perseverance in proclaiming the message that, in the gospels, Jesus asks from his disciples.

Question: When is it most difficult to take a stand and announce that I hold Christian principles? Do I manage to do this?

Second reading: Christ, the Second Adam (Romans 5.12-15)

Christ is the saviour, but how does he save? The Letter to the Romans is Paul's fullest explanation, and the heart of that teaching is that Christ is the Second Adam. Adam's sin in the Garden of Eden, as described in Genesis, is not a simple historical story of one particular sin. It is the paradigm of all sin, the paradigm or analysis of all human failure, the process of turning away from God's commandments in pride and independence: 'I know better than God what is good for me.' We are children of Adam in so far as we have sinned, and Adam's sin sums up that of all humanity. At the same time, Adam is not only the type, but also the founder of all humanity. Christ, by way of contrast, is the second founder of all humanity. His act of perfect obedience to his Father on the cross transcends and heals this act of disobedience committed by the first Adam. Only Christ's act of loving obedience could be great enough to do this. It had to be an act of a man, but not of a mere man. We are members of this new humanity in so far as we join ourselves to Christ, put all our trust and hope in him.

Question: Can you see any similarity between the sin of Adam and our own sins?

Gospel: The Mission of the Apostles (Matthew 10.26-33)

This whole chapter of Matthew brings together and sums up what Jesus has to say to his apostles about declaring his teaching in the face of hostility and persecution. Jesus himself was fearless in proclaiming his message. He 'taught with authority', as the gospel constantly tells us. His disciples are sent out to do the same. We do not often meet with real persecution, although it may yet happen. The martyrs of communist Russia or Vietnam lived many years of peaceful Christianity before unexpectedly facing martyrdom. The monk martyrs of Algeria did not reckon on martyrdom when they went to Algeria. The only preparation for martyrdom can be fidelity and prayer. More often we face mockery for holding to Christian principles, and that too can be difficult to bear. We can be accused of narrow mindedness, lack of appreciation of human values, blind obedience, sentimentality, naivety, and a host of other hurtful slurs. Jesus did not promise that the Father would prevent the sparrows falling to the ground! Neither is it always easy to respond to such slurs with the patience and generosity as well as the truthfulness which Jesus would have shown. 'A spoonful of honey attracts more flies than a barrelful of vinegar', said St Francis de Sales.

Question: Should I prepare for martyrdom? How?

Thirteenth Sunday

First reading: Elisha and the Woman of Shunem (2 Kings 4.8-12a, 14-16)

This is a lovely story of hospitality repaid; it is given to us here to illustrate one sentence in the gospel, that hospitality given to a prophet earns the reward of a prophet. In fact, we are here told only half the story, for later the child suddenly sickens and dies (possibly of sunstroke), and the prophet bring the child back to life. Almost the same story is told of the prophet Elijah in 1 Kings 17; the similarities in the way the story is told show that the evangelist Luke had this in mind when he told the story of Jesus raising to life the son of the Widow of Naim, which ends with the popular acclaim, 'A great prophet has risen among us; God has visited his people' (Luke 7.11-16). In Luke, Jesus is frequently presented as a prophet and more than a prophet, for instance in his opening manifesto in the synagogue at Nazareth, where Jesus likens his mission to that of Elisha and Elijah (Luke 4.16-30). The Ascension is also described in terms of the prophet

Elijah being carried up to heaven, while his disciple looks on (2 Kings 2.11).

Question: How is the aspect of Christ as prophet helpful to our understanding of him?

Second reading: Baptism into Christ (Romans 6.3-4, 8-11)

Last Sunday's reading from Romans explained to us how Christ is the Second Adam, by his obedience undoing the disobedience of Adam. The reaction may be, 'But what has that to do with me? How does it benefit me?' The answer here given is that we were baptized into Christ's death so that we are joined to him and will be transformed by his Resurrection. The Greek *baptizo* means 'plunge into': we are plunged into Christ's death. Our life is now Christ's life, although not yet transformed like his. Paul coins a whole series of new words beginning with 'syn-' (a formation similar to 'synchronized' or 'synthetic') to show how our life is merged into Christ's. The most expressive of all is that we are *synphytoi* with Christ: this word is used in medical terminology to express how two parts of a broken bone grow together again and merge into a bond stronger than the original. By my baptism into Christ's death, his death becomes mine. Christ's story becomes my story. Christ's strength becomes my strength. Christ's body becomes my body. Christ's risen life becomes my risen life.

Question: What effect should this identification with Christ have on our relationships with other Christians?

Gospel: Hardships of the Apostolate (Matthew 10.37-42)

At the end of this collection of sayings of Jesus about the mission of the Christian apostolate, Matthew puts a whole series of daunting challenges. Luke gives almost all the same sayings, but scattered in different contexts. The last saying is only in Mark as well. Believing as we do that the composition of the gospel is inspired, even to the selection and ordering of the sayings of Jesus, we can see this group of sayings as a series of challenges not to take up Christianity without serious forethought. There is no such thing as non-apostolic Christianity, but by becoming Christians we take on a share in Christ's own task of spreading the Good News. The challenge is great but the reward is certain.

First comes a trio of sayings to show the absolute priority of Christ's claims, over the closest family ties, over life and finally over possession of one's own self. Then comes a quartet of promises of rewards to those who welcome Christ's messengers. The envoy is placed equal with the principal:

Christ's messenger is as Christ, Christ as his Father. Then in detail the reward for welcome of a prophet, of any upright person, and finally of the Christian in need.

Question: What is the closest tie you have on earth? Can Jesus be more important than that?

Fourteenth Sunday

First reading: The King on a Donkey (Zechariah 9.9-10)

The link of this reading to the gospel reading is not immediately obvious, at least in English translation. The use of a donkey as a mount is a sign that the king will be humble, just as Jesus in the gospel says that he is humble of heart. This is even more literally fulfilled when Jesus makes his messianic entry into Jerusalem on Palm Sunday mounted 'on a colt, the foal of a donkey'. In the spirituality of the centuries after the Babylonian exile and leading up to the coming of Christ, this quality of humility, rejection of all pomp and pride of position was very central. Israel could claim no success of distinction of its own, and was forced to rely on the Lord. The poor and humble were the chosen ones of the Lord. Especially in the Lukan stories of Jesus' infancy, it is made clear that the blessing comes to the poor and humble. Mary and Zechariah, father of John the Baptist, are both poor and disadvantaged. Mary can find no decent place to give birth to her son. Jesus is greeted by impoverished, hireling shepherds. Joseph can afford only the turtledove, offering of the poor. Simeon and Anna have the disadvantage of advanced old age.

Question: Gentleness is all very well, but does pomp have any place?

Second reading: The Spirit is Alive in You (Romans 8.9, 11-13)

Chapter 8 of Romans, from which readings for the next three Sundays are chosen, is the chapter of the Spirit. We have seen that the Christian, baptized into Christ, lives with his life, the life of the Spirit of Christ. This means that the Christian's whole value system is that of the Spirit, the reverse of the values of the 'flesh'. 'Flesh' in Paul does not mean, as it often does in modern parlance, only the grosser, 'carnal' desires such as sex, gluttony, drunkenness. In the Letter to the Galatians 5.18-21 (and in many ways Galatians is a preliminary to Romans), the 'works of the flesh' includes such non-physical things as sorcery, rivalry, quarrels, malice. The concept of 'flesh' therefore centres on unchecked or unschooled natural desires, self-indulgence as opposed to self-control. To live by the law of the Spirit is therefore not to live by the Law of Moses, which merely checks external actions; neither is it to live by the law of the flesh, but it is to live by the Spirit of Christ, from which spontaneously well up love, joy, peace, patience, kindness, trustfulness, gentleness and the other Christ-like motivations. In this sense, the Law of Christ does not restrain from without but impels from within.

Question: Can the interior impulse really replace an external law?

Gospel: Father and Son (Matthew 11.25-30)

This much loved and encouraging passage tells of the intimacy of the relationship between father and son in a way that no other passage of the synoptic gospels does. It is reminiscent of those passages in John 5 that unfold the equality of father and son: the son does nothing but what he sees the father doing; the father loves the son so that he entrusts all things to the son, and the son gives life just as the father gives life. Then comes the gentle invitation of the son to all who are overburdened. The 'yoke' is often a symbol of the Law of Moses, which could seem burdensome with its many commands, though it was also valued as God's revelation of himself to his own people in love. Christ is not a tyrannical master, but is a sympathetic, gentle and humble leader who shares his life with his followers. The 'yoke' or Law of Christ, as we saw with regard to the second reading, is the interior impulse of the Spirit. It cannot be burdensome, since it is a joy to carry, a way of living with Christ and by his Spirit. Even the joy of martyrs, subjected as they are to physical pains, is a constant feature of accounts of martyrdom.

Question: What does Jesus mean by his 'yoke'? Do you find it comfortable?

Fifteenth Sunday

First reading: The effective Word of God (Isaiah 55.10-11)

This poetic passage from Isaiah about the word of God may be understood on two levels. On one level, it prepares for Jesus' parable in the gospel reading about the sower and the seed. But while Isaiah stresses the effectiveness of the word of God, Jesus reflects on the failure of his word with many sections of his hearers, as well as on the brilliant success of his word in those who bear fruit 'thirtyfold, sixtyfold, a hundredfold'. On another level, it prepares for the meditation on the Word of God in the prologue to the gospel of John: 'In the beginning was the Word; the Word was with

God and the Word was God.' This helps to explain just how God, the awesome and inexpressible, can be manifested and active in creation. In Genesis, God created by his Word ('Let there be light, let there be a vault, etc.'), so the Word is seen not as something separate from and independent of God, but as the concrete expression of God's will, the manifestation of divine power. The Word that comes forth from God's mouth and does not return unfulfilled is, on this level, the creative power of God, unstoppably fulfilling the will of God in the world.

Question: What does the image of Jesus as God's Word convey?

Second reading: Creation Freed from Corruption (Romans 8.18-23)

In our reading of Romans 8 on life in the Spirit of the Risen Christ, we have missed out (they are used on a separate occasion) a few crucial verses on our adoption as sons, enabling us – both men and women – to call God '*Abba*, Father'. This intimate Aramaic family name, used by Jesus to his Father in his agonized prayer in the Garden (Mark 14.36), can be used by all his followers who share his life. With Jesus, we are heirs of God, sharing his inheritance. Not only ourselves, however, but the whole of creation is renewed and re-created by the Spirit. It all takes on a new dimension and a new life, groaning in the Spirit to be released from frustration. This is a new reason for renewed human beings to care for God's creation. In the first place, we were created in the image of God to further and to complete his creation. Now, re-created as adopted sons and heirs of God, our responsibility is increased and intensified. As yet, we have only the first fruits of the Spirit, but first fruits make sense and have their value only in view of the fullness and completion of the harvest.

Question: In what sense is creation groaning in the Spirit to be set free?

Gospel: The Parable of the Sower (Matthew 13.1-23)

Like any good teacher, Jesus uses pictures – or parables. Ever heard the one about the elephant and the wasp? Or electricity like a toy train going round a room? Anyway, for the next three weeks we have some of these pictures, to show us what Jesus is trying to do. This first one is rather sad. Whatever he does seems to fail: seed pecked up by birds, scorched by the sum, choked by thistles. What are my pecking birds, my scorching sun, my choking thistles, which annihilate the seed Jesus sows in me? Different for every one of us. But some, just a little, of the seed bears a fantastic harvest. There must be something I can show to the Lord with pride and gratitude: 'Look, this is the seed you gave me; it has grown, developed, and here is your harvest.' Jesus, too, reflected on his mission to establish his Father's sovereignty on earth. Jesus, too, got depressed and wondered if he was getting anywhere. It was only when he had failed utterly, alone, deserted and tortured, that his perseverance won the crown. Jesus doesn't want the successful. He wants the failures as his followers – and that is where the harvest lies.

Question: Does this parable show Jesus optimistic or disappointed?

Sixteenth Sunday

First reading: The Leniency of God (Wisdom 12.13, 16-19)

The Book of Wisdom was written in Greek, shortly before the birth of Jesus, for the Greek-speaking Jews of Alexandria. Much of it concerns the harsh treatment of the Hebrews in Egypt before the Exodus under Moses. Here the author has moved on to describe luridly the depravity of the inhabitants of Canaan before the Israelites arrived in the Holy Land. Nevertheless, God cared for them and treated them with leniency, giving them opportunity for repentance. This has two lessons for the readers of the Book: first, they too must pardon the sinner and be kindly with God's own kindness. Second, God always gives a chance to repent of sins and follies, and this applies to us, too. This leniency is a sign of God's strength. Leniency and generosity are always signs of strength rather than of weakness, just as it is always the stronger person who apologizes first. The reading is appointed to be read today in order to pair with the gospel reading, emphasizing a possible reading of the Parable of the Wheat and the Darnel: the owner of the field leaves the darnel in place until harvest, that is, until the final judgment, thus leaving the wicked a chance to repent.

Question: Is God's forgiveness really a sign of divine strength?

Second reading: Prayer in the Spirit (Romans 8.26-27)

This is an encouraging confirmation by Paul that when we pray our own miserable prayers are supplemented by the Spirit of Christ praying within us. What does this mean? Is Paul referring to praying in tongues, which certainly occurred in his Corinthian community? He himself says that he had the gift also, although he did not frequently exercise it. It is surely wider than this. If we pray to praise the glory of God and give thanks for God's kindness to us, our own prayer can only be inadequate; but it is supercharged by the Spirit. Our prayer of repentance likewise, for our repentance can never be adequate. The same with our protestations of loyalty and commitment. What about our prayer of petition? We pray desperately for a fine evening for the barbeque (or for rain for the garden), but perhaps the Spirit deepens this prayer to our real profound desire to be brought nearer to God by whatever he decides is best for us and those for whom we care! 'The prayers that the Spirit makes for God's holy people are always in accordance with the mind of God' – they go beyond our petty and ephemeral requests, for Christ is praying within us.

Question: Does this make a difference to the way we pray?

Gospel: Parables of Growth (Matthew 13.24-43)
The Gospel of Matthew gathers together a whole set of pictures that Jesus used to describe the society of God's servants he was intent on setting up. Matthew calls it 'the Kingdom of Heaven'. Jews avoided bandying around the name of 'God', so Matthew calls it by the place where God is enthroned, heaven.

The first picture, the wheat and the darnel, shows that in some of those called the good seed has been overlaid by weed. In its early growth, this weed, the inedible darnel, is incredibly difficult for a non-farmer to distinguish from good barley. No more can we presume to sort out who is seeking God and who is not; it is dangerous to despise or to dismiss anyone at all. The explanation given by Matthew constitutes a warning that the harvest, the judgment, will come in the end.

The other two pictures form a pair. A mustard seed is but a tiny grain, but shoots up in a few months to form a big plant. So a pinch of yeast makes a whole loaf of bread rise. Jesus could have told these to his disciples when they were depressed: 'Cheer up! Even a spark of goodwill can set a whole forest ablaze!'

Question: What do you learn from these parables about the Kingdom of God?

Seventeenth Sunday

First reading: Solomon's Prayer for Wisdom (1 Kings 3.5-12)

How many of our modern politicians and monarchs would do well to imitate this prayer of Solomon as he comes to the throne! He is touchingly conscious of his own inadequacies and inexperience. He does not ask for anything for his own advantage, but just for the skills he needs to rule his people well. In reply, the Lord promises him plenty of material rewards.

Immediately afterwards, as illustration of the wisdom given to him, we have the famous story of 'The Judgment of Solomon', how he settled the dispute between two prostitutes, each claiming as her own the live baby of two, the other of whom had died. His wisdom became so renowned that several collections of witty and pungent proverbs in the Bible are attributed to him. The Lord made him a canny businessman too, for he built up a fortune as middleman, selling horses from Asia Minor to Egypt, and chariots to go with them from Egypt to Asia Minor, as well as mining the minerals of the land. No wonder the Queen of Sheba was bowled over! The reading is given here perhaps to pair with the gospel picture of the disciple who in the parables brings out wisdom new and old.

Question: What gift above all would you ask from God?

Second reading: Moulded to the Image of his Son (Romans 8.28-30)

It is time for Paul to start summing up the benefits of the Spirit he has detailed in this chapter. In his excitement, he switches to high rhetoric, using a triple chain figure which he uses also elsewhere in his exalted conclusions: 'destined – called, called – justified, justified – glorified'.

The content about which he is justifiably so excited is that God's chosen ones are moulded to the image, shape or pattern of his Son. Not merely co-heirs but conformed. To underline this assimilation to Christ, Paul uses every metaphor he can find: con-crucified with Christ, con-buried with him, con-risen with him, congruent with him. Living with Christ's life, moulded to the pattern of Christ, the Christian takes on Christ's history as his or her own. This is the personal aspect of being plunged into Christ's death at baptism. The community aspect will be explored in the letters to the quarrelsome community at Corinth: as all Christians live with Christ's life, Christians form one single body, vivified by the same life-giving Spirit, and therefore must help and serve one another as members of the same body, each contributing a different gift, one being an ear, one an eye, one a hand.

Question: How would you explain to a non-Christian the Pauline idea that the Christian lives with Christ's life?

Gospel: Treasures New and Old (Matthew 13.44-52)

Three final pictures this week from Matthew's collection of Jesus' images of the Christian community. Matthew likes pairs of parables: the dragnet pairs with last week's darnel parable, the treasure pairs with the pearl. The Kingdom is an exciting and unexpected treasure that can change our whole life, like winning the pools or the lottery – except that God's gifts change us only for the good, and fill our lives with meaning and joy. Of course, we know that God's call is demanding: you've got to pay a price for the field in which the treasure lies, or the genuine pearl found in a junk shop.

The very last picture – the householder bringing down different food packets, pots and jars off the shelf – is encouraging, too: some are old favourites (perhaps the Christian values and prayers we inherited from our families), but some also add new flavours, which we have discovered or been taught ourselves. If we listen, the Spirit is always there to show us new ways of living out our Christian call, an opportunity for prayer or help or service. This 'householder' is often thought to be Matthew's own secret signature: he brings out old and new in the Christian message.

Question: Which is your favourite among all these images?

Eighteenth Sunday

First reading: Invitation to the Banquet (Isaiah 55.1-3)

Our approach to God and to things divine has two contrasting aspects. On the one hand, we must be aware in awe of the splendour of God and of our own terrifying littleness; this engenders a hushed stillness in us. On the other hand, there is joy and celebration of what God has given us. Particularly in Christianity this is a family and community joy, celebrating our oneness in Christ; the obvious way to celebrate this is a party with noise, food and drink. The readings on this Sunday are all about joy and celebration, and the first and third about a party. Isaiah hands us an invitation to the party. The invitation has two particular notes. First, it is in similar terms to the biblical invitations from God's Wisdom to come and share the banquet prepared by Wisdom for those who wish to learn God's ways. Second, it is a fulfilment of the tradition of the covenant dominating the Bible: God made an alliance, a special bond, with special promises to Abraham, renewed it and intensified it to Moses and again to David. When Israel shattered that covenant by constant rebellion, God promised a new covenant, ratified again at a party, at Jesus' Last Supper with his disciples.

Question: Should the Eucharist be more obviously a joyful celebration?

Second reading: A Celebration of God's Love (Romans 8.35, 37-40)

This lively expression of delight and confidence really concludes and sums up the explanations of God's love for us, as it is manifested and given to us in the saving act of Jesus. This has been the fullest explanation given by Paul of just how Christ saves us, and how we are made a new creation and now live by the Spirit of Christ. After that, the Letter to the Romans goes on to particular consequences and applications of this. There will be another such outbreak of joy from Paul which we read in three weeks' time (Romans 11.33-36). It is Paul at his best and most ardent. First, just before our reading, comes a series of excited rhetorical questions: 'What can we add?', 'Can anyone condemn?', 'Are we not certain?' Then the expression of Paul's total confidence in God's saving love, from which nothing can cut us off. In the biblical mind, seven is the perfect number, signifying completion: Paul first gives seven hardships and trials that cannot cut us off, then seven hostile powers that are powerless against the love of God. The message is: there isn't anything that can separate us from the love of God.

Question: If nothing can separate us from the love of Christ, is anyone in hell?

Gospel: A Family Day Out with Jesus (Matthew 14.13-21)
Every mother knows the disaster situation of the family day out when the shops turn out to be closed and the emergency supplies were left at home. This lot have been three days on the trot, and there must have been nothing left at all. Jesus turns the disaster into a party for that huge crowd of people. Left to our own resources we are helpless, but Jesus can deal with that. How many were there? We don't know, for the numbers are symbolic. In the Bible, '12' alerts us to the tribes of Israel. So the 12 baskets of scraps show that the crowd is the 12 tribes of Jesus' new Israel. The way Jesus takes the bread and says the blessing must remind any Christian of the Eucharist. So this gigantic field party was a sort of Eucharist, Jesus at the centre of his people, entertaining them and cheering them. It probably wasn't very orderly. There would have been children enjoying the food and then running around and tripping up themselves and others as they sat on the grass. An African Mass is often like that, with lots of singing and dancing and celebration. That is why the Sunday Mass is so important: meet your friends and celebrate Christ together!

Question: Would such a picnic-style Eucharist increase our understanding of what is going on?

Nineteenth Sunday

First reading: Elijah's Encounter with the Lord (1 Kings 19.9, 11-13)

This awesome story of Elijah's encounter with the Lord is read today to pair with Peter's encounter with Jesus, the Son of God, on Lake Galilee. Mount Horeb, where it occurred, is an awesome place, a rocky mountain on Sinai. No earth, vegetation, or animals, just stark rock, some iron ore red, some granite grey, some almost sulphur green. It was here that Moses and the People of Israel had their experience of God, too, and the silent mountains almost speak of God. Elijah was fleeing from the threat of persecution, a trek of 40 days and 40 nights. There are experiences that cannot be put into words, whether it is the ecstasy of love or music or beauty. No one can adequately express in words the experience of an encounter with God, and Elijah's is described quite differently from that of Moses, who experienced God in thunder, lightning and earthquake. The 'light, murmuring sound' is literally 'a sound of silence'. In any case, the experience strengthened him enough to return to his mission. It is because of these encounters that Moses and Elijah are present at the Transfiguration, when the closest disciples experience the divinity of Jesus on the Holy Mountain.

Question: What terms would you use to describe an intimate experience of God's presence?

Second reading: The Holy People of Israel (Romans 9.1-5)

After his exposition of Christ's saving work Paul turns to the question that tortures him: how is it that Israel, so long prepared, failed to recognize the fulfilment of the prophecies? Paul was a Jew through and through, and was deeply wounded by the failure of his own people to welcome Jesus, despite all the privileges given them and which he here details. For Paul, Christianity is the conclusion to which Judaism was meant to lead. But God never revokes his gifts, and these gifts still belong to the Jews; it can never be said that the Jews have been superseded and lost their status as God's Chosen People. For the next two chapters, Paul quotes every conceivable scripture to show that the rebellions of the Jews against God throughout their history made it inevitable that they would fail to recognize the Messiah. Nevertheless, he insists, a remnant will turn to the Lord in the end. The dead branches have been cut off to make room for the gentiles to be grafted in, and the old branches will be grafted in again at the end. The horticultural image obviously does not work – you can't graft in dead branches – and finally Paul simply throws up his hands and praises the inscrutable wisdom of God.

Question: In what sense is the Jewish people still the people of God?

Gospel: Jesus and Peter on the Water (Matthew 14.22-33)

The Christian people is often depicted as a boat, with Peter at the helm. As in a boat, everyone has their part to play: kids to bring the excitement and the challenge, parents to take the responsibility, grandparents just to be there to comfort and reassure. Without Jesus they were getting exhausted, frustrated and probably bad tempered and quarrelling. When Jesus appears everything changes: first, terror and awed amazement, then Peter rushes to meet him – and loses confidence, only to be swiftly rescued. How does Jesus come to me? In the joys of family? In the unwelcome criticism of an angry neighbour, who tells me the truth about myself? In the worries of a job or the agonies of a failed relationship? In the staggering beauty of creation? In physical pain? All these can bring God's presence, and without that presence we cannot expect to cope. Jesus does not force himself on us. He just jogs us, and says, 'Here I am if you want me.' He may disappear into the sea mist again for a time, and we may sink into the water like mistrustful Peter. But it all ends with a welcome and a recognition that Jesus can cope even with a life-threatening situation.

Question: Why is Peter such a good role model for us?

Twentieth Sunday

First reading: God saves all nations (Isaiah 56.1, 6-7)

One of the great results of the disastrous Sack of Jerusalem by the Babylonians and the exile of the Jews in Babylon was the growing realization that Israel had been chosen to bring God's healing not only to her own people but to the peoples of the world. I shall lead them all to my Holy Mountain, promises the Lord. In the gospel, we will see this put into action when Jesus is manoeuvred into healing the Canaanite woman's daughter, beyond the bounds of Israel. What does this mean for us today, in the twenty-first century, whose watchword – as Nelson Mandela once said – is globalization? Our God is concerned for the salvation of all peoples, and it is for us to bring the values of Christianity to all nations. But our God is truly God of all nations, and we have no right to force our own appreciation of God's ways of acting onto other civilizations who understand in their own way what we express by the Lordship of God, the salvation won by Christ's loving obedience, and spread by the Spirit of Christ. To fail to appreciate the other great religions of the world is an act not of homage to the Christian God but of failure to appreciate the divine omniscience and omnipotence.

Question: How is it that believers in other religions are still saved by Christ?

Second reading: The Obedience of all Nations (Romans 11.13-15, 29-32)

It is by chance that the reading from Romans coincides with both the other two readings, for Paul is here really meditating on, and distraught by, the failure of most of the Jews to respond to the salvation promised to them in Christ. It is indeed a devastating puzzle that God should have prepared his people for the completion of his Kingdom in Christ and that, despite all this, they did not respond. But were the Jews especially unresponsive, especially rebellious? Or are they just typical of us all? One of the reasons why the New Testament makes such a meal of the failure of the Jews to respond is surely as a warning to us. We have been chosen. We have been buried into Christ's death and now live with Christ's life, and yet our response is pretty lukewarm and spasmodic. To use Paul's dramatic image of the olive tree of Israel, if the true branches can be cut off to make room for the gentiles to be grafted in, then surely the grafted branches can fail to take on the life of the vine. However, such is Paul's conviction of the power of Christ and the victorious Lordship of Christ that he never even mentions hell or eternal punishment. He does not seem to envisage that anyone could escape the saving power of Christ.

Question: Are the Chosen People still the beloved of God?

Gospel: Jesus and the Canaanite Woman (Matthew 15.21-28)

This is an especially significant scene in two ways. Mark's Gospel was the first to be written, and Matthew edits and expands it, using other sources as well. In Mark, this scene is the only explicit encounter between Jesus and a gentile – and a woman at that! At first, Jesus is reluctant to do anything for her, for his mission was primarily to Israel. He puts her off, and is really quite brusque to her. However, she wins through by her persistence and her determined confidence in his powers: the disciples get fed up with her shrieking after them, and ask Jesus to cure her daughter, which he does. We need to be persistent in our prayers and in our efforts. God does not grant a casual request. Second, it shows a lot about Jesus' relationship to women and about his sense of humour: they seem to tease one another with their repartee. There is the same repartee in the account of Jesus' meeting with the Samaritan woman in the Gospel of John: she stands up to him with her cheeky repartee. They are both obviously enjoying this playful scene. It suggests that not everything is solemn and serious in heaven, and there is room for a sense of humour!

Question: Is Jesus rude to her, or is he merely challenging her?

Twenty-first Sunday

First reading: The Master of the Palace (Isaiah 22.15, 19-23)

This reading from Isaiah is chosen to pair with the gospel reading about the appointment of Peter, for there Peter is appointed as head of Jesus' own team. In this first reading, Isaiah predicts that Eliakim will take the place of Shebna as master of the king's palace in Jerusalem, and that God will invest him with authority. To open and close the doors of the palace was the privilege of the master of the place. To the Hebrew mind such a pair of opposites often signifies everything in between, so that opening and closing the doors mean having control of everything that goes on. No one else may interfere. Similarly, by the pair of opposites 'binding' and 'loosing', Peter is given total authority over the assembly or community of Jesus that is the Church. Equivalently, as Eliakim is given the key of the palace on his shoulder (or, as we would say, round his neck), so Peter is given the keys of the Kingdom of Heaven. Peter is sometimes pictured as the doorkeeper of heaven, but 'the Kingdom of Heaven' is far wider: it means 'God's sovereignty', which Jesus came to establish on earth, in which all obey, worship and give glory to God.

Question: How does this Old Testament reading contribute to our understanding of the gospel?

Second reading: God's Wisdom and Knowledge (Romans 11.33-36)

After his long and thorough exposition of the way in which the work of Christ won our salvation, and by his loving obedience wiped away the proud sin of Adam's disobedience, Paul has been agonizing about how the Jews can have failed to recognize this fulfilment of God's promises to Abraham. Quoting one passage of scripture after another, he finally comes to the conclusion that, in the end, in God's good time a remnant of Israel will be saved. How this will be he really cannot explain. Throwing up his hands in incomprehension, he can only burst into this wonderful hymn of praise to God's inscrutable Wisdom. We simply cannot understand God's plans and methods. This concluding passage comes close to the marvellous passage at the end of the Book of Job. Job has rejected the shallow explanations for his sufferings suggested by his friends, when God intervenes to show Job how mighty and wise he is. Job can only admit that God's Wisdom surpasses anything human beings can conceive, and God's might infinitely transcends any human power. So Paul willingly grants that God must run his own world, and we cannot even attempt to challenge God's reasoning, for everything begins and ends in God.

Question: Are faith and reason at all compatible?

Gospel: Jesus Claims Peter as Rock (Matthew 16.13-20)

At last Peter recognizes that Jesus is the Messiah, the Christ. At last he realizes that in Jesus they can see the action of God. The disciples followed Jesus as soon as he called, but for a long time they were puzzled what to make of him, of his wonderful teaching and his godlike personality. Now comes a shaft of light and understanding. We too often take some time to appreciate the true worth of someone we know well: a little gesture can sometimes reveal just how generous and thoughtful they are. Peter suddenly grasps that there is God, acting among them, a daunting or even terrifying thought. Jesus replies to Peter's recognition with his own generosity, giving him a new name, 'Rock', for this is what 'Peter' means. If you name something, you make it your own, take it to yourself. This is just what Jesus does with Simon who becomes his own Peter. That is the importance of the naming of a child at baptism: Jesus takes us to himself and we become his. The early Christians called themselves 'Those over whom the name of Jesus has been called'. We may have been named Mary or John, but the name of Jesus has been called over us and we have become his.

Question: What are the implications for us of Jesus' promise to Peter?

Twenty-second Sunday

First reading: Jeremiah Complains to God (Jeremiah 20.7-9)

As we saw some weeks ago (the twelfth Sunday of the Year), Jeremiah had a tough time, telling the citizens of Jerusalem that their city was to be besieged and destroyed, and that they themselves were to be dragged into exile. He tried to evade his duty of announcing this dire message, but the Lord gave him no peace, no matter how much he tries to drive the message from his mind. So God overpowers or seduces the prophet and compels him to proclaim the message. Both images are important, for it is a tough, but at the same time a willing and joyful compulsion. Jeremiah almost has a sort of love–hate relationship with the Lord. In the same way, Paul says he has no choice but to proclaim the message of Christ. In the gospel reading, Peter suggests to Jesus that he should avoid the way of suffering, and Jesus refuses to take any escape route. In all these cases, the natural human tendency to take the easier path crashes headlong into the brick wall of God's will. We are always slow to accept the way of suffering. In the gospel, each time Jesus teaches that he can achieve his glory only through suffering, the disciples seem to refuse to listen.

Reflection: 'Lord, if that is how you treat your friends, no wonder you have so few of them' (St Teresa of Avila).

Second reading: The People of God (Romans 12.1-2)

Paul has concluded his account of the saving work of Christ and its consequences for Israel. Now he goes on to detail some of its implications for the Christian life. The overall banner headline is that Christian behaviour must be totally different from the values of the world, for the Christian is a new creation with a new set of values. Two aspects are most striking in this introductory passage, first, the novelty, second, the motivation. In Chapter 8, on the Spirit, Paul repeatedly stresses that not only Christians but the whole of creation is straining to be set free from slavery to corruption; the presence of the Spirit of Christ makes all things new; it is a totally new world. In today's passage, again he stresses the renewing of our minds. Second, Paul stresses that the motivation comes from within: it is a matter no longer of the external compulsion of the Law, but of inner compulsion, for the Christian has become a living sacrifice, dedicated to God with minds transformed, discerning personally the will of God and acting on this discernment. This is Christian personal responsibility: we must 'discern for ourselves what is the will of God'.

Question: How do I set about 'discerning for myself what is the will of God'?

Gospel: The Cross of Jesus (Matthew 16.21-27)

What a turnaround! Last Sunday Peter was being congratulated on at last realizing the Jesus was the Christ. He was promised the keys and authority to make decisions valid in heaven. Now Jesus shoos him away and tells him that he is Satan, the Tempter. Why the change? Jesus had told Peter that his role as Christ Messiah was to suffer and die in order to achieve his purpose, and Peter shied away from it. What is your particular soft option? What is the difficult task Christ is asking of you, and you avoiding? We are no better than his first disciples! In the gospel, this will happen twice more: three times Jesus foretells his Passion and each time the disciples simply fail to understand. Each time Jesus again puts it bluntly that you cannot be a Christian without following Jesus in carrying a cross. We see people suffering the whole time, physical disabilities, breakdown of relationships, heartless treatment from others, financial worries – and then we grouse at a twinge of pain or a hurtful word. Carry the cross behind Jesus? Yes, of course I will, but if you don't mind, I'll just take that section that is well padded and fits my shoulder nicely. No point in unnecessary splinters in my neck.

Question: How does this tally with 'My yoke is easy and my burden light'?

Twenty-third Sunday

First reading: The Task of the Prophet (Ezekiel 33.7-9)

Why did the church choose this passage, about the prophet warning sinners, to pair with the gospel reading about reconciliation? Partly because every person's sin or failure affects the whole Church. If I fail in my duty to my brother or sister or spouse or child or other dependant, this harms the holiness of the whole Church. I can't shrug it off as no concern of mine: 'I can't be bothered', 'too busy', 'nothing to do with me, anyway'. Of course, it is all very well for the prophet Ezekiel to point out other people's faults: that is the job of a prophet, to show others how God sees them. Heaven forbid that I should go round telling people their faults! Contrariwise, just occasionally I can learn some home truths about myself when someone flies off the handle; that is the time to listen and learn! Jesus did not denounce sinners: he dined with them. For myself, there are countless people and occasions on which a healing word, a healing touch can begin the process of growth over the scar tissue. But it must be a healing in love, and unless there is real, overflowing love, keep clear!

Question: Is it a good rule to praise four times for every time you correct someone?

Second reading: Love and the Law (Romans 13.8-10)

Paul has described the process of salvation, won for us by Christ's loving obedience to his Father. Now he gives his instructions how we should live as Christians; he merely slips into the basic command of Judaism: love your neighbour as yourself. Each of these negative commandments he mentions contains a clutch of positive values. If I really love and bond with my spouse, it will never come to adultery. 'You shall not kill' implies also the values of furthering life in all the ways we can. 'You shall not steal' involves also the respect for the property and wellbeing of others. The only debt I owe to anyone is love. It is easy to kid ourselves that we are practising love, when in fact it is self-interest, self-justification. It is easy enough to be loving to our friends (most of the time!), but that is not what Paul means. In his earlier letter to the Corinthians, he gave us that searching test for true love, 'Love is always patient, never jealous, not boastful or conceited, never rude, never seeks its own advantage', and so on. I can't look many of those qualities in the face without some embarrassment.

Question: Can you think of a better set of criteria for real love than 1 Corinthians 13?

Gospel: Reconciliation (Matthew 18.15-20)

In working through the Gospel of Matthew for this year's readings, the Church has had to be selective. In this eighteenth chapter of Matthew on relationships within the community, it is striking that the Church has chosen this passage to put before us. The first part is all about sorting out disagreements and about forgiveness. Despite the presence of Christ in the Christian community, there are going to be disagreements and misunder-standings in every community and every family. The vital thing is to sort them out and not to let them fester. So here we are given a safe process. Just afterwards, this is supplemented by Jesus' teaching that we have to forgive not just seven times (the perfect number) but 77! That means again and again, without limit.

We also get the reminder that Christ is present always in his community. The same promise is given at beginning (the name *Emmanuel* means 'God with us') and end of the gospel ('I am with you to the end of time'). Therefore the decisions of the community will be considered binding in the sight of God. It is especially striking that the same promise is here given to the Church as had earlier been given to Peter himself. Peter on his own wields the authority of the Church.

Question: Would you add anything to this process of reconciliation?

Twenty-fourth Sunday

First reading: Vengeance and Quarrelling (Ben Sira 27.30–28.7)

It is some months since we had a reading from this wise old scribe. He was on the staff of the Temple at Jerusalem (or at any rate moved in these circles), and clearly has the greatest love and respect for the Temple and the Law of God. He gathered together and reflected on the wisdom of the ancients, aware all the time that the Lord God is the source of all true wisdom. Most of his proverbial wisdom accords with that elusive quality, common sense, but it is none the worse or less important for that! Here he already looks forward to the message of today's gospel parable: the quality of God which we know best is the divine mercy and forgiveness. The very meaning of the divine name revealed to Moses on Sinai is 'God of mercy and compassion', and this echoes again and again down the scriptures. We are made in the image of God, and our glory is to imitate in our own poor, human way, this divine forgiveness. Once we see love and forgiveness as our divine mode of living, our whole relationship with other people changes. The last few lines give us a good, commonsense summary of the foolishness of quarrelling.

Question: Why is it so hard to forgive?

Second reading: Life as Christ's Community (Romans 14.7-9)

The context of this wonderful statement of Paul is the moral exhortation to the Roman Christians towards the end of his letter. Paul has been insisting that no one should tamper with the conscience of another. He has been discussing a particular problem of the time, whether eating meat which had once been offered to idols implicated the eater in idol worship. He states his own opinion, but will not force it on anyone else. For Paul to be living with Christ's life gives every Christian a dignity, a trustworthiness and a freedom ultimately to make his or her own decision. It is a delicate balance: Paul gives his opinion, which means that we must listen to the voice of the Church and its teachers. At the same time he realizes the presence of the Spirit of Christ, guiding every individual Christian who is genuinely living for the Lord. To a modern believer this raises a host of questions. Have I really listened? Am I being simply stubborn, deceiving myself into avoiding truths that I find inconvenient? What is the Voice of the Church? Whatever the answers, Paul's confidence in the guidance of the Spirit shows the dignity of the Christian and the respect with which the Christian must be honoured.

Question: How do I form my conscience?

Gospel: The Unforgiving Debtor (Matthew 18.21-35)

This is a favourite parable of Matthew, continuing and concluding his theme that forgiveness is the life's blood of any Christian community. We cannot live together without upsetting one another, unwittingly, or even deliberately. So forgiveness is the vital step. So important is it that two consecutive Sunday gospels are devoted to it. It expands and stresses our petition in the Lord's Prayer: 'Forgive us our trespasses as we forgive others.' The importance of this petition was already underlined by Matthew; it is the only petition of the Lord's Prayer to which he adds at the end a confirmatory saying of Jesus. Like so many of Matthew's parables, this one revolves round contrasting characters, the 'goodie' and the 'baddie' (wedding guests and guest without a wedding garment; the two who use their talents and the one who hides it; the girls with and without oil for their lamps; the sheep and the goats). The contrast between the two sums of money is deliberately fantastic: the first slave owes millions of dollars, a sum no private person could ever repay, let alone a slave; it is more than a year's tax for a whole Roman province The second owes a couple of months' wages of a casual labourer.

Question: 'Forgive and forget'? Or can forgiveness become a bond of friendship?

Twenty-fifth Sunday

First reading: 'My Thoughts are not Your Thoughts (Isaiah 55.6-9)

This is the triumphant conclusion of the second major section of the Book of Isaiah: God's ways are utterly different from human thinking. The passage is obviously chosen because it looks towards God's 'irresponsible' behaviour in the gospel for this Sunday. In many ways, it is comforting to think that God is not like us. One reason why we cling to God is to be liberated from ourselves and to be brought into his marvellous light, living a life freed from the restrictions, frustrations and self-centeredness that surrounds and penetrates us. Obviously, God does not have our faults of selfishness, laziness, malice, lust and greed. More than that, not being bodily or limited in any way, God does not plan or think like us. God does not think things out, with 'yes' and 'no', working in concepts or sentences. God does not laboriously plan what to do, weighing consequences, advantages and disadvantages! Even our love is always tinged with self-interest and concern for ourselves. God's love is entirely generous and outgoing, a limitless cascade of love, deluging and penetrating each of us.

Question: Is it comforting or daunting to think that God is so different from us?

Second reading: Paul Yearns to be Free (Philippians 1.20-24, 27)

This is the first of four Sunday readings from Paul's letter to the Philippians. They were his favourite community, linked to him with a strong bond of affection and intimacy, the only community from which he would accept gifts of money. Paul writes this letter from prison, not sure whether he is to live or die, not sure either which is his stronger desire. For life is his bond with the Christian communities he has founded, and who still need his help. But the centre of his life is the total rootedness in Christ, of which death can only be the completion. As he writes elsewhere, the Christian has been baptized into Christ's death, dipped into Christ's death, and so is soaked in Christ's death, waiting only for it to be completed in Christ's Resurrection. If we really believe this with the strength of Paul's conviction, it gives a whole new centre to life, a whole new perspective on the life that is Christ's. Death will then not be a matter of fear and dread, but only a slipping into the glory of the Resurrection.

Question: Is it right to fear death?

Gospel: The Payment of Wages (Matthew 20.1-16)

'It is not fair! They have hardly had time to roll up their sleeves, and the latecomers get the same wage as I do, having sweated it out right through the heat of the day.'

OK, but God is unfair. What are you going to do about that?
'But they didn't deserve it, whereas I worked all day.'
OK, you worked. But how did you deserve even to exist?
'Well, God gave me existence, but he might at least be fair.'
OK, and where would that leave you, if God were fair and gave you what you deserve? Do you want a God in your own image, vengeful, scheming, lazy, punishing (other people), complacent, selfish?
'Hold on! Not completely like me, but at least I **am** fair.'
No. God isn't fair at all. That is why Jesus enjoyed having parties with sinners and scum with whom you wouldn't be seen dead.
'Well, they will be different then, when they and I are dead – they'll be sort of cleaned up.'
Up to your standards, you mean? Are you sure God wants them 'cleaned up' like you? Perhaps God loves them just as much as you. Could Jesus ever have said "Blessed are the hungry and dirty and dishonest"?

Twenty-sixth Sunday

First reading: Attitudes to Sinners (Ezekiel 18.25-28)

The prophet Ezekiel was speaking in Babylon during the exile of the Jews there after the destruction of Jerusalem. Not surprisingly, the second generation of exiles were questioning why they should suffer for the failures of their forefathers. This was, however, a new phase in the development of morality, for beforehand the sense of solidarity with family or clan had been so strong that it was assumed that punishment for the sins and failures of an individual would affect the whole clan or family. Now the individual is to be held responsible for his or her own sins only. Furthermore, the individual cannot simply rely on good deeds of the past, or feel irremediably condemned for failures in the past. Conversion in both directions is possible: just as the good person can become evil, so the evil person can change direction. At the end, the Lord promises conversion to the good, a new heart and a new spirit, so that even the sinner can repent and live.

Question: What sort of qualities are needed to help a person change their ways?

Second reading: A Hymn to Christ (Philippians 2.1-11)

This is a wonderful hymn of Christ's self-emptying and his exaltation and vindication by the Father, probably an ancient Christian hymn celebrating the triumph of Christ, which Paul adopted and used for himself. In the first half of the reading, Paul shows the warmth of his joy as a pastor in the fellowship of his young community at Philippi, although the fact of this strong appeal for unity may suggest that he is painting an optimistic picture of their single mindedness! He also gently chides them for their vanity, and the reason why he includes the hymn is to show that the path of humility is the way to exaltation. The hymn itself contrasts Christ, the Second Adam, with Adam (that is, humanity) who fell, who wanted to be like God, who tried to escape death, tried to exalt himself and was humbled. The last verses are one of the clearest statements in Paul of the divine character of Christ. A verse from Isaiah 45.23 is applied to Christ. In Isaiah, the verse describes the homage due to the Lord alone, and no one else. In the hymn, this divine homage is paid to Christ – and this is to the glory of God the Father. The concept of divinity is expanded to include Christ.

Question: What would your answer to this be? A Muslim once said to me: 'If you say your Jesus was God, you just don't understand what God is.'

Gospel: Parable of the Two Sons (Matthew 21.28-32)

Matthew loves giving parables of Jesus contrasting 'goodies' and 'baddies' like these two contrasting sons. Matthew's parables put everything in black and white with no shades of grey (wise and foolish wedding attendants, sheep and goats). Luke uses a different kind of parable, in which the characters – just like us – often do the right thing for the wrong reason. The sayings of Jesus were transmitted by word of mouth for some years before being written down. Did the straightforward contrast in Matthew (it is odd that both change their minds without a reason) develop into Luke's parable of the Prodigal Son? Both times the 'goodie' son ends up bad, and the 'baddie' son ends up good, but in Luke's version both changes of mind are motivated, and there is great emphasis on the son's repentance and the father's overwhelming joy at getting him back. The lesson in Matthew's story is given also by Jesus' word in the Sermon on the Mount, 'It is not anyone who says to me, "Lord, Lord" who will enter the Kingdom of Heaven, but the person who does the will of my Father in Heaven.' It is no use simply saying that Christ is our 'Lord', we have to express it in our behaviour.

Question: What does this say about hypocrisy in religion?

Twenty-seventh Sunday

First reading: The Vineyard of the Lord (Isaiah 5.1-7)

A vineyard needs a lot of devoted care, pruning, manuring, tying back. In the rocky soil of Israel, even more special care is needed, such as gathering the stones to form retaining walls to keep the soil from eroding, building a lookout tower against thieves and a vine press for crushing the grapes. Then the right fruiting vine has to be grafted onto the sturdy stock, as here the vine dresser grafts on fine grapes. Imagine his disappointment when all he gets for his pains is inedible wild grapes! After this haunting parable of Isaiah, the vineyard became a stock image of Israel, swathed in God's loving care, and all the dwellers in the rich vines of the hill country of Israel would be aware that it was an image of the love lavished on the vineyard. So when Israel goes into Exile, Psalm 80 laments: 'You brought a vine out of Egypt. Why have you broken down its fences? Every passer-by plucks its grapes. Wild beasts feed on it.' The prophets also, especially Ezekiel, use the image. Jesus' hearers would immediately recognize what he meant.

Question: Can one transfer the image of the vineyard unchanged to the Church?

Second reading: A Greeting (Philippians 4.6-9)

This warm and affectionate little passage was probably originally the end of a letter from Paul to the community at Philippi which he loved so well. It is a lovely conclusion to a letter. Paul encourages them in every way to be cheerful in the Lord, but especially to be grateful. If we really appreciate that the Lord is near, we cannot worry and the peace of God will rest upon us. Then also gratitude and thanksgiving will be our mode of thought, penetrating all our thoughts on every subject. The word Paul uses for 'thanksgiving' is the word used for the Eucharist, which is the great prayer of thanksgiving, offered by Christ to the Father in the name of us all. It is the summing up of all prayer, petition, gratitude and admiration. No doubt Paul is thinking of it as the high point of all prayer (148).

Question: Is Paul encouraging us to live in a fools' paradise, or can we really be without fear or worry?

Gospel: Wicked Tenants of the Vineyard (Matthew 21.33-43)

Jesus' understanding of the sovereignty of God brought him the violent opposition of some of the Jewish leaders. Were they corrupt, or just closed to any new way of thinking, so closed that they could not see that Jesus was the promised Messiah? Anyway, Jesus used this story about the tenants of a vineyard to show that they were not leading the people as they should. Everyone would immediately understand the image of the vineyard. The prophet Isaiah – and many others after him – had used this image in a well-known poem eight centuries earlier to show that the vineyard of Israel refused to yield a good harvest to God, whatever care God lavished on it. God expected *fairness of judgment* and all he found was a *shriek of agony* (the same word in Hebrew apart from one letter). What does this mean for us? Not that we have to follow every new idea. But it does mean that we must be open to the idea that we may be wrong, that our service of the Lord may be faulty, that people we find tiresome or unacceptable may have more good in them than we credited. God's ways are not our ways, and we need to watch out for the bend in the road.

Question: Are the tenants of God's Christian vineyard any better than the previous tenants? Who are they, anyway?

Twenty-eighth Sunday

First reading: The Banquet of the Lord (Isaiah 25.6-10)

The reading begins with the image of the messianic banquet, the banquet that the Lord is preparing for the end of time, an image which Jesus takes up in the gospel story of the wedding feast. After the first lines, the image changes to the removal of the mourning veil and the destruction of death, every tear wiped away. In the earlier parts of the Bible, the dead are thought to lead a wretched existence in Sheol, a life that is no life, a sort of half-existence without power or substance, when the dead cannot even praise God. Gradually, Israel comes to realize that God's love is so enveloping and so enduring that God cannot desert or abandon his faithful even in death. Even death cannot cut off the faithful from God. This is one of the crucial passages where the permanent, saving strength of God's love is expressed. Speaking to the Sadducees (who did not believe in the Resurrection) Jesus will say: 'God is the God not of the dead but of the living.' Paul will say, 'Neither death nor life can separate us from the love of God which is in Christ Jesus.'

Question: What is heaven like? Is this too simplistic an image?

Second reading: Philippians 4.12-14, 19-20

Paul has reached the final greetings of his letter. Even when he is writing to his beloved community at Philippi, from whom alone he would accept gifts, Paul is anxious to maintain his independence. In the ancient world, as in the modern world, a favour demands a return favour: 'There is no such thing as a free dinner'! So Paul points out that he could manage without the gift they have given him, since all his strength comes from God. But he also wishes them the blessing of the fulfilment of all their needs from the glory of God in Christ Jesus. This is an incomparable blessing, whose awesome value is obscured by our careless use of the term 'glory'. The glory of God is a term frightening in its richness. No human being can see God and live, but Moses can for a moment glimpse God's glory – after which his face is so seared that he must wear a veil over it. It is a glory that, by contrast, fills Isaiah with dread at his own sinfulness, which makes Ezekiel fall to the ground. It is the experience of the limitless power and majesty of God.

Question: Am I ready to face the glory of God?

Gospel: The Wedding Banquet (Matthew 22.1-14)

A wedding is a time of joy and completion after long preparation, a time of love and of complete satisfaction. In Judaism at the time of Jesus, the coming of the Messiah is often compared to a wedding feast. The marriage feast at Cana must have been some party! At Mary's request, Jesus produced 900 litres of wine. The Letter to the Ephesians teaches that the love in a human wedding is only a pale shadow of Christ's love for his bride, the Church. In this story of the royal wedding, however, two things go drastically wrong. First, the original wedding guests refuse to come. Not only do they refuse, but they brutally maltreat the innocent messengers, and the king (who must stand for God) relentlessly burns down their city. This must be an adjustment to Jesus' story, applying it to the Sack of Jerusalem, captured and burnt by the Romans in 70AD, a few years before Matthew was writing. Second, the man who has no wedding garment is slung out. A wedding garment is a standard Jewish image for works of generosity expected of every faithful Jew. For us Christians, too, the story constitutes a double warning.

Question: Are we alert and listening for God's call? Do we rest secure in being called Christians and leave the dirty jobs to others?

Twenty-ninth Sunday

First reading: I am the Lord and There is no Other (Isaiah 45.1, 4-6)

This passage of Isaiah must have been written at the very end of the exile in Babylon, as Cyrus, King of Persia, was approaching to take over the city and decree that the captives, Jews and other nations, should be sent home to their own countries. In this, the Jews saw Cyrus as God's own envoy. It must have finally confirmed them in the new understanding, reached by being sunk into the hostile and alien civilization of Babylon, that their God, the Lord, was God not just of Israel but of the whole world. Before the exile, of course, they were convinced that the Lord was their own special God and protector, but what of other nations? Confronted with the alien and materialistic gods of Babylon, they realized that God, their own intimate and loving Lord, was the God not just of Israel but of the whole world, the whole universe, the creator of light and darkness. If no other lesson were learnt from the Exile, this was a major advance in understanding. Do we have other gods to worship? Do we accept the Lord as key to every door in the universe, even the door of our own hearts?

Question: Do I try to worship other gods as well as the Lord?

Second reading: The Earliest of Paul's Letters (1 Thessalonians 1.1-5)

This Sunday we start reading First Thessalonians, the earliest of all Paul's letters. It is read for the next five Sundays. Paul moved so rapidly round the new Christian communities that he founded he could never instruct them fully at the first founding. We, too, need to go on learning more about our faith. So Paul needed to keep in touch, answering questions, solving difficulties, showing his 'concern for all the Churches'. They are real letters, each responding to a different set of circumstances. Each of Paul's letters begins with a warm greeting, 'grace and peace'. 'Grace' is God's affectionate and powerful smile, drawing us into God's loving protection, and empowering us to live and work for him. Then, with his thoughtful courtesy, Paul encourages them (where possible – the Galatians get no compliments, for they have let Paul down badly) with praise for their achievements in Christ. Here he praises their faith, their love and their firm hope, and also the effectiveness in their lives of the power of the Spirit. It never does any harm to look for the best in people, and show that their efforts have been recognized!

Question: How much does faith need to seek understanding?

Gospel: The Question of Taxes (Matthew 22.15-21)
They must really have thought they had their victim sewn up! If Jesus said he paid the Roman taxes, he recognized the Emperor, not God, as his Lord. If he said he did *not* pay, he was a traitor to Rome. Jesus turns the question back on them. First, he makes them admit that they recognize Rome as overlord by carrying a Roman coin, for the coin would carry the Emperor's head. Next he puts to them a question: what do *they* consider is due to Caesar? Finally, he goes beyond their question, to interrogate their ultimate loyalty: in the last analysis, just what is due to God? At a superficial level, this seems a little verbal tussle, in which Jesus outwits his opponents. But the story was remembered and passed on in the Christian community not because of Jesus' cleverness, but because, at a deeper level, it is a question that Jesus puts to each of us: just where do our loyalties and priorities lie? In money? Respect? Sex? Fame? A good holiday? Comfort? Power? Jesus is not a dictator who imposes his will. He just asks the question and leaves us to give our own answer. To those who question him, he gives no easy answer, but always replies with another question.

Question: Where do my priorities lie – in money, sex, power, fame, leisure?

Thirtieth Sunday

First reading: Fair Treatment for the Poor (Exodus 22.21-27)

These are the very primitive laws of the Old Testament, the heart of the first law code laid down for Israel in the desert of the Exodus, before the Israelites even reached the Holy Land. 'Primitive'? Does our modern society equal them and the values they express? The principle is to help everyone who needs help, even foreigners, widows and orphans – just as God helped the Hebrews when they were slaves in Egypt. Men and women, made in the image of God, are God's representatives on earth, and must continue God's work of caring and healing. Anyone in need must not be humiliated, but must be given full human dignity, allowed to stand tall before his or her neighbours. The creditor may not enter the debtor's house to hassle him, the worker must be paid on time to get his dinner, the homeless must get back his cloak for the night. The vulnerable are not to be exploited. Jesus will put this, 'You must love your neighbour as yourself', but here, too, he is only quoting the Old Testament (Leviticus 19.18).

Question: Is the dignity of the individual sufficiently honoured in our society?

Second reading: Facing the Glory of God (1 Thessalonians 1.5-10)

At every Mass after the consecration, we remind ourselves, 'Christ will come again', and the Thessalonians to whom Paul is writing were especially alert to this 'Second Coming' as they waited for Christ to come from heaven. Paul had taught them that Christ has conquered death, that death is no more, and they mistakenly took this to mean that Christians would not physically die. Paul will answer this difficulty later in the letter. We do not know what this 'Second Coming' of Christ will be, but for Christians, history has a purpose and a direction. We do know that each of us will face Christ for our individual judgment when we die. There will be no question of Christ doling out suitable penalties to me. 'No human being can see God and live.' Faced with the stunning purity of the glory of God I know that I will be filled with longing and love, but will know that I am not fit to enter into the pure and overwhelming love of God. Only when the dross is purged away will I be fit to enter Christ's embrace.

Question: What does the Second Coming of Christ mean for me?

Gospel: The Great Commandment (Matthew 22.34-40)
Familiarity with Jesus' answer to the question about the greatest commandment blunts our awareness of its startling directness. Answers could be given, singling out one of the ten commandments as the greatest, the most important basis of society. A frequent answer to the question was and is the golden rule, existing in many cultures: 'Do not do to another what you would not have done to you.' This is basically a selfish answer, protecting my own interests. By contrast, Jesus' answer slams home, turning away from self to God. 'Love', not 'obey' or 'adore' or 'fear' or 'reverence'. Love is not the warmth of companionship or of sex, but is the willing generosity of mother to helpless young child or daughter to helpless old parent, of wife to alcoholic husband or husband to paralysed wife, seeking no reward but the happiness of the receiver. Paul gives a useful checklist in First Corinthians 13. The First Letter of John gives a shorter checklist: 'No one who fails to love the brother or sister whom he can see, can love God whom he has not seen.' The real interests of the recipient of love may not always be easy to find, but the spirit of giving is unmistakable.

Question: Whom do you know who really practises the commandment of love?

Thirty-first Sunday

First reading: A Corrupt Priesthood (Malachi 1.14–2.2, 8-10)
In the three-year cycle, there are only two Sunday readings from the prophet Malachi. He could be called 'anonymous', for 'Malachi' means only 'My Messenger'. The book is printed at the very end of the Old Testament – conveniently, because it ends with a message about the coming of the final messenger of the Lord before the Day of the Lord; this leads on perfectly into the New Testament and the gospel of Matthew. The book was probably written soon after the return of the Jews from exile in Babylon. The prophets of this time show that the enthusiastic return was soon followed by a period of disillusionment and slackness in the performance of religious duties: they could not even get started on rebuilding the Temple. Today's passage denounces the religious leaders for their failure truly to give glory to God, both by their sacrifices and by their failures in moral leadership. Are they really striving to give leadership in celebrating the covenant between God and his people? The reading is obviously chosen to pair with the gospel reading, in which the religious leadership at the time of Jesus is also fiercely criticized. Slackness in religious observance is a danger in any age, even our own.

Question: Is the Church in our day becoming slack and lukewarm?

Second reading: Paul's Care for his Converts (First Thessalonians 2.7-9, 13)

This is the earliest of Paul's letter that we possess, and he stresses, as he often does later, his unremitting care for the Churches he has founded around the eastern Mediterranean region. He seems to be defending himself, perhaps against a charge that he had neglected them. Certainly the urgency with which he moved from one city to another cannot have left him time to instruct them fully; this is why his letters to them are so rich in teaching for us! They supplement the rudimentary instruction that he gave to them when he was present. Elsewhere he underlines how heavily this anxiety for the wellbeing of these young communities weighs on him. The vividness and excitement of his letters show how earnest and eager he was. Writing to the Corinthians, at the end of a recital of the persecutions, dangers and hardships he has undergone in the service of Christ and the gospel, he adds, 'beside all the external things, there is, day in, day out, the pressure on me of my anxiety for all the Churches' (2 Corinthians 11.28). Paul's self-defence stands in sharp contrast to the criticism in the first reading of the slackness of the religious leaders.

Question: What do we expect from our pastors?

Gospel: The Scribes and Pharisees Denounced (Matthew 23.1-12)

This is the fiercest of all the hard things that the gospel of Matthew has to say about the scribes and Pharisees. It introduces a sevenfold curse on them. The Pharisees were the party of the Jews most concerned for the exact observance of the prescriptions of the Law of Moses. The 'scribes' were lawyers to whom they would turn in the case of a clash between two laws. Their attention to detail and their fussiness often made them lose sight of the real purpose of the Law. However, Jesus was prepared to meet them on the Pharisees' own ground and debate with them in their own terms. In the gospels, and especially in Matthew, written towards the end of the century, the hostility to this group has obviously become fiercer, no doubt because of their persecution of the followers of Jesus. As Matthew warns: 'They will flog you in their synagogues.' One of their concerns was obviously the status of the religious leaders. It looks as if they were turning into little gods on their own. So here the gospel stresses by contrast that all the disciples of Jesus are equal: in Christianity, there is only one Father, only one Teacher for all.

Question: Should we use titles such as 'Father' within Christian practice?

Thirty-second Sunday

First reading: The Search for Wisdom (Wisdom 6.12-16)

For the Bible, wisdom is not knowledge, such as scientific or philosophical knowledge acquired by study and learning, or even the sound judgment acquired by experience and maturity. It is the reflection of God's own Wisdom, the Wisdom by which God creates the world and guides humanity. Wisdom is, therefore, divine, a reflection or image of God, 'the reflection of the eternal light and the image of his power'. Everything created is good in so far as it expresses this Wisdom of God. In the New Testament, Jesus is seen as the incarnation of God's own Wisdom as well as the incarnation of the 'Word' of God, for Jesus is both the firstborn and the summit of God's creative purpose. In Greek, 'wisdom' is a feminine noun, and therefore divine Wisdom is often represented as a female character, a hostess inviting to her banquet all who desire true Wisdom. We need to seek out this Wisdom. It can be granted only by God, but God is eager to share divine Wisdom with those who truly seek it. This reading is given here to pair with the gospel reading, through the image of keeping awake to seek for the banquet of Wisdom.

Question: Is my skill at cookery or car maintenance the same as me or a part of me? Is God's Wisdom the same as God?

Second reading: The Last Trumpet (First Thessalonians 4.13-18)

The first Christians were unclear about many things in their faith. The Thessalonians were obviously worried about the fate of Christians who had died. Had not Paul taught them that Christ had conquered death? What was this talk about an imminent final coming of Christ to bring history to its end? How soon would it occur? Paul gives an answer in terms of a familiar image, a Roman triumphal procession. After a great victory in battle, a Roman general could be granted a 'triumph', marching through the streets of Rome with his victorious army amid cheering crowds, like a successful football team or local regiment coming home. There was no need to worry about Christian friends and relations who had died, for they would come with Christ in his triumphal procession, and the rest of us would join him on the way. All this, of course, is imagery. Neither Paul nor anyone else had any idea *when* it would occur. But he teaches with firm confidence that it *would* occur. The timing is irrelevant. We don't mind waiting a bit, so long as we can be sure that we will all be reunited in the joyful triumph of Christ's victory over death.

Question: Do we need to know any more about the end of the world than this?

Gospel: The Ten Wedding Attendants (Matthew 25.1-13)

Of course, they weren't *bride*smaids! According to the custom of the time, the girls were attendant on the bride*groom*, to greet him with their lamps as he arrived at the wedding reception. Anyway, half of them weren't ready, let him down, and then found themselves shut out. There is a subtle difference between the parables given in Mark's and Matthew's gospels. In Mark, they are all about the sudden coming of God's Kingship in history, at the time of Jesus. Jesus proclaimed that the crisis was *now*. In him, God's reign had arrived: it was time to take drastic action. Matthew's parables take a longer term view: there will be a final judgment at the end of time, for which we, in the Church and in the course of history, must prepare. Some will, some won't. Some will be found to be wheat, others to be weeds. When the catch of fish comes in, some fish will be thrown away, some kept. Some will be sheep and others goats. Each year, as the liturgical year draws to a close, the Church reminds us of this. And it will be sudden and unpredictable, like a burglar on the one night I forgot to lock the door, or like a mousetrap snapping shut, or like the unpredictable moment of birth pangs.

Question: Can't I just forget about the whole thing? I am not going to die tomorrow.

Thirty-third Sunday

First reading: A Woman about the House (Proverbs 31.10-13, 16-18, 20, 26, 28, 31)

The gospel parable is about a man who is a wise administrator, and this first reading delicately pairs it with a woman who is a shrewd businesswoman, running her household and her cottage industry capably, wisely and generously in reverence for the Lord. The Bible is often felt to be unduly male oriented (an accusation often made also against the Church), and this was the normal state of society in those days. Nevertheless, a succession of remarkable women moves through the pages of the Old Testament, real partners to their husbands, and often providing the motive force in pursuit of God's promises. In the New Testament, too, besides Mary and Jesus' female followers in the gospels, we see Jesus valuing women. Particularly the playful scenes between Jesus and the Samaritan woman and the Canaanite (or Syro-Phoenician) woman spring to mind. Especially in Paul's letters and apostolate women play important roles, even leadership roles, working with Paul to establish his communities, Chloe, Phoebe, Junia. The first convert to Christianity in Europe was a woman, Lydia.

Question: Do you think the Bible is unduly male oriented? So what?

Second reading: A Thief in the Night (1 Thessalonians 5.1-6)

Paul had obviously taught the new Christians at Thessalonika that Christ had conquered death, so that death had no more grasp on Christians. So they were puzzled that Christians nevertheless died. Paul explains in the letter that Christians who have died will be the first to rise up and join the returning Christ in his triumphant procession. Only after them will come those who are still alive. However, Paul's principal stress is on the unpredictability of the Day of the Lord, that final day when the Lord will set right all injustices. It makes little difference whether I meet the Lord in some sort of imagined vast Judgment Day, or whether my meeting with the Lord is merely personal at my own death. I know that I will not be ready – if only I had just a little more time to prepare! – and that I will not be in a fit state to face the glorious, pure wonder of Divine Love. The day will come as unexpectedly as a thief in the night or the pains of childbirth, with that same finality and inescapability.

Question: What will be your reaction on meeting God?

Gospel: A Story about Talents (Matthew 25.14-30)

It is encouraging to think of all the talents that friends and neighbours have and that I don't have. It is all part of the gifts of the Spirit, which Paul sees as making up the whole Body of Christ. Everyone has a special contribution to make. As for me, it is extraordinary that God created me with all my twists, defects, fears and failures, and it is precisely because of those boils, sores, abscesses that God loves me, helps me and guides me to work out my salvation. And it is just possible that there may be friends who can think that God has given me talents that make a tiny contribution to the happiness and goodness of the world. What of the man who has only one 'talent', digs it into the earth, and is so severely treated? This is surely someone who resolutely turns his (or her) back on the goodness she (or he) has received and refuses to work with it for the Lord's purposes or anyone else's. Such a talent goes to waste and merely rusts and corrupts. If

I know anyone like that it is just worth asking whether, with infinite and patient kindness, I can just help that person to release the talent and bring it to blossom.

Question: What are your chief talents and how do you use them?

Thirty-fourth Sunday, Christ the King

First reading: The Loving Shepherd (Ezekiel 34.11-12, 15-17)

Is this really an appropriate reading for the Feast of Christ the King? All about sheep? Shouldn't it be about crowns, medals, processions and majesty? No, it should not! Christ's Kingship is modelled on God's Kingship, or rather, Jesus came to show us what God's Kingship is. 'The Kingship of God has come upon you', was his first proclamation. In the British countryside, we can usually leave the sheep to graze on their own. In the hilly country of Palestine, there is always a shepherd to look after them, to stop them wandering over a cliff or stave off attack from wild animals. Sheep are silly creatures, can be guaranteed to wander, wide eyed and gormless, in front of a passing car and then run the wrong way. We are silly creatures, too, and do just the same. We need God's care to keep us on the right path. Jesus as the Good Shepherd cherishes us, guards us, heals us, calms our fears, and even gives his life for us. That is what his Kingship is.

Question: What can I do to make Christ's Kingship more a reality in the world?

Second reading: King Jesus Presents the Kingdom (1 Corinthians 15.20-26, 28)

What will happen at the end of the world? How will the world be brought to an end? We simply do not know, and it is not the sort of thing the Bible needs to teach us. For us Christians, three things are certain – and this is what Paul teaches us here in vivid picture language. First, God's sovereignty will extend over the whole of creation in peace and harmony. Second, this will be through Christ's work of mediation, for Christ is Lord of the Church, the 'backbone' of the Church which is his Body. When Paul says 'he has put all his enemies under his feet', he is quoting a messianic Psalm about the priest-king of Jerusalem, frequently applied to Jesus. Third, Christ is the first fruits of the Resurrection: where he has led the way, we are to follow.

Question: What does this reading tell us of the relationship of Father to Son?

Gospel: The Last Judgment (Matthew 25.31-46)

This is the last of Matthew's great parables. The world is finally divided into 'goodies' and 'baddies'. The great dramatic scene here depicted will not necessarily happen all at once, but we shall each of us at the moment of death face the judgment of our divine Lord in his glory. This confrontation will be an experience far more awesome and shattering than any description can express, and yet fulfilling and reassuring. We will know at last in a naked way our own filth and also our own infinite value to this transcendent figure.

Two striking points are stressed in the parable. First, we will be judged uniquely on our treatment of those in any kind of need. Not on our prayer life. Not on our asceticism or penances undertaken. Only on our respect for others, how far we look to see what they need and what we can give. Each of the ten commandments in the Old Testament, each of the eight beatitudes in the New can be resolved into this: telling the truth, financial honesty, honouring father and mother (or children), hunger for justice, peace making. The second striking point is the reason for the first: that Christ is in each person. What we do to others, we do to Christ.

Question: What does it really mean that Christ is in me and all other people?

Year B

Second Sunday of Year B

First reading: The Call of Samuel (1 Samuel 3.3-10, 19)

In the readings of Sundays 'in ordinary time', the first reading normally links to the gospel reading, and this is a superb example of such a link: the call of Samuel and his response prepare for the call of the first disciples of Jesus.

The call of the young boy Samuel into the Lord's service is always a favourite. It is easy to imagine the boy lying, dozing on his mat in the half-darkness, hearing the voice murmur 'Shmuel' (the Hebrew form of his name). Was it really a call, was it the old prophet calling, or just the wind in the pillars of the Temple? He has all the directness, willingness and simplicity of a child, the sort of qualities needed for the Kingdom of God. Often, however, in the same way we do not know whether an 'inspiration' is really the call of God or our own imagination. Prayer and advice help in discerning the genuine call from a madcap scheme! Others may know us better than we know ourselves, and God's call is always fitted to our true nature.

Question: How is God's call heard?

Second reading: The Body Belongs to Christ (1 Corinthians 6.13-15, 17-20)

This is the first of six consecutive Sunday readings from Paul's letter. The Christian community at Corinth was a troublesome lot, and seems to have lacked any resident human guide. They relied on the Holy Spirit, backed up by several letters from Paul. Here we have Paul's most forceful reason for sexual self-control: as Christ lives in us by his Spirit, all our bodily members are Christ's, and Christ is involved in every movement of them. This should give us a wonderful reverence for our bodies, knowing that we implicate Christ in all our body's activities. The most powerful expression comes in verse 16 (omitted in the public reading, perhaps as being too pointed) 'anyone who attaches himself to a prostitute is one body with her, since the two become one flesh'. This drives the lesson home: Christ, too, becomes involved with the prostitute. Christ is involved in a wonderful way in the sexual act of procreation, giving a couple the inestimable privilege and joy of sharing in God's work of creation. But Christ is also abused by a Christian's abuse of sex.

Question: How does it affect me that my body is Christ's body?

Gospel: The First Disciples (John 1.35-42)
This year the ordinary Sunday gospel readings are taken from Mark, enabling us to get a full picture of that gospel. But Mark is the shortest of the gospels, and is not quite long enough, so just occasionally a reading from John slips in to complete the picture.

This story of the call of the first disciples takes place in the Jordan valley, where John was baptizing. The first two to be called are disciples of John, so had joined his group of those waiting for the Messiah. They were ready when John pointed him out. It is striking that Jesus first calls them to be with him, and first of all they remain with him for a time. First in our call to follow Christ comes prayer and getting to know Christ, before we can actively work for Christ and bring others to share his joy. Only after this repose with Jesus do they sprint off in their enthusiasm and bring others to join in the benefits they have received from the tranquillity of keeping company with Jesus.

Question: As a disciple of Jesus, do I spend enough time simply being with him?

Third Sunday

First reading: Nineveh Changes its Ways (Jonah 3.1-5, 10)

The story of Jonah (whale and all) does not even pretend to be historical. For one thing, it takes about 10 minutes to walk across the ruins of Nineveh. The story is a joke by Jews against Jews who think they alone can be saved: Jonah the Jew tries to run away from God, whereas the gentiles at Nineveh repent as soon as they hear God's message – even the animals wear sackcloth! Like the story about St Peter showing Protestants round heaven: he points to a high wall: 'Hush! The Catholics are behind there. They think they are the only people here.' The reason why this reading is chosen to pair with the call of the disciples is the immediacy of their response. They take the message to heart without hesitation.

Question: Why is the message of Christ so neglected in the world today?

Second reading: This Passing World? (1 Corinthians 7.29-31)

The earliest Christians were very aware that the Resurrection of Christ ushered in the last period of the world. With the fulfilment of God's promises in Jesus' death and Resurrection everything important had happened. The end was imminent, and it was urgent for everyone to get ready. What must we think of this attitude 2,000 years later? Yes, it is urgent for every individual to respond to God's call, and there is no time to lose. Every decision counts; every step along the path leads in one direction or the other. However, this is an instance where the message of the Bible must be seen as a whole, one teaching balancing another. 'The Kingdom of God is upon you!' does not mean that the world will end tomorrow. Matthew's gospel is quite clear that there is time before the last judgment to practise good works of prayer and generosity. At the last supper, Jesus teaches that his disciples have a task to do in the world, guided by the Holy Spirit. So Paul is not teaching here that Christians should 'down tools' and sit waiting for the end, but that we must not absorb the values of those around us who think that the supermarket, the sports centre and the holiday cottage are the only realities worth thinking about.

Question: Can I do anything to live the gospel more fully?

Gospel: The Call of the Disciples (Mark 1.14-20)
What is going on? Last Sunday we had the story of the first two disciples joining Jesus. One of them was Andrew, the other unnamed. Now we get another story, in another place, of other first disciples being called. So the Church underlines, two weeks running, the importance of Jesus' new community. The first thing he does is call disciples. He can't do everything on his own, and that is the point of the Church. He calls disciples to make a new people, a new Israel. We all have our part to fill in Jesus' play (sometimes it seems like a pantomime), old, young, middle aged. Tired old people, busy parents, lively youngsters, each of us can make a unique contribution, especially since Jesus has chosen us himself. An odd choice, some of us! What did he want *me* to do in the new family of Jesus?

The two different places show that at least two different people told the story. When two people tell the same story, there are bound to be variations. The place didn't matter, or the order in which they were called. The point of the story was the call, the response and the companionship, working together.

Question: To whom would you point as having left everything to follow Jesus?

Fourth Sunday

First reading: The Second Moses (Deuteronomy 18.15-20)

Moses was the messenger who gave the Law to Israel on Mount Sinai. In their difficult and lonely journey of 40 years through the desert, he was their leader. It was his legal decisions on cases presented to him that formed Israel. His prayers gave them manna in the desert, water from the rock and protection from their enemies. Israel remembered him ever afterwards as the founder of their people. In the Book of Deuteronomy, the last of the five books of the Law, God had promised that he would raise up another leader, a Second Moses. At the time of Jesus God's final messenger, who would put everything to rights, was thought of in these terms. This is why Matthew especially represents Jesus in these terms: just like Moses, he was persecuted at birth by the king, and later had to flee into exile until his persecutor was dead. He taught his Sermon on the Mount just as Moses gave the Law on the mountain. He gave bread in the desert just as Moses had done. So when Jesus taught 'with authority' in the synagogue at Capernaum, he was seen as acting like Moses, the teacher.

Question: Is it helpful or harmful to have a Church that teaches with authority?

Second reading: Marriage or Celibacy? (1 Corinthians 7.32-35)

Paul's reasons for celibacy can be read on two levels. The first, superficial, level is that both husband and wife may be divided in mind, may have loyalties divided between the Lord and their spouse. They have to be preoccupied with pleasing the other partner in the marriage. In itself, this is a very important part of the marriage, a vital part of being 'one flesh', one thinking, living person. At this level, such concern is very much part of 'the Lord's affairs', and cannot stand in opposition to them. At another level, however, there may be tension, for each marriage partner is concerned to provide a firm material basis for family life, and so is bound for the sake of the family to get involved in worldly values, providing a good standard of living for the family. The point of celibacy is that the celibate must stand as a witness that these material values are of less importance than the eternal values of the Lord's service. Important as the values of family life are, the celibate has the opportunity to turn wholly away from this scale of values. Celibacy does not make sense unless the values of the Kingdom of God fill the celibate's whole horizon.

Question: How valuable is celibacy as a witness in the Church?

Gospel: Jesus teaches with Authority (Mark 1.21-28)

This story goes one step further in showing the growing authority of Jesus, which is the theme of the early part of Mark's gospel. He has already called the disciples. He calls and they simply follow. It seems that he is a total stranger to them, yet with such authority that they drop everything to follow him. Now, in the synagogue, he teaches on his own authority. He does not quote the interpretations of others, as rabbinic teachers did, saying, 'Rabbi X says this, Rabbi Y says that.' No, Jesus teaches, 'I say to you …' He seems to be master even of the law. But it is God's Law. Only God has authority over it, so who does he think he is? At least he is the teacher comparable to Moses, who is to come into the world, the teacher prophesied in today's first reading. Then, to confirm his authoritative teaching, he shows his authority by overcoming the dreaded unclean spirit, wringing from it the snivelling protest, 'Have you come to destroy us?' and the acknowledgement that he has a special link with God.

Question: On the human level, why did people follow Jesus so enthusiastically?

Fifth Sunday

First reading: Job's Suffering (Job 7.1-4, 6-7)

In the whole three-year cycle there are only two Sunday readings from the lovely and tragic Book of Job. The Book puts at its most acute the problem of sickness and suffering: why should I suffer? Job has lost everything, wealth, family, health. He sits on a rubbish heap, scratching his sores with a broken pot. In this passage, he gives a painful picture of the sick person's frustration, the slow and pointless passage of time, the crazy, distorted imaginings. He feels that God is oppressing him, but yet clings to God as his one hope of release. Undeserved sickness and death is worrying for anyone who believes in a loving God. On the natural plane, sickness is a reminder that things are out of order and could get worse. To the believer, it is a reminder that this brilliant, complicated, sophisticated creation cannot continue developing for ever, but must return to God in God's own good time. As Jeremiah explains, the pot cannot complain to the potter: 'Why did you make me like this?' But couldn't a loving God have made something so that it never went wrong? Or is it the consequence of our revolts against God that confidence in God has given way to fear and mistrust?

Question: How is the love of God compatible with unmerited suffering?

Second reading: Paul, the Servant of All (1 Corinthians 9.16-19, 22-23)

As we work through this letter to the Christians of Corinth, we find Paul's reflection on his own task. His teaching is firm enough. Under the compulsion of his divine call, he has no choice but to teach the truth. Yet in his desire to win them for Christ, he is sensitive to the needs of all people. Here he has just been giving a ruling on whether it is allowed to eat food that has been dedicated to pagan gods. His first point is this: as such gods don't exist, dedication to them does not affect the food. But his most important point is that you must not upset other people's consciences. In other words, the overriding principle is to be sensitive and caring towards the needs of individuals. If we are anxious to do the right thing, we can often be quite hard about acting 'on principle', trampling on the feelings of others without regard for their own sincerely held beliefs. For Paul, the highest principle in his treatment of people is always love.

Question: Should you always follow your conscience?

Gospel: Jesus at Capernaum (Mark 1.29-39)

The snippets gathered in the gospel reading give us a sample of Jesus' activity at Capernaum, the little fishing village on the edge of the Lake of Galilee: healing and prayer. The first incident, the healing of the relative of his friend and follower Simon Peter, reminds us that Jesus does respond if we pray for the needs of our nearest and dearest. Then the summary of his evening activity shows his concern to bring healing and wholeness. Just so any Christian will desire to follow his example: we can harm or heal those around us in so many ways. It does not need to be a miracle! A greeting, a look, a smile, a touch can bring the peace of Christ to someone in desperate need of reassurance – and no less can they harm and wound. But the third little story, of Jesus going off to pray in the early morning, shows that the wellspring of all his activity was his union with the God whom he called his Father. We cannot say what Jesus' prayer was, any more than I can say what your prayer is, but the confident communication between Father and Son must have been the source of his strength and compassion.

Question: What is the best time and circumstance for prayer?

Sixth Sunday

First reading: Leprosy (Leviticus 13.1-2, 45-46)

This reading from the law sets the scene for Jesus' healing in the gospel reading. Leprosy in its modern medical sense (*Mycobacterium leprae*) is a devastating disease, leading to the loss of fingers, and then even whole hands and feet. These biblical regulations were, with good reason, designed to prevent contagion. In biblical times lack of precise diagnosis led to other skin diseases, such as psoriasis and even acne, being lumped together with it. So the worst thing about many of the lesser forms of 'leprosy' would have been the isolation, for 'lepers' were cut off from all human society. The priests were involved not so much as sacred ministers but as reliable persons to judge the symptoms, although, of course, the sacrifice of thanks for disappearance of the disease was a genuine religious thanksgiving.

Question: Which was worse, the isolation or the disease?

Second reading: Liberty and Love (1 Corinthians 10.31–11.1)

This is the last reading this year from First Corinthians, the end of a section of the letter, so summing up. Paul has just quoted a slogan that that difficult community threw in his face: 'Everything is permissible.' This was the conclusion they drew from the abolition of the restrictions of the Jewish Law. Paul's principle was that the Spirit was an inner guide, so that no external restrictions were necessary. With their slogan, the Corinthians jumped to the conclusion that there were no limits, so Paul now adds various pieces of guidance: 'Do everything you do for the glory of God!' If the glory of God is always before our minds, we can hardly go wrong. 'Never be the cause of offence', that is, never lead anyone else into sin. It is easy sometimes to put people in a situation in which they are bound to fail, through fear or anger or frustration, or just because they are unequal to the task. 'Take me as your pattern, as I take Christ for mine.' To us moderns, this may sound arrogant, but Paul regarded himself as the Servant of the Lord Jesus, just as Jesus regarded himself as the Servant of the Lord. So Paul is encouraging the self-confident Corinthians to put themselves in a position of servants, serving the community for the glory of God. No matter what our position, we can always do something more for the community.

Question: Are 'ministries' in the Church really acts of service or of self-importance?

Gospel: Jesus Heals a Leper (Mark 1.40-45)

Mark shows the warmth of Jesus' humanity and his concern for the leper. The leper had no right even to approach Jesus, but must have felt that he would get a favourable response, no word of reproach. 'Jesus felt sorry for him' is a weak expression; the Greek is far stronger: colloquially, it can literally be translated 'was gutted'; Jesus felt it to the depths of his being. Then Jesus touched him, both touching someone ritually impure and risking the infection. There have been famous repetitions of this brave and heartfelt gesture: Francis of Assisi kissing a leper's hand, Princess Diana shaking hands with an AIDS sufferer (when the sickness was thought to be contagious by touch). One can imagine the awestruck horror of the bystanders at this outrageous expression of love and sympathy. Why, then, does Jesus 'sternly send him away'? A more faithful rendering would be not 'sternly' but 'in anger'. It is possible that the anger is directed at the leprosy, considered as an exterior invasion, so 'sent *it* away'. At least Jesus' whole-hearted emotional involvement with the sufferer is palpable.

Question: Why was Jesus so moved, or even angry, about the leprosy?

Seventh Sunday

First reading: The Forgiveness of Israel (Isaiah 43.18-19, 21-22, 24-25)

This reading is taken from the second part of Isaiah, written during Israel's Exile in Babylon, but when they were already expecting the release of the captives after 70 years of slavery. The banner headline at the beginning was 'Console my people; she has received double punishment for all her sins' in the exile and enslavement. The prophet makes no secret of Israel's infidelities, but details their slackness and the failures of their sacrificial rituals. Nevertheless, the prophet protests that the Lord will take no more notice of such failures. Instead, he will guide the people across the desert, even renewing the wonders of the Exodus, by making 'a road in the desert and water in wastelands' as at the Exodus from Egypt. The gospel sees the fulfilment of this in Jesus by the quotation in the first verses of Mark of 'A voice crying in the desert, "Make his paths straight"'. The Church sees the fulfilment of it in Jesus by pairing this reading with the gospel reading about Jesus' forgiveness of sin.

Question: Is there anything that is really unforgivable?

Second reading: Jesus, the 'Yes' of God (2 Corinthians 1.18-22)

This is the first of eight consecutive Sunday readings from Second Corinthians, interrupted this year by the seasons of Lent and Easter. Paul is explaining to the Corinthians why he did not fulfil his promise to visit them again, and insists that he does not say 'yes' and 'no' at the same time. (He goes on to explain that he changed his plans in order to spare them a severe rebuke, since they had rejected and insulted his messenger.) On the contrary, he follows the trustworthiness of God's own promises in Christ, who is the 'yes' of the Father's promises. Paul uses a neat play on words, for the Hebrew word 'amen' means 'yes' or 'firm'. When we say 'amen' to someone's prayer, we signify our agreement. In just the same way, Christ is the firmness of God's promises, bringing them to completion. Paul may be referring to the Great Amen at the end of the Eucharistic prayer when he says 'it is through him that we answer "Amen".' All this is also interesting as showing that Paul, despite stemming from the Greek city of Tarsus, seems to think in Hebrew.

Question: How important is it to keep your word? Absolutely?

Gospel: The Double Cure of the Paralytic (Mark 2.1-12)

It is a double cure because the sick man is cured of both sin and disease. Mark often relates his stories in 'sandwiches', that is, he puts one story between two halves of another story (like the ham in the slices of bread). Later on, in Jesus' Jerusalem ministry, the Cleansing of the Temple is sandwiched between the Cursing and the Withering of the Fig tree, to show its significance: the fig tree of Israel is withered. In this case, the ham is the forgiveness of sin. The bap is the physical cure. The two stories reflect on one another, since the visible cure is evidence for the invisible forgiveness. The link joining the two stories is 'said to the paralytic' in verses 5 and 11. The scandalized scribes materialize only for the ham story, which seems to them blasphemous. Indeed, it is, and deliberately so! They are right that only God can forgive sins, for sin injures God's world in a way that finally only God can put right. If I run over or maltreat a child, only God can heal the scar. So the impression of Jesus' authority continues to grow until the only possible conclusion is that this is God among us.

Question: Should or can past sins be totally washed away?

Eighth Sunday

First reading: The Lord's Love for his Spouse (Hosea 2.14-15, 19-20)

The Prophet Hosea is the poet of God's love. His own wife was repeatedly unfaithful to him, but he continued to love her passionately and to pursue her ceaselessly. In a later passage, he also see the relationship as the love and devoted care of parent for child, 'I have brought my son out of Egypt …'. But the response of Israel, the beloved, was short lived as the morning mist that floats away. Hosea's inspiration was to see that his love for his wife was an image of God's love for Israel. No matter how often Israel was unfaithful and rebellious, the Lord continued to draw her back to him. Here Hosea harks back wistfully to the 'honeymoon period' of 40 years in the desert at the exodus, when Israel and the Lord were alone together without distraction, bonding and growing together. Israel continued to see the covenant relationship in terms of the marriage bond, which would be brought to perfection when the marriage became firm and unbreakable. Jesus, too, uses the image of the wedding feast as a parable of the final consummation of the relationship. In John's gospel, Jesus symbolically begins his public ministry with the marriage feast of Cana, a presage of the marriage feast of heaven.

Question: How stable is our marriage bond with the Lord?

Second reading: A Letter written on Human Hearts (2 Corinthians 3.1-6)

After Paul's first letter to the Corinthians, his relationships with that community went through a rocky period. Hearing of their dissensions and quarrels, he had been pretty rough on them, sluicing them down severely with sarcasm about their selfishness and arrogance. After that, relations needed some careful repair! However, the situation was also complicated by other Christian teachers, who seem to have questioned Paul's authority. In today's passage, he suggests that these teachers were undermining his authority by pointing out that the Corinthians had never received any letters of reference about him. He might be a total impostor! Paul's reply is that the Corinthian Christians are themselves his letter of reference. Presumably he means that the works of the Spirit of Christ among them, sparked off by Paul's mission among them, are testimony that Paul's mission was from God. With a delicate reference to Jesus' own words at the Last Supper about the 'new covenant in my blood', he suggests that these works of the Spirit are the fulfilment of the New Covenant foretold by the prophets: it would be written not on stone but on human hearts, and would be a source of new life. This nice compliment would help to assuage any hurt feelings.

Question: Is the presence of the Spirit and the new covenant equally obvious in your Christian community?

Gospel: Fasting at a Wedding? (Mark 2.18-22)

Today's reading comes from Mark's collection of several confrontations between Jesus and the Pharisees in Galilee. The Pharisees were sticklers for observance of the practices of the Jewish Law. Fasting was originally a sign of sorrow and repentance – if you are really upset, as at a death in the family, you don't want to eat much. Presumably the disciples of John the Baptist fasted also as part of their change of lifestyle or conversion in preparation for the coming of the Messiah. Jesus' reply shows that the joyful moment of the coming of the Messiah, the coming of the Kingship of God, has already burst upon them. It is a time not for mourning but for an explosion of joy. He appeals to the idea of the splendid wedding feast, to be celebrated when the sovereignty of God is completed and God's love for his people sealed in a marriage bond. But he adds the warning that a time is coming when the bridegroom will be taken away. Is he referring to his own Passion and death, or to a time of seeming absence of Christ from his Church? Then comes a little group of images, perhaps sayings of Jesus originally independent, all teaching that our behaviour must be totally new: it is no good mixing new habits with old.

Question: Why is a marriage feast a good image for the end of all things?

Ninth Sunday

First reading: The Sabbath Day (Deuteronomy 5.12-15)

What place has the Sabbath Day for Christians? Well, of course it is the foundational element in today's gospel stories about Jesus. But, surely, the Jewish Sabbath celebrated God's day of rest at the end of creation, while we Christians have moved the Day of the Lord to Sunday, the day of Christ's Resurrection. That is the day we all celebrate nowadays, the weekly day of Resurrection. There are several elements to a Sunday: first and foremost, acknowledgement to God of our gratitude for creation, and our own existence and especially of Jesus' Resurrection, which brings us also new life. Second, our natural need for rest, recreation and relaxation, probably with the family we love. This makes it a celebration of the life and love of the family, another gift of God, a chance to renew and refresh relationships with parts of the family we have neglected. Third, it is a day on which we can be ourselves, not working for someone else, but independent, reminding us of the God-given individuality of each person. Fourth, it is often a day of expeditions and novelty, whether we go to the country or to the family in the next street, seeing new sights and rejoicing in God's creative goodness and in human skills.

Question: What does Sunday mean to you?

Second reading: The Light of Christ (2 Corinthians 4.6-11)

Paul, the apostle of Christ, reflects on his ministry. On the road to Damascus, he was brought to Christ by seeing a light from heaven. Thenceforth, he sees Christ as enlightenment, bringing light into the darkness of human existence. He sees his ministry also as a ministry of light, revealing the truth of the glory of God. But he is realistic, too, about the hard knocks that our task as beacons of Christ's light may bring. Here he uses the image of the games. Every two years at Corinth the Isthmian Games were held, more famous in the ancient world than the Olympic Games – better prizes, easier access, better toffee apple stalls, more distinction (but just try pronouncing it!). Paul would have been familiar with this from his stay in Corinth, and, as a tent maker, may have made tents for the tented village of the competitors. It would have included rough sports, such as boxing and wrestling and even gladiatorial contests, so competitors and spectators would have known all about pursuits, being knocked down and scarred, possibly even deaths. The Christian is not daunted, but like a courageous gladiator, springs up and carries on through all difficulties.

Question: How does Christian ministry bring light? Does it bring hard knocks too?

Gospel: Jesus and the Sabbath (Mark 2.23–3.6)

For today's gospel reading, we are given two separate confrontations between Jesus and the Pharisees over Sabbath observance. The first is especially interesting because we see Jesus arguing with the Pharisees in their own way. They challenge him for allowing his disciples to work on the Sabbath, for harvesting was considered work, and a stickler could just say that the disciples were harvesting. Jesus replies by quoting a precedent in scripture for breaking the ritual laws. His attitude to the Law is far broader than their petty, detailed observance, going back to the real purpose of the Law and of creation. As so often, he turns back to one of the basic texts of the Bible, the story of creation in Genesis 1. Then he finally settles the question with a magisterial general statement, which shows his command even over the Law. The second controversy is especially significant because at the end of it we see that already in this early stage of his ministry, Jesus is annoying some of the Jews so much that they start plotting his death. In the end, however, the Pharisees take no part in his arrest and execution. Christian witness must be fearless and uncompromising.

Question: Should laws always be obeyed?

Tenth Sunday

First reading: The Aftermath of the Fall (Genesis 3.9-15, 20)

The story of the Fall is an analysis of human temptation and sin as it always happens, rather than a historical account of what happened once long ago, when human beings first evolved on earth. Sin brings shame on us: we do our best, like both the man and the woman, to blame someone else, but in the end we know we are defenceless and naked before God. We know that we deserve our penalties, but the wonderful thing about the biblical story is that God continues to care for us: he himself thoughtfully sews clothes for the man and the woman to hide their embarrassment. More important, God promises that evil will not triumph for ever. The penalties of hard labour and pain come not from divine vindictiveness but from human sinfulness: we are no longer in perfect harmony with God. If we were in harmony with God our confidence in him would spare us the pain. The reading pairs with the gospel reading, since it introduces Satan, the Tempter. The final bit is a 'Just So Story' of the animal world, explaining how the sinewy snake came into being: the proud, fiery serpent lost its legs and was reduced to being a mere big worm.

Question: What does the story teach us about human sin?

Second reading: The Weight of Glory (2 Corinthians 4.13–5.1)

Is this an older Paul, who feels that he is failing ('this human nature of ours falling into decay'), and is looking forward to death, or rather to the weight of glory at the Resurrection? In last Sunday's reading, he was positive enough, bouncing up again after the hard knocks received in the gladiatorial combats of life. Contrariwise, in Philippians 1.21, he is caught in a dilemma and writes: 'Life to me, of course, is Christ, but then death would be a positive gain.' Such is his faith and conviction of the saving power of Christ that he longs to be fully united with Christ. He looks forward to 'the weight of glory' that must be the goal of every Christian. Glory is a specifically divine property. Moses was allowed to see the awesome divine glory, but the face of God he could not see. Isaiah was bowled over by his experience of the divine glory in the Temple, contrasting with his own awareness of his uncleanness. It seems that for Paul to feel 'the utterly incomparable, eternal weight of glory' is to be bathed in the divine presence and to enjoy eternally the company of God.

Question: No one can see God and live, but how do you imagine the 'weight of God's glory'?

Gospel: Jesus Rejected (Mark 3.20-35)

The first stage of Jesus' ministry comes to an end. He is rejected as 'out of his mind' by his own family. Then he is rejected by the scribes as being in league with Beelzebul. Finally, his family again arrive, looking for him, and he turns to those who are listening to him as his true family. This all leads into the Parable of the Sower, which seems to be Jesus' reflection on his rejection by most people, and his fruitful acceptance by a small number of disciples. It is, of course, significant that the scribes cannot deny that he drives out evil spirits. If even his enemies are forced to admit it, it must be true. The best they can do is sarcastically to ascribe his powers to the chief of evil spirits, here named 'Beelzebub' or 'Beelzebul' (two different versions of the text). The former name means 'lord of the flies', probably a mocking corruption of the latter, which means 'lord prince', the title of a local deity. The whole scene presents an agonizing picture of the isolation of Jesus. In Luke's version of the scene, by a very slight adjustment, Jesus' mother and brothers are the prime example of those who hear the word of God and keep it.

Question: Did Jesus feel disappointment and isolation as we do?

Eleventh Sunday

First reading: The Noble Cedar (Ezekiel 17.22-24)

The task of prophet Ezekiel was to keep up the spirits of the Jews exiled to Babylon. For them, it seemed that the Sack of Jerusalem was the end of all hope: they had lost their homes, their King, their Temple and even their covenant with God.

Ezekiel was a person of fantastic imagination, not afraid to indulge in wild and daring mimes to force through his message that God was still in charge and still caring for Israel. He mimed the siege of Jerusalem by building a mud brick model and escaping through the wall. His visions are also daring and inspiring. Perhaps the best known is the Valley of the Dead Bones, prophesying that Israel will come to life again, and read at our Easter Vigil. The present chapter is an imaginative allegory about a great cedar tree despoiled by two eagles, that is, Israel despoiled by Babylon and Egypt. Our reading is a tailpiece, promising that Israel will again become a great cedar tree, in whose shade the nations will come to take shelter. The gospel parable uses the same figure of a great tree in which all peoples will shelter. The great cedars on the mountains of the Lebanon are an awesome and unforgettable sight, stretching far into the sky and wide across the hills, a suitable refuge for great birds.

Question: Is the Church a refuge in which we may shelter?

Second reading: At Home with the Lord (2 Corinthians 5.6-10)

Paul uses several different sets of imagery to convey the goal of the Christian life for which he is longing. We know that all imagery is inadequate, but especially such pictures as heaven 'up there', in the clouds, playing harps. In 1 Corinthians 15, Paul used images of participating in God's power, incorruptibility and glory, transformed into a new mode of being by the Spirit. In last week's reading, he spoke of the 'weight of glory'. In today's reading, he speaks of 'being at home' with the Lord in contrast to being in exile. Now that we are adopted children of God, to be with the Lord is our natural family homecoming. In the final sentence, he envisages also the final judgment when we are laid bare for what we truly are, the frightening but comforting moment at which we see ourselves as God sees us, when we can cease putting on an act and keeping up appearances. Before God, there is neither need nor possibility of pretence. All masks are stripped off. This, too, is an aspect of being at home, for there is no pretending before the family. This fills him with courage and optimism on his journey home from exile.

Question: How do you envisage 'heaven'?

Gospel: The Seed Growing (Mark 4.26-34)

Jesus was a countryman, from the rich agricultural plains of Galilee, where wheat and fruit trees abounded. It was natural from him to use such imagery for the Kingship of God which he was proclaiming. Today's gospel reading offers us two of the many images in Mark's chapter of parables. What did Jesus want to teach by them? Images can carry many layers of meaning. First, the seed growing secretly. Perhaps Jesus meant that God's purposes are accomplished in spite of our feeble and fumbling efforts. Perhaps it was a warning that after long waiting the time for decision, the time of harvest, had come with Jesus' own mission. Then the mustard seed: was this a reply to the discouraged disciples – or perhaps Jesus' critical opponents – that his motley little group of undistinguished peasants, fishermen and tax collectors would grow into God's own mighty tree. Perhaps this is a first hint that Jesus' mission is for all nations, not just for Israel. All nations would come, nest and find a home in its branches, just as in the first reading they nest in the branches of the great cedar tree. At any rate, both images show that God is in charge, and has great plans that will be fulfilled, in spite of our own inadequacies.

Question: What does Jesus mean to teach by this parable?

Twelfth Sunday

First reading: Job's Agony (Job 38.1-4, 8-11)

The Book of Job is a brilliant, evocative piece of writing, exposing in all its anguish the problem of the suffering of innocent people. It is a timeless plaint, expressing the incomprehension and frustration of all those who suffer undeservedly. It may well have been provoked by the second generation of exiles in Babylon, suffering for sins that are not their own. But it is a problem that brings agony in every age. Why should my child die young? Why should I be subjected to long and humiliating illness? Here, at the beginning of the saga, Job is so wound up that he curses the very day he was born. Throughout his struggle to understand, he has a love–hate relationship with God, wanting to be free of God's persecuting hand, but at the same time depending on and attached to that same protecting hand, confident that there is a solution. Despite what he sees as God's unacceptable bullying, he remains convinced that God's love will never forsake him. The two conflicting emotions seethe together throughout the Book, until the final vision of God's incomparable wisdom and glory convinces Job that God's purposes are beyond human reasoning. Job is calmed and comforted by the experience of the awesome and incomprehensible glory of God.

Question: How is the suffering of the innocent compatible with the idea of a loving God?

Second reading: The New Creation (2 Corinthians 5.14-17)

In this reading of Second Corinthians, Paul is explaining that the Resurrection of Christ has radically changed everything. In this new creation, all our standards, hopes and expectations have undergone a transformation. He is perhaps already tilting at people who prided themselves on having known Jesus during his earthly life, and pitted their authority against Paul's own. Certainly, later in the Letter, he sets out to dispute the claims of some people of Jewish background who considered themselves 'super-apostles'. Salvation is not achieved by this knowledge of the earthly Jesus. The message of the gospel makes sense only in the light of the Resurrection. The Risen Christ is the firstborn from the dead, and his Resurrection is the model for ours. This is the ultimate answer to Job's question: whatever sorrows earthly life may bring, if we are baptized into Christ's death, we will also share his Resurrection. We already share Christ's life and are being transformed into him. The life we are experiencing now is only a preparation for its fulfilment in Christ's Resurrection.

Question: Is Paul exaggerating when he says that with the Resurrection everything old has passed away?

Gospel: Jesus Calms the Storm (Mark 4.35-41)

Jesus certainly seems to have chosen a pretty dim and unappreciative group of disciples. They do call him 'Master', but after all these wonders they still don't really trust him, and have no hesitation about addressing him rudely and brusquely. Did you say, 'Just like me'? Well, perhaps I am just as untrusting. We often behave as if Jesus were quietly snoozing, quite unconcerned about our troubles and concerns, as we struggle hopelessly, up to our necks in the mud and sinking rapidly. However, once Jesus' attention has been roused, once they have put their trust in him, he effortlessly remedies the situation. This incident is the climax of a series of wonders, when we see Jesus' authority and command gradually increasing. First, he imperiously called the disciples and they followed. Then, he taught authoritatively in the synagogue as no other had ever taught. Next, he had the effrontery to forgive sins, as only God can do. Now, he controls the elements. Only God controls the wind and the waves, as in the psalms God 'walks on the backs of the waves'. Hence, the astounded, awestruck reaction of the disciples. But, just like me again, they soon forget again and are surprised when Jesus comes to their rescue.

Question: What are the qualities required by a disciple of Christ? Why did Jesus choose such an unappreciative bunch?

Thirteenth Sunday

First reading: Immortality (Wisdom 1.13-15; 2.23-24)

The first reading, as so often, looks towards the gospel reading, where Jesus raises the little girl from death. It takes the opportunity to reflect on death in God's scheme of things. For those who have no faith, death rules everything. It is the absolute end, perhaps a release from suffering, but always a tragedy for somebody, the awesome end point from which there is no return. The Book of Wisdom was written at a time when belief in immortality and the Resurrection was finally emerging in Israel. Earlier Israel had believed that the dead dwelt in a sort of powerless half-life in Sheol (not unlike the Greek Hades), where it is impossible even to pray. Now Israel realized that the love of God for every person was so strong that it could never be broken off by death. As Jesus was to say, God is a God not of the dead but of the living. This reading is wonderfully positive and ebullient, for God is a God of life in all its positive forms, all of which are a reflection of God's own life. The fullest of all these reflections is the life of each human individual, created in the image of God.

Question: How should we envisage or imagine life after death?

Second reading: Generous Giving (2 Corinthians 8.7, 9, 13-15)

Paul's Letter to the Galatians shows that there was a major disagreement in the early Church between those who held that Christians must still obey the Jewish Law and those who did not. The Law party was led by the Church at Jerusalem under James, brother of the Lord. After all, Christianity is the fulfilment of the promises to Abraham, the fulfilment of Judaism! Paul set about healing the breach by making a great collection from his gentile Churches to take to the Church at Jerusalem as an act of homage and friendship. There seem to have been many poor people at Jerusalem, whom the people of such a bustling and successful harbour town as Corinth could help. Paul writes in this Letter giving the basic principle of Christian generosity: the imitation of Christ, who gave himself wholly in love. Yet he also gives the invaluable principle that each individual's conscience is the only yardstick. Not all of us can reach our human fulfilment by living in the destitution of St Francis, and each must judge his giving by his own conscience. Some Christian communities prescribe one tenth of their income in giving. Paul avoids any mathematical formula, for circumstances and obligations differ – as well as generosity.

Question: In some countries, giving to the Church is part of tax. Is this a good idea?

Gospel: Two Cures of Women (Mark 5.21-43)

The author of the Gospel of Mark likes to combine incidents to show their joint significance, often, as here, sandwiching one story between the two halves of another. In this instance, the significance is surely that both recipients of Jesus' healing love are women. Only a minority of Jesus' miracles concern women, and the bringing together of these two, one a girl and the other an old woman, serves to stress their importance to Jesus. It is unfair to accuse the Bible of being male dominated. A mother's devotion is a frequent image of God's love. There are plenty of feisty women in the Old Testament, who put their menfolk to shame by their courage, enterprise and initiative: Rebecca, Tamar, Deborah, Ruth, Esther, Judith. Jesus' own relationships with women seem to have been easy and even humorous. One need only think of his playful bargaining with the Syro-Phoenician over the cure of her daughter, or the jokey exchange between Jesus and the Samaritan woman at the well, not to mention his delicacy towards the woman taken in adultery or the sinful woman who showed her love by weeping at his feet. Paul also clearly relied in many ways in his apostolate on the ministry of women.

Question: What is Jesus' attitude to women? Is the Church fair to women?

Fourteenth Sunday

First reading: The Call of a Prophet (Ezekiel 2.2-5)

This is the story of the call of Ezekiel to be a prophet. There is an obvious parallel between the rejection of Ezekiel as a prophet and the rejection of Jesus by his own people of Nazareth. A prophet is not simply someone who foretells the future. The task of a prophet is to tell people how God sees things, for the prophet sees things as God sees them. This directness of vision is not always popular, for we don't always like being told home truths about ourselves. The truth about ourselves is often unwelcome, particularly when it involves criticism and demands change. Ezekiel was sent to the people of Israel, exiled in Babylon, to encourage them and tell them that, despite their disastrous losses, all was not lost. The hope of Israel was in them, rather than in the remnant left in Jerusalem. They were 'stubborn and obstinate' and refused to listen. We are prepared to listen to criticisms of others merrily enough, and agree heartily. However, the word of God often comes to us in ways that we do not recognize, criticisms of ourselves, perhaps spoken in anger, or only 95 per cent true, but no less a valid criticism for that.

Question: Name a dozen different ministries in the Church. How can you tell to which you are called?

Second reading: Paul's Weakness and Strength (2 Corinthians 12.7-10)

In this final part of the letter Paul, is defending his apostolate against a rival group of preachers whom he caricatures as 'super-apostles'. They claim to have authority greater than his. Paul replies by claiming that he is more fully a servant of the Lord Jesus. Most of his claim is an invaluable autobiographical sketch. He grounds his claim on three factors. First, he outlines the sufferings and persecutions he has undergone in the service of Christ. Just as Jesus sees himself as the Suffering Servant of the Lord prophesied by Isaiah, so by his sufferings Paul sees himself as the servant of the Lord Jesus. Second, Paul speaks of his heavenly vision, the experience or revelation of 'words that may not and cannot be spoken by any human being', obviously the core inspiration of his life. Third, in this passage, he stresses his own weakness, which makes him rely on God's strength. What this weakness was we do not know. Neither is its exact nature significant. The point is that it prevented Paul becoming proud and made him rely on God's strength to counteract it. We probably all need a whacking great fault or failure to curb our pride. I'd be too ashamed to tell you mine.

Question: What is the weakness of which you are most ashamed?

Gospel: Jesus Rejected at Nazareth (Mark 6.1-6)

The very last sentence of the reading speaks of their lack of faith. What was this lack of faith? They recognized in Jesus an extraordinary wisdom and a power of miracles, but this seems not to have been enough. What more was needed? Faith is not the acceptance of a set of propositions, 'I believe that the earth circles the sun', etc. It is putting all my trust in God as my only hope. Abraham, the model of faith, went out into the desert, leaving everything on which he relied, everything that made him what he was. He even trusted God to get him out of the unbearable fix when God told him to sacrifice his only son. The townsfolk of Nazareth presumably thought they knew Jesus through and through. They were prepared to acknowledge his wisdom and his miracles. But they were not prepared to go further and see that God was at work in him, that he was the manifestation of God among them. It is all very well to admire Jesus, to think him a fine teacher and a heroic, honourable man, who gave everything for his high ideals; but unless we see God in him, the divine transcendence of all that is human, he cannot work the miracle of taking us to himself.

Question: Would Jesus have been hurt by their failure to recognize him? How was it that they did not react more favourably?

Fifteenth Sunday

First reading: The Unwilling Messenger (Amos 7.12-15)

Amos had a tricky task on his hands. He was sent unwillingly by God from the neighbouring kingdom of Judah to tell their bitter rivals in Israel to change their ways, to stop exploiting the poor and the weak, to bring sacrifices which were a real expression of homage to God who champions the needy and the powerless. No surprise that he was booted out of the national shrine and told to shove off home and mind his own business. We don't like prophets who try to shake us out of our comfortable ways, pointing out our inadequacies, challenging us to be true to God's plans for us. In vain, Amos insisted that he was not a professional troublemaker, that all he had wanted was a quiet life looking after his flocks and herds and sycamore trees. And then the Lord had insisted on giving him this special task. The exciting thing about being a Christian is that we never know when we will be called by the Lord to do some special task, great or small – even if it is only welcoming the unexpected and tiresome visitor and remembering that he or she is in the place of Christ.

Question: If a prophet came today, what would he (or she) have to say about God's will for our society?

Second reading: The Cosmic Plan of God (Ephesians 1.3-14)

Today we start reading the great letter to the Ephesians, the first of seven Sunday readings. Many scholars think that it was written not by Paul himself, but by a follower steeped in Paul's thought. Gone are the old problems of Jew and gentile. Reflections are on a cosmic scale, and Christ is evaluated in terms of the cosmic powers. The Letter is quite different in style and develops many of Paul's ideas. Perhaps it is the first commentary on Paul.

The sevenfold blessing with which it begins sums up God's plan of salvation for humanity. The climax is in the centre, 'to bring everything under Christ as head'. Christ is the Wisdom of God, the plan according to which and through which all things were created. Christ is also the completion of the creation, and the unity of all things in Christ is a special emphasis of the Letter. All things are under Christ as head creation, all nourishment for creation and all guidance of creation. These are the functions that a head performs for a body, which Christ performs for creation.

Question: What is meant by saying that everything is summed up or brought to a head in Christ?

Gospel: Instructions for Missioners (Mark 6.7-13)

The instructions for missioners are shaped by the urgency of the Kingdom. They are to travel light for speed. They should wear sandals rather than go barefoot, also for speed and security. They are to rely for their provisions on the welcome they receive, and if they are unwelcome, they should not waste time on those who reject them. Did Jesus think that the Kingdom or Kingship of God would finally burst on the world in his own time, that there was so little time to spare? In one way, it did – at his death and Resurrection, which fulfilled God's plan and restored us to friendship with God. In another way, it is still in the future: the reign of peace and justice is not yet established. There is still sorrow, distress, enmity, fraud, jealousy and plenty of other evils that fracture God's Kingship. We are still imperfect reflections of the light of Christ, still pilgrim members of a pilgrim Church. Our efforts are feeble, even in Christ's footsteps. We cannot sit back complacently, any more than the missioners of Jesus' own time, and the task of establishing the Kingdom is still imminent.

Question: How can missioners best bring Christ's light and God's joy to the world?

Sixteenth Sunday

First reading: The Lord will shepherd Israel (Jeremiah 23.1-6)

The choice of this reading looks towards the gospel. It is quite unlike so many passages in Jeremiah, when he was obliged to prophesy doom and disaster for Israel. As well a doom for the current shepherds of the people it foretells a time when the Lord himself will shepherd his people through his own shepherds, a king in the line of David. The promise shimmers between God as himself the shepherd and his representative being the shepherd. The exile in Babylon must still intervene, but it will give way to the reign of 'The-Lord-is-our-Saving-Justice'. This name is roughly equivalent to the Kingdom of God proclaimed by Jesus, for the Kingship of God is a Kingship of God's justice and salvation. God's 'justice' is not like human justice, which consists in observance of and obedience to the law, whether it be the Jewish law or civil law. God's justice consists in fidelity to his promises, the promises made originally to Abraham, and repeated to Moses and David, the repeatedly renewed covenant, the promise of patronage and protection, if only they will put their trust in the Lord. This is what makes it a saving justice, the hope of Israel, fulfilled in Jesus.

Question: In what way is God's 'justice' or 'righteousness' a saving justice?

Second reading: The Unity of Believers (Ephesians 2.13-18)

The Letter to the Ephesians celebrates the unity of the Church, returning again and again to this subject. In this passage, the 'you that used to be so far off' denotes the gentiles, and the 'us' the Jews. The two groups of Christians, sprung from Jews and gentiles, which formerly were so much at loggerheads, are united by the blood of Christ and the single Spirit to form the single new man which is Christ's Body, the Church. This particular division between believers is no longer the prime worry in our problem of disunity, for the scandal of disunity within Christendom becomes more acute as the proportion of Christians in the world population shrinks. However, the uniting of these two groups brings to mind that Christ won salvation for all the world. In some mysterious way, all who are saved are saved by Christ, even if they are not explicitly aware of this. One great theologian called such people 'anonymous Christians'. One wonders whether believers who seek the truth in Buddhism and Islam would be happy to be so described! Is it enough that they should profess Christ's values and be aware of our human inadequacy to save ourselves?

Question: Do you find that the Church is a source of peace? How could this be improved?

Gospel: The Feeding of the Five Thousand (Mark 6.30-44)

This account introduces a series of six Sunday gospels on the Eucharist. As this year's gospel, Mark, is too short to provide readings for the whole year, it is after this account of the Feeding in Mark that the Church moves on to insert five Sundays of John's Bread of Life Discourse. The story can be read on several levels. It is a foretaste of the Eucharist, the disciples gathered round Jesus as the new Israel (12 baskets for the 12 tribes) for a fully satisfying meal, the messianic banquet. Jesus is the good shepherd who feeds his flock, according to Psalm 23, on the green pastures beside the restful waters of the Lake of Galilee. Jesus is the prophet like Moses who provides manna for his people in the desert, or more exactly like Elisha in 2 Kings 4 (next Sunday's first reading). The story is recounted in terms that deliberately recall these and other biblical scenes, concentrating more on the meaning than on the historical facts. There must, of course, have been a wonderful feeding at the base of the story, but it is difficult to re-establish exactly what this was.

Question: Would you say this meal was a Eucharist or not?

Seventeenth Sunday

First reading: Elisha feeds the Crowds (2 Kings 4.42-44)

The prophet Elisha was renowned for the wonders he worked; others are related before and after this incident. Here, he is repeating Moses' miracle of providing bread or manna for his followers. For Christians, however, the greater interest is that the miraculous feeding by Jesus is recounted in terms that deliberately recall this incident: the chance comer who provides barley loaves and more, the prophet's command, the disciple's incredulous question, the repeated command, the feeding and the food left over. The same six steps may be seen in the gospel. So Jesus is repeating the Moses miracle after the pattern of Elisha, only a thousand times as generously: instead of 20 'loaves' (small pitta breads) among 100 men, Jesus shares out five among 5000. What is the point of this modelling of the story? For John, Jesus is a second Moses, standing in the same tradition but greater than Moses, making God known just as Moses had done, bringing to completion all that Moses had begun. 'The Law was given through Moses, grace and truth have come through Jesus Christ.'

Question: If the story is adjusted to show the similarity of the two incidents, is it a true story? In what sense?

Second Reading: The Unity of the Church (Ephesians 4.1-6)

The continuing disunity among Christians makes this passage difficult to read with a clear conscience. It is perhaps the strongest plea for unity in the New Testament, with the possible exception of Jesus' prayer at the Last Supper. Is there really a 'peace that binds you together'? One Lord, one faith, one baptism, one God and Father of all – all this is undeniable. One faith? Perhaps not in the sense of a set or list of beliefs, but all Christians profess the same awareness of inability to save ourselves; we all rely on and put our trust in God's promises, fulfilled in Jesus Christ. In itself, that awareness should be enough to draw us together. What can still justify our disunity? One comfort is that immense strides have been made in a lifetime since the annual Week of Prayer for Christian Unity was established, a heartening desire to understand one another and our still separate traditions. The work of the one Spirit is clear in that the generation that began this search can hardly have hoped for such rapid convergence. Gradually we discover that the traditions in different Church communities express the same funda-mental values in slightly different ways, with slightly different emphases.

Question: What else could you do to foster the unity of Christians?

Gospel: The Feeding of the Five Thousand (John 6.1-15)
Just like Mark's story (last Sunday's gospel), John's version of the miraculous feeding reminds us of the Eucharist, when Jesus 'said the blessing' over the bread. Since this gospel has no account of the institution of the Eucharist at the Last Supper, it is here particularly significant. The feeding is also described as one of the 'signs' that Jesus works. The first part of the Gospel of John is often called 'the Book of Signs' because Jesus works a number of signs which show his true quality. First comes the sign at the marriage feast of Cana, where his sign of turning the water into wine is a sign of the messianic banquet. Other signs are the raising of the royal official's son, a sign of Jesus' gift of life, and the cure of the blind man in the Temple, as sign of Jesus' gift of light and revelation. Several of the signs are followed by an extended discourse, explaining the meaning of the sign, as this is followed by the discourse on the Bread of Life, explaining the significance of Jesus' gift of himself as the Bread of Life, the Wisdom of God received in the Eucharist.

Question: If you were going to have supper with Jesus, how would you prepare?

Eighteenth Sunday

First reading: Manna from Heaven (Exodus 16.2-4, 12-15, 31)

The journey of the people of Israel through the desert of Sinai is regarded in the Bible from two quite different angles. From one angle, it is the time of perfect harmony between God and his people, the honeymoon period when Israel was sublimely faithful to the Lord. From the other angle, it is seen as the beginning of murmuring against the Lord, which will grow into the infidelities that eventually led to Israel's punishment by the Exile to Babylon. This account of bread from heaven shows both Israel's impatience with the Lord and the Lord's supreme patience with Israel. The historical basis is that God cared for his people and provided them with food during a generation's wandering in the savagely inhospitable desert of Sinai, a huge, infertile expanse of rock and sand, where virtually nothing grows. This care is focused on manna, a sweet substance excreted from bushes on Sinai in a way Israel found miraculous. The story has grown in the telling: it is linked to keeping the Sabbath, for it could not be harvested on the Sabbath. Second, with typical Hebrew word play, this odd substance is linked to the Hebrew expression *manhu*, meaning 'What is it?'

Question: Is Israel's pattern of rebellion repeated in the Church?

Second reading: A New Creation in Christ (Ephesians 4.17, 20-24)

In his great classic letter to the Romans, Paul teaches that by being baptized into Christ's death, we have been joined with Christ in his Resurrection and become a new being, fused with Christ or grafted into Christ. He sees us as living with Christ's life principle, the Spirit, rather than our old corrupt life principle. In First Corinthians, he enlarges on the ways of life that this brings, the varied gifts of the Spirit that together make up the Christian body, the Body of Christ. Now, in Ephesians, we see a consequence of this. The Christian body is repeatedly described as a New Man, a new creation, after the model of the Second Adam. What does all this talk of 'new creation' amount to in real terms? First, it poses the question whether we have really been renewed. Are my values and attitudes radically new as a Christian? Do they differ from the priorities that I would have without Christianity? Particularly with regard to the Body of Christ and its ministries, do I play my part in the web of Christian activities that go to make up the Christian community? Do I really exercise my talents in a way that builds up the community?

Question: What priorities in fact need a Christian have which clash with those generally held?

Gospel: The Bread of Life (John 6.24-35)
After the account of the miraculous feeding of the 5000, Jesus explains the significance of the event. First, he stresses that its importance lies not in the food that goes bad, but in that of which it is a sign. They must understand the sign value of the food, its ultimate fulfilment in Jesus of the manna in the desert: we live not by bread alone but by every word that comes from the mouth of God. The whole explanation is built on a contrast between Moses and Jesus, between the food given by Moses and that given by Jesus. Jesus is the bread of life not only as the Eucharistic bread, but first of all as revelation. We often concentrate exclusively on the Eucharistic meaning of this chapter. It is, however, belief and understanding that is first explained and first required, and only then is attention turned to eating the Eucharistic bread. The explanation is situated with Jesus in the synagogue at Capernaum, and – after the manner of Jewish sermons of the time – each phrase of the scriptural quotation from the Book of Exodus is commented in turn: *Bread from heaven/he gave them/to eat.*

Question: If this incident is a sign, of what is it a sign?

Nineteenth Sunday

First reading: Elijah's Breakfast (1 Kings 19.4-8)

The wicked Queen Jezebel had slaughtered all the prophets of the Lord except Elijah. Elijah had then mounted a competition with the prophets of Baal, challenging them to bring fire down from heaven to consume the bull they were sacrificing to Baal. Despite Elijah's taunts, they had failed miserably, leaving the field to an easy victory by Elijah, whose God produced a flawless display of pyrotechnics, climaxing in a splendid holocaust. Nevertheless, Elijah still felt threatened, fled and announced that he had had enough of life, whereupon he fell asleep in a sulk. God's reaction to this petulant behaviour is touching. First, he wakes Elijah up to an excellent breakfast, then he provides a sufficiently substantial lunch to fortify Elijah for a 40-day trek through the Sinai desert. Typical of God's forgiveness and indulgence! His chosen ones complain to him roundly, and he treats them pretty roughly at times. Look at the relationship between Jeremiah or Job and God! Teresa of Avila put it like this: 'If you treat your friends like that, no wonder you have so few of them.' At least it shows that we are expected to treat God with intimacy and frankness, voicing our complaints to our Father.

Question: What have you to complain about to God?

Second reading: The Seal of the Spirit (Ephesians 4.30–5.2)

In the early Church, confirmation was known as the sealing in the Spirit, a rather beautiful image, which stems from this passage. In the ancient world, long before general literacy, everyone had a personal seal to mark documents or possessions. We are the soft wax, which by confirmation are permanently set as belonging personally to the Spirit of God, so we are his. It is one unfortunate consequence of the gendered nature of the English language that we have to call the Spirit 'he'. The Greek for 'Spirit' is neuter gendered, but we can hardly call a Person of the Trinity 'it'. The Hebrew for both 'Spirit' and 'Wisdom' is feminine. If the Latin for 'Spirit' had not been uncompromisingly masculine, perhaps the tradition of the western Church might have opted for the feminine and addressed the Spirit as 'she'. Could we have a feminine Person of the Trinity? God is certainly described as having some feminine traits, such as a maternal affection, outdoing even a mother's love for her baby. The Spirit is ever alert to our needs, supporting us before we realize our need of support, wise in guidance, unlimited in generosity, tireless in forgiveness. Being sealed by the spirit commits us to the same sort of consideration for others.

Question: Is the Church unduly male dominated, or do women now have a fair place?

Gospel: Belief as Eternal Life (John 6.41-51)

We always think of this Bread of Life Discourse as centred on the Eucharist, but the first part of it – just like the Liturgy of the Word in the first part of the Mass – is centred on the bread of life, which is the revelation of God. The ruling quotation for this kind of Jewish sermon is, as we saw last week, from the Psalm, 'Bread from heaven he gave them to eat.' Then half-way through comes a quotation from the prophets, a sort of half-time booster quote. This quotation from Isaiah comes in today's reading, 'They will all be taught by God.' Its context is the personal relationship of each believer to the Lord. The Lord will sow in our hearts individually the knowledge of himself, so that each of us has a personal, secret link, to be cultivated by prayer. If we listen to the Father and learn from him, we come to Jesus, who has seen the Father. So in this reading the emphasis is on listening, seeing, believing the revelation of the Father. This is no abstract set of truths but a personal knowing, just as we know those we love on earth. Only at the end do we move on to the final topic of eating the Bread of Life.

Question: How do we hear the Word of God in the Church today?

Twentieth Sunday

First reading: The Invitation of Wisdom (Proverbs 9.1-6)

In the Old Testament, divine Wisdom is often represented as a woman (the word 'wisdom' is feminine in both Greek and Hebrew), inviting to her banquet all who are willing to come. The only qualification is to be simple and open to learning, those whom Jesus in the gospel will call 'meek and humble of heart'. Especially after the Exile in Babylon, the Israelites realized that they could not rely on their own strength and wisdom, but must turn to God in humility and confidence. Such lowliness is a feature of the post-exilic prophets and their spirituality. It is seen to be exemplified also in the Infancy Narratives of the gospels, especially in Luke, where all the characters are poor and destitute, powerless to help themselves, and relying on the Lord's favour: the parents of John the Baptist and of Jesus, the shepherds, ancient Simeon and Anna. This invitation prepares for the imagery of the messianic banquet, and in the gospels especially the meals where Jesus is seen feasting and relaxing with his often disreputable and disadvantaged friends. It prepares also for Jesus' invitations to the banquet of the Eucharist, where we are those helpless and disreputable friends!

Question: How can we acquire this divine Wisdom?

Second reading: Songs of the Spirit (Ephesians 5.15-20)

Singing is a natural expression of joy and united harmony that has always occurred in Christianity from the very beginning, to express the joy and gratitude of Christians in the Lord. It seems that this instruction in the Letter to the Ephesians only continues and encourages the tradition. Already in Paul's letters, there are buried a number of hymns, unlikely to have been written by him, but more probably heard and picked up by him from the different communities. They are in a style far more rhythmical and balanced than his own excited and argumentative writing. Special examples are the hymns to Christ in Philippians 2.6-11 and Colossians 1.15-20, but the letters to Timothy and Titus have several examples of snatches of hymns. There is also a snatch of a hymn immediately before this reading from Ephesians. The earliest outside witness to the Christian liturgy, a letter from the provincial governor Pliny to the Roman Emperor, also describes the Christians meeting on a set day (presumably Sunday) to sing hymns 'to Christ as to a God' before having what he describes as a perfectly ordinary a meal together (presumably the Eucharist). So the singing of hymns has a venerable tradition in Christianity.

Question: What is your favourite hymn, and why?

Gospel: Eating the Bread of Life (John 6.51-58)

This is the last of the readings from the Bread of Life discourse. It moves on from seeing Christ as the Wisdom of God, who must be accepted and believed, to the sacrament of eating the bread of life. These correspond to the two halves of the Mass, first the service of the Word, then the Eucharistic banquet. We are all so diet conscious nowadays that it is quite obvious that the food we eat affects us. By eating Christ, we are assimilated into him. But, just as, if I am sick, food does me no good and can even harm me, so if I eat Christ sacramentally without wanting to be moulded into him, it does me no good at all. That is why Paul complained that the Corinthians were answerable for the death of Christ. And drinking the blood of Christ? Blood is the sign of life – if there is no blood, there is no life – and God is the Lord of life and death. So if I receive Christ's blood, I take on his life, his divine life, as the gift of God. That has alarming side-effects: it means

I share Christ's life with other Christians. We all live with the same life's blood. Do I really share my life, my talents, my goods with others, knowing that I share the same bloodstream?

Question: How do you hope to grow by receiving the Eucharist?

Twenty-first Sunday

First reading: Renewal of the Covenant at Shechem (Joshua 24.1-2, 15-18)

This final chapter of the Book of Joshua shows Israel settled into the 'land flowing with milk and honey', having concluded the great trek of the Exodus. At Shechem they held a great assembly of all the tribes, and renewed the covenant, with promises of loyalty to the Lord. The renewal of the covenant was necessary because in the course of their desert wandering a number of various tribes had joined Moses' original group of escaped slaves, and not all of them had been present at the original covenant. This scene at Shechem is put in parallel to today's gospel reading because Joshua challenged them to make up their minds whether or not they intended to remain loyal to the Lord, in the same way as Jesus challenges the disciples at the end of the Bread of Life discourse. The similarity is not only a challenge to loyalty, but specifically to covenant loyalty, since the Eucharistic context of the discourse puts the failure of some of the disciples and the acceptance by Peter and the others into the context of refusing or accepting the New Covenant made by Jesus at the Last Supper.

Question: What is the connection between the Covenant and our Eucharist?

Second reading: The Mystery of Christ's Love (Ephesians 4.32–5.1-2, 21-32)

This final reading from Ephesians is rightly a favourite reading for weddings. The first sentence, of course, is vital to avoid the impression of male chauvinism: wives should be subject to their husbands, but also husbands to their wives! The really enriching teaching, however, is that the devotion and self-sacrifice of husband for wife is seen as a parable for the love of Christ for his spouse, the Church. The love and devotion of spouses for one another – and it works both ways – gains greater dignity from this Christological truth. It is designated as a 'mystery', which in Pauline language does not mean 'something I can't understand'. It means the great profound truths about God that are to be finally revealed in these, the last times. In this case, the 'mystery' is the depths and intensity of Christ's love for his Church, of which the love of spouses for one another is only an echo. The bonding and binding love and self-sacrifice of spouses echoes and reveals Christ's love for the Church. From this comparison, we gain understanding and awe for both members of the comparison. It also nicely sums up the repeated message of Ephesians about unity in the Church.

Question: What can we learn from married love about Christ's love for the Church?

Gospel: Lord, to Whom shall We Go? (John 6.53, 60-69)
This parting of the ways at the end of the Bread of Life discourse is not primarily about belief in the Eucharist. It is the starting point, but the lesson is wider. The Gospel of John is like a series of great forks in the road, one after another leading off the true path. A series of decisions is called for, whether to follow Jesus or not. Or it is like a series of court scenes, except that people are not judged; they judge themselves by their reaction to Jesus: at the marriage feast at Cana, the disciples believe, then in the Temple 'the Jews' reject. Nicodemus sits on the fence. The Samaritan Woman moves from cheeky scepticism to fervent apostleship. The great scenes in Jerusalem (the man at the Pool of Bethzatha, the blind man in the Temple) ironically show the Jews rejecting Jesus in such a way that they drive others to accept him. Finally, before Pilate, 'the Jews' think they are condemning Jesus when, in fact, they condemn themselves by, 'We have no king but Caesar.' What about the Lord as King of Israel? Day by day the challenge is aimed at ourselves too: do we believe or betray?

Question: In what does the choice for or against Jesus consist?

Twenty-second Sunday

First reading: The Gift of the Law (Deuteronomy 4.1-2, 6-8)

What was special about the Law laid down for Israel? Many of the laws are known also from law codes of neighbouring peoples, written on stone or clay tablets and recently discovered; some are more primitive, some more sophisticated. Running through them all, however, are two threads. First, if you want to be the People of God, this is the way you must live, to be like him and keep company with him and be his very own. So the Law was a testimony of love, and obedience to it is an expression of grateful love: 'Be holy as I am holy.' A second thread is respect for human dignity, and especially that of the poor and needy. In other law codes, nobles have more honour and privilege than commoners, free men and women than slaves. In Israel, all have equal respect, and every faithful Israelite must remember that God's protecting hand hovers over those who are in any misfortune: created in the image of God, you must treat the widow, the orphan and the immigrant as I treated you when you were strangers in Egypt. All this was enshrined in the written Law, interpreted by the oral traditions of the elders – not always so successfully, as we see in the gospel.

Question: What have love and holiness in common?

Second reading: Putting the Word into Action (James 1.17-18, 21-22, 27)

For the next few weeks we will be reading the Letter of James, the longest of the seven so-called 'catholic' epistles, written not to any particular person or community but to the Church universal, throughout the world (which is what 'catholic' means). The real author is unknown, but it purports to come from James, the first leader of the Jerusalem community after Peter's departure. As we know from Paul's letter to the Galatians, James continued to value the Jewish way of life and observance of the Law, even while following Jesus. The Letter accordingly contains many practical lessons about fulfilling the Law of Christ, stressing especially – as at the end of this reading – the need to care for the poor and the weak. It is full of striking, pithy images, like that of looking in the mirror and then going off and forgetting what one saw (verses omitted in the middle of this reading). The author applies this to care of the poor: it is no good glancing at the Law and then claiming to be religious while neglecting those in need. Religion consists not in 'piety' but in putting one's beliefs into action.

Question: Do you prefer to live by law, where everything is cut and dried, or by the challenge of the Beatitudes?

Gospel: Clean and Unclean (Mark 7.1-8, 14-15, 21-23)
Legal observance has its dangers, for it is sometimes easy to obey the law exactly while forgetting its purpose. It is no good driving doggedly just below the speed limit while endangering life and limb. The more exact the laws, the greater the temptation to manipulate them to evade their purpose. The Pharisees were as aware of this danger of distortion as is the modern stickler for exact observance. But the Pharisees have a bad press in the gospels because, at the time the gospels were written, hostility between Christians and Pharisaic Judaism was at its height. During Jesus'

own lifetime their opposition was not so obvious. For instance, they had no share in the Passion and Crucifixion of Jesus. In any case, Jesus' own final saying here, while it may apply to the Jewish ritual law, has much wider application than the observance of Jewish rules for clean food. It is more akin to the saying in Matthew: 'A sound tree cannot bear bad fruit, nor a rotten tree bear good fruit. By their fruits you shall know them.' A person's true qualities are seen by that person's actions; their true intentions and character, what comes from the heart, becomes visible in their words and actions.

Question: Is there any danger in Christianity of a 'dead' obedience to law?

Twenty-third Sunday

First reading: The Day of the Lord (Isaiah 35.4-7)

While Israel was still in being, the Day of the Lord was a threat, a day of expected punishment. Once the axe of the Babylonian exile had fallen, and disaster had come upon the whole of Israel and Judah, the Day of the Lord becomes a promise of salvation. Hence this lovely, joyful poem, looking forward to the coming of the Lord to heal Israel and take vengeance on her tormentors. It looks forward to the coming of the Lord himself, not of his representative. We call it 'messianic', as if it concerned the coming of the Lord's anointed. But in the expectation of the deliverance of Israel, even up to the time of Jesus, it was not clear whether God would visit the earth personally (whatever that would mean) to effect the total reversal of all things and the healing of all misery, or whether his messenger and herald would come first. In the late prophecies of Malachi, not long before the Incarnation, the prophet Elijah will come as the Lord's herald, to prepare the way. So was John the Baptist this Elijah figure, preparing for Jesus? Or is Jesus preparing for the Lord? Or is the coming of Jesus the coming of the Lord?

Question: What would the coming of God's rule or Kingship mean in real terms?

Second reading: Shabby or Chic? (James 2.1-5)

The Letter of James has been described as 'a manifesto for social justice', and among all its pieces of advice this is certainly a strong emphasis. Concern for the poor and the less fortunate runs right through the Bible. Human beings were created in the image of God, and this is one of the ways in which this image must be expressed. So Israel is constantly told: 'You must treat the stranger among you as I treated you when you were strangers in Egypt.' Similarly, widows and orphans are the special object of God's care. In the beatitudes of Luke's gospel, the poor, the hungry and those who weep are assured of God's blessing. In more modern times the great Papal Encyclicals on social issues gave the first official teaching anywhere on the rights of exploited classes after the Industrial Revolution, the right to a just wage, to healthcare, to form trade unions, and so on. However, it is always instinctive and natural – as this witty and poignant reading shows – to give more honour to the lord mayor at the front than to the tramp who shuffles in at the back of the Church, forgetting that in God's eyes they have just the same value.

Question: Are Christians sufficiently aware of the social demands of the gospel?

Gospel: Jesus cures a Deaf Man (Mark 7.31-37)

We have been prepared to see the true meaning of this incident by the first reading, for in his wonderful cures Jesus is fulfilling the prophecy of Isaiah. Jesus' activity as he goes around 'doing all things well' is the coming of God into the world, the Day of the Lord when the tongues of the dumb will sing for joy. Jesus is the sacrament of God. In him, God is active in the world, bringing peace, healing and joy. In him, people met and experienced God. His gestures of putting his fingers into the man's ears and touching his tongue with spittle are affectionate ways of showing that God is physically at work in him. In a modern hygiene-conscious world such gestures might be frowned upon. But if we are truly acting as the members of Christ's body in the world we cannot hold back, and from time to time will be involved physically and totally in helping others. One such courageous gesture was Princess Diana's handshake with an AIDS sufferer when it was still believed that the condition was physically contagious. We too can bring Christ's healing in countless simple, but often costly and courageous, ways.

Question: Is there any connection between sin and sickness?

Twenty-fourth Sunday

First reading: The Servant of the Lord (Isaiah 50.5-9)

As we shall see, the gospel reading is a turning point; it concentrates on two matters, of which this reading from Isaiah relates to the second. This part of the prophecy of Isaiah contains four interrelated poems of a Servant of the Lord, who willingly undergoes suffering and humiliation for his ministry to the Lord. Jesus' own sayings on service and suffering show that he was aware of these songs, and that he saw himself as this Servant of the Lord: 'The Son of Man came not to be served but to serve.' Many details in the story of the Passion correspond to the songs, in today's reading the flogging, the mockery and the insult, and also Jesus' voluntary failure to resist or to defend himself: at each trial he amazes the 'judge' by his silence. At the same time these songs are marked by a confidence in the Lord: whatever happens, the Lord will not desert his faithful Servant. Especially in the fourth song, the suffering and humiliation of the Servant lead to his eventual vindication and the triumph of God.

Question: How is this reading echoed in the story of Jesus' Passion?

Second reading: Faith and Works (James 2.14-18)

The interconnection between faith and good works has been a puzzle from the beginning of Christianity – and before. At some times people seem to have believed that it was possible to earn salvation. However, you cannot bargain or negotiate with God. As the psalms say: 'No one can buy their own ransom.' All we can do is hang on by our fingertips to God's promises, put our trust in God's limitless forgiveness. Faith is not a matter of believing first one doctrine and then another. Primarily, it is a matter of where my trust and confidence is lodged. What, then, is the point of good works? If our faith in God's generosity and forgiveness does not lead us to act with similar generosity and forgiveness, it is a strange slap in the face for God, the demonstration of a strange conception of God! We are made in the image of God, so that, if we recognize this, we will attempt to carry on God's work with at least an echo of the divine generosity and forgiveness. When James says that otherwise our faith is dead, he really means that it is a withered faith that is not faith at all.

Question: Is a faith that does not show itself in behaviour a real possibility?

Gospel: Peter's Declaration of Faith and Jesus' Reply (Mark 8.27-35)

This is the turning point of Mark's gospel. Up until now the stories we have heard have all shown ever increasing wonder and amazement at Jesus' personality, his goodness and his authority. But even his closest disciples do not seem to have seen what this implies. Then suddenly Peter comes to the realization that Jesus is the Messiah, the Anointed of God, for whom everyone was waiting. However, Peter still does not understand what this implies. Jesus is not a conquering political hero, who will simply wipe out all opposition by overwhelming force, and make every path smooth and gentle. Jesus begins to show his disciples that the road to fulfilment is through suffering. Three times Jesus repeats this prophecy, and three times the disciples fail to grasp the lesson: first Peter, then the disciples who are arguing about precedence, then the two sons of Zebedee, who want the best places for themselves. So three times Jesus repeats that if you want to follow Jesus you must follow him to the cross. Neither are we, later followers of Jesus, any quicker that the first disciples to learn this lesson. We greet with indignation and resistance any suffering that comes our way.

Question: Why does Jesus rebuke Peter so fiercely?

Twenty-fifth Sunday

First reading: The Good Man Taunted (Wisdom 2.12, 17-20)

This is the first reading this year to be taken from the Book of Wisdom. This book was written probably at Alexandria, and was written in Greek, so is not included in the Protestant canon of scripture, which includes only the books written in Hebrew. A major theme of the book is the contrast between divine Wisdom and folly. It also includes a wonderful poem on God's Wisdom, by which he created the world, 'the reflection of the eternal light, and the image of his goodness'. In this reading, we have the taunts that those who refuse divine Wisdom make against those who embrace Wisdom. It is remarkable that, in Matthew's gospel, the taunts of the chief priests, scribes and elders against Jesus as he hangs on the cross use these very words. This use of scripture is typical of Matthew's irony, and shows just how wrong they were. The reading therefore both prepares us for the prophecy of the Passion in the first part of the gospel reading and contrasts these boasts with the wisdom of simplicity represented by the child in the second part.

Question: Is there such a thing as specifically Christian Wisdom?

Second reading: Peace and Prayer (James 3.16–4.3)

The reading from the Letter of James first contrasts quarrelling and ambition, and their evil effects, with the true wisdom which brings peace. Then it goes on to some stern words about prayer that is not heard, 'because you have prayed for something to indulge your own desires'. Is it wrong, then, to ask God for what we want? What about 'Ask and you shall receive, seek and you shall find'? The problem of unanswered prayers of petition is a difficult one. We do not really believe that we can change God's mind and intentions by praying. Nevertheless, we express to God our needs and desires, although we are well aware that he knows them already. This is what a child does to a loving father, 'Please, please!' We even link arms with our mother, Mary, or even our brother and Saviour, Jesus, to increase the persuasive power. But every prayer of petition, just as a child's prayer to a loving father, contains the hidden text that our Father knows best. The child or the praying Christian can want something desperately, but for true prayer must submit in obedience, sometime puzzled obedience, to the Father. Only so is the prayer an expression of trust and affection.

Question: What is the point of petitionary prayer?

Gospel: The Second Prophecy of the Passion (Mark 9.30-37)
Mark gives us three formal prophecies of the Passion, of which this is the second. He uses the triple number frequently to stress the importance and sureness of an event. So Peter denies Jesus three times, and Pilate three times asserts Jesus' innocence. Jesus is shown to be fully aware of the fate that awaits him: he goes into it with his eyes open, and accepts his Father's will, especially in the awareness that his Father will not desert him, but will vindicate him by the Resurrection.

Again the disciples fail to understand the message: while Jesus had been giving them the message of triumph only through suffering and humiliation, they had been thinking about who would be first. So Jesus sets before them a child as the model. In what way is a child a model? Children are notably and innocently selfish. Neither are they straightforward, for they can be devious and scheming from an early age. Is it that they know they cannot control a situation, and trustingly accept what they are given? The final saying suggests that it is this quality of dependence that Jesus proposes: the child is dependent on the will of the Father.

Question: Why does Jesus put forward a child as a role model for us?

Twenty-sixth Sunday

First reading: Openness to the Spirit (Numbers 11.25-29)

This is a curious little scene, and the corresponding scene in the gospel is no less curious. It is part of the story of Israel's wanderings in the desert. Moses' father-in-law wisely suggests to Moses to appoint assistants to deal with all the complaints, quarrels and lawsuits among the people. So some of the divine spirit of judgment which was on Moses descends upon these 70 elders. However, there seems to have been some sort of irregularity in the appointment of Eldad and Medad, which leads to objections even by Joshua, Moses' faithful servant and successor. Nevertheless, the message finally given is that the Spirit of God is to be welcomed wherever it may be found. It is a valuable reminder that the Spirit of God is greater than human regulations and crosses human boundaries. The wisdom of God may be found beyond the organization of the Church. Genuine holiness may be found also beyond the limits of the Church. We must respect the freedom of God to give what he wills where he wills it, and we must be prepared to learn from those who do not belong to our own tradition.

Question: Is holiness to be found beyond the limits of the Church?

Second reading: The Dangers of Wealth (James 5.1-6)

This final reading from the Letter of James is a denunciation of the selfishness of the rich in the style of the Old Testament prophets, with a wealth of daunting imagery. This strength of expression is somewhat surprising in the early decades of Christianity, for it seems that wealth was not one of the temptations to deflect the early Christians. There do seem to have been rich Christians in the community at Corinth, but, on the whole, the Christians seem to have belonged to the lower classes and slaves. James, the presumed author of the Letter, was the leader of the Jerusalem community. The Church at Jerusalem seems to have been in chronic financial difficulty: Paul was asked to help it out, and took a collection from the gentile Churches up to Jerusalem. In the early second century the pagan Celsus denounces Christians as ignorant and ill educated. However, these warnings are still relevant today. It is still tempting to ease cash flow by postponing payment of bills! The power and immunity given by wealth can still have a corrosive influence that blinds the owners to the needs and susceptibilities of others.

Question: Is wealth necessarily a distraction from our true goals?

Gospel: Helps and Hindrances (Mark 9.38-43, 45, 47-48)

The gospel gives us a rich insight into two entirely separate matters, for this part of Mark is a collection of sayings about discipleship. The first little story tells us that we must accept good wherever we can find it, not only in our own group and where we expect it to be. It is the same lesson that came in the first reading. The Spirit of God is at work not only in Catholics, not only in Christians, not only even in explicit believers. As Vatican II teaches so strongly, the Holy Spirit is at work even in those who are seeking the

Kingdom under signs and symbols. They can be better people and better Christians than those who sit back and do nothing, secure in the belief that they are members of the Church!

Second, the gospel gives some dire sayings about 'scandals'. The word so translated means not stories about evil people or evil doings, but a trip stone which makes people fall over. The dire sayings are about leading other believers into evil and about the trip stones in ourselves, the disordered desires, that lead us into evil. Jesus' sayings here must be taken with the utmost seriousness, but perhaps not literally to the extent of self-mutilation.

Question: Name a really good person whom you admire who is not a Catholic or even a Christian.

Twenty-seventh Sunday

First reading: God gives Man a Partner (Genesis 2.7, 15, 18-24)

The whole of these stories at the beginning of Genesis are intended to explain how God designed things to be. They are, of course, not meant to be historical, but their teaching is of the highest importance, as showing how things were meant to be. By giving the animals their names, the man is taking part in their creation. Made in the image of God, the man's task is to promote God's work and foster creation and foster life, just as God himself does. The creation of human beings is the climax of creation, which means that human beings have a responsibility towards the rest of creation. The warm ideal relationship between God and the man before the Fall is particularly touching. God's care for the man, putting him to sleep before the surgical operation and sewing up the wound himself is delightful. So is God's careful moulding of the woman and the presentation of his handiwork to the man. It is important to see that there is no unevenness between the sexes, each is personally moulded by God. Their welcome for one another is the author's pictorial way of showing that the bonding between them in marriage is a divine institution.

Question: Is the equality of the sexes sufficiently valued in Christianity?

Second reading: The Leader to Salvation (Hebrews 2.9-11)

The Letter to the Hebrews is going to be read for the next seven Sundays, right up until Advent. Its author is completely unknown, but it was clearly written for Hebrew priests, who had become Christians and were missing the traditional rites of their people. It assumes knowledge of the Jewish ritual, and with many allusions to scripture, it circles round two themes. First, it shows that the Jewish sacrificial rituals were a pale shadow, of which the reality and fulfilment comes in the perfect sacrifice of Jesus. Second, it points out that the People of God are still on pilgrimage. God's promise that they would reach a place of rest was not fulfilled by their arrival in the Holy Land; it will be fulfilled only in heaven. In today's reading, we glimpse part of the first theme. Jesus humbled himself to become man, only a little less than the angels (the author is alluding to Psalm 8), in order to become perfect through his suffering. He had to become fully human, so that by being made perfect he might lead all his brothers (and sisters) to the same perfection.

Question: How did Jesus learn by suffering? How do we?

Gospel: Two become One Flesh (Mark 10.2-16)

The Pharisees are putting a trick question to Jesus, as is clear in Matthew's fuller account. They knew the Law, which permitted divorce, and they will quote this Law to Jesus. The Law allowed divorce for 'indecency', but teachers were divided about what this meant: did it mean adultery or a lesser fault? So their real question is what Jesus considers grounds for divorce. As so frequently in his discussions with the legal experts, Jesus goes beyond the question: God made man and woman such that they should bond together permanently and become one thinking, living being. The word used for one 'body', or one 'flesh', really means one entity, not a hunk of meat, but a single, vibrant personality. God's intention was not that they should be separable again. So Jesus does not answer the question about grounds for divorce at all. It is striking that here – and on other occasions – Jesus' authority is such that he feels able to alter the sacred Law of Moses. For the Jews the Law of Moses was God's own gift, sacred and unalterable by any human authority. By altering it, by annulling the permission for divorce under certain circumstances, Jesus is implicitly claiming divine authority.

Question: Why has divorce become so frequent? Is there anything Christians can do?

Twenty-eighth Sunday

First reading: The Riches of Wisdom (Wisdom 7.7-11)

Unusually, the first reading seems to pair both with the second reading and with the gospel. It pairs with the second reading because divine Wisdom and the Word of God are similar: each is the way in which God makes himself known to us. It pairs with the gospel reading because the author of the Book of Wisdom esteems riches as nothing and prefers Wisdom, just as the rich man in the gospel is encouraged by Jesus to prefer the following of Christ to his riches.

The Book of Wisdom was written a bare half-century before the birth of Christ, at a time when all hope of a personal Messiah in the line of David seemed remote. The only way in which God might enter into this world seemed to be by his Wisdom. This chapter goes on to show how God created the world and continues to rule it by his Wisdom. Divine Wisdom is described as the 'mirror of God's active power and image of his goodness', language seeking to describe how Wisdom is in God and yet is not exactly identical with the Creator. This language will be used also by Paul and John to describe the incarnation of the Word of God.

Question: What does it mean to say that Divine Wisdom became incarnate in Jesus? How does it enlarge the way we think about God?

Second reading: The Word of God (Hebrews 4.12-13)

The Word of God can here be understood on two levels. The Word of God that is the scripture penetrates to the human soul. That is why we need to read the scriptures to come to know the ways of God. By this prayerful reading, we can come to understand the world and even ourselves as God sees them, gradually growing in understanding of his will for us, how I personally can be penetrated by the Spirit of God and grow closer to the Lord. The author of the Letter is inviting readers to reflect on the psalm that speaks of the 'place of rest' for the People of God, and to understand that their arrival in Canaan after the wanderings in the desert was not the final 'place of rest' designed for them by God; they are still on pilgrimage. The Word of God can also be understood as the Word which became flesh, as in the Prologue to John's Gospel. Jesus is the Word of God become flesh, the image of his goodness, by which we can come to know God. The two senses are combined in the glorious vision, at the beginning of the Book of Revelation, of the Risen Christ, the Lord of the Church, from whose mouth issues a two-edged sword, by which he judges the world.

Question: Beneath its imagery, what does this reading mean by saying that the Word of God is sharper than a sword? How does it 'penetrate' us?

Gospel: The Rich Man's Question (Mark 10.17-30)

This exchange between Jesus and the rich man is often read with Matthew's parallel in mind, where Jesus tells the *young* man to sell his possessions 'if you would be perfect'. There are no such two levels in Mark's story. The questioner has a certain age, for he has kept the commandments 'from my earliest days'. He is in the full flush of wealth, and getting rid of his riches is not a mere counsel of perfection. Jesus is stressing the danger of possessions for everyone. It is a curious fact that for many people, the more they have, the more they want. Conversely, the less people have, the more generous they are, knowing the value to other needy people of the little they have. It is not merely that we need to be free of the preoccupations and distractions of wealth. Wealth can be a good preoccupation if the worry comes from awareness of the responsibility it brings. Repeatedly, however, in the history of the Church, from St Anthony of the Desert, St Francis of Assisi and others, people have interpreted these words heroically and stripped themselves of all possessions to concentrate on the Kingdom of God. God's blessing is especially on the poor.

Question: Is money a blessing, a distraction, a worry or an opportunity?

Twenty-ninth Sunday

First reading: The Suffering Servant of the Lord (Isaiah 53.10-11)

The whole of the Fourth Song of the Suffering Servant is read at the liturgy of Good Friday. Today we have only a part, but enough to show that the Servant's suffering somehow fulfils God's purposes, brings glory to the Servant and salvation to others. We do not know who the servant originally envisaged by the author was, perhaps the prophet himself, perhaps the people of Israel, suffering in exile in Babylon. But the Word of God also has a fuller meaning. We know from Jesus' own sayings that he saw himself as the complete fulfilment of these poems: 'The Son of man came not to be served but to serve and give his life as a ransom for many.' He saw his life as one of service and of perfect obedience to the Lord, his Father. He saw his task to be the establishment of the Kingship of God on earth, which would bring salvation to all, and that the opposition to this Kingship would bring him suffering and eventually death. This selfless obedience of Jesus would undo the stubborn disobedience of all humanity, featured in the sin of Adam. It would bring to completion the Lord's designs for the world and for all creation.

Question: Whom did the prophet mean by the Suffering Servant?

Second reading: The Supreme High Priest (Hebrews 4.14-16)

The Letter to the Hebrews contrasts the supreme High Priest with the transient high priests of Judaism. In order to bring humanity to perfection, Jesus had to share completely in our humanity. He was 'tempted in every way that we are', sexual temptations, temptations to anger, to intolerance, to cut people down to size. He was 'capable of feeling our weaknesses', fear, frustration, laziness, boredom. In the gospels, few of these are mentioned: his exhaustion at the well in Samaria, his grief at the death of his friend Lazarus. But, as he had a very human personality, he must have suffered the fears and incomprehension of childhood, the frustrations of adolescence, as well as the more complex troubles and sorrows of adulthood, not to mention the unremitting opposition of those who rejected him – all under the overarching passion for his Father and his Kingship. All this would have enriched his personality still further, until he offered the whole of his humanity in obedience to his Father's designs. Just as martyrdom is the crown of a life of Christian fidelity, so Jesus' final sacrifice was the crown of a life of love, obedience and generosity.

Question: Do you know anyone who has been enriched or made a deeper personality by suffering?

Gospel: A Life of Service (Mark 10.35-45)
Three times in Mark's gospel Jesus formally tells his disciples about his coming Passion, and each time they seem entirely deaf to it. So each time Jesus counters their misunderstanding by repeating the need of a disciple to follow him in suffering. Today's reading begins just after the third prophecy, and – true to form – the sons of Zebedee reply with a request for the best seats at the banquet of the Kingdom! Matthew spares the two disciples by putting the request in their poor mother's mouth. Only in a second exchange with Jesus do they woodenly accept to share Jesus' 'cup' and 'baptism'. Do they really know what they are accepting, or do they just blithely agree? The indignation of the other disciples prompts Jesus to his clearest statement in words that authority in the Church is a service. His clearest statement in action is the smelly business of washing their travel-gnarled feet at his last meal with them. The lesson is difficult to assimilate, for authority corrupts even at this level. At the ordination of a priest the Church still speaks of 'the dignity of the priesthood' rather than 'the service of the priesthood'.

Question: Is ministry in the Church treated too much as a dignity rather than a service?

Thirtieth Sunday

First reading: Israel is my firstborn son (Jeremiah 31.7-9)

The most remarkable feature of this prophecy of Jeremiah is that Jeremiah spoke it when the destruction of Jerusalem was certain. The city was about to collapse and its inhabitants be dragged into captivity across the desert on meat hooks. Yet Jeremiah proclaims that the Lord has saved his people! It is so certain that Jeremiah can speak of it in the perfect tense: it has virtually already happened. In the midst of disaster, he declares that the Lord is a father to Israel, and Israel his cherished firstborn son! Even the blind (ready for the gospel miracle!) and the lame will be gathered in. They will have to wait for the fulfilment, but the promise remains a beacon of hope. There are times in everyone's life when everything goes wrong and irremediable disaster strikes. In those dark moments we know that the same promise holds for us. In the Spirit, we can still cry out '*Abba*, Father'. The household of the Lord is a Church composed entirely of firstborn sons. According to the Law of Israel only sons had a right of inheritance, so even the daughters of the Church are rightly described as firstborn sons.

Question: How can people 'from the farthest parts of earth' call God 'Father' if they have never heard of God?

Second reading: High Priest of the Order of Melchizedek (Hebrews 5.1-6)

'He can sympathize with those who are ignorant or uncertain.' To single out these two characteristics and to grant that Jesus could be uncertain or ignorant is a bold assertion of Jesus' full humanity. Yet ignorance and the ability to learn is a condition of humanity: the child Jesus must have learnt how to deal with fire and knives and other dangers, and there is no way of learning so sure as initially getting it wrong. Similarly uncertainty is a crucial human condition, at once an openness to learning and a reminder of humility. How certain was Jesus of what would happen in his Passion? He must have known that 'his head was in the noose', but the detailed predictions of the Passion are surely subsequently phrased in the light of the actual events. The two unique elements of his priesthood are total ability to sympathize with us, and his unmediated link to his Father. These make his priesthood, his representation of ourselves to the Father, and his whole-hearted offering of himself in obedience to the Father, far more immediate than any formal priesthood, such as that of the priestly line of Aaron, could ever be.

Question: As a man, did Jesus really learn? How much did he know of what the future held?

Gospel: Blind Bartimaeus (Mark 10.46-52)

There are several remarkable things about this story. First, the scene is just when Jesus is leaving Jericho. Jericho is about three hours' walk from Jerusalem, up a great, rocky canyon. When you leave Jericho, you know you are just about coming to Jerusalem. It is the last village on the way, and the excitement of the great revelation of Jesus at the Passion is already upon them. The cured beggar dances on the way with them. Second, he is the only person in Mark to call Jesus 'Son of David', drawing attention to Jesus' messianic ancestry, ready for his messianic entry into Jerusalem. Third, in Mark Jesus says 'Your faith has cured you' only twice. The first time was to the woman with a haemorrhage, who had shown her faith with great courage by daring to touch Jesus' garment in the crowd. Now Bartimaeus shows the same stubborn courage in carrying on shouting despite the attempts to silence him. So they both show with courage that they really do put their trust in Jesus and are confident that he will help. If our faith is to save us, it needs to be real, courageous and stubborn. Lukewarm, tentative faith is not enough.

Question: How do we show our faith and trust in Jesus?

Thirty-first Sunday

First reading: 'Hear, O Israel' (Deuteronomy 6.2-6)

This reading is very special: it is the command that rules Israel's life, and the life of every true Christian. The faithful Jew recites this passage morning, noon and night, and in prayer carries the text literally before the eyes, on the hands and on the doorposts of the house, so that one is always aware of the most important loyalty in life. This is a symbol that love of God must dominate all our actions and thoughts; it must be always in our minds and thoughts, and must be the guide of all our deeds and motivations. God is a God of love and warmth of the heart, not a God of threats or compulsion. To serve God is a joy and happiness, bringing light and colour into our lives. If God is not in our lives and thoughts, we are the poorer for it, and lack not only truth but also the warmth of an unspeakable, personal friendship. The only difference the New Testament brings, as St Paul explains, is that for Christians there is not merely one Lord God. For us there is one God, the Father, from whom all things come, and one Lord, Jesus Christ, through whom all things come.

Question: What would life be like without God?

Second reading: The Perfect High Priest (Hebrews 7.23-28)

The pagan idea of sacrifice was to make reparation to a demanding and often angry god, to divert a capricious god from our own failings by flattery and gifts. The blood of the victim that was shed was a substitute for human blood, paying the price for a life which should have been forfeit. The Christian idea is entirely different. Christ is the perfect human being who is also divine, united to his Father in a perfect and permanent act of love. This reached its highest expression in the offering of his life in loving obedience. It was not a barbaric act of paying a penalty that I should have paid, but a return in tender love in which I may share. Christ still remains with or before the Father in this permanent, timeless act of loving obedience or loving embrace, accepted and vindicated by the Father in the Resurrection, which raises Christ onto a new plane of existence in God. The Letter to the Hebrews, written for Christians of Jewish origin who still hankered after the rituals of the Temple, makes clear that Christ's offering is the perfect fulfilment of all the objectives and devotion imperfectly expressed in the rituals of the Temple.

Question: What is the basic difference between pagan and Christian sacrifice?

Gospel: The Great Commandment (Mark 12.28-34)

The basic command of Judaism, which should dominate all life, was love of God above all things. Jesus audaciously adds to this another commandment of the Old Testament, the love of neighbour. This is the only case in the gospels where a scribe positively approves Jesus. Why is this the case? The scribes were the experts in the law and its interpretation. To stress the importance and the equality of the second commandment of love, Jesus uses a technique of interpretation common and approved in Israel. If the same words are used, you may set two passages of scripture on a level with each other. In these two commandments, and only here in the whole of the Bible, are the words used, 'And you shall love...' with a direct object. This enables Jesus to put the command on the same level – and the lawyer approves his interpretation. The first Letter of John puts it: 'No one who fails to love the brother whom he can see can love God whom he has not seen.' This was, of course, not a new commandment; it was the equality of the two commandments of love that was new in the teaching of Jesus.

Question: What sort of person do you find it most difficult to love?

Thirty-second Sunday

First reading: Elijah and the Widow (1 Kings 17.10-16)

This story about Elijah and the widow of Zarephath is chosen to pair with the story in today's gospel about the generosity of the widow in the Temple. It is also, of course, about a widow's generosity, but this story is more about her trust and obedience to the command of the prophet. In a way, trust in the Lord is the subtext of all generosity: we trust that the need presented to us is presented to us by the Lord, a request for our help. We trust that God, our Father, knows what he is doing. Realizing that we are no more than stewards of God's good things, we respond to the need which God presents. This story also has something special about it, for this widow in the territory of Sidon is mentioned in the manifesto speech that Jesus makes in Luke's gospel in the synagogue of Nazareth: his mission is not confined to Israel any more than that of the prophets was. The gentiles, too, are the children of God, the object of his loving care, and are to be saved no less than the Jews. In Jesus' mission, the gentiles also form part of the Chosen People of God.

Question: What recent incident really called for your trust in God?

Second reading: Christ's Sacrifice Once and for All (Hebrews 9.24-28)

Addressed to Jewish priests converted to Christianity, this Letter to the Hebrews seeks to show them that the sacrifices they had formerly valued so much were only a shadow of the reality in Christ. There is no time in heaven! Those sacrifices were of their nature temporary and unsatisfying; Christ's is of its nature eternal and all sufficient. The image of Christ, permanently presenting his sacrifice and his blood before the throne of God, is ultimately reassuring. It signifies the permanent and unbreakable union of humanity to God, welded by the obedience of Jesus on the Cross. Although the language is largely similar, the sacrifices of the Bible are not to be thought of in the same way as pagan and Greek sacrifices. They are not appeasing an angry god, but are celebrating unity with God. They are shared meals, and in the great annual sacrifice of the Day of Reconciliation, blood is sprinkled on people and altar to signify the renewed union with

God. Especially reassuring is the mention of Christ's blood, for blood is the symbol of life. Christ's blood, given to us, is the sign and sacrament of the gift of divine life, offered to us, if only we will accept it.

Question: Why was Jesus' self-offering so valuable to God?

Gospel: The Widow's Offering (Mark 12.38-44)

We are presented with a contrast between the dignitaries of the Temple, parading in their splendour, and the least of the least. These little coins are called *lepta*, meaning 'light', hardly more than shavings of copper, hardly worth picking up. Yet the value of a gift depends not on its absolute worth, but in the love with which it is given. The value of a birthday present depends on the love it expresses, and the care that has gone into choosing or making it. One can imagine the widow debating with herself: could she survive without these two little coins, if she made this supreme gift to the Lord. What would she have to go without? As with the Sidonian widow in the first reading, this paltry gift is a rich expression of her trust in divine love and care, of her wanting to do something for the Lord. The little gift would go unnoticed among the riches of that exquisite and lavish building, for its splendour was the wonder of the eastern Mediterranean, but it is a heartfelt expression of her love. Just so with our prayer of praise: it does no good to God, but is for us the joyful outpouring of our love and wonder.

Question: What makes a gift really valuable?

Thirty-third Sunday

First reading: The Resurrection of the Dead (Daniel 12.1-3)

We are coming towards the end of the Church's year. This passage looks towards the end of all things. It is a crucial passage, for here, for the first time in the Bible, the Resurrection of the dead is proclaimed. The Book of Daniel was written during a great persecution of the Jews a couple of centuries before Christ. It was then that finally the Resurrection of those who remain true to the Lord was revealed. The earlier Israelites pictured the afterlife as a sort of powerless, shadowy half-existence in Sheol, where the dead could not even praise God. Yet there had been many hints of conviction that God would never desert those who love him: 'I know that my Redeemer lives, and that from my flesh I will look on God', said Job. Only now, under the stress of the death of martyrs in the persecution, is the full truth revealed: at the end of time God will intervene to draw his own to himself in fullness of life. In this reading, 'many will awaken' does not mean that some will not awaken; it merely indicates a vast number, the almost limitless multitude of the dead.

Question: Which of the martyrs in modern times do you admire most?

Second reading: One Single Sacrifice (Hebrews 10.11-14, 18)

In this, our last reading from the Letter to the Hebrews, Christ is pictured in the terms of the coronation song, Psalm 110, as the Son of God, sharing God's throne. His sacrifice on the Cross was not an act of vengeance by God, inflicting on Jesus the pains which we deserve, after which God suddenly changed his mind and rehabilitated Jesus. It was the consummate act of loving obedience, by which Jesus, on behalf of all humanity, reversed the disobedience of Adam and united us all to God. The Resurrection, by which Christ was raised to glory, the Son of God in power, was the recognition of this renewal of life. The sacrifices of the Old Law were partial, temporary and needed to be repeated. Christ's offering in obedience was complete, and could never be repeated. Writing to the Corinthians Paul uses the same psalm to show that Christ is waiting to put the last great enemy, Death, under his feet, and so present the Kingdom to his Father. This is the glorious awakening described in the first reading.

Question: What is the importance of the Resurrection?

Gospel: The Coming of the Son of Man (Mark 13.24-32)

Jesus saw his mission to be the establishment of the sovereignty of God, the kingship and rule of God over the world, even in rebellious human hearts. Using the language and imagery of his time, he described this 'earth-shaking' event in terms of cosmic disturbances. The coming of God, the Day of the Lord, would constitute the end of the world as we know it. As Christians we must acknowledge that the death and Resurrection of Christ utterly changed the world for ever; it was the Day of the Lord. And yet the world still continues, and we have still to prepare for the Day of the Lord, when we will come into that awesome presence. That meeting can be pictured only in terms of collapse and upheaval, our world turned upside down. At death all our familiar realities cease, even the ticking of the clock. At death, time ceases to have meaning. We do not know, and have no need to know, when or how this will occur. For all it will come, for each it will be an individual meeting, but will it be all together or each individually? The Son of Man will gather his own, in great power and glory.

Question: Should we be afraid of death or should we look forward to it?

Thirty-fourth Sunday, Christ the King

First reading: One Like a Son of Man (Daniel 7.13-14)

This prophecy of Daniel was written in the dark days of the Syrian persecution of Judaism a couple of centuries before Christ. First, the evil empires that persecuted Judaism are described under the imagery of ravening beasts, tearing their prey to pieces. Then comes this altogether different image of a noble human being on whom God confers all power and sovereignty on earth. In the original vision, this human figure is the personification of the Jews, 'the holy ones of the Most High', who will be freed from this persecution and exalted to glory. In the New Testament, this prophecy is applied to Jesus. He uses the mysterious expression 'Son of Man' to describe his authority on earth to forgive sins and to prescribe rules for Sabbath observance. He uses it also to soften the prophecy of the suffering and death by which he will achieve his final Resurrection. In the final commission of the Risen Christ to his disciples in Matthew, he goes even further: to him has been given all authority both in heaven and on earth, and in this power he sends out his apostles, promising that he will be with them always.

Question: Did the man Jesus have something that showed his authority?

Second reading: The Lord of the Churches (Revelation 1.5-8)

The Book of Revelation opens with a vision of the Risen Christ as Lord. This passage is rich in quotations from the Old Testament, allusions to several passages of the Bible to express the dignity, power and sovereignty that belong to Christ. He is described even in divine terms, the first and last letters of the alphabet signifying that he is the beginning and end of all things, their origin in creation and their goal. He spans the whole extent of time, past, present and future, until he comes again. More specifically, also, in his glorified humanity Christ is the Lord of the Church, since he has taken the Church to himself, cleansed it, and made it a Kingdom of Priests to serve God. This too is a biblical expression, for Israel is described as a royal priesthood; it will find its fulfilment in the Church. Like the prophecy of Daniel, the Book of Revelation was written in time of persecution, to assure the persecuted faithful that they were safe in the protection of God, whose power would eventually prevail to rescue them and bring them to triumph and security.

Question: In what sense is Christ the Lord of the Church?

Gospel: Judgement before Pilate (John 18.33-37)
In some ways, this dreadful scene is part of the climax of John's Passion Narrative. Throughout the narrative, John stresses the ultimate significance of the events, taking the stress off Jesus' suffering and humiliation, and laying it on his triumph. Finally, Jesus will die only when he has completed his mission, and hands over his Spirit to the newly formed Christian community of Mary and the Beloved Disciple. In this scene, the Jewish authorities have denounced Jesus as claiming to be King of the Jews, not knowing how true that claim is. Jesus declares that his Kingdom is no earthly kingdom, but far more powerful and meaningful. By his statement, he invites Pilate to declare himself for the truth, as any judge should do. Now Pilate three times declares Jesus innocent, but at the same time makes a mockery of himself, as he stands before Truth itself, and asks what is truth. Then he seats Jesus on the Judgement Seat, robed and crowned as a king. Before this Jesus, enthroned as judge and king, the Jewish authorities deny themselves and their faith by declaring, 'We have no king but Caesar.' If God is not king, Judaism has no reason to exist.

Question: Why is the Feast of Christ the King put at the end of the Christian year?

Year C

Second Sunday of the Year

First reading: The Wedding Feast of the Lord (Isaiah 62.1-5)

The marriage relationship is perhaps the most intimate of the personal relationships we know, designed to become ever deeper and more absorbing. Even the relationship of mother to child cannot equal it. So, in the Bible, the relationship of the Lord to his people is described in this way. But, like many human marriage relationships, it went through bad patches. Israel was so determinedly unfaithful to the Lord that eventually he was compelled to bite the bullet and forsake her to those with whom she had prostituted herself. This could not be permanent: Israel could not go on being called 'Abandoned' and 'Forsaken'. The past would be forgotten. After the return of Israel from exile in Babylon, Isaiah prophesies the final wedding in terms of the unalloyed joy of a fresh wedded couple. So in the gospels Jesus uses the figure of the final wedding feast, and the image of himself as the bridegroom in the joy of the festival. He always gives us another chance, an unalloyed welcome.

Question: How many sayings and parables of Jesus can you remember which use this image?

Second reading: Gifts of the Spirit (1 Corinthians 12.4-11)

At the beginning of each year the Church gives us some six Sundays of readings from Paul's first letter to the Corinthians, that troubled community. Corinth was a thriving port town of southern Greece, with a very heterogeneous community, rich and poor, academics and dockers. There were no human leaders in the community, and reliance on the Spirit for guidance in the problems of living as Christians did not always provide a solution. These three Sundays show Paul trying to help. Yes, the Spirit is at work in them in many different ways. There are many different gifts, all necessary for this varied community. The trouble seems to have been

234

that each person valued their own contribution so much that the gifts of others seemed insignificant. Paul's stress on the variety of ways in which the Spirit works to build up a community gives us the occasion to reflect on the variety of gifts which the Spirit has poured out on our own Christian community, and on every individual member of it. I can rejoice in gifts which God has given to me, but only if simultaneously I think of all the gifts which others have and I lack.

Question: Apart from love, would you say that any gift is more important to the community than any other?

Gospel: The Wedding Feast at Cana (John 2.1-12)
Year C is the year of Luke's gospel, but we start with this reading from John, the symbolic beginning of Jesus' ministry. It is full of riches. After the first reading from Isaiah, it is impossible not to see this 'sign' (as John calls it) as a sign of that final wedding feast of God and his people. Furthermore, in Jewish thought water represents the law: in an arid land water is the sign of life and is precious – just so the Law of God is precious and gives life. Jesus transforms this water of the Law into the wine of the New Covenant – and in such generous quantities, over 100 gallons of wine! Then there is Mary's part: Jesus says his hour has not yet come (and the reader knows that the Hour of Jesus will be the moment of his exaltation at the Cross and Resurrection), but Mary's confident plea is a reminder to us of the power of her intercession. She will be mentioned no more in this gospel until she is present at the Cross, sharing the Passion of her Son and joined to the Beloved Disciple to form the first Christian community.

Question: What was Mary thinking while she waited for something to happen?

Third Sunday
First reading: Ezra Reads from the Law (Nehemiah 8.2-6, 8-10)

The Book of Nehemiah, from which today's reading is taken, is the latest historical book of the Hebrew Bible. It describes the re-establishment of the People of Israel, now the Jews, in and around Jerusalem, on their release from exile in Babylon. In the 70 years of exile they had developed a way of life based on the law and marked by Sabbath, circumcision and ritual food, which distinguished them not only from the Babylonians, but also from those inhabitants of Judaea who had not been dragged into captivity. It was only those who were passionate for the Lord and this way of life who returned to the ruins of Jerusalem. Others stayed in more comfortable exile! Ezra, the expert in the Law, and Nehemiah, commission by the King of Persia (in whose empire Judaea lay), were at different times leaders of the community. In this scene, Ezra reads out and so promulgates the Law in Jerusalem, to the acclaim of the people. What a contrast to the scene in the synagogue at Nazareth where Jesus reads out the passage from Isaiah that is the clue to his way of life and that of his followers, only to be rejected by his own people!

Question: How would you explain to a non-believer that God's Law is a joy and a treasure?

Second reading: The Body of Christ (1 Corinthians 12.12-30)

Following directly on last Sunday's reading, in today's passage, Paul shows just why the different gifts of the Spirit must be used for the common purpose of building up the community. He compares the community which lives with Christ's life, the life of the Spirit, with a human body. For the effective functioning of the human body each highly diverse organ must play its part, contribute its own particular speciality. To prevent the individual Corinthians becoming proud and possessive of their own particular gifts, he stresses that, like parts of the body, none is more important than any other. Is it less serious if your liver fails than if it's your kidneys? This comparison of a community to a human body is common in ancient literature, but nowhere else is the community as a body described as the body of a particular person in the way that Paul designates the Corinthian Christian community as the Body of Christ. The Body which lives by the life principle of Christ's Spirit is Christ's own Body.

Question: What makes the Body of Christ different from any other body?

Gospel: Jesus Proclaims his Message (Luke 1.1-4; 4.14-21)

Today's gospel passage starts the series of readings from Luke that will continue throughout the ordinary Sundays of the Year. It is composed of two separate passages: first, it gives Luke's introduction to his gospel, in which he explains how and why he wrote it. Then, jumping over the preparatory stories of Jesus' infancy, baptism and testing in the desert, it comes directly to his programmatic manifesto in the synagogue at Nazareth. The gospel is offered to Theophilus – a Greek name – and is written for gentile communities. So Luke stresses that Jesus' message is not just for Jews but for the peoples of the whole world. Twice in this short passage, which gives Jesus' programme, Luke stresses that Jesus is moved by the Spirit of the

Lord. As we saw in the second reading, the Spirit was palpably at work in the early Christian communities. This was no more than a continuation of the Spirit's activity from the very beginning of the Christian movement. In Luke's stories of the annunciation, birth and infancy of Jesus, the presence of the Spirit is constantly noted. In the earliest stories of the Church in the Acts of the Apostles, the same guidance directs every move.

Question: Is the Spirit given enough prominence in the Church today?

Fourth Sunday

First reading: The Prophet Rejected (Jeremiah 1.4-5, 17-19)

Jeremiah was given a tough assignment. His task was to proclaim doom to his fellow citizens under the threat of invasion by the overwhelming might of Babylon. Unless they returned to God and put their trust in the Lord rather than in their own feeble manoeuvrings, they were doomed to slaughter and exile. To stop the people hearing this message their leaders arrested him and dumped him in the squelchy mud of an almost empty well, fed on one loaf a day. It is only too human to block out the message one does not want to hear. So, while Jeremiah steadfastly held his ground, Babylon advanced, destroyed the city and Temple of Jerusalem, and led the people into exile. Bruised in exile, they learnt the hard way. As Jeremiah put it, God took from them the heart of stone and gave them a heart of flesh, to respond not just as a nation, but individually in tenderness and love. Jeremiah's steadfast preaching in the face of opposition is presented to us as a preparation for that of Jesus, which we hear in today's gospel reading.

Question: What parts of Jesus' message do we just not want to hear?

Second reading: Authentic Love (1 Corinthians 12.31–13.13)

The Christians of Corinth saw that they had a variety of gifts and talents. Paul gladly admits this. He only complains that this led them to squabbling and rivalry, for they were blind to the reasons for which these gifts had been given. Like all our talents, and especially those of interpersonal relationships, they were given by the Spirit that gives life to the Christian community. Their ultimate purpose is not to puff up the holder of the gift but to build up the community. The gift must be applied and exercised in love, for love is the highest gift of all gifts. Love alone builds the community. Then Paul paints a picture of what real love is. Few of us can read or listen to it without realizing our own failures and selfishness, as Paul puts his finger on one after another of our own failures. The passage acts as a testing ground of whether our love is genuine or whether we are merely deceiving ourselves. The final part of Paul's argument is also encouraging, not merely because of the durability and long-lasting nature of love, but also from the picture of heaven it conveys: in the perfect maturity, to which we look forward, there will be nothing left but love.

Question: Can you hold up this passage and get a metre reading on your loves?

Gospel: The Rejection of Jesus at Nazareth (Luke 4.21-30)

The reaction of the villagers of Nazareth to Jesus' proclamation of Good News for the poor, the handicapped and disadvantaged is predictable. We have all suffered from failure of our own people to recognize our talents! In this case, it is also fuelled by a paradoxical jealousy: in the moment of rejecting Jesus' message they also want to reap the advantage of his miraculous healings. The rejection of Jesus by his own people provokes Luke to continue the lesson to an extent not given by Mark or Matthew: Jesus quotes instances that show God's care for those outside his traditional 'Chosen People'. God's love is universal, not limited by ethnic or any other boundaries. The Chosen People were chosen not for their own selfish privilege but to bring salvation to the whole world. In the same way, in the New Dispensation of Christ, his people, the Church, are chosen not just to enjoy God's benefits and love for themselves, but as the instruments of his love for all. It is the same message as that of Paul: true love has no limits. Luke is especially aware that Jesus sends his message beyond the limits of the Chosen People. I have been chosen not for my own advantage but as an instrument to bring Christ to others.

Question: Does God love some people more than others?

Fifth Sunday

First reading: The Holy One of Israel (Isaiah 6.1-8)

In the collection of the sayings of Isaiah subsequently made, this vision is not the first, but it certainly recounts the first vocation of the prophet. For Isaiah, God is primarily the Holy One of Israel. This vision of the triple Holy, seated on the throne of glory in the Temple, does all that is possible to convey in words the daunting otherness of the One whose glory fills the whole earth. The human reaction to it can only be acute awareness of uncleanness. Isaiah can only shrink away until his uncleanness has been purged by the cauterization of his lips. No human being can see God and live. The glory seen by Isaiah (and by Moses on Mount Sinai) is but the outer fringe, but it leaves the human visionary stunned and aghast at the contrast between the divine holiness and human unworthiness. Throughout the Book that bears his name, Isaiah will revert again and again to the awesome holiness of the Lord. God is our loving Father, but there can be no neglecting the distance lying between Creator and created. At the same time we are attracted and daunted.

Question: How does your idea of holiness fit with Isaiah's?

Second reading: The Earliest Gospel (1 Corinthians 15.1-11)

The most precious element of this reading is the first traditional recital of the Good News of Christ's death and Resurrection, which the earliest Christians already saw as fulfilling the scriptures. We can tell that by Paul's time this recital was already traditional. First, Paul here uses the terms used by the rabbis for the handing on of tradition, 'I *taught you* what *I had been taught* myself.' Second, the language is not quite Paul's own; for instance, for scriptural fulfilment Paul always writes 'as it is written', whereas here we twice have 'in accordance with the scriptures', which Paul himself never says. To witness to the Resurrection of Christ was the primary task of the apostles. For us, too, it is the primary task; not merely by our words, but by the way we behave, we need to live in the awareness that Christ's Resurrection after his endurance of humiliation and dreadful suffering is the basic fact of life. The basic factor in Christian faith and witness is not the empty tomb but the experience of the apostles in meeting the Risen Christ. This is what unbelievably transformed them from being a defeated and hopeless rabble, huddled in hiding, into courageous and enterprising witnesses.

Question: Is this the nucleus of Christian faith that you would write?

Gospel: The Call of the First Disciples (Luke 5.1-11)

There were obviously several different versions circulating in the early Church of the call of the first disciples. In Mark and Matthew, Jesus is passing along the shore of the lake when he calls two pairs of disciples. In John, it takes place where John the Baptist was preaching. The story in Luke has many similarities to the story at the end of John's gospel after the Resurrection, when the risen Christ commissions Peter: a night of failed fishing, followed by a huge catch in obedience to Jesus' instructions. The Church has always seen this as a sign of the need for obedience to Christ.

Luke's version here combines the same play on words as in Mark and Matthew about fishing for people. Luke sets the story a little later: in Mark, the fishermen have never seen Jesus and follow him blindly; in Luke, Peter and his friends have already got to know Jesus before they are commissioned. A special feature in Luke is Peter's cry that he is an unworthy sinner. Luke often teaches us that no one can be a disciple of Jesus without first admitting their sinfulness: Zacchaeus the tax collector, and the woman who wept at Jesus' feet (Luke 7.36-50) are other examples.

Question: What do you find special and important about Luke's account of the call of the disciples?

Sixth Sunday

First reading: A Curse and a Blessing (Jeremiah 17.5-8)

Actually, it is neither a curse nor a blessing. It is not invoking or wishing on a person the blessing or the curse. Instead, the prophet is here saying that people who behave in these two ways are respectively blessed and accursed. There is no need to wish it on them, for their own behaviour merits it and brings it on themselves. Such statements of blessing and its opposite are frequent in the Bible; an example very similar to this is in Psalm 1. In Jeremiah's prophecy here, unlike most of the instances in the Bible of 'beatitudes', in both Old and New Testaments, there is no list of ways of moral conduct, it is simply a matter of trust or faith. It is not a person's achievements that count, for we cannot earn blessedness; we can only trust in God. However, if God is the real centre of our trust and reliance, we will try to behave as we were created, in the image of God, imitating the divine generosity, forgiveness, attentiveness to human need, fostering life rather than restricting it. This will mean that our heart is truly turned to the Lord, and the Lord will care for the rest.

Question: How true is it that we bring blessing and curse on ourselves?

Second reading: A People of the Resurrection (1 Corinthians 15.12, 16-20)

As he nears the end of his great letter to the Corinthians, which we have been reading for five Sundays, Paul teaches about the Resurrection, the bedrock of Christian faith. Last Sunday he was rehearsing the most primitive proclamation, that Christ had truly risen from the dead and had encountered a host of witnesses. Now Paul comes on to the Resurrection of

Christians, of which Christ's Resurrection is the first fruits and the model. The importance of Christ's Resurrection is not only that it places him in glory at his Father's right hand, but also that it is the forerunner of our own Resurrection. We can know little about the transformation that will take place in us at the Resurrection. We will be physical, but physical in a quite different way. The glorified body is a body, but not like any body that we know. The traditional Christian picture of clouds and harps is not to be taken too seriously. The only important thing is that we will be wrapped or wrapt in the joy of the presence of God, enveloped in utter contentment. Nothing else will matter but the enjoyment of the most lovable of all beings.

Question: Why will it not be possible to get bored in heaven?

Gospel: The Beatitudes (Luke 6.17, 20-26)
Matthew's Sermon on the Mount and Luke's Sermon on the Plain are both collections of sayings of Jesus about the basic conditions of Christian living. Each begins with a set of 'Beatitudes', announcing who is specially blessed by the Lord. One frisky modern translation renders them, 'Congratulations to you who are …!' Matthew's set of eight Beatitudes focuses more on spiritual qualities, poor *in spirit*, hunger and thirst *for justice*, whereas Luke's four are more directly on the circumstances of life. The stress is, therefore, on the reversal of values brought by Jesus. Jesus turns the world upside down. His gospel or 'good news' comes to the poor, the neglected, the oppressed. True blessedness does not consist in wealth, fame or festivities. It is those who struggle now who will receive a lasting reward. Are the four negatives that follow too hard on the rich, the contented, the frivolous, the famous? Through this gospel runs a thread of warning about the dangers of contentment, and we seldom pay attention to warnings unless they are overstated! The worry of those who have plenty, about how they should use their advantages responsibly for others, must be as least as great as those who worry to survive.

Question: Is money a positive bar to eternal happiness, or a challenge?

Seventh Sunday

First reading: David spares Saul (1 Samuel 26.2, 7-9, 12-13, 22-25)

This delightful story of David occurs when Saul is pursuing the young David in the wilderness of Judah, above the Dead Sea. The successful young warrior was getting too ambitious for the liking of King Saul, who, in a bad mood, tried to pin him to the wall with a spear, and then threw him out of court. David then gathered a band of outlaws, and Saul attempted to hunt him down. The result was this story. Was David magnanimous, or was he already thinking that one day he, in his turn, would be the Lord's anointed? The assassination of the king would be a bad precedent! David was a fantastic leader, the sort of person whom anyone would follow anywhere. He was also a great sinner, committing adultery and murdering the cuckolded husband to make his own guilt seem less. But he was a great penitent too, a lovable and very human figure. Above all, he was the real founder of the Israelite monarchy and of the 'line of David' from which Jesus would come. To him were the promises made that God would be a father to the Son who would reign for ever on his throne.

Question: Was David calculating or generous?

Second reading: Transformation in the Resurrection (1 Corinthians 15.45-49)

This is the third of the four Sundays on which Paul is explaining the meaning of the Resurrection of Christians. The Resurrection of Christians follows the model of Jesus' own Resurrection. As the firstborn from the dead, Christ is the founder of the new humanity, just as Adam is the founder of fallen humanity. 'Adam' means 'man', and the story of the Fall in the Book of Genesis is not so much a story of an event long ago as the story of every human temptation and sin. However, the obedience of Christ, the Second Adam, undoes the disobedience of the First Adam. Just before this passage, Paul has explained that in the Resurrection we will all be changed, and transformed into the heavenly sphere, in the image of the Risen Christ. What was weak will be strong with the strength of God, what was corruptible will be incorruptible with the incorruptibility of God, what was contemptible will be glorious with the glory of God. He refuses to say what sort of bodies we will have, but he sums up the other changes by saying that whereas the life principle was the soul, in the Resurrection it will be the Spirit of God.

Question: What does the Resurrection of the body mean in the light of this teaching?

Gospel: Unlimited Love (Luke 6.27-38)

Luke's version of the Beatitudes, which formed last Sunday's reading, puts the emphasis not on Christian attitudes, as Matthew's version does, but on the blessing on those in real, dire need. Now he continues this with our duty to respond to those in need, even if they are hostile, even if they hate us. There must be no calculation whether we will get back money or property lent, no limit to how much we lend or give. At first it seems as if Luke is concerned only with money, and indeed he is so concerned, for he is always warning of the danger of possessions and the need to use them for those who have none. Luke is proclaiming Christ's Good News to a more affluent society than do Mark and Matthew, and places all the more emphasis on the danger of wealth. But, after dealing with money, Luke goes on to other acts of generosity. We must not judge, but must forgive in order to obtain forgiveness. Most of all, we must be compassionate. Whereas Matthew ends his instructions here with the general, 'Be perfect just as your heavenly Father is perfect', Luke focuses on compassion, 'Be compassionate just as your Father is compassionate.' It is an affair of the heart: we must be emotionally involved with those in need.

Question: Which is the more important, compassion or generosity?

Eighth Sunday

First reading: The Test of Speech (Sira 27.4-7)

The wise sage of Jerusalem collected many proverbs and pithy sayings. Most of them are severely practical, as in this short reading. Here he presents us with four images of testing someone by their speech. He does not deny that there are other ways of proving a person's worth and generosity, but these four aspects of testing by speech are as clear as any. This reading is chosen to introduce the sayings of the gospel reading on discerning people by their fruits. There is no way of telling what people are except how they act.

In fact, the Book of Sira is rather a favourite with Luke. He takes at least two of his sayings and transforms them into parables to illustrate two of his special emphases in Jesus' teaching. Luke is the evangelist of prayer, and a saying on a widow's earnest prayers (Sira 35.14) illustrates the need to persevere in prayer in Luke 18.1-8 (the Parable of the Unjust Judge), and the Rich Fool (Sira 11.19) is used to illustrate the acute dangers of hoarding wealth in Luke 12.16-21.

Question: Which is the most testing of the criteria given in this reading?

Second reading: Christ's Victory over Death (1 Corinthians 15.54-58)

For most people, death is a terror: the one thing certain about life is that it will end in death. For Paul, death is a triumph which he awaits eagerly, longing to be fully united with Christ and to share fully in Christ's victory. This Christian attitude, totally at variance with the views of those who do not know Christ, and with our natural human instincts, is the reason why the Church has given the last four Sundays to meditation on the transformation that will take place at Christian death. Paul is so convinced of the overwhelming power of Christ and his victory over sin that there is no hesitation: this mortal body will put on immortality. Quite how this will be is still not entirely clear: Paul says it is foolish even to ask what sort of body the dead will have. But he insists that there is continuity: the seed that dies is transformed, but 'each kind of seed has its own kind of body'; the risen person is in continuity with the person in this life. There are no conditions attached, no threat or fear of hell, being cast into outer darkness 'where there is weeping and gnashing of teeth', as in so many of Matthew's parables.

Question: Why does Paul never mention the word 'hell' or consider it?

Gospel: Judging Others (Luke 6.39-45)

Matthew gathered together the teachings of Jesus on the basic requirements of Christian morality into the Sermon on the Mount; that formed a sort of manifesto for the Kingdom of Heaven, starting with the eight Beatitudes. Luke gathers many of the same teachings into his 'Sermon on the Plain', starting with four Beatitudes. This has provided the gospel readings for the last three Sundays. Matthew, writing for Christians of Jewish origin, stressed Jesus' teaching on the law, and how Jesus made it more interior and often more demanding. Luke, always aware of the needs of the poor, stresses more our social obligations. As he draws to a conclusion, he gives us two of Jesus' warnings, expressed in the vivid language and with the fierce exaggeration and wit that is so characteristic of Jesus' teachings. The first, the splinter and the log, warns us to use the same standards in judging ourselves as we use in judging others. The second, the sound and rotten fruit, is perhaps a double warning. You can judge people only by their actions. More profoundly, it is also a challenge: don't flatter yourself on your achievements until you are good through and through, until the store of goodness in your heart is really overflowing.

Question: Is it ever helpful to point out other people's faults?

Ninth Sunday

First reading: God of all Nations (1Kings 8.41-43)

This prayer is presented as the conclusion of Solomon's prayer at his dedication of the Temple in Jerusalem. In fact, it is tacked on at the end of the prayer, and is looking back from a later time, when Israel had become aware that God is God not only of the Chosen People but of all the world. From the Babylonian Exile onwards the Jews became more and more conscious of their role in bringing God's salvation far beyond the borders of their own land. This will be exemplified in today's gospel story of the centurion who turns to Jesus for help. As Christians, we believe that there is one God of all the universe, who loves all and saves all who turn to him in good faith and conscience, even if they revere God under a quite different set of concepts, naming God as 'Allah', or – as the great religions of the East – seeking enlightenment or awakening rather than salvation. Our Hebraeo-Christian revelation of God is not the only path of enlightenment, for God can also be sought, as the Second Vatican Council puts it, 'in shadows and images'. We have no warrant for confining the work of the Holy Spirit to our own set of concepts, for we cannot begin to understand the ways of God.

Question: How are non-Christians saved by Christ?

Second reading: Introducing the Galatians (Galatians 1.1-2, 6-10)

For the next six Sundays we will be reading Paul's Letter to the Galatians. This was written to a group of Churches in Galatia (a central area of Turkey), where there was a strong Jewish presence. After they had become Christians some envoys arrived from Jerusalem, telling them that they must observe the Jewish Law, presumably because Christianity is the completion of the hopes of Judaism. Some of these new Galatian Christians accepted this and began to practise the Law. It was obviously unclear as yet what the status of the Law was for Christians. Paul was furious and wrote a scathing letter – the only letter that does not begin with a complimentary greeting – to tell them that observance of the Law was pointless. He forcefully states his own authority as personally called by Christ to be an apostle. He even publicly rebuked Peter, the chief of the apostles, for returning to the observance of the Law. We are saved by Christ, he says, not by the Law. The gifts of the Spirit that they can see among them come from Christ, not from the Law. The Law was only a provisional guide, leading us to Christ. Now that Christ has come we are adopted to sonship as free, adult co-heirs with Christ.

Question: Is there continuity between Judaism and Christianity?

Gospel: The Centurion's Servant (Luke 7.1-10)
This story is particularly important to Luke. In Jesus' first appearance in the synagogue at Nazareth, he had promised that, like the prophets Elijah and Elisha, he would bring healing to the gentiles. Now he proceeds to do this, for the centurion is a gentile, although not necessarily a Roman – there is no sign of Roman troops in Galilee for some decades after Jesus' time. Luke is writing his gospel for a gentile audience, and misses no opportunity to underline the openness of Jesus to gentiles, and even the hated Samaritans. The centurion is the right person to benefit from this first cure of a gentile, for not only does he show a fine deference to Jesus and humility, but also he has made generous use of his position and what wealth he had, in building the synagogue. Wealth is always a danger unless it is used well, and an opportunity if it is. Above all, we see his complete trust in Jesus' healing power, even without physical contact between Jesus and the servant, a trust that Jesus had not experienced even from the Israelites themselves. This trust has won him a place in the Mass, in our prayer of humility immediately before communion.

Question: Does Jesus love non-Christians too?

Tenth Sunday

First reading: Elijah raises a Boy to Life (1 Kings 17.17-21a, 22-24)

This is the second of two stories about Elijah and the widow of Zarephath. Jesus alludes to the first story in his programmatic speech at Nazareth in Luke 4.26. This is an example of a miracle worked outside Israel, a reminder that Jesus' mission was not only to the Jews, but also to the gentiles. Elijah was sent to her when there was no food in Israel, and she provided something for him out of her meagre supplies. As a result, the supplies did not run out. However, at first, she seems to get little satisfaction for this, since her son now dies suddenly. But then, he is brought back to life by the prophet, and all ends well! More or less the same story of raising the son of the prophet's hostess to life is told of the prophet Elisha, the successor of Elijah; it must be either that there was confusion between them, or that there was a deliberate attempt to show the similarity of their missions. In the rabbinic tradition, a very similar story of raising a boy to life is told of one of the charismatic Galilean rabbis contemporary with Jesus. The story prepares us for the gospel story.

Question: Are we bound to believe that Jesus' miracles were unique? In what way were they unique?

Second reading: Paul's Mission from God (Galatians 1.11-19)

Galatians is one of the very early letters of Paul. His authority could be, and was, questioned. Other missioners had come down from Jerusalem to the Churches of Galatia, and had contradicted Paul's message that Christians need not obey the Law of Moses. In reply, Paul forcefully insists that his authority was not dependent on the apostles of Jerusalem, but that he was directly called by God, and – like the prophet Jeremiah – set apart from his mother's womb. To show the power of God's call, he recounts how utterly opposed to Christianity he had been before he was called, violently persecuting Christians. It was a total reversal. So certain was his call that he had no need to confer at the time with the human authorities of Christianity, and only spent a short time with Peter and James after three years. In fact, he goes on to relate, he even stood up to Peter and told Peter that he was in the wrong, so that Peter changed his stance. Henceforth, Paul is careful in his letters to make explicit that he was 'called to be an apostle', not merely appointed as a delegate of other human authorities. His message is the message of God.

Question: What can we do to help overcome divisions and quarrels in the Church?

Gospel: The Son of the Widow of Nain (Luke 7.11-17)

In his gospel, Luke is always careful to point out that women are saved no less than men. Mark tells the story of the raising to life of the daughter (woman) of Jairus (man). Luke now tells the story of the raising to life of the son (man) of this widow (woman). Similarly, an angel announces the miraculous birth of John the Baptist to his father, and of Jesus to his mother – and who comes out of it better? Zechariah is struck dumb, and Mary is blessed! The Markan story of the man losing a sheep is balanced by the Lukan story of a woman losing a coin; each rejoices as an image of the rejoicing in heaven. The story of the widow's son is told with typical Lukan delicacy. He stresses that this was her only son, so her only hope in the world, and that Jesus feels for her. At the end we are reminded of the Old Testament stories by the acclamation that a great prophet has arisen. In Luke, Jesus is often characterized as a prophet: his foreknowledge and prophesying are stressed, and finally his Ascension is described in terms reminiscent of Elijah's ascent into heaven in a fiery chariot.

Question: Has the Church returned to equal treatment of women and men?

Eleventh Sunday

First reading: David's Repentance (2 Samuel 12.7-10, 13)

The account of David's adultery with Bathsheba is a great story. When Bathsheba tells him she is pregnant, he tries to disguise his crime by persuading Uriah, her husband, to sleep with her. When Uriah refuses, David has to have him killed, in the hope of escaping the charge of adultery. This is where our reading begins, as David's own prophet, Nathan, tells David the score. His is a story of rags to riches, shepherd boy to king, outwitting Saul at every step, winning his way into the counsels of the Philistines, gradually building up his powerbase. For all his charismatic leadership, courage, ability to charm both men and women, skilled (and often crooked) diplomacy, David's greatness lies in his repentance. In the Bible, he is the model of the great sinner and the great repentant, the great public penitent, for he repents humbly and unremittingly. Amid all his faults, David's warm and open relationship to the Lord is his salvation. It is glimpsed often in his story, and, although it does not save him from his great fall, it brings him back in heartfelt penitence. The story is, of course, chosen to pair with today's gospel reading.

Question: Why is David seen as such a favourite of the Lord?

Second reading: Crucified with Christ (Galatians 2.16, 19-21)

We plunge straight into the middle of Galatians, for this is the third of six readings from the letter. Paul had brought a group, probably mostly Jewish, to see that the promises to Abraham were fulfilled in Christ. Then some other Jewish Christians came down from Jerusalem and told these new Christians that they must still observe the Jewish law. Paul was furious, calls them 'Fools!', and reasserts his teaching that one must only trust in Christ and his Resurrection. He asks them the source of the works of the Spirit, which were plain for all to see among them. Was it the Law or is it the issue of Christ's life living in them? Half measures will not do, and Paul goes on to tell of the total commitment of his own life to Christ. Once a burningly zealous Pharisee, he is now dead to the Law and lives only with the life of the Spirit in Christ. We cannot win salvation by any actions of ours. We can only hang on by our fingertips to the salvation won for us by Christ.

Question: Does this mean that the Jewish Law no longer has any significance?

Gospel: The Woman who was a Sinner (Luke 7.36–8.3)

This is a story of devotion and repentance, but a story also of the welcome of Jesus. He does not rebuke the sinner or interrogate her. He sets no preconditions, demands no promise of improvement. The details of her sin are unimportant to him; the heartfelt repentance is all that matters. Of all the evangelists Luke especially stores up stories of the return of sinners: the Prodigal Son, the Pharisee and the Tax Collector at Prayer, Zacchaeus, the Good Thief, perhaps the Woman taken in Adultery. To Matthew's story of Joy at the Man's Found Sheep, he adds the story of Joy at the Woman's Found Coin (typically adding woman to man). In contrast to all this, stands the host at the dinner party, Simon the Pharisee, not evil, but a stickler for observance of the Law, and judgmental of others. However, Jesus is delicate even to Simon, giving him a question he can answer, so that Jesus can affirm him before he points out his shortcomings. At the end of the scene, Luke points out the importance of the part played by women in Jesus' ministry. In Paul's ministry, also women will play a vital part, not only as hostesses, but themselves spreading the Good News – Chloe, Pheobe, Junia, Priscilla and others.

Question: Is Jesus too indulgent to the woman or too hard on Simon or neither?

Twelfth Sunday

First reading: The One whom they have Pierced (Zechariah 12.10-11)

The meaning, the translation and even the text itself are quite obscure. This, one of the latest of prophetic passages, perhaps even in the second century before Christ, is expressing confidence in the restoration of Jerusalem. It has been dominated by foreign powers, but God will pour out on it his favour and compassion. The deliverance of Jerusalem is somehow connected with 'one whom they have pierced', for whom there will be great mourning. For us the importance is that in the New Testament this obscure 'one whom they have pierced' and the 'only son' is looked upon as prefiguring Jesus, the only-begotten Son and Suffering Servant of the Lord, whose Passion and death is the means of salvation of the whole world. The passage is applied by John to Jesus whose side was pierced by the soldier's lance in the gospel, and again in the opening vision of the glorious Risen Christ in the Book of Revelation: 'He is coming on the clouds; everyone will see him, even those who pierced him.' His triumph will be acknowledged by the whole world, and his wounds will be his glory. This passage therefore prepares for the gospel passage.

Question: Is it legitimate to look through this prophecy to the suffering of Christ?

Second reading: Baptized into Christ (Galatians 3.26-29)

In a state of fury, bluntly calling them 'fools', Paul is writing to these new converts to Christianity to counter the instructions they have received from messengers from Jerusalem. These had insisted that they must still obey the Jewish Law. Paul replies that those who have been baptized into Christ are wholly renewed. All previous conditions, sex, status, race, have fallen away, and all are simply adopted sons and daughters of God. To 'baptize' means to 'dip', as in a river, and Paul's image is that those who have been dipped into Christ's death rise with him in his Resurrection, dripping and soaked through with Christ. This is not merely external clothing, but it means living with Christ's own life – 'I live now, no, not I, but Christ lives in me' – and the only feature that matters at all is that we are adopted to sonship with Christ, and so have become in him heirs to the divine promises given to Abraham. Living with Christ's life, we can address God with the intimate Aramaic family word, *Abba*, used by Jesus himself, and are free of all other obligations.

Questions: If I use the family word *Abba* to God, must I qualify or supplement it at all? Is there anything to be said for delaying baptism until the age of understanding?

Gospel: Peter's Profession of Faith (Luke 9.18-24)

Peter's profession of faith in Jesus as God's anointed messenger occurs, of course, in each of the first three gospels, but each relates it in his special way. Luke, for whom prayer is so important, stresses that Jesus was at prayer, as he was at so many special moments, such as the choice of the disciples, the Transfiguration, the moment when the disciples asked Jesus to teach them how to pray. In Mark this is the turning point of the gospel, a breakthrough for Peter after a long and frustrating period of inability to understand who Jesus was. But only a partial breakthrough, for he still cannot grasp the message that Jesus' mission involves suffering. Matthew strengthens Peter's confession to 'the Christ, the Son of God' and then has Jesus congratulate Peter with the promise of the keys. He also intensifies both Peter's protest at the idea of Jesus suffering, and Jesus' correspondingly fierce rebuke to Peter. This Sunday's Lukan version gives neither praise nor blame to Peter, but hurries straight on to the message of suffering. Neither Jesus nor his followers can win through to the crown of Resurrection without first undergoing the Passion. Luke quietly generalizes the message, for Jesus speaks not just to his disciples but to 'all'. What? Me, too?

Question: Do I learn more about Jesus through joy or through sorrow?

Thirteenth Sunday

First reading: The Call of Elisha (1 Kings 19.16b, 19-21)

This story is clearly chosen by the Church to pair with the latter part of the gospel reading, or even possibly in reverse, for Jesus' call to the unnamed disciple seems to be modelled on Elijah's call to Elisha. Elisha must have been a rich man to have 12 yoke of oxen ploughing his field – a large field and a hefty herd. Elijah's gesture of throwing his mantle over Elisha is to claim Elisha as his own. When Elijah is taken up to heaven his mantle falls on Elisha again, giving him a double share of his spirit. By slaughtering the oxen and burning the tackle, Elisha destroys his own livelihood, but he is allowed to take leave of his family before taking up the life of a prophet. Elijah was a fearless prophet of Israel, inspired by the vision of God (at the cave on Mount Horeb) and uncompromisingly defending the rights of God against idolatry (the prophets of Baal) and injustice even by the king (Naboth's Vineyard). He was expected to come again to herald the final coming of God, and many saw him in John the Baptist. Elisha was perhaps more a political operator, furthering God's plans by the appointment of rulers.

Question: Does Elijah think that Elisha is too slow to respond? Do you?

Second reading: Freedom to Love (Galatians 5.1, 13-18)

Paul is still, as last Sunday, warning the Galatians against regarding themselves as bound by the Jewish Law. This is an external restriction, whereas Paul wants them to be led only by the interior Spirit of God, which will lead them in the paths of love. It is important to understand correctly the distinction between the flesh and the Spirit. The sins of the flesh are not merely 'carnal' sins like sex, greed and overindulgence. They include also such things as rivalry, jealousy, quarrels and malice. So 'the flesh' is more generally self-indulgence and lack of self-discipline, perhaps unrestrained natural desires. These are not in themselves evil, but they need to be harnessed and directed by the impetus of the Spirit. By the same token, the Spirit is the life of Christ in us, and motivates everything that leads to Christ, not only – as Paul here lists – 'love, joy, peace, patience, kindness, gentleness and self-control', but also everything that builds up the community in love, loving guidance, teaching, the healing touch, as well as the more striking gifts like speaking in tongues. In 1 Corinthians, he explains that each member of the community has a special gift, and all these are needed for a healthy community.

Questions: What gifts can you contribute to the life of your Christian community? What gifts do you lack that you see in people around you?

Gospel: Uncompromising Discipleship (Luke 9.51-62)

The latter half of Luke's gospel, as Jesus embarks on his great journey to his death at Jerusalem, is marked by Jesus' teaching on the difficulties and challenges of discipleship. Right at the beginning comes the little lesson that the disciple must not be surprised or take vengeance at rejection. Then three lessons on the uncompromising demands of discipleship. These are not 'counsels of perfection', but demanded of every disciple of Jesus. First, the Son of Man has nowhere to lay his head. The disciple has no right to creature comforts. Second, perhaps the most counter-cultural of all Jesus' demands, for burying a dead father was regarded as a sacred duty, and yet not even this may stand in the way of a response to the call of Jesus. Third, a more rigorous condition than even Elijah demanded of Elisha, no backward glance even to bid the family farewell. Not even the most sacred of natural ties may stand in the way of the demands of following Jesus. These conditions may seem unfeeling and unacceptably harsh: Jesus expresses his teaching with maximum vigour. This is partly the nature of the Semitic language, which rarely uses a comparative, 'more than …' It is either day or night, no dusk! But we must beware of softening what must remain hard.

Question: Can there be a clash between family loyalty and loyalty to Jesus?

Fourteenth Sunday

First reading: As a Mother Comforts her Child (Isaiah 66.10-14)

We are used to the imagery of God as Father, the creator and initiator of all things. But there is no gender or sex in God; these distinctions are human and animal; God infinitely transcends such human limitations. So there is also room and need for a gentler image of God as mother: 'As a mother comforts her child, so will I comfort you', promises this passage, even daring to invoke that most maternal and intimately loving and trusting image of the child feeding at its mother's breast. Such imagery for God as mother comes in other passages as well, such as Psalm 131, where the contentment of the believer in God is compared to that of a little child in its mother's embrace, or Hosea 11.1-4, in which God's loving care is described in terms of a parent leading and feeding a child – the child is now growing up, and God's maternal love continues throughout our lives. One of the chief Hebrew words describing God's love for his people is *rahamim*, the plural of *raham*, which means a mother's womb. It appeals, therefore, to the instinctual gut feeling of a mother for her child, which can never be destroyed or overruled.

Question: What are the implications in prayer of this imagery of God as mother? What is scripture teaching us by the imagery of God as father?

Second reading: The Triumph of the Cross (Galatians 6.14-18)

This is the final reading for this year from the fiery letter to the Galatians. It also provides the entry antiphon for Maundy Thursday, as we enter upon the celebration of the Lord's Passion and Death. Paul is finally again comparing the law and the Cross. Instead of glorying in the physical mark of circumcision, the symbol of subjection to the law, he glories in the Cross 'branded on' his body – he must mean in a symbolic sense by baptism, unless he means the scars of the floggings he received – which makes him a new creation. Everything is new about the Christian baptized into Christ, having left behind the old, mundane preoccupations to embrace the new freedom inspired by the Spirit. This sounds all very well, but we know, and Paul knows also that it is a constant challenge to bring this new life and new scale of values into reality: 'The good thing I want to do, I never do; the evil thing which I do not want – that is what I do', he laments writing to the Romans. We are already reconciled to God, but only once does Paul say we are already saved. Even then it is 'saved in hope', which puts it into the future.

Question: How far does my new life in Christ express a new scale of values?

Gospel: The Mission in Action (Luke 10.1-12, 17-20)
The instructions to the 70 sent out are direct and simple. They are really sent out like lambs among wolves, without food, without distractions, without baggage, without spares. The version in the Gospel of Mark allows them

sandals, presumably to enable them to make more speed on their journey, for the urgency of the task is paramount. They are not to be distracted by picking and choosing their accommodation or their food. Direct, too, is their method: to impart the blessing of peace and to heal. No second chance: if the blessing is rejected, away they go, leaving the town to a fate worse than that of Sodom! Last Sunday's gospel demanded an uncompromisingly whole-hearted response to the call from the apostles themselves. This Sunday they demand the same response to their own message. Again the absolute demands of Jesus! There is a wonderful simplicity about this message of the coming of the Kingdom: all that is involved is peace and healing. No squabbles, no fripperies, no complications of doctrine. If these can remain the focus of our Christian vision, we may make some progress towards bringing the Kingdom of God to reality in our own surroundings.

Question: What sort of healing can I bring? Is this the most important aspect of the Kingdom?

Fifteenth Sunday

First reading: Moses' Final Counsel (Deuteronomy 30.10-14)

The Book of Deuteronomy, purporting to be written by Moses, but, in fact, penned some centuries later, consists of four great discourses on the Law. This lovely passage concludes the last discourse, after which the death of Moses is recounted. It encourages the people to observe the Law. The Law is not obscure, or difficult, or far away. They do not need to travel far or search deeply. The author is saying that it is Israel's natural inheritance, and is natural for them to observe, almost – as we would say – second nature. The Law was for Israel God's most precious gift, a revelation of the divine nature and the divine ways to the world, so a source of light and life. It revealed how Israel must behave in order to be God's faithful people. So observance of the Law was not a tiresome obligation but a response in love to this gift made in love. For Christians, the Law is brought to perfection in the incarnate Word of God, who is the perfect revelation of the Father, and is the Way, the Truth and Life. Israel saw the revelation of God's will, and so of his nature, in the Law; Christians similarly see the full revelation of the glory of God in Christ Jesus.

Question: How can I come to know God's ways? Answer: Read John's Gospel in the awareness that Jesus is the Way, the Truth and Life.

Second reading: Christ the Firstborn (Colossians 1.15-20)

This first reading from Colossians is a hymn to the pre-eminence of Christ. It falls into two stanzas, the first his pre-eminence as firstborn in creation, the second his pre-eminence as firstborn from the dead. As firstborn in creation, he is the image of the invisible God, in whom all is created, just as, in the Book of Wisdom, Wisdom is called the image of God, the reflection of the eternal light and the mirror of God's active power. In Wisdom, in Christ, God can be seen. In the second stanza, as firstborn from the dead, Christ brings all things to perfection and completion. The hymn is a sort of parabola, starting with God in creation, descending to Christ as Lord of the Church, and returning with Christ to completion in God. In the two closely related letters, Colossians and Ephesians, the author is concerned to define Christ's superiority to the so-called spirits of this world, 'thrones, dominions, rulers and powers', which must have been revered in that region of Asia Minor.

Question: What is the relationship of image, reflection, mirror to reality? Does this help to an understanding of the divinity of Christ?

Gospel: The Good Samaritan (Luke 10.25-37)

To many a Jew at the time of Jesus, the hatred of the Samaritans was such that a Good Samaritan was a contradiction in terms. It is striking that Luke changes the dialogue about the two commandments. In Mark's and Matthew's accounts, Jesus answers the question about the commandments, while in Luke, Jesus challenges the questioner, who then himself gives the right answer. It is also striking that, in his reply at the very end, the lawyer, despite Jesus' praise of him, cannot bring himself to pronounce the hated name, 'Samaritan', and says 'the one who ...'. The dry humour of the story consists in the conscientious dilemma of the priest and the Levite: if the huddled traveller turns out to be dead, they will incur corpse defilement and be unable to perform their sacred duties! This legal dilemma makes the Samaritan's attentive generosity all the more poignant, for a Samaritan is free of any such hang-ups. Love shown to the unfortunate and the downtrodden is always a major theme for Luke. But note also the Samaritan's careful administration of his funds: he gives not a blank cheque but two days' wages, which he will supplement on his return if necessary!

Question: Is the main point of Jesus' story to be generous or not to be judgmental?

Sixteenth Sunday

First reading: Abraham's Hospitality (Genesis 18.1-10a)

This splendid story of Abraham entertaining the three strangers is chosen by the Church to pair with the gospel reading of Martha and Mary as an example of hospitality. But it has many other aspects. In the story, the three men shimmer between being one and three. Since they clearly represent God – in a delightfully human way – this has been understood from the time of the earliest Church writers to be a hint of the Trinity, although the Trinity is not revealed until the New Testament. Another vital aspect is that it features the beginning of the fulfilment of the promise of a great posterity to Abraham. Abraham's faith has been tested by having to wait until both he and his wife are well beyond the normal age of conception, and now at last the Lord shows his care for them. A charming aspect comes just after the end of the reading: Sarah *laughs* at the idea of a child at her age: this makes a pun on Isaac's, her son, name, which means *laughs* or *smiles*. This pun recurs several times in the Isaac story. For the sequel to the story, Abraham's bargain with God, we must wait until next week!

Question: How has God tested your faith?

Second reading: Paul's Sufferings for Christ (Colossians 1.24-28)

The letter to the Colossians, begun last Sunday and read over four Sundays, is one of the latest of the Pauline letters. Some scholars think it was written not by Paul but by a disciple, thoroughly familiar with his thought, applying his master's ideas to a new situation. In any case, it is part of inspired scripture. The mystery revealed only at the end of time, which Paul was commissioned to proclaim, is that the salvation promised to Abraham and his kin now extends to all people. This is the riches of his glory. Paul is also very aware that his own sufferings and tribulations in the apostolate mirror and complete those of Christ. When he says that he is 'completing what is lacking in Christ's afflictions' he does not mean that Jesus' Passion was somehow faulty or deficient. Rather, he means that, as the Body of Christ, the Church in every age must be a suffering Church. His confidence rests in his sufferings, for they enable him to say that he is the Servant of the Lord Jesus in just the same way as Jesus is the Suffering Servant of the Lord. In 2 Corinthians, when others claim more authority than he has, he replies by saying that he has suffered more.

Question: Is suffering part of our mission as members of the Church? Why? How is this fulfilled?

Gospel: Martha and Mary (Luke 10.38-42)

Martha and Mary have become the classic figures in the Church representing two different styles of life, the active and the contemplative vocation, an active apostolate or a life of prayer. Carried to an extreme, this opposition is, of course, merely silly. No active apostolate can thrive unless it grows out of a life of prayer, for we cannot draw others to the knowledge and love of a God whom we do not ourselves know and love. Neither can a life of prayer be genuine unless it leads to care for others and concern for the salvation of all those whom the Lord loves. Even a strictly enclosed community cannot claim to be a part of Christ's body unless its fabric is one of love and concern for all the members, and especially those in need, the elderly, the sick and the young. In fact, Jesus does not present any such choice between two different religious ways of life. His speech is always in terms of absolutes. He does not use comparatives; he says that Mary has chosen not 'the better' but 'the good part'. Any 'good' life must be founded on listening devotedly to the Lord and responding to what we have heard.

Question: How important a part does listening to the Lord play in my life as a Christian?

Seventeenth Sunday

First reading: Abraham bargains with God (Genesis 18.20-32)

This delightful story continues the episode of last Sunday's first reading. It is reminiscent of a scene of bargaining in an oriental bazaar, a scene of deadly earnest, yet playful bargaining. Abraham goes on pushing his luck, using laughably inadequate logic, until he has gone well beyond the point of any sort of reason. His partner in this game continues to show good-humoured tolerance, and, above all, an unbelievable willingness to forgive. Some might find this process of bargaining to lack reverence for the almighty power of God, but it is an expression of Israel's intimate affection for the Lord. This attitude is all expressed in the special Hebrew name for God, which is never pronounced. The Lord himself will later show Moses the meaning of this intimate name of Israel's own God as 'God of mercy and forgiveness'. This sacred personal name of the Lord is never pronounced, partly out of reverence (for the glory of the Lord is too awesome for that name to be on human lips), but partly also out of intimacy, just as we do not noise around in public the intimate terms of affection that are used only within our close family circle.

Question: Can I bargain with God in this way?

Second reading: Baptized into Christ (Colossians 2.12-14)

In this powerful passage, we see the strength of Paul's image of our sharing in Christ's death and Resurrection. Our life is hidden with Christ in God, since we were baptized into Christ's death and raised in his Resurrection. We emerge with Christ from the tomb, sharing his life, co-heirs with him and calling God our Father. Paul sees the sin of Adam not as something that happened long, long ago, but as an analysis of our own sin, for 'Adam' means 'man' or 'humanity'. This sin, every sin, is a sin of disobedience to God. Christ is, in Pauline thought, the Second Adam. By his obedience to his Father on the Cross he wiped away, dissolved or overrode the sin of disobedience of the first Adam, the sin of humanity. The sacrifice of Christ on the Cross is the complete expression of obedience to the Father, which restores our loving relationship to the Father. This is forcefully expressed by saying that Christ nailed to the Cross the record of our debt to the law. Circumcision was of no avail; it was only by being baptized into Christ's death and raised in his Resurrection that we could be restored.

Question: What are the implications for Christian behaviour of sharing Christ's life?

Gospel: The Lord's Prayer (Luke 11.1-13)

Luke is the evangelist of prayer. Again and again he shows us Jesus praying. At all the important moments of his life he needs this intimacy with his Father. So he is praying at the baptism; before the choice of the disciples he prays through the night; at the Transfiguration he is praying. Now the prayer of Christians picks up his own prayer. Luke's rendering of the prayer he taught the disciples is slightly shorter than the version in Matthew. It begins with the simple call 'Father', rather than 'Our Father in heaven', a noble and affectionate simplicity. 'Thy will be done' is omitted, for it is Matthew who often insists on doing the will of the Father. Instead of 'give us this day our daily bread' Luke gives the insistent 'give us each day', which stresses the continuity of our dependence on God. After this prayer follows a series of parables and images underlining the importance of persistence in prayer and continual prayer after the model of Jesus himself. Elsewhere, Luke will give us other parables: the Unjust Judge, again teaching perseverance in prayer, and the Pharisee and the Tax Collector, teaching the importance of humility in prayer.

Question: Have there been occasions when God has answered your prayers in a way you did not expect?

Eighteenth Sunday

First reading: Vanity of vanities (Ecclesiastes 1.2; 2.21-23)

This is the only Sunday reading from the Book of Ecclesiastes. The Book is dramatically attributed to King Solomon, but it must have been written several centuries later, even after Alexander the Great. This late book of Wisdom is full of disillusionment and restless questioning of all the old certainties, not even sure of the afterlife. It queries whether happiness is anywhere to be found, certainly not in hard work! In this, it partners the gospel reading about the rich fool, although the rich fool is condemned for his selfish hoarding, while the author of Ecclesiastes despairingly thinks that no toil can win any worthwhile result. Why is this Book included in the collection of the revealed truth? Perhaps because it is always useful to question our certainties again and make up our mind again. Certainly it blows away the assumption of earlier Israel that happiness is to be found in wealth and distinction, and that wealth is a sign of God's blessing.

Question: Where do you place your security and happiness?

Second reading: Risen with Christ (Colossians 3.1-5, 9-11).

This final reading from Colossians is full of the hope of the Resurrection. Indeed, it is prescribed for reading also on Easter Sunday morning. The Pauline theme of being baptized into Christ and so sharing his risen life is familiar from the earlier letters. Adopted into sonship with Christ, we have cast off all the old ties, and there is no room for all the old vices. But there is a fascinating and inspiring change of viewpoint. In the earlier letters, Paul said that we were already reconciled to God but not yet saved. In the later Colossians and Ephesians, we have already been raised with Christ, but this risen life in Christ is still hidden in God and merely has yet to be revealed. Once we have been baptized into Christ, we have been taken on as his own, and can securely address God with intimacy as Father. This gives us confidence in our continuing struggle to shake off all evil and allow Christ to take control of every aspect of our lives. We still 'are being transformed into Christ', but the battle is already won.

Question: If my natural dwelling place is now with Christ 'at the right hand of the Father', what difference does this make to my priorities?

Gospel: The Dangers of Wealth (Luke 12.13-21)

Luke's language and style make it clear that he comes from a reasonably privileged background. In his stories, he uses far larger sums of money than Mark. He understands about investment banking and rates of interest. This makes it all the more striking that he continually warns against the dangers of wealth. Jesus brushes aside a dispute about inheritance. The parable of the Rich Fool is perhaps the most condemnatory of all the parables; nowhere else in the gospels is anyone called outright a 'fool!' Salvation comes first to the poor, the shepherds of Bethlehem, through a baby cradled in a cattle trough. Only Luke says that the apostles left 'everything' to follow Jesus. In the ideal young community of the early Church in Jerusalem, he insists that everything was held in common. The guests invited to the Great Supper refuse the invitation because they are distracted by their new purchases. The only hope for the rich (for example in the parable of the Rich Man and Lazarus) is to use their wealth to make friends in heaven.

Question: Would Jesus approve of my property situation and the use I make of my money?

Nineteenth Sunday

First reading: A Contrast between Israel and Egypt (Wisdom 18.6-9)

The Book of Wisdom is possibly the latest book of the Old Testament, written not in Hebrew but in Greek, for the Greek-speaking Jews of Alexandria, just a few years before the birth of Jesus. The book is written against the background of considerable hostility between the Jews and the Egyptians. It vigorously attacks their worship of idols and especially of sacred animals, but is also vividly aware of Israel's vocation to bring salvation to the whole world. The final section of the book, from which this reading is drawn, makes a series of rhetorical contrasts between the Egyptians and the Israelites at the time of the Exodus. At the very moment at which the Israelites were being delivered from Egypt, the Egyptians themselves were undergoing the destruction of the firstborn. The promises to Abraham to make his children God's people were being fulfilled, while their enemies were being punished. This was the moment of the Passover, when Israel offered sacrifice and agreed to the Divine Law. Most first readings relate to the gospel reading; however, this reading prepares for the second reading, which is a meditation on the journey of God's People.

Question: The Christian Passover of the Lord is the Eucharist. How can we make is a moment of commitment to Christ's covenant?

Second reading: The People of God on Pilgrimage (Hebrews 11.1-2, 8-19)

The Sunday reading of the Letter to the Hebrews is divided between Years B and C. The author of the letter is unknown; there is no reason to think that it was written by St Paul. Its purpose was to strengthen Jewish priests who had joined the Christian community and were yearning for the sacred rites of Judaism. So it sets out to show that the rites of Christianity are superior. This year we have four readings from the later part of the Letter, of which this reading is the first. The principal theme is the journey of the People of God in faith. The faith of the ancestors of Israel, as they journeyed in faith through trials and difficulties, reliant on God's faithfulness, is still an inspiration. Outstanding among their acts of faithful obedience was Abraham willingness to sacrifice his only-begotten son, Isaac, seen by the Church as a foretaste of God's willingness to sacrifice his only-begotten Son to reconcile the world by his obedience. But whereas the resting place that Israel reached was not their final heavenly homeland, the Christian People of God is on pilgrimage to the final place of rest.

Question: What is it in the Church that nourishes our faith and sustains it?

Gospel: Being Ready for the Master's Return (Luke 12.32-48)

The reading begins with a separate three verses that once again warn of the danger of worldly possession. This is a danger against which Luke, writing to a prosperous audience, continually warns. Then comes a series of warnings to be alert for the final meeting with the Lord, and a series of blessings on those who are so ready. Luke does not have a great scene of a universal final judgement, like Matthew's parable of the sheep and the goats. There is no need to wait for a great final judgement scene at the end of the world. Luke, with his Greek frame of mind, is more interested in the individual judgement, for each of these parables concerns a single individual who is rewarded or punished. This is fully compatible with the notion that each individual's final judgement is at death, rather than all together at the end of the world. The most wonderful and startling is the first promise that the master will himself serve the faithful servant. A second parable concerns the thief who (literally) 'digs through' the wall of the house when the master is off his guard. A third lesson is framed in terms of a slave who misuses his authority over other slaves, and so concerns the misuse of authority in the Church.

Question: How do you imagine your final judgement? What is its most awesome element?

Twentieth Sunday

First reading: Jeremiah in the Well (Jeremiah 38.4-6, 8-10)

The prophet Jeremiah was a peaceable person, whose mission was to threaten the people of Jerusalem with destruction by the might of the approaching Babylonian armies. Their only hope lay not in military efficiency and power or in alliance with foreign nations, but in fidelity to the Lord. This was not the only message he had to give, for he also foretold that the Exile would bring a new covenant and forgiveness of sin as they repented their infidelities in exile and returned to the Lord. In any case, he tried to escape this mission by pretending to God that he had a stutter, but the Lord told him to quit pretending and get on with the job. The King systematically tore up his prophecies as they were read out, sheet by sheet, but at the same time he had a nasty, sinking feeling that Jeremiah was right. However, his military personnel overruled him and silenced Jeremiah by dumping him in the mud at the bottom of an underground water storage tank. This reading is chosen to pair with the gospel reading, and so to teach that the message of fidelity to the Lord and to Christ is bound to be a sign of contradiction and to provoke opposition.

Question: Jeremiah promised that the Lord would write his Law on their hearts (31.33). What did he mean?

Second reading: Jesus, the Pioneer and Perfecter of our Faith (Hebrews 12.1-4)

Last Sunday's reading from Hebrews celebrated a long procession of figures from the Old Testament who had been sustained by their faith through difficulties and disappointments. This 'great crowd of witnesses' had kept their faith alive heroically on their pilgrimage towards the goal. The supreme figure, of course, is Jesus, who disregarded the shame of the Cross, and so has taken his seat on the throne of God. With Jesus, a whole new dimension of faith begins. The two words translated 'pioneer' and 'perfecter' are carefully chosen to express the beginning and the completion of our faith. The former means that he set it in motion and led from the front, not merely a leader but an initiator, without whom it would never have happened. What is meant by 'perfecter'? Jesus brought it all to completion. It is the same word stem as occurs in Jesus' last word on the Cross in John: 'It is complete.' What is complete? The life of Jesus? Jesus' own work? The first Christian community, formed from Mary and the Beloved Disciple? The plan of God? The promises of scripture?

None of these can be excluded, for in each of these senses Jesus is the completion.

Question: In what way is our faith different from that of the Old Testament figures?

Gospel: Fire to the Earth (Luke 12.49-53)

What is this? Jesus came to bring peace and harmony, to perfect the fond unity of society and families. How is it then that he can here say exactly the opposite? And without apology! There is no, 'I am afraid there may sometimes be disagreements in the family.' Rather, 'I have *come to bring* disagreements in the family.' To make things worse, in Judaism, the family is the basic unit that sticks together through thick and thin. Any Jew will be thoroughly shocked by this passage. We have seen repeatedly that Jesus' statements are often fierce and extreme: 'If your hand causes you to fall, cut it off'; 'Let the dead bury their dead.' Elsewhere he says 'It is easier for a camel to pass through the eye of a needle than for a rich man to enter the Kingdom of Heaven' – and the traditional let-out clause that he is talking about a small gate in Jerusalem is simply wrong; there was no such gate! Jesus is teaching that the most sacred earthly ties are less important than loyalty to him. He chooses the family deliberately because it is so sacred and important, but even so, less important than following him.

Question: What are the hardest circumstances in which you have to make decisions for or against the demands of Jesus?

Twenty-first Sunday

First reading: Salvation to the Nations (Isaiah 66.18-21)

The first and third readings today are both inspiring and daunting. The first reading comes from the very last chapter of Isaiah. Israel has returned from exile, and settled down back in Jerusalem. It has outgrown the frantic worry about mere survival under threat of extinction, and can afford to look outwards. Just so, a sign of a child's maturity is when she or he grows less self-preoccupied and can begin to be aware of the needs of others. In the same way, Israel now sees that the vocation of the Chosen People is not to be turned in on itself, but to bring the Lord's salvation to others. Isaiah prophesies that this wonderfully outlandish list of far distant lands, Tarshish, Put, Lud, Tubal and Javan, will come to draw salvation from Jerusalem, and will take part in Jerusalem's own sacred worship. It is the immediately preparation for the spread of the gospel. As Christians we believe that all nations will somehow be saved by Christ, even though they do not know him. 'Nor is God far distant from those who in shadows and images seek the unknown God', says the Constitution on the Church of Vatican II.

Question: How can those who have never heard of Christ be saved by him? Is it by admitting the failure of human nature and our need to rely on someone else?

Second reading: The Discipline of Suffering (Hebrews 12.5-7, 11-13)

What is the sense of all the suffering in the world around us, the constant pain, worry, loneliness, fear, frustration? Is all this distortion and misery really compatible with the belief in a God of love? The Letter to the Hebrews here gives one explanation: it is the loving training and discipline of a father to bring us to peace. In a world without pain, would we ever turn to God? When all is going well, many of us can manage nicely without God! If our world falls apart, we need God to put it together again. Paul puts it slightly differently, seeing suffering as the privilege of sharing in Christ's own redemptive suffering. By enduring Christ's suffering in every age, the Church ensures that it truly is the body of Christ, the Servant of the Lord. But we can never be content with suffering. Jesus himself understood suffering, and he went out of his way to heal it in all its forms. We should also remember, that, in an age in which so many decry the selfishness and materialism of society, the generosity shown by so many for the alleviation of suffering, the care of the sick, the betterment of the underprivileged, is one of the signs of Christ at work in his society.

Question: Is it true, or just pious, to say that by tending the sick we gain more than we give?

Gospel: The Narrow Door (Luke 13.22-30)

The gospel reading puts the point directly opposite to the first reading. There the inhabitants of distant lands will come to draw salvation from Jerusalem. This is repeated in the gospel, but the daunting corollary is also given to those nearer home, and expecting to find their way in easily: don't sit back in complacent contentment that we have been called, or you may find the door slammed in your face. Matthew 7.21-23 has the same warning: it is not enough to keep calling out, 'Lord, Lord!' without actually doing the will of the Father. He also has a similar, more developed parable of the wedding attendants, five wise with oil in their lamps, and five unprepared for the wedding feast. They too vainly cry, 'Lord, Lord!' from outside the door. This is almost a centre piece of the instructions to the disciples as they make their way with Jesus up to Jerusalem and to his Passion and death. There is no cheap way in: each disciple must take up the cross behind Jesus and follow to the end of the road. This teaching is the more striking in Luke, who stresses that both Jews and gentiles will take part in the festival.

Question: In that case, is a good pagan better off than a lukewarm Christian?

Twenty-second Sunday

First reading: No need to boast (Sira 3.17-20, 28-29)

Readings from this book of Ben Sira (or Ecclesiasticus) come only half a dozen times on the Sundays of the three-year cycle. It is probably the oldest of the Greek books of the Bible, written in Hebrew by an experienced scribe at Jerusalem a couple of centuries before Christ. The version we have was translated into Greek for the Jews of Alexandria by the grandson of the author. The book is full of worldly as well as divine wisdom, and a real appreciation of human nature. There is often a streak of dry wit as well. Here he reminds us that pride is often a cover-up for insecurity. The truly great person has no need to create an impression, can afford to be open and appreciative and ready to learn from others. Such openness is attractive and winning among our fellow human beings. More important, it gives a solidity and authenticity that leave us open also to the quiet word of the Lord. 'To the humble the Lord reveals his secrets.' This is the quality of Jesus who is 'meek and humble of heart', who rides as king into Jerusalem not on a prancing warhorse but on a donkey.

Question: Do I ever really convince other people (or even myself) by showing off?

Second reading: The City of the Living God (Hebrews 12.18-19, 22-24)

This final reading from the Letter of the Hebrews brings together the two main themes of the Letter, the superiority of the priesthood of Christ to that of the Old Law, and the theme of pilgrimage, concentrating here on its goal. Just like the Israelites in the desert of the exodus, the Church is still a pilgrim Church, wending its way unsteadily towards it final goal. In soothing the nostalgia of the Hebrew priests who still yearned for the old rites of the Temple, the author compares the two pilgrimages of the

Old and New Testament, and points to the superiority of the goal of New Testament pilgrimage. The pilgrimage of the Old Law was to Sinai and to the unbearably awesome experience of God on the mountain. The goal of the Christian pilgrimage is the heavenly Jerusalem, where all is peace and perfection. There is the contrast also of the two covenants, the one made on Sinai, destined to be broken repeatedly throughout the history of the Chosen People, and the eternal new covenant mediated by the priesthood of Christ, destined to remain for ever as the secure basis of our adoptive sonship and inheritance.

Question: Is the Church still on pilgrimage? Do you see it as advancing or stationary?

Gospel: Invitations (Luke 14.1, 7-14)
Two parables about invitations to table. Both are from Luke's special material, without parallel in the other gospels. He moves in a higher stratum of society than Mark and Matthew, and often has in mind the implications of the gospel for their situation. The first parable, however, like several of Luke's parables, seems to be developed from a little Old Testament proverb: 'Do not give yourself airs, do not take a place among the great; better to be invited, "Come up here", than to be humiliated' (Proverbs 25.6-7). At first sight, this seems a merely worldly precaution, a false humility engineered to gain attention. But, for Luke, a banquet is always an image of the heavenly banquet of the Lord. So the message is a moral one too: don't think yourself better than you are. The message is also typical of Luke's open and straightforward approach. One is reminded of the Parable of the Pharisee and the Tax Collector at prayer, where the latter prays only 'God be merciful to me, a sinner.' The second parable also is typical of Luke, his stress on the inherent danger of wealth, on the need to use wealth well, and his concern for the poor and neglected in society.

Question: Who would be thrilled with an invitation and could never return it?

Twenty-third Sunday

First reading: In Praise of Divine Wisdom (Wisdom 9.13-18)

This lovely passage is the conclusion of Solomon's prayer for heavenly Wisdom, saying that heavenly Wisdom and the true knowledge of the things of God are beyond human grasp. If we cannot penetrate to an understanding of the visible world around us, how can we hope to reach an understanding of the divinity beyond the grasp of all our senses? The prayer is put in the mouth of King Solomon, who in the Old Testament is almost the personification of human wisdom, but artificially, for the Book of Wisdom was composed at Alexandria only shortly before the birth of Christ. The recognition at this moment that Divine Wisdom lies well beyond the reach of all human faculties is all the more impressive in view of the achievements of the great philosophical schools of Alexandria. Such occasional poems, scattered through the Wisdom Books of the Old Testament, are a valuable reminder that God is beyond all human comprehension in wisdom, strength and beauty. Perhaps the most beautiful and overwhelming of all is the experience of God conveyed in the poems of Job 38–41. These poems may also be seen as praise of the Wisdom of God which will become flesh and be manifest to us in Christ Jesus.

Question: 'Of what we cannot speak, it is better to keep silent.' Is this true of God?

Second reading: Paul and Philemon (Philemon 9b–10, 12–17)

Paul's letter to Philemon – and this reading makes up about half the letter – is a friendly little note from Paul to Philemon about a slave of Philemon's called Onesimus, who has been serving Paul in his imprisonment, and has become a Christian. There are two theories as to why Onesimus was with Paul: either Onesimus ran away from his master and took refuge with Paul, or Philemon lent Onesimus to Paul for a limited period. In either case, Paul is now sending Onesimus back, and, at the same time, pressurizing Philemon to send him Onesimus for a further period. The most important and attractive element in the Letter is Paul's affectionate brotherhood with the slave, now a Christian. After long centuries of the toleration of slavery within Christianity, Christians will realize that the affection and brotherhood here expressed make slavery among Christians intolerable. A further step taken later will be that any enslavement of human beings is incompatible with Christianity, and that all human beings must be treated as brothers and sisters, equal before the Lord. It is a classic case of the slow deepening of the understanding of Christian morality.

Question: And what about the position of women in Christianity?

Gospel: The Cost of Discipleship (Luke 14.25-33)

Jesus does not pull his punches, and here delivers a series of devastating body blows to anyone who is looking for easy discipleship. All through this journey up to Jesus' own death at Jerusalem the cost of discipleship has been a recurrent theme: 'Let the dead bury their dead' (thirteenth Sunday), the Parable of the Rich Fool (eighteenth Sunday), 'From one to whom much has been entrusted, even more will be demanded' (nineteenth Sunday), 'Father against son, son against father' (twentieth Sunday), and now 'Hate father and mother' and 'Give up all your possessions'. A certain amount of the vigour of these demands may be attributed to a Semitic mode of expression, ease of superlatives and lack of comparatives, but there is no doubt about the absolute demands made on the disciple. When Jesus made these demands he knew what lay ahead of him, and was only asking his disciples to follow his own course. We must count the cost before beginning to build the tower. Most of us have, of course, already started to build the tower. There is no turning back from the plough (thirteenth Sunday), only prayer for a courage and loyalty which exceed our own powers.

Question: Does Jesus really mean we must hate father and mother?

Twenty-fourth Sunday

First reading: Israel Rebels in the Desert (Exodus 32.7-11, 13-14)

We start off with a fine argument between the Lord and Moses. 'Your people, whom you brought out of the land of Egypt', says the Lord to Moses. 'Your people, whom you brought out of the land of Egypt', says Moses to the Lord. Like parents, each blames the other for a misbehaving child. As soon as Moses' back was turned, Israel made itself an idol in the form of a golden calf – or rather a golden bull, called a 'calf' merely to be derisory – after the model of the local storm gods. The principal point is that, for all his blazing anger, the Lord cannot maintain his wrath against the people to whom he has promised an eternal inheritance. Once again, God changes his mind. His love of his people triumphs over his anger. In the next chapter, he passes before Moses and cries out the meaning of the name 'the Lord': a God of mercy and forgiveness, slow to anger, rich in faithful love and constancy, a meaning of the name that will echo down the pages of the scripture. The reading prepares us for the story of the Prodigal Son in the gospel.

Question: Is God always ready to forgive? Can anything stop it?

Second reading: Paul the Sinner (1 Timothy 1.12-17)

We read the two letters to Timothy over the next seven Sundays. Many scholars hold that, in accordance with a contemporary convention, the letters to Timothy and Titus were not actually written by Paul, but by a faithful disciple, still inspired by Paul, who puts what Paul *would have* said in the particular circumstances. Paul is represented as directing his two principal co-operators in their organization of Church structures. These letters present a valuable picture of the problems of the Church, a generation or two after Paul, settling into an organizational pattern towards the end of the first century, and finding its way among the values of Hellenistic society. In the present reading, Paul's open confession of his ferocious way of life before his conversion to Christianity, and the mercy he received from the Lord, pairs well with the record of divine mercy in the other two readings. The final little confession of faith in Christ as Saviour is one of the many declarations of Christological doctrine that give a special richness to these letters. Traditional formulations of doctrine are especially valued guidelines in these letters.

Question: Pray about an occasion when the grace of God drew you back from disaster.

Gospel: Forgiveness (Luke 15.1-32)
Today's gospel gives us three particularly attractive Lukan stories of forgiveness. The first two form a typical Lukan pair. First comes the story of the lost sheep, which comes also in Matthew. Luke, however, puts all the accent on the joy in heaven at the return of the sinner. Then, to the story of the man looking for his sheep, Luke adds the story of a woman looking for her lost coin. He is always careful to show that women have an equal part in the Kingdom with men. So he deliberately pairs Zechariah and Mary, Simeon and Anna, Jairus' daughter raised to life with the Widow of Naim's son, and so on. The main story, however, is the Prodigal Son, told with all Luke's love, artistry and delicacy of character study: the wastrel son who goes back home simply because he is hungry; the loving father perpetually on the lookout, running to meet the son, interrupting the carefully prepared speech and pampering the returned wastrel; the disgruntled stay at home who invents slanders about the other's 'loose women' and is gently corrected by his father's 'your brother'. An unforgettable picture of the overflowing love and forgiveness of God.

Question: Is there anyone you have not yet forgiven?

Twenty-fifth Sunday

First reading: Racketeering (Amos 8.4-7)

Amos is one of the first of the prophets whose sayings were gathered together and written down. He was peacefully pasturing sheep in the southern hill country near Bethlehem, when the Lord summoned him to trudge northwards and denounce the racketeering of rich against poor in Samaria. Archaeologists have shown us the traces of it. The capital was moved westwards to link with Mediterranean trade: marriage alliances with merchant princes, grand palaces displacing slum dwellings, expensive (and idolatrous) ivory inlays on the furniture. The fat cats would not listen to Amos, told him he was not welcome in their country, sent him packing and continued to fleece the helpless poor, for they controlled the money supply and the means of exchange – until the mighty power of Assyria swept down and destroyed them all. For us today perhaps the equivalent is rich nations profiteering from poor, unequal business deals, unfair trade, 'international aid' packages to dispose of excess production, the rich growing richer, the poor growing poorer in a thousand ways. The message of Amos is linked to the gospel by the final sentence: use wealth to make friends in heaven by your generosity.

Question: Can you do anything to prevent exploitation of the poor?

Second reading: Universal Salvation (1 Timothy 2.1-7)

As the gospel message moved out of the restricted world of Judaism, and came into contact with the larger world of the Greco-Roman Empire, new questions arose for Christians. The first question here was relationship to the civil authorities, and the answer: accept them and pray for them, in their attempts to provide a worthy framework for human life. The second question, a pressing one in our post-Christian society, can non-Christians be saved? Here the scripture tells us that God wills all people to be saved and come to knowledge of the truth, and that there is one mediator, Christ Jesus. How is this so? Is it enough to grope towards a God 'in signs and symbols' (Vatican II), accepting a power outside ourselves, to which all are indebted for existence itself, the ultimate authority in human life? And the mediator? How can people be saved by Christ if they do not know him? Is it enough to acknowledge our human deficiencies and failures and lay them in hope at the feet of a loving Saviour whom this unknown God will surely provide to bring the creation to fulfilment? What a responsibility have we, in expressing our values in such a way that others may share them?

Question: How can all people be saved by Christ, even those who do not know him?

Gospel: The Dishonest Steward (Luke 16.1-13)

This parable can be deeply disquieting if we take it as an allegory, that is, if every element in the story is meant (as in Matthew's Parable of the Wheat and the Tares) to have an equivalent in reality. We can't have God praising the steward for his frauds! No, the point of the story is simply the steward's energy and inventiveness, his shrewdness as a 'child of this age'. A lot more thought goes into how to make money than into how to spend it to the best advantage of others! The danger and encumbrance of wealth is such that inventiveness and energy is needed in using it to win friends in heaven. The full cleverness of the story is more subtle: Jews were forbidden to lend to Jews at interest. The steward cuts off the interest from the bills of his master's debtors, for oil was commonly lent at 100 per cent interest, and wheat at 25 per cent. It was easy to return olive oil adulterated with cheap sesame oil, but if I scatter handfuls of chaff in the grain I give you back, you will spot it immediately. So the steward makes his master obey the Law! The sayings added at the end hit the nail on the head: no slave can serve two masters, God and money.

Question: Do I take more trouble over what I want for myself or what I owe to God?

Twenty-sixth Sunday

First reading: Couch potatoes (Amos 6.1a, 4-7)

'Alas for those who lounge in front of the telly, munching their crisps and slurping their lager. Alas for those who zoom the streets, singing raucously along with their blaring radios.' Is Amos simply a middle-aged spoilsport, castigating the evils of his time? The real question is whether they manoeuvre themselves off the couch for the sake of the needy person at the door, whether they spring out of the car to help the blind person across the road. Following that, what *is* our society coming to, what can I do to help remedy the fundamental ills of our society, whatever I conceive them to be? What can I, helpless and half-hearted as I am, do to build on the ruins? How far can Jesus push me? One thing is sure, it is always one step further than my comfort zone. The Lord may not want me to go and be a Charles de Foucauld, a Romero, a Mother Teresa, but he always wants me to go one step nearer, whatever my state of life, one step at a time out of my comfort zone in response to his challenge. I can never say I have done all I need to do.

Question: What more am I able and willing to do for one person in need?

Second reading: Sevenfold Praise (1 Timothy 6.11-16)

The letters to Timothy contain several little hymns of praise to Christ. After his final exhortation to Timothy to perseverance and to witness, the author gives this concluding doxology as an inspiration for his (and our) devotion to Christ, enumerating seven titles of Christ's pre-eminence. In this egalitarian world, where TV has almost abolished the mystique of royalty, the first three titles of royalty (sovereign, king of kings and lord of lords) may not move us too much. But who would absent themselves if even a 'minor royal' was coming on a visit to office or factory, let alone the Lord of all Lords? The other awesome titles cannot fail to draw us. He possesses as his own the immortality for which we crave. He dwells in the sphere of faultless light that we cannot even envisage, let alone enter. He is beyond our sight, our comprehension, even our imagination. His are power and honour without end. We can only be amazed at how far he is beyond us, and yet that he walked beside the Lake of Galilee with his chosen friends, and allowed himself to be humiliated before his exaltation.

Question: How can we envisage God's glory?

Gospel: The Rich Man and Lazarus (Luke 16.19-31)

This story of Jesus comes only in Luke, another of those dreadful warnings of the danger of wealth, for Luke gives us always the gospel to the poor. Luke shows us those who blithely turn down their invitation to the banquet of the Kingdom in order to try out their new holiday cottage, their latest Porsche or the refitted yacht. Through the Crafty Steward he reminds us that those who want to make money are often sharper than those who want to make the Kingdom. Through the Rich Fool he reminds us that well-stocked barns are no remedy against death. For me, there are three particularly horrible features of this parable: first, the flea-ridden dogs licking Lazarus' sores: there are no pets in Palestine; dogs are either bristling guard dogs or mangy curs. Second, the Rich Man's continuing self-absorption even after death he still does not recognize Lazarus' existence and thinks only of his own burning tongue; contrast Abraham's gentleness: it almost looks as though he would cross the chasm if he could. Third, the obdurate brothers; they are just not willing to listen, even to the most startling event; nothing will distract them from their own selfish preoccupations.

Question: When was the last time I turned my back on someone who needed my help?

Twenty-seventh Sunday

First reading: The Righteous Person lives by Faith (Habakkuk 1.2-3; 2.2-4)

This fascinating passage has two entirely different meanings; the first is the meaning of the original Hebrew prophet, the second is the meaning of 'faith' in the gospel passage with which this first reading pairs. The drift of the passage in the Hebrew prophet Habakkuk is endurance. 'Make it plain on tablets, so that a runner may read it' – that is, as you whisk past, running your Marathon, you see an encouraging placard in the crowd, 'Keep it up!', 'Keep going!' So the message in the last line is that, however tough and unpromising the course, the righteous person lives by endurance, perseverance, fidelity. The message was originally intended to keep up the spirits of the Jews as the Babylonian armies approached: it will be tough, but stick it out, for the Lord will not desert you. However, the Apostle Paul is using the Greek translation of the Hebrew text – of course, he is writing in Greek – which reads 'the righteous person lives by fidelity/faith'. Paul uses the text in Romans 1.17 and Galatians 3.11 to prove that justification is by faith. Luther adds a further complication by adding, without justification, 'alone': 'The righteous person lives by faith alone.' For Paul, faith expresses itself in action.

Question: How does Christian hope make life different?

Second reading: The Sound Teaching of the Gospel (2 Timothy 1.6-8, 13-14)

Today we start with the first of four Sunday readings from Second Timothy. The letters addressed to Timothy and Titus, those two central members of Paul's staff, are generally considered not to have been written by Paul. However, they are all part of the inspired word of God, and a handful of reputable scholars considers that Second Timothy is indeed by Paul. In 1 Corinthians 16.10-11 the Corinthians are urged to treat Timothy gently, and here again the author seems to be encouraging Timothy himself against timidity; perhaps he was a naturally hesitant person. One of the principal emphases of all three letters is the adherence to 'sound teaching': they are encouraged not to show initiative but to keep to the tradition already established. This is, of course, already implied by the laying on of Paul's hands, for a Jewish rabbi would learn much by heart, and at the end of his training was commissioned to carry on the tradition in the name of his own teacher. Such methods would have been important for the preservation of the teaching of Jesus during the Pauline period, before it came to be written down in the gospels.

Question: Is it sufficient to keep to what we have been taught?

Gospel: The Reward of Faith (Luke 17.5-10)

The two sections of this gospel reading appear at first sight to be entirely separate, the first about faith, the second about the reward of service; but they do fit together. The faith required consists not in reciting a creed but in hanging on by one's fingertips, through thick and thin, to God's power and will to save. In nothing else is there any hope, not in my own power or ability. That is why, in the second section, we have no right to expect any sort of reward as our due from God. Our work is valueless; only our admission of helplessness and our trust in God's power can save us. However, not all parables should be taken as allegories. The severe master here is not necessarily God, any more than the master who in another parable praises his crooked steward. When we hear the unyielding command of the master to the slave to expect nothing and to set about serving at supper, we cannot forget that at the Last Supper it was Jesus who put on his apron and washed his disciples' feet. We may be worthless slaves, but this gives us confidence that our Master ministers to us.

Question: Do I really serve anyone? Am I a useless servant?

Twenty-eighth Sunday

First reading: Naaman the Syrian (2 Kings 5.14-17)

This little excerpt is the stub end of one of the most delightful stories in the Bible (read it!). It pairs with the gospel reading. In his opening proclamation in the synagogue at Nazareth, Jesus declares that he has come to save the gentiles too, just as Elisha did, citing Naaman as an example. Today we read just the cure itself. The odd bit about 'two mule-loads of earth' is the result of the belief, still persistent at that time, that the God of Israel could be worshipped only on the soil of Israel – so take some soil with you! Naaman wants to express his gratitude at home, too. At that time the Lord was accepted as God of Israel, the Sovereign and Protector of Israel, but this implied nothing about other nations. It was not until the Babylonian Exile, when Israel was confronted the multiple gods of Babylon, that Israel advanced a step and saw that the Lord was the God of the whole earth, the whole universe, and that all the other deities, such as sun and moon and stars, were simply timing devices plugged into the vault of heaven by the Lord himself. God reveals himself to Israel, and to us, gradually.

Question: How has your faith deepened or developed in the last years?

Second reading: The Grounds for Hope (2 Timothy 2.8-13)

If Paul is chained as a criminal, at least he gives the grounds for his hope and his security: 'The saying is sure.' The kernel of the Good News is the Resurrection, and that is enough. If Christ is risen from the dead, no more is required; this in itself is the fulfilment of the promises to David. Paul then quotes a little symmetrical hymn that was no doubt sung by the early Christian congregations. The earliest external evidence to the Christian liturgy is a letter from Pliny, governor of a province in what is now northern Turkey, in the early second century, only a few decades after Second Timothy. He has examined Christians under torture and sends his findings to the Emperor: they meet on a set day (presumably Sunday), make oaths of loyalty to one other, sing a hymn 'to Christ as to a God', and then have a meal (presumably the Eucharist). The last lines of this reading could be part of just such a hymn, under the pressures of persecution, celebrating the union of Christ with his followers, and Christ's fidelity to his own people, whatever they do to him.

Reflection: If we are faithless, he remains faithful.

Gospel: The Samaritan Leper (Luke 17.11-19)

Now we see why the story of the cure of Naaman the leper formed the first reading: in the gospel reading, we find another cure of a foreigner, and not an ordinary foreigner, but a hated foreigner. There was a cordial hatred between Jews and Samaritans – a wretched hybrid race, who accepted only part of the Jewish Bible, and had their own ideas about the coming Messiah. Yet we have already had the story of the Good Samaritan, who succours the wounded traveller, neglected by Jewish priest and Levite. Now only a Samaritan comes back to thank Jesus for the cure from leprosy. Samaritans are the foreigners geographically nearest to Jesus, but hated by the Jews. If the Samaritans can set an example to the Jews, so can many other foreigners. In his initial proclamation, Jesus promises salvation to the gentiles, and Luke misses no opportunity to show us gentiles ripe for salvation, the centurion of Capernaum who built the synagogue and whose son is cured, the guests for the banquet, called in from highways and byways. He is preparing for the second volume, the Acts of the Apostles, where the Good News will spread to the ends of the earth, to Rome itself.

Question: Is any race superior to any other? Why or why not?

Twenty-ninth Sunday

First reading: Perseverance in Prayer (Exodus 17.8-13)

This battle scene seems to us nowadays a bit of an odd passage to choose to reinforce the gospel lesson of perseverance in prayer. Can we still pray for the slaughter of our enemies? An important value of these bloodthirsty passages of the Old Testament is to remind us that revelation is gradual: we cannot take in everything at once. Look how long it took us to realize that the logical consequence of Paul's little letter to Philemon is the total abolition of slavery! Paul didn't realize it, and neither did most Christians for 1700 years. Future generations may think our morality primitive, too, as we or our successors come to understand Christianity ever more fully. However, prayer can be exciting and uplifting, but it can also be boring and exhausting, with just that sinking feeling of exhaustion: 'I can't hold my hands up any longer.' That is when we need really get on and hang on in there, expressing that God is not just one Mr Fixit among many possibles, but is our only hope and dependence. Cupboard love alone will not do, neither will a last-minute turn to someone about whose existence we had practically forgotten.

Question: When is it important to turn to prayer?

Second reading: The Uses of Scripture (2 Timothy 3.14–4.2)

The inspired writer seems to be devoting much of his space to the use of scripture in preaching and controversy, but most of all the scriptures 'instruct you for salvation'. We have to receive the message, and take it to our own hearts before we can pass it on to others. This is by seeing the variety of ways in which God cares for us, his ever present forgiveness in all our idiotic mistrust and shying away, our stubborn preference for our own search for happiness. Only by immersing ourselves regularly in the scriptures and growing to love these varied glimpses of God can we come to draw out their richness and sweetness. And there are plenty of difficulties to be overcome: the strangeness of language and ancient ways of thought, the barbaric primitiveness of the Chosen People of God, the boring instructions on sacrifice and purity. Don't rush it or gobble it up. Go your own pace, and remember that it began as God's Word to Abraham, Moses, David or whoever, or Jesus helping his contemporaries to understand about the Kingdom, or Paul responding to the queries of his half-instructed converts. But now it is God's Word to you.

Question: What is your favourite passage of scripture?

Gospel: The Answer to Prayer (Luke 18.1-8)

We often think of prayer as mere asking, and this parable encourages us to pester God as the wronged widow pestered the Unjust Judge. But that is only one aspect of Luke's teaching on prayer. He also shows us what our attitude in prayer should be, by the parable immediately following in the gospel, the Pharisee and the Tax Collector: the tax collector wins approval because he just stands there, admitting his sins. Most instructive, however, is Luke's teaching on Jesus at prayer: he reminds us that Jesus is always quietly at prayer to his Father. He needs to slip away to spend the night in prayer. Especially he prays at the most important moments of his life, at his baptism, when he chooses his team, before he teaches them to pray, at the approach of his Passion, finally forgiving and comforting others at his death. Paul tells us we should pray continually. The prayer of asking must be built on a relationship of love and dependence, just as the request of child to parents is built on that loving relationship. It does not matter if the child is naughty, as long as the relationship is one of love; so we do not need to be perfect to make our requests to our Father.

Question: When and how do you find it best to pray?

Thirtieth Sunday

First reading: The Prayer of the Humble (Sira 35.15-17, 20-22)

The Book of Sira was translated into Greek by the grandson of the author. The grandfather wrote in Hebrew. He was a wise, witty and sometimes cynical teacher of Jerusalem, who gathered and built on the pithy sayings of the sages. The first part of this reading, about the widow's persistent appeal to the Lord, may well be the basis of last Sunday's parable of the persistent widow and the unjust judge. Did Jesus build his parable on this piece of wisdom of the ancients, or did Luke use the Book of Sirach to expand Jesus' teaching? So also the second part of the reading, which prepares us for today's parable of contrasting suppliants, proud and humble, in the Temple: did Jesus build on the ancients or Luke? Jesus certainly heard and learnt from the holy books of Judaism. Whether Jesus directly used it or not, the message of the two parts is clear in the phrase that joins them: whoever whole heartedly serves God will be accepted. There is no pretending in prayer. As a wise old priest once said to me: 'In prayer you can stop pretending to be Queen Victoria or a poached egg.'

Question: What is the best short prayer you know?

Second reading: Paul's Farewell (2 Timothy 4.6-8, 16-18)

This is the last Sunday reading from the 'Pastoral Letters', addressed to Paul's assistants, Timothy and Titus. Fittingly, it is a summing up and defence of his mission, according to the literary conventions of the time. We do not know where the trial he mentions took place, or the eventual outcome, although the tradition holds strong that he was martyred in Rome (and his severed head bounced three times, giving rise to three fountains, the famous Tre Fontane). In his letters, Paul several times mentions imprisonment, but nowhere a formal trial, so that we can only guess. Did he set out on further journeys, even to Spain, after his confinement in Rome? We do not know. The sporting images of 'the good fight' and the 'race' are typical of Paul, and also the image of a libation, the first few drops from a cup of wine, offered in homage to a divinity. But most of all we are reminded that Paul had long yearned for death and to be fully united to his Lord and ours: 'Life to me, of course, is Christ, and death would be a positive gain' (Philippians 2.21), although he was held back by the positive need for his energetic guidance.

Question: Can you make any of Paul's self-defence your own?

Gospel: The Pharisee and the Tax Collector (Luke 18.9-14)
These two figures are stock characters, sketched with Luke's brilliant wit and sensitivity. The gospels invariably give the Pharisees a bad press, since after the destruction of Jerusalem they were the only surviving branch of Judaism, so stand for the vigorous opposition of Judaism to Christianity at that time. The Jewish historian, Josephus, paints a sympathetic picture of them, and Matthew's picture of them as the personification of hypocrisy may be a caricature of their fussiness of observance. Jesus played them at their own game in the careful interpretation of scripture, although with more profound understanding; was he a Pharisee too? Preoccupation with exact observance of rules can often appear to outsiders as hypocrisy. At that time a tax collector was the epitome of malpractice, extortion and abandonment of all decent standards. He worked for the hated Roman occupying power; he had to make his own living by extorting excessive tax. So this is one more example of the reversal of all expected values, and Jesus' outreach to those generally despised, the woman notorious in the city as a sinner, the woman taken in adultery, Zacchaeus and the 'good thief'. It beautifully fulfils the first reading: 'the prayer of the humble pierces the clouds.'

Reflection: God be merciful to me. I am a sinner.

Thirty-first Sunday

First reading: God's Love for All (Wisdom 11.22–12.2)

On the occasion of the conversion of Zacchaeus, read in today's gospel, the Church presents us also with this reading from the Book of Wisdom, which is one of the strongest statements in the Old Testament of God's mercy on all and God's desire that all people should be saved, 'since if you had hated something you would not have made it'. Again and again the Book of Wisdom makes much of God's forbearance, that sinners may have every chance to repent. This presents us with the clash: our love for God must be free, so that it is possible not to choose God. If our choice of God must be free, rejection of God must also be a possibility. And yet, would God have created anyone who did not choose him? We do not know that anyone actually has rejected God. Hell must be a possibility, but is it empty? We have no right to judge the consciences even of the monsters of history, and it is hard to say that anyone has been without some spark of generosity or gentleness or goodness.

Question: How is the concept of hell compatible with that of a loving God?

Second reading: The Final Coming of the Lord (2 Thessalonians 1.11–2.2)

The earliest Christians were confused about the final coming of the Lord. Jesus proclaimed that the Kingship of God was imminent. Did this mean that the world was coming rapidly to an end? How rapidly? Was the gist of his teaching principally that his death and Resurrection changed everything, even the whole constitution of the world? Then Paul taught that this world was passing away, that Christ would soon come in a great triumphal procession. Some saw the Fall of Jerusalem in 70AD as an urgent sign of the end. The Book of Revelation seems to teach that there will be reign of Christ for 1000 years after the first Resurrection and before the final struggle with Satan and the second Resurrection. Today's reading suggests that some thought the Day of the Lord had already arrived. Each year, as the cycle of readings draws to an end, the Church reminds us of this final coming of the Lord. When will it be? All we know is that it is imminent, in the sense that we must live in the spirit that God's final reckoning is urgently impending, and 'it is not for you to know the times and dates that the Father has decided' (Acts 1.7).

Question: How much do I need to know about the future and the end of all things?

Gospel: Zacchaeus (Luke 19.1-10)

The story of the rich little tax collector of Jericho is always a favourite. It was a constant complaint of defenders of the Law and its prescriptions that Jesus kept disreputable company – tax collectors, lepers, Samaritans and prostitutes! He took part in their carousals and seemed to enjoy their company. Tax collectors are never popular, and everyone thinks they are overtaxed. Under Roman rule the tax farmers were moral outcasts, especially because they worked for the hated foreign dominators, and surely added their own percentage to the tax demanded. Jesus does not even seem aware of their uncleanness. He does not wait for them to repent and approach him, but positively goes out to them and summons them into his company. Zacchaeus had given no sign of good intentions. This unpopular little man was simply inquisitive, wanting to see what Jesus looked like, not even trying to get near him. One can imagine his open mouthed and delighted amazement, perched in his sycamore tree, as Jesus invited himself to supper over the heads of the intervening crowd. 'Why should Jesus choose me?' No conditions attached, no previous guarantee of good behaviour or repentance! So Jesus draws out our good intentions before we are even really aware of them ourselves.

Question: Did Zacchaeus invite any friends to join him and Jesus? Did he have any friends?

Thirty-second Sunday

First reading: Rising to New Life (2 Maccabees 7.1-2, 9-14)

This is the only reading from the Books of Maccabees in the Sunday cycle of readings. In the year 167 BC the Syrian Empire dominated Palestine, and King Antiochus IV decided to make an important step towards unifying his empire by wiping out the singular worship and religious customs of the Jews. He met stronger resistance than expected, and a great persecution was necessary. The resistance was led by three brothers who were given the name 'Maccabee' or 'Hammer'; they give their name to these two biblical Books (and also to an excellent beer in Israel!). Our reading gives one incident in that persecution. The lasting importance of such a heroic stance was the development of the doctrine of Resurrection to new life. Until that time Israel had seen the dead confined to Sheol, a wretched half-life, where the dead had no strength and could not even praise God. Now they saw that God would raise up to new life those who had died for their faith in the persecution. By the time of Jesus this belief in the Resurrection of the dead to new life was standard in Israel. Only the traditionalist Sadducees did not accept it.

Question: How different would your life be if there were no Resurrection?

Second reading: 2 Thessalonias 2.16–3.5

A reading from Thessalonians heralds the end of the liturgical year, for Year A ends with 1 Thessalonians and Year C with this second letter. Both letters are concerned with the Second Coming of Christ at the end of time. The little community at Thessalonika were worried. Paul had taught them that Christ had conquered death: for those baptized into Christ death was no more. But then Christians had died! So Paul wrote to them that Christ would soon come in a triumphal procession, bringing with him his followers who had already died. This must have thrown the Thessalonians into a frenzy of excitement at such an imminent Coming, for Paul writes to them this second letter to calm them, explaining that the Coming is not so utterly imminent. They must continue to live life in the world, for there must first be a period in which evil is still at work, a period in which the Word of the Lord is still spreading, as it is among them, and in which they need protection from evil (or the Evil One). The Christian cannot opt out of the world, so needs the strength of the Lord to live the ways of the Lord in a world which fundamentally fails to recognize such ways.

Question: What is meant by 'the forces of evil'?

Gospel: The Sadducees' Riddle (Luke 20.27-38)

Since they did not believe in the Resurrection or any sort of life after death, the Sadducees are trying to make fun of Jesus. By the Levirate Law of Judaism, if I marry and die without begetting a son, my nearest male relative is bound to marry my widow and raise up a son in my name to carry on my line. The Sadducees' neat mockery is to ask what happens if this is repeated seven times (and worse than that, for the perfect number 'seven' means 'ad infinitum'). Jesus, again with typical neatness, turns their argument by returning to this fundamental text of scripture, God's reply to Moses at the Burning Bush. Not only is this in the present tense, 'I *am* (still) the God of patriarchs long dead', but it is the fundamental text that guarantees God's rescue and protection to his people through thick and thin. This is one more instance of Jesus' deep control of scripture, of the way he passes over the flippant and superficial arguments of his opponents to penetrate to the basic sense of scripture. To God, no one is 'dead and gone', but we all remain safe in his hands.

Question: Do Abraham, Isaac and Jacob have any advantage over me? If so, how?

Thirty-third Sunday

First reading: Burning like an Oven (Malachi 4.1-2)

Each year the Church takes the end of the liturgical season to remind us that the Day of the Lord is coming. This 'Day of the Lord' has several different levels. In the Old Testament, it was the great and terrible day, pictured in ever more cataclysmic cosmic images, when the Lord would come to set right all injustice. In today's world, this would be some upheaval! Rags to riches, riches to rags, slumdog millionaires, emperors wearing no clothes! Then Jesus came, declaring that the Kingdom was at hand, that the Day was dawning. And so it did, at the Hour of Jesus, completed on the first Easter Sunday, when the world and life were changed for ever. Yet in another sense, at another level, the Day is still to come. Christians are different from every other people, in that we live in expectation, in the knowledge that, at some time, everything will be brought to completion. The sun of righteousness shall rise, with healing in its wings. Christ will hand over the Kingdom to his Father, having put all things under his feet, even the last enemy, death. Whatever these images mean, that is the shape of history.

Question: How do you imagine the Day of the Lord?

Second reading: 2 Thessalonians 3.7-12

In his earlier letter to the Thessalonians, Paul had warned them that the Day would come 'like a thief in the night', like an unexpected trap suddenly sprung, the dreaded roadside bomb. The recipients of the letter seem to have been so panicked that some simply downed tools and sat waiting. So now Paul chides that anyone who does not work should not eat either. This charge does not refer only to earning our bread and butter; it is also symbolic. Paul himself, after all, both earned his bread and butter by his leather working and set the fire of the gospel alight all around the eastern Mediterranean. In all his writings, he is acutely aware of the pressure from the end point, although he has no idea when it will come. We don't get any nearer perfection, or any nearer the state in which we would like the Lord to find us, simply by sitting and waiting. Even those who are chair bound, and can indeed only sit and wait, can at the same time mightily advance the Kingdom by bringing the light and joy of Christ to their surroundings.

Question: What should we do to prepare for the Day of the Lord?

Gospel: Perseverance (Luke 21.5-19)

Luke was writing his Gospel after the devastation of Jerusalem by the Roman armies in 70 AD, and the way he frames the words of Jesus suggests that he had witnessed the devastation. Massive blocks of stone, thrown down from the walls, are still lying there as they fell, scattered at the base of the Temple. The message of this passage is, then, the same as Paul's: the end is sure, but is not yet. Jesus prepares his followers for what is to come before the cataclysmic finale. He warns against false Messiahs, political leaders or other saviour figures who claim to 'put the world to rights'. His followers will be continually challenged to give an account of their beliefs, harassed and martyred in every age, betrayed by those they thought their friends. There is a promise that Jesus will give the words and wisdom for reply; there is a promise of protection from real harm; but there is no promise that it will be a quiet and easy life. A constant theme in Luke's Good News is that the followers of Jesus must follow him in his difficulties and trials. Only with like endurance will they keep in his footsteps.

Reflection: Recall an occasion on which the Lord gave you wisdom beyond your own.

Thirty-fourth Sunday, Christ the King

First reading: David Anointed King (2 Samuel 5.1-3)

David is a fascinating character. As a leader, he had a charm and charisma that were irresistible. There is no doubt that he was ambitious. When the women sang, 'Saul has killed his thousands and David his tens of thousands', it was music to his ears. The king's son fell in love with him and gave him his own prince's gear. The king's daughter fell in love with him, and he accepted her as a good dynastic marriage; but he never had children by her, although he was not lacking in sexual drive (Bathsheba was to come later). He set up a protection racket in Judah and so won the loyalty of the tribal leaders there; they first anointed him king of Judah at Hebron, the southern tribal capital. Finally, after Saul's death, the elders of the northern tribes, Israel, came to anoint him king as well, to reign over the whole country. But he also took the first steps to setting up the Temple cult, and was ever after remembered for that. It was to David that the promises of God's eternal monarchy were given that were to be fulfilled in Jesus. These promises echo down and down the scriptures; they were the basis of all Israel's hope.

Question: What do you consider leadership qualities before God?

Second reading: The Kingdom of Forgiveness (Colossians 1.12-20)

Way back in the summer, on the fourteenth Ordinary Sunday of the Year, we heard all but the first part of this reading, for it celebrates the unrivalled position of Jesus as firstborn not only in the order of creation, but also in the Resurrection. In the order of creation, Christ is the image of the unseen God, the model or template on which God created the world, the Wisdom of God, so the firstborn and yet himself uncreated. In the order of the Resurrection also he is the firstborn, bringing all things to perfection, and so the crown of creation. Before this we today have a significant preface. Paul is writing, with a slight air of surprise, to the gentiles: the gentiles too are enabled to enter into this inheritance, to join Christ in this kingdom, promised to David and fulfilled in Jesus. As this year's gospel readings have taught us again and again, it is not a kingdom that we can earn. All we need to do is to submit ourselves for forgiveness. Not all that easy, perhaps! Put it the other way round: all we need to do is stop pretending to others and ourselves that we are perfect.

Question: What sickness in myself is the most frequent cause of falling?

Gospel: The King of Forgiveness (Luke 23.35-43)

The crucifixion scene in Luke, as in all the gospels, is the climax. And Jesus is stressed as being King. The soldiers mock him as such, but the gospel's use of irony ensures that we understand that they are saying more than they realize. They mock him also as Saviour ('Save yourself and us as well!'), and especially in Luke, from the Infancy Stories onwards, is Jesus seen as the true Saviour God. In Luke, the crucifixion scene is primarily a scene of forgiveness, in which Jesus carries on to the very end his work of forgiveness, which Luke has underlined throughout the gospel. It begins with the women of Jerusalem mourning for Jesus, and ends with all the spectators departing, beating their breasts, recognizing their universal guilt. Jesus spontaneously forgives his executioners, asking for them God's forgiveness before they even ask themselves. He welcomes into his Kingdom of Paradise the bandit who spontaneously acknowledges his guilt. It is the climax of the reversal of values that we have seen throughout this gospel that the King should be the wretched figure dying on the Cross, and that homage should be paid to him not by dignified courtiers, but by another wretched figure, dying by his side.

Question: What sort of person should a citizen of the Kingdom of Forgiveness be?

SOLEMNITIES WHICH TRUMP SUNDAYS

Feasts of the Lord and Solemnities

2 February The Presentation of the Lord

First reading: The Coming of the Lord (Malachi 3.1-4)

This first reading from Malachi is dire and threatening. The Lord will come to his Temple and refine it. The reading seems to fit better the coming of Jesus to cleanse the Temple in the final days of his ministry than the coming of the child Jesus in helpless innocence. Yet the searing, final coming is already presaged in the coming of the young Jesus to the Temple to be greeted by Simeon as the fulfilment of God's promise of salvation or completion. Malachi prophesied the purging of the sons of Levi, and no one can deny that a dreadful purging of the sons of Levi took place at the Sack of Jerusalem in 70AD. They had failed to recognize their Lord. This cannot but give us pause to reflect whether we, who have theoretically committed ourselves to Christ, have, in fact, responded and been converted and purged. Are we in any way better than those who were condemned and suffered, or are we merely more secretive, better at concealing out faults and secret distortions from others? The thoughts of all hearts will be laid bare in the end. It might be as well to start laying them bare, or purging them now.

Question: How is it that the majority of Jews failed to recognize Jesus?

Second reading: The Faithful High Priest (Hebrews 2.10-11, 13b-18)

The inclusion of this reading is unbelievably moving: the child presented in the Temple is also to suffer, the sword will pierce Mary's heart. But it is because Jesus is fully human, and now a helpless child, that his loving obedience to the Father will save the human race. 'What was not assumed was not saved', say the Fathers. In Jesus, the source of our salvation, the disobedience of Adam was washed away. Adam is the representative of us all, personifying the human race. Adam's sin is the myth or analysis of the sin of us all, and Jesus had to be like his brothers and sisters, to share their full human nature if he were to save their human nature. He shared our baby helplessness, our adolescent anguish, our fear of death, our loss of friends whom we thought were faithful. In all this, he knit himself into the human race, and by taking it upon himself, saved it by joining it once more into the Father's love. The language of high priesthood is used in this Letter to the Hebrews because the letter is written to Hebrews who were pining for the rituals of the Temple. But the priesthood is radically different, according to the order of Melchizedek (an unknown priesthood), in the line of Aaron.

Question: What was the purpose of Jesus' death?

Gospel: The Child Destined for the Rise and Fall of Many (Luke 2.22-40)

The story of the Presentation of the child Jesus in the Temple is dominated by Simeon's welcome, 'a light to enlighten the gentiles and the glory of your people Israel', and by his warning to Mary, 'a sword will pierce your heart'. Simeon reiterates the angel's promise that the child would fulfil the destiny of Israel and Israel's task to the nations. Much like any family life, the promised future included the delights of the growing, developing child, and the background fear that the great destiny of each child may include sorrow and even heartbreak. How much did Mary and Joseph know about the precious child they were nurturing? As he grew to independence, did he become more loving and supportive? How did his contemporaries find him? Was he a leader? Did he stand out from the pack? Each of us has a private picture of the child, the boy, the adolescent, the young man. If he were fully human, he had the same frustrations and worries as every child growing in youth and through puberty. All we know for sure is that 'the child grew to maturity', and that Mary 'pondered all these things in her heart', with Simeon's welcome and warning before her mind.

Question: Imagine Jesus' first serious conversation as an enquiring child with Mary.

25 March The Annunciation of the Lord

First reading: A Girl is with Child (Isaiah 7.10-14; 8.10d)

The prophecy in this first reading was given in 736BC, when King Ahaz of Judah was about to be forced into an alliance, in a vain attempt to oppose the crushing military power of Babylon. Isaiah goes to him and warns him that the alliance would be fatal: he had better trust in the Lord. Isaiah promises a sign, which Ahaz refuses. He does not want to be convinced!

What is this sign? The original Hebrew reads: 'A girl is with child and will bear a son.' Mary did not know the Greek translation, 'the *virgin* is with child', but she knew the prophecies of the Messiah who would save Israel, and she must have recognized that she was being asked to undertake the motherhood of this child. A daunting challenge, to change her life and bring her to the heart of God! On her the future of her people would depend, and perhaps circles wider yet. The end of her carefree childhood, her own plans for marriage and family, dedicated entirely to the God she served. We cannot know how much she realized, but she must have heard the prophecies from the Sabbath readings of the Prophets, and known that a daunting task was offered to her.

Question: Why is Mary's virginity important in the Church's teaching?

Second reading: 'I Have Come to Do Your Will' (Hebrews 10.4-10)

This reading from Hebrews is a beautiful commentary on and interpretation of the Incarnation itself. The Letter is written to those, probably Jewish, priests who had embraced Christianity, who were pining for the old rites. It explains that the old rites could never accomplish God's purpose. How, then, could the sacrifice of Jesus? The purpose of Jesus' sacrifice was not the bloodshed, as if an angry God demanded blood from someone as reparation, and the blood of Jesus was more effective than mere animal blood. This is the pagan idea of sacrifice, to turn away the wrath of a god by offering a little gift! The meaning and effectiveness of the sacrifice of Jesus was a consummate act of loving obedience, an obedience that washed away and annulled the disobedience of Adam, that is, the disobedience of the human race. Why death? The whole of the human life of Jesus, which begins at this sacred moment of the Annunciation, the moment of conception, is an act of loving obedience to the Father. But this obedience reaches its climax in the full expression of it at the crucifixion: Jesus was prepared to give himself totally, even to death.

Question: Should we say that the Annunciation was the moment of our salvation?

24 June The Nativity of John the Baptist

First reading: Formed in the Womb to be God's Servant (Isaiah 49.1-6)

The first reading from Isaiah, written in the dark days of the Babylonian Exile, introduces a Servant of the Lord, formed in the womb to be the

Lord's Servant and to bring light both to Israel and to the nations. It is read on this feast of the birthday of John the Baptist because he too, as the story of the annunciation to Zachariah recounts, was chosen and given a task from his mother's womb. 'Chosen from his mother's womb' does not imply that some are not, but is a way underlining the importance of the person's task in proclaiming the Good News. Paul uses the same expression of himself and his ministry in Galatians 1.15. In the original prophecy of Isaiah, is this an individual whose mission is to bring Israel back to the Lord, or is it the nation of Israel, destined to bring the gentile nations to the Lord? The words of the Voice at the baptism of Jesus are the opening words of the first Song of the Servant in Isaiah. The sayings of Jesus about service – the Son of man has come not to be served but to serve – show that he too saw himself as this Servant of the Lord.

Question: Are we not all chosen from our mother's wombs?

Second reading: The Mission of John the Baptist (Acts 13.22-26)

In this reading, Paul is proclaiming the Good News to the Jews of Antioch, showing how John prepared for Jesus, the Saviour of David's line. John's task was to prepare a community of repentance. This was not merely a community of people who moped over their sins, but a community of those who were prepared to change their ways and take on the new way of life of the Kingship or Sovereignty of God, symbolized by the washing away of their old way of life in the River Jordan. As God's prophet he prepared the community for Jesus and pointed out Jesus himself as the Lamb of God. Not the least notable feature about John was his wonderful humility: he insisted that Jesus, who came after him, should pass before him, that Jesus should grow greater and he himself grow less. Jesus gave him the greatest of all recognitions: 'of all the children born to women there has never been a greater than John the Baptist' (Matthew 11.11). In his fearless proclamation of the message of morality to Herod and in his death as a witness, he showed himself a true precursor of Jesus.

Question: What do you find the most striking element in John the Baptist's mission?

Gospel: The Birth and Naming of John the Baptist (Luke 1.57-66, 80)

The birth stories of John the Baptist and of Jesus are told in such a way as to bring out the parallelism between the two figures, and the special position of each. Of each, the parents are models of the fidelity of Israel, and of trust in the Lord. An angel foretells the miraculous birth of each.

The birth and naming of each is an occasion of great joy. In each case, John is great but Jesus is greater still: The exalted position of John serves to exalt the position of Jesus even further. John will prepare the way; Jesus will be seated on the throne of his father David. Zechariah doubts and is struck dumb; Mary humbly enquires and is blessed. John's name means 'God is gracious', Jesus' name is 'Saviour'. At the birth of John there is joy in the family, at the birth of Jesus the joy and singing are by the angels. At the end of this passage, John goes out into the desert because it was from the desert that the Messiah was expected to come, and John will be the herald voice, crying in the desert in fulfilment of Isaiah, 'Make straight his paths.'

Question: What would you have advised John the Baptist to do in the desert?

29 June Saints Peter and Paul

First reading: Peter is Released from Prison (Acts 12.1-11)

The early chapters of the Acts of the Apostles show the earliest Church at Jerusalem being led by Peter. The later chapters recount the mission of Paul to the gentiles. This story tells of a near disaster, averted by divine intervention. Had Peter, as well as James, been martyred at this early stage, the Church might have been left without leaders and could hardly have survived. It is one of the many accounts of divine intervention to free the apostles from the prisons to which their fearless witness to Christ brought them. Several times the whole group of apostles had been imprisoned by the Jewish authorities for their witness and miraculously released. This full account is paralleled by the release of Paul from prison in Thessalonika through an earthquake; the stories of Peter and Paul are parallel in many ways. The lesson is that the Holy Spirit was guiding the Church at every stage, and was looking after its members as they proclaimed the gospel. The story is superbly told, with the amusing picture of Peter, still half-asleep, being guided at every step by the angel, like a sleepy child, woken up in the middle of the night.

Question: Would the Church have collapsed had Peter been executed?

Second reading: Paul's Farewell (2 Timothy 4.6-8, 17-18)

Writing to his follower Timothy, Paul sums up and defends his mission, confident in the divine help he has received throughout his trials as an apostle. We do not know what this 'rescue from the lion's mouth' was, but he was shipwrecked several times on his missionary journeys, and also imprisoned, beaten and flogged by both Jews and Roman authorities. He persevered in his apostolate, but he yearned to be fully united with his Lord and ours. He was very conscious that he and all Christians are baptized into Christ's death, rise with Christ in his Resurrection, and so live with Christ's life: 'Life to me, of course, is Christ, and death would be a positive gain' (Philippians 2.21). He was held back by the positive need for his energetic guidance by the communities he had founded all over the eastern Mediterranean. The sporting images of 'the good fight' and the 'race' are typical of Paul. The games were as important as football matches today. He uses also the image of a libation: in Roman society the first few drops were poured out from a cup of wine, as a symbol of offering to the gods. Paul now feels that he is approaching the end of his journey.

Question: Can you make any of Paul's self-defence your own?

Gospel: Jesus Claims Peter as Rock (Matthew 16.13-19)

At last in this gospel reading, Peter recognizes Jesus as the Messiah, the Christ and Son of the living God. At last he realizes that in Jesus they can see the action of God. The disciples had followed Jesus as soon as he called, but for a long time they were puzzled what to make of him, of his wonderful teaching and his godlike personality. Now comes a shaft of light and understanding. We too often take some time to appreciate the true worth of someone we know well: a little gesture can sometimes reveal just how generous and thoughtful they are. The impulsive Peter suddenly grasps that there is God, acting among them, a daunting or even terrifying thought. Jesus replies to Peter's recognition with his own generosity, giving him a new name, 'Rock', for this is what 'Peter' means. Jesus makes Peter the Rock on which his Church is founded. The promise of authority which Jesus here gives to Peter he also gives to the community itself, 'where two or three are gathered in my name' (Matthew 18.18–19). Peter is the rock of unity in the Church; he and his successors speak in the name of the Church.

Question: Why did Jesus choose such an impetuous and unreliable character as Rock?

6 August The Transfiguration of the Lord

First reading: One Like a Son of Man (Daniel 7. 9-10, 13-14)

This prophecy of Daniel was written in the dark days of the Syrian persecution of Judaism a couple of centuries before Christ. First, the evil empires that persecuted Judaism are described under the imagery of ravening beasts, tearing their prey to pieces. Then comes this altogether different image of a noble human being on whom God confers all power and sovereignty on earth. In the original vision, this human figure is the personification of the Jews, 'the holy ones of the Most High', who will be freed from this persecution and exalted to glory. In the New Testament, this prophecy is applied to Jesus. In the trial before the High Priest, he will claim this exalted position as his own, saying, 'You will see the Son of man seated at the right hand of the Father and coming on the clouds of heaven.' The High Priest recognizes this as a divine claim and cries out, 'Blasphemy!' This title, and the claim to share the Father's throne, are indeed claims to divinity. It gives sense to Jesus' other claims to divine power, the power to forgive sins and to complete the Law. In this power, he sends out his apostles to teach and baptize all nations.

Question: What does Jesus mean by calling himself 'son of man'?

Second reading: Peter's Witness to the Transfiguration (2 Peter 1.16-19)

In fact, the Second Letter of Peter was probably written not by Peter but by an unknown author, writing in Peter's name and with his authority. For the author, the event of the Transfiguration takes a central place in spirituality, 'as a lamp shining in a dark place', providing a confirmation of the prophetic message and an inspiration until the dawning of the final day. The description of the place as 'the Holy Mountain' is a reminder that we do not know where it took place, but that, wherever it occurred, it is a parallel to the appearance of God on the Holy Mountain of Sinai, which was the occasion and basis of the choice of Israel to be God's People. There Jesus was honoured with glory conveyed to him by 'the Majestic Glory'. In the Bible, 'glory' is properly a divine property. It is an awesome term, for glory belongs to God alone, although 'heaven and earth are full of his glory', as the angels sing in Isaiah's vision of God in the Temple (Isaiah 6.3). As the Beloved Son of God, Jesus shares the same glory. It was, therefore, for the chosen disciples who witnessed it, properly and experience of the divinity of Jesus.

Question: Is it possible to experience in any way the glory of God in creation?

Gospel: The Transfiguration (Year A: Matthew 17.1-9; Year B: Mark 9.2-10; Year C: Luke 9.28b-36)

Mark's was the first Gospel to be written; he gives the basic account which Matthew and Luke both use. This commentary looks first at Mark, then at the changes made by Matthew and Luke.

Mark's Gospel has been described as 'a Passion Narrative with extended introduction.' In this second half of the Gospel, everything is overshadowed by the Passion of Jesus. The disciples are going to be stunned and shaken by the Passion, when their loved and awesome leader is taken from them and tortured to a humiliating death. So beforehand God allows them to see the other side, to see Jesus for what he really is. They see his features as a heavenly person, transformed with the divine light and clothed in dazzling garments. With him are the two heavenly figures who had experience of God on the Holy Mountain, Moses and Elijah, for this is an experience of Jesus as God. The overshadowing cloud is further evidence of the divine presence. The Voice that spoke to Jesus at his baptism now speaks to them all, authenticating Jesus as God's Son and chosen teacher. The disciples are literally 'gob stopped', and want to preserve the experience by building three shelters for the heavenly visions. But such an experience, like any mystical experience of the divine, is not to last. They must return to the business of living their daily lives in the light of this overwhelming experience.

Matthew's account is almost the same as Mark's. He adds the detail of Jesus' face shining like the sun. This was the case with Moses when he encountered God on the Holy Mountain, and Matthew, writing for Jewish Christians, is always keen to stress that Jesus was a Second Moses. He also changes the reaction of the disciples: in Mark, they are so scared that they do not know what to say, but in Matthew, they fall to the ground and do reverence, and Jesus gently raises them up.

Luke stresses that Jesus went up the mountain to pray. He frequently stresses Jesus' constant need for prayer, and many of Luke's parables are about prayer (the Importunate Widow and the Unjust Judge, the Pharisee and the Tax Collector). Luke also details that Jesus, Moses and Elijah were conversing about his journey up to Jerusalem, a journey that is the theme of the latter half of Luke's gospel.

15 August The Assumption of the Blessed Virgin Mary

First reading: The Woman Robed with the Sun (Revelation 11.19a, 12.1-6, 10ab)

This vision of the woman giving birth and of the huge red dragon is bewilderingly rich in biblical symbolism. The context of the Book of Revelation is the struggle between the Church and the demands of Roman paganism, particularly the demand that all should worship the emperor as God. The purpose of Revelation is to reassure the faithful of victory, despite the threat of martyrdom. The woman represents Israel, the people of God, who gives birth to a son, the true ruler of the universe. The dragon, of great sagacity and immense power, is the Roman Empire. The son is unhesitatingly whipped up to heaven in triumph, frustrating the evil dragon of its prey and issuing immediately in the hymn of triumph. The perspective is, of course, foreshortened, omitting the details of Christ's earthly life, to show the certainty of the son's triumph. Secondarily, tradition sees in the woman the earthly mother of the Saviour, Mary, mother of Jesus and mother of the Church, who triumphs over all the powers of evil. The secondary symbolism, therefore, is that Mary is the great sign in heaven of triumph over evil. Evil has no hold on Mary, and her children are sure of victory.

Question: Is this a fair picture of the history of the Church?

Second reading: Christ, Firstborn from the Dead (1 Corinthians 15.20-26)

On the Festival of the Assumption of Mary it is important to get things in the right order. Christ is the firstborn from the dead. In him, all will be brought to life, but all in their proper order. Mary is the first after her Son, and raised by her Son because she is part of his Body, the Church. The perfection of the Mother of the Saviour is won for her by her Son. He draws her after him in his retinue. In this chapter, Paul is teaching about bodily Resurrection. This is not merely immortality of the soul, but the Resurrection of the whole person, an animated body, not a soul hidden in a body. It is particularly fitting with regard to Mary, the physical mother of Jesus, who gave to him her genes, her personality, her features and her talents. If any son takes after his mother physically, it must have been Jesus. The declaration by the Church of the Assumption of Mary is an assertion of the saving value of all our activity, the healing touch, the conquest of pain, exhaustion, moodiness and physical temptation in all its forms. That is why Mary goes ahead of us all and leads the way to full Resurrection.

Question: What is the best way to honour Mary?

Gospel: Mary's Visit to Elizabeth (Luke 1.39-56)

The core of this gospel reading is Mary's canticle of thanksgiving for God's gifts to her. It is, however, fitting that, on the Feast of the bodily Assumption of Mary, it should begin with her bodily attention to the bodily needs of her elderly relative. With her own baby on the way, she would have plenty of other priorities, making her long journey an act of real kindness. Her canticle, sung daily in the liturgy of Evening Prayer, sums up God's faithfulness to his promises, focused on his gifts to this simple peasant girl. It combines a wonderful sense of the holiness of God with warmth of gratitude, showing the thoughts that revolved constantly in her mind. As is fitting in the mouth of a girl whose only knowledge of books was the Bible, Mary's song is a texture of scriptural phrases. We cannot assume that Luke wrote it down at Mary's dictation, for putting words in the mouth of his characters is a feature of Luke the historian; but it must reflect her thinking. If any theme resounds again and again throughout the Bible, it is God's care for the poor, the simple and those in need. It is this that sets the Hebraeo-Christian tradition apart from the ways of the world

Question: Why is the Assumption an important doctrine of the Church?

14 September The Exaltation of the Holy Cross

First reading: The Healing Snake (Numbers 21.4-9)

This story about a bronze snake explains a bronze snake that was long kept in the Temple at Jerusalem as a reminder of God's healing power, which lasts from age to age. Eventually, in a purge of dubious objects of veneration, the reforming king Hezekiah decided that the snake was idolatrous, and destroyed it. One still sometimes sees a snake curled round a stake as a medical sign, a promise of healing. The Church sees that healing sign as a preparation for the great healing sign of the Cross. During Lent and Passiontide we remember the Cross chiefly for the suffering of Christ. Now, months later, we can celebrate the triumph of its healing power and the triumph of Christ's victory. The Feast originates in the victory of the Christian emperor Heraclius, when he won back from the pagan Persians a great relic of the Cross they had taken from Jerusalem. The crucifixes hanging in our homes must be seen as symbols not only of Christ's suffering, but, above all, of his triumph over death.

Question: How should Jesus be represented on the Cross, in triumph or in suffering?

Second reading: Christ, the second Adam (Philippians 2.6-11)

This lovely reading seems to be a very early Christian hymn that Paul had heard and incorporated into his letter. It contrasts the first Adam with the second Adam, Jesus Christ. The first Adam, the representative of the whole human race, tried to be like God, he wanted to escape death, he was disobedient and was humiliated. The second Adam, the founder of the new humanity and first fruits from the dead, was in the form of God, but did not capitalize on his divinity. In full obedience to the Father, he accepted death, a humiliating death, and was raised up by the Father. The last lines give one of the fullest pictures of Christ's divinity in Paul: Christ receives the divine name, the Lord, which belongs to God alone. To Christ, every knee must bend, as it must bend only to God. And yet, this does not take away from God's glory, since – on the contrary – it is 'to the glory of God the Father'. Paul never actually calls Christ 'God', but here he shows precisely that, by attributing to him the reverence and adoration that are due only to God.

Question: Do you find this poem an attractive centre of devotion? Why?

Gospel: The Son of Man must be Lifted Up (John 3.13-17)

In this gospel reading we are listening in to a conversation between Jesus and Nicodemus, a Pharisee who came to Jesus by night (presumably because he did not want his colleagues to know). Do you mind your colleagues knowing that you are a Christian? Jesus is talking about an incident during the Exodus journey, when the Israelites were struck by a plague of snakes. Moses hoisted a bronze snake on a pole as a recovery totem. It sounds superstitious, but presumably to depend on it was an expression of trust in God. Jesus now says that this snake is to be seen as a promise of the salvation to be won by trusting in his Cross. The Cross remains our sign of victory. To wear it and welcome it is increasingly, in this increasingly material world, a statement of where our heart and our confidence lie. However, the Cross is not complete in itself. Some people find it 'morbid' or 'morose', but to Christians it contains also the victory and reassurance of the Resurrection. The Cross makes sense not by the crumpled figure on the wood, but by God's acceptance of that obedience. The triumph of the Resurrection is too glorious to be represented by anything visible.

Question: Should a fervent Christian home be dominated by representations of Christ crucified?

1 November All Saints

First reading: The Martyrs in Safe Keeping (Revelation 7.2-4, 9-14)

The Book of Revelation, from which this reading is taken, was written during the first persecutions of the Christians. It is built on the promise that, after persecution, those who are faithful to God and to Christ will be delivered and gathered into the peace of God's presence. At the time of writing, the persecuting force from which they were to be delivered was the might of the Roman Empire, with its immorality, its materialism, its consumerism, and, above all, its demand that all its subjects should worship the emperor as God. For Christians at that time, the late first century, the great test was whether they would accept the standards of the Empire or remain faithful to the demanding standards of Christianity. The same decision stands before Christians in today's world. Who is my Lord, Christ or the standards for which the emperor stood, carelessness about sexual morality, materialism, consumerism, putting myself first in everything without regard for the cost to others? Do I connive at and approve standards of behaviour that are built on a morality far from that of Christ? More pressingly, do I accept those standards for myself?

Question: What are your criteria for sanctity? Is martyrdom too much stressed?

Second reading: We Shall be Like Him (1 John 3.1-3)

The second reading also contains hints of an opposition from a godless world, but concentrates much more on union of God's children to God himself. We are already God's children, because we have been adopted in Christ and can cry '*Abba*, Father!' What are the implications of this adoption to sonship? Sometimes a son is almost absurdly like his father in looks, gestures, mannerisms and ways of approaching any task. For ourselves, we cannot yet fully know what this likeness will consist in, but we are promised that in the fullness of revelation we will be assimilated to God. Not only must we be close to our Father in prayer, but we must also show the qualities of God in our actions, God's generosity, his forgiveness, his openness. Part of this must be that we will find that God has developed in us all the qualities we most love and admire in others, sons assimilated to their father. It will be a world of universal joy and appreciation, as all is suffused with the generosity and love of the Father. 'We shall be like him because we shall see him as he really is', and this means that the vision of God will be so overwhelming that we cannot but become like him.

Question: What are the elements you look forward to in heaven?

Gospel: The Beatitudes (Matthew 5.1-12)

These eight blessings stand at the head of the Sermon on the Mount, pointing out eight ways in which we can welcome God into our lives. They are ways of living out God's blessing, possible only if the hand of God is upon you. That is why the first and the last knit them all together with 'theirs is the kingdom of heaven'. Jesus came to proclaim the Kingship of his Father, and these are ways of living it. For each of them, do you know someone in the parish or elsewhere in your life who exemplifies the attitude? Or one of the saints who typifies each of them to you? What is your own favourite? For most of them there are gospel incidents in which Jesus sums them up, like the entry into Jerusalem on a donkey as the gentle king, or the love he shows in his welcome to sinners, or his bringing peace to those tortured by disease or contempt, or his purity of heart in his single-minded preoccupation with his Father's will, and finally his acceptance of persecution for what he knew to be right. Any Christian may suddenly find herself face to face with this shattering challenge.

Question: Are the beatitudes an adequate summary of Christian holiness?

9 November The Dedication of the Lateran Basilica

First reading: Dead Bones (Ezekiel 47.1-2, 8-9, 12)

In a hot, arid country water is an obvious sign of life. Even in Britain, many people carry a bottle of water with them! In this marvellous picture of water flowing from the Temple the water brings life and fertility to the wastelands and dusty deserts, and even to the hot, salty, smelly Dead Sea. It brings unexpected and unbelievable beauty and fruitfulness to what had been useless and infertile. Ezekiel meant this as an image of all the richness and productiveness that would flow from the new Temple at Jerusalem. The Lateran Basilica in Rome (not St Peter's) is the Pope's own church, and so the sign of the unity of the Church built on the apostles, a unity sealed by union with the Bishop of Rome, the successor of Peter. On this feast of that Lateran Basilica, the Church applies this image to the fruitfulness that the Church brings to all life. Do I see the tradition of the Church as bringing life and richness to all activity and being? As a representative of the Church am I seen as enriching life, a messenger of good news?

Question: Does your local Church community really enrich the surrounding society?

Second reading: The Master Builder (1 Corinthians 3.9-11, 16-17)

In the Bible, there are many enlivening images of the Church, a flock of sheep, a vineyard, a cultivated field, but here St Paul uses the image of a building. Each stone makes its own contribution. Pull one out and the whole building may collapse! Every stone rests on another and forms the basis for a further stone. But it isn't the building of stone and metal, the solid basilica, that matters, but the living stones that make it functional. The point of this building is that it is a living and breathing building, heaving and bursting with life, each stone winking at every other and breathing in unison, because it lives with the life breathed into it by the Spirit of God. Paul writes all this to the Christian community at Corinth, an extraordinarily disunited and disparate group (dockers and professors, magistrates, athletes, teachers and slaves) to remind them that they form a single building on the foundation stone which is Christ. If they, with all their quirks and oddities, could constitute a single building with one common purpose, any community can manage it!

Question: What are you doing about building blocks that don't quite fit your plan?

Gospel: Rebuilding the Temple (John 2.13-22)

The Temple at Jerusalem was an amazing complex of buildings, covering the area of 20 football pitches. At the end of the 46 years of construction, 38,000 workers were made redundant. And Jesus says he will rebuild 'this Temple' in three days! In the Gospel of John, Jesus often plays with misunderstanding ('living water', 'born again', 'true bread') to reach a deeper meaning. So the Temple was only the symbol of Jesus himself, the meeting place between God and human beings, the channel of divine life. The really important Temple is the Risen Christ, filled with the Spirit that also gives the same life to the Church. The Feast of the Lateran Basilica is the feast of the one life of the whole Church, in which the Risen Christ promised that he would always be present, strengthening the whole. Of that presence and that corner stone, and the unity that it provides to the Church, the Bishop of Rome is the symbol. The symbolic 'rubbishing' of the Jerusalem Temple by Jesus reminds us that it is a Church of sinners, always in need of purification, throwing out the rubbish and letting the fresh air in through the windows.

Question: What can be done to further the unity of the broken Christian Church?

8 December The Immaculate Conception of the Blessed Virgin Mary

First reading: The Aftermath of the Fall (Genesis 3.9-15, 20)

The story of the Fall is an analysis of human temptation and sin as it always happens, rather than a historical account of what happened once long ago, when human beings first evolved on earth. Sin brings shame on us: we do our best, like both the man and the woman, to blame someone else, but in the end we know we are defenceless and naked before God. We know that we deserve our penalties, but the wonderful thing about the biblical story is that God continues to care for us: he himself thoughtfully sews clothes for the man and the woman to hide their embarrassment. More important, God promises that evil will not triumph for ever. The penalties of hard labour and pain come not from divine vindictiveness but from human sinfulness: we are no longer in perfect harmony with God. If we were in harmony with God, our confidence in him would spare us the pain. The reading pairs with the gospel reading, since it introduces Satan, the Tempter. The final bit is a 'Just So Story' of the animal world, explaining how the sinewy snake came into being: the proud, fiery serpent lost its legs and was reduced to being a mere big worm.

Question: What can we learn from this analysis of sin?

Second reading: The Cosmic Plan of God (Ephesians 1.3-6, 11-12)

The sevenfold blessing with which the Letter begins sums up God's plan of salvation for humanity. The climax is in the centre, 'to bring everything under Christ as head'. Christ is the Wisdom of God, the plan according to which and through which all things were created. Christ is also the completion of the creation, and the unity of all things in Christ is a special emphasis of the Letter. All things are under Christ as head of creation, as nourishment for creation and as guidance of creation. These are the functions that a head performs for a body, which Christ performs for creation. The Immaculate Conception of Mary was the beginning of the completion of this plan: it was fitting and necessary that the mother who would form and shape the Son of God should be totally without blemish, a shining example of faultless motherhood, a perfect role model for her Son. The aspect of conception in the womb of her mother is only a symbol of the totality of Mary's goodness.

Question: What do we owe to our mothers?

Gospel: The Annunciation (Luke 1.26-38)

What was the young girl Mary doing when the message came? Kneeling piously? Feeding the sheep? Fetching water? Sweeping the mud floor? What was she thinking? Engaged to be married, surely about her approaching wedding to Joseph and about the children she would mother. Then came the message that she could accept or refuse, the message on which hung the future of the world: her child would be different from all others. How 'different'? Her thoughts were turned back to the promise to David. It had been read to her so often in the Bible, and now the words were drummed into her mind: 'His reign will have no end.' This would all be the work of the Spirit that she had so often heard read out in Isaiah; 'the Holy Spirit will come upon you', the Spirit that was to come upon the Servant of the Lord, the Spirit of Emmanuel, 'God with us'. Her young body was to grow, nourish and develop this child. Then she would have the child in her arms to cherish and shape as both Son of God and her own son.

Question: How was Mary's life changed by this message?

Index of passages commented